# FIGHTING POLITICAL GRIDLOCK

For Mike + Cindy
Hope you take some
good ideas away from
this book about states.
Best
David T. Carmine

# FIGHTING POLITICAL GRIDLOCK

How States Shape Our
Nation and Our Lives

DAVID J. TOSCANO

Foreword by Senator Mark R. Warner

University of Virginia Press

CHARLOTTESVILLE AND LONDON

University of Virginia Press
© 2021 by the Rector and Visitors of the University of Virginia
All rights reserved
Printed in the United States of America on acid-free paper

First published 2021

9 8 7 6 5 4 3 2 1

Library of Congress Cataloging-in-Publication Data

Names: Toscano, David J., author.
Title: Fighting political gridlock : how states shape our nation and our lives / David J.
    Toscano.
Description: Charlottesville : University of Virginia Press, 2021. | Includes
    bibliographical references and index.
Identifiers: LCCN 2020058636 (print) | LCCN 2020058637 (ebook) | ISBN
    9780813946467 (hardcover) | ISBN 9780813946474 (ebook)
Subjects: LCSH: State governments—United States. | State governments—Virginia. |
    Policy sciences—United States. | Policy sciences—Virginia.
Classification: LCC JK2408 .T58 2021 (print) | LCC JK2408 (ebook) | DDC
    320.60973—dc23
LC record available at https://lccn.loc.gov/2020058636
LC ebook record available at https://lccn.loc.gov/2020058637

To state lawmakers throughout the land,
searching for solutions in the "laboratories of democracy"

# Contents

# Foreword

I first met David and his wife, Nancy, in the early nineties, when I was serving as chair of the Democratic Party in Virginia and David was a new member of the Charlottesville City Council. We've been friends since then, close to thirty years, and I've always known David to be both thoughtful and solutions oriented, so this book could not come at a more important time.

With the departure of President Donald Trump after a single term and the election of President Joe Biden on a bipartisan mandate, it's clear that Americans long for an end to the gridlock and dysfunction that have characterized our national political institutions for too long. To that end, President Biden and the new Democratic Congress would be well served to look toward state capitals such as Richmond as a model for what is possible when elected officials and politicians are rewarded for solving problems, not merely for kicking the other side.

I'm honored that Virginians have put their trust in me to represent them in the U.S. Senate, reelecting me in 2020 for a third term— but it's no secret that serving as governor was, in many ways, the best job I've ever had. As a Democratic governor from 2002 to 2006, I worked with a Republican-controlled state legislature to reform the tax code, get our budgetary house in order and save Virginia's AAA bond rating, and make the single largest investment in K–12 education in Virginia history. By the time I left office after four years, Virginia ranked nationally as the best-managed state, best state in which to do business, and the best state to get a public K–12 education.

The fact that we were able to accomplish so much in just four years, despite having a legislature controlled by the other party, is a testament to the ways in which state governments differ from where I work in Washington, D.C. As COVID-19 has brought into stark relief, many of the decisions that most affect your everyday life—your children's education, your health—are made not in our nation's capital but in statehouses around the country.

While I didn't serve with him, I was a close observer as David was elected to the state legislature in 2005—holding a seat once occupied by Thomas Jefferson—and quickly rose to be Democratic leader in 2011. Coming to Richmond from Charlottesville, David represented one of the most notoriously progressive parts of the Commonwealth in the state capital. As House minority leader, he often had to balance what his constituents demanded with the diverse needs of the entire Democratic caucus, who hailed from rural Virginia, Northern Virginia, and the urban cores of Richmond and Hampton Roads—and he never failed to do so with both grace and style.

As the publication of this book demonstrates, David still has much to contribute to the political and civic dialogue—not only in Virginia but across the country. In *Fighting Political Gridlock: How States Shape Our Nation and Our Lives*, David thoughtfully examines the ways in which our state governments still form the backbone of our civic and political governance. Though the work—or lack thereof—in Washington often hogs the proverbial spotlight, our political system is, at its heart, decentralized. The federalist system devised by our founders two and a half centuries ago ensures that core services of government, such as the administration of criminal justice, and even more existential questions of representation—such as redistricting and how voters choose their representatives—are decided primarily at the state and local level. This is what enables states to serve the needs of their citizens even as it often seems that national consensus and action appear increasingly out of reach.

With this book, David Toscano has thoughtfully highlighted the opportunities and challenges facing our state governments. I am confident that this work will soon be considered essential reading for students, policymakers, and public officials alike.

Mark R. Warner
U.S. Senator, 2009–present
Governor of Virginia, 2002–2006

# Acknowledgments

This book began as an effort to synthesize my fourteen-year experience as a state legislator with policy debates taking place in Virginia and nationally during the first decades of the twenty-first century. What emerged was a manuscript that was too long and overly complicated for what I was attempting to do, that is, to show why states matter in this great nation of ours. Fortunately, my editor at the University of Virginia Press, Nadine Zimmerli, suggested that I remove much of the Virginia-specific material for a future undertaking and concentrate on the national scene. It was a good move, and allowed me to focus on the unique character of various state policies and their impact, leaving much of the Virginia material for later. Her keen insight and editorial touch helped tremendously in generating this book.

This undertaking benefits greatly from many others as well. My former legislative aide, Erin Monaghan, spent countless hours reading and editing various iterations of this manuscript; being a lawyer, she was invaluable as I tried to make legal concepts more comprehensible. A number of exceptional Virginia historians, among them Brent Tarter, Ron Heinemann, Ed Ayers, George Gilliam, and Elizabeth Varon, helped me understand Virginia's history and the state during Reconstruction in greater detail. Much of material on Virginia's history is included in an upcoming volume, but the insights helped shape this narrative in several key places. Law professors Carl Tobias and Richard Schragger provided new insights into judicial selection processes and the interplay between state and local government. Jeremy Anderson, president of the Education Commission of the States, Peter Blake, director of Virginia's State Council on Higher Education (SCHEV), and Robert E. Anderson, president of the State Higher Education Executive Officers Association (SHEEO), all reviewed the sections on higher education and provided useful insights. Chris Bast, Thomas Hadwin, Albert Pollard, and newly installed Virginia State Corporation commissioner Angela Navarro were kind enough to comment on the energy chapter and helped clarify some of the complex issues I had either neglected or inadequately explained. Constitutional scholar A. E. "Dick" Howard, a key drafter of Virginia's 1972 Constitution, helped me think about state constitutions in new ways. Former US congressman L. F. Payne was an early and insightful reader of portions, as were Delegates Mark Sickles and Rip Sullivan. Friends Richard and Meg Zakin, Ned Martin, and David Gies provided feedback on the introduction.

Larry Sabato of Virginia's Center for Politics encouraged me along the way; his insights into state and national politics are the measure by which many analyses are judged. Former and present Virginia governmental staffers such as Bill Leighty, who served with distinction in Republican and Democratic administrations, and Paul Reagan and Larry Roberts provided further background on how decisions are made in the executive branch. I owe a special debt to all the delegates and senators with whom I served—not only because they work to make the commonwealth a better place to live and are the source of great stories, but because they provided critical insights about how state policy is made. Special gratitude goes to the governors with whom I served, Ralph Northam, Tim Kaine, Bob McDonnell, and Terry McAuliffe, all of whom I watched balance the competing needs of the commonwealth and their constituents with skill and commitment; and, of course, thanks to Senator Mark Warner, who penned the foreword and brought a new political dynamic to our commonwealth. Former governor Bob McDonnell and Speaker Bill Howell, as well as Virginia attorney general Mark Herring, gave graciously of their time in discussing some of the hot-button issues we faced while serving together. Norm Oliver and Lillian Peake assisted with my understanding state responses to the pandemic. This volume benefits greatly from the National Conference on State Legislatures (NCSL), whose staff was always available to answer questions and whose publications are essential reading for anyone interested in this field. Shoutouts to Laurie Jinkins and Eileen Filler-Corn, two path-setting women who took on House Speakerships in Washington State and Virginia at the same time, just before COVID-19 disrupted everything, to Dahlia Lithwick, with whom I commiserated about the state of American democracy, and to others like Gold Star parent Khizr Khan and Susan Bro, both of whom have shown grace and commitment in the aftermath of incredible tragedy.

The staff at the University of Virginia Press were consummate professionals. Nadine Zimmerli took a chance on me and helped shape the final manuscript in important ways. Marjorie Pannell improved the manuscript with expert editing, improving my writing to help tell this story in an objective fashion. Ellen Satrom, Emily Grandstaff, Emma Donovan, and Jason Coleman got us across the finish line. I also want to thank my former legislative assistants, Jenny Hogan, Sarah Buckley, Carmen Bingham, Erin Monaghan, and Jane Dittmar. The job of a delegate is tough; they helped make it easier.

Above all, I have been fortunate to enjoy the strong support of my family during my years in politics. People frequently read about "political wives," and my wife of forty-five years, Nancy Tramontin, could write a book on the subject—or a series of books. I could not have come close to achieving what I have without her total support. She brought joy and enthusiasm to the social and policy side of this work and never wavered in her support, whether it was editing my writing, providing technical support on the computer, giving solicited (and often unsolicited) sound political advice, or putting up with my various rants about people with whom I disagreed. Without her, I would never have been in a position where I could have contemplated writing this book, much less done so.

Our son, Matthew, offered his enthusiastic support during my years in public service, which spanned his years from birth to age twenty-three, and brought a Gen Z's point of view to politics, reminding me often of using language that evolves and is reflective of the times. It is impossible for public officials to adequately represent their constituents without the support of family. I am forever in debt to mine.

# FIGHTING POLITICAL GRIDLOCK

# INTRODUCTION
## Fights of Our Lives

As election results flashed across TV screens late into the evening of November 3, 2020, some thought they were witnessing a replay of 2016. Like Hillary Clinton, Democratic candidate Joe Biden had jumped to a lead in the popular vote but remained behind in several key states that could provide incumbent president Donald Trump with a second term. As in 2016, the polls in the weeks and months leading up to the election had reported large leads for Biden, both nationally and in the key battleground states. Some Democratic operatives suggested that Florida, Georgia, and even Texas were not only competitive but might actually give Biden wins on the way to a landslide. Consequently, the early results were received in some quarters with disbelief. Florida reported early, and it appeared likely that Trump would win the Sunshine state. Texas numbers also appeared favorable to the incumbent. Even Virginia, which had voted for Democrats in every presidential election since 2008, reported an early lead for Trump that continued late into the evening. How could a president whose approval rating never reached 50 percent for his entire presidency possibly win reelection? And how was it possible that he could garner over 70 million votes?

As the night's focus quickly turned to the states of Michigan, Wisconsin, and Pennsylvania, it was again clear that the race for the presidency is not really a federal contest but instead a combination of fifty state contests, and the candidate who assembled enough electoral votes by winning these discrete and individual races would become the next president. In the race for the presidency, states matter: the winner is determined not by popular vote but instead by the allocation of each state's electoral votes in the Electoral College. Beyond that, Americans were coming to understand that each individual state has a wide array of rules that determine how votes are counted and reported, a nuance that, as it turned out, had implications both for the result of the race and for how it was interpreted by the public. On election night, the possibility briefly existed that the 2020 presidential election would be the third in twenty years in which the candidate who received the most popular votes would not win the presidency.

The role of the states was especially prominent in 2020, if only because this was an election unlike any other. The COVID-19 pandemic that began in February had knocked the country on its heels, and now was gathering greater strength. More than 225,000 Americans had died of the disease by Election Day, and the trajectory of infection appeared to be out of control. State leaders were doing their best to protect their citizens, but the lack of a coordinated response was crippling much of the effort. The country had not seen such a health crisis for the best part of a century, and most officials believed conditions would worsen substantially before they got better. In response, almost every state made changes—some temporary, others permanent—to give citizens greater opportunities to vote by mail.[1] But each of these changes also came with very different rules for counting the votes. And, as it turned out, those different rules influenced the public's perception of how the election was unfolding. Fortunately for democracy, the public remained calm as the vote counting dragged on into Friday and Saturday, and final margins were sufficiently large that the lawsuits brought by the Trump campaign were viewed as political theater that would not change the results.

The outcome could easily have been different. Included among the states allowing mail-in voting were the swing states of Arizona, Florida, Wisconsin, Pennsylvania, Michigan, Ohio, Nevada, and Georgia, with their collection of 117 electoral votes, certainly enough to decide the presidential election.[2] Pennsylvania and Nevada even permitted the counting of votes received after Election Day if they had been postmarked before it. Close followers of the election understood that these state procedures probably meant that the election result would not be known on November 3.

For months, President Trump and his allies had railed against mail-in voting, suggesting, against any evidence, that it generates rampant fraud. Democrats cast early votes in droves, but Trump's pronouncements had the effect of encouraging his followers to vote on Election Day. Since many states count and report those votes cast on Election Day before those received by mail, the president assembled early leads in several key states, including Pennsylvania, where he had amassed a 500,000-vote margin by the end of the night. Lost in those numbers was the fact that Democrats had cast millions of votes in advance of Election Day to ensure their voice would be heard without having to risk going to the polls during a once-in-a-lifetime pandemic.

As Biden built small leads in Arizona and Nevada, the former vice president saw a clearer path to assemble the 270 electoral votes to win. But no one could discount the possibility that the outcome might depend on numerous lawsuits, not just in one state, as occurred in 2000, but in several, each of which had its own unique rules about who could vote and how votes would be counted. As a result, some scenarios predicted a close presidential contest whereby Trump would claim victory based on November 3 vote totals and then litigate the legality of the mail-in votes in numerous states.

On election night, the different state laws that would dictate the winner and the perception of the process became clear. Since Florida allows mail-in votes to be opened and counted prior to Election Day, it reported its results very quickly. When the state was called for the president, those who believed that Florida could break for Biden were not only disappointed but wondered whether their hopes for victory would again fall prey to the vagaries of the Electoral College. The same vote counting arrangement, however, did not apply to key states such as Michigan, Wisconsin, and Pennsylvania. Knowing that the volume of mail-in votes in those three states would be so great that final results might not be known for days, their governors had asked their Republican-controlled legislatures in the fall to change state law to permit early counting. They were rebuffed, and the state election officials could not review mail-in ballots for errors, much less count them, until Election Day. This caused a delay in reporting results in key states and played into the narrative spun by Trump supporters that the election was being stolen.

The impact of these state policies was felt most acutely in Pennsylvania, the state that ultimately made Biden the winner when it was called for the former vice president on Saturday, November 7. The Keystone State reported higher mail-in voting than its fellow midwestern swing states of Wisconsin and Michigan, with over 2.6 million citizens voting by mail, including over one million in Philadelphia area alone.[3] But these ballots were not counted until the in-person voting results had been tallied and, on that basis, Trump had jumped to a substantial lead. The mail-in vote results were dramatically different, especially in key Midwestern states. Biden posted landslide-type numbers, in some cases outpolling the president by as much as nine to one. As Biden's margin over Trump increased, so too did the protests from Trump loyalists, who took to the streets with placards proclaiming "Stop the Steal." With the reporting of each new batch of votes, Trump's lead continued to erode until Biden passed him, ultimately garnering a margin that ruled out a recount. A similar dynamic occurred in Georgia. By the end of the state's early voting, nearly 3.9 million Georgians, or about 51 percent of the state's registered voters, had voted either in person or by absentee ballot.[4] When those counts were released, Biden had overcome an early Trump lead and won the Peach State's sixteen electoral votes. Biden won the popular vote by over seven million votes and his Electoral College margin would exceed by thirty-six the 270 needed to become president. Biden's victory was clear and decisive.

President Trump and his allies found defeat difficult to accept, and kept blustering about election fraud and how Trump had won. Secretary of State Mike Pompeo asserted that we would see a smooth and peaceful transition— to a second Trump term. Attorney General William Barr initially called for an investigation of voter fraud. At the same time, Trump continued to purge federal officials who appeared to be disloyal. When he fired Secretary of Defense Mark Esper and dismissed four others from the Defense Department's high command whom he perceived to be disloyal,[5] anxiety grew as to whether the president was trying to ensure the loyalty of the military in the event of a constitutional crisis.

It was difficult to determine the precise strategy, if any, the president had devised to retain the White House. But for any plan to succeed, states would need to cooperate. Trump would first need the secretaries of state in key states to refuse to certify their voting results. If this occurred, state legislatures could possibly intervene and appoint their own electors, who might then vote to provide him a second term. The two Republican US senators in Georgia who failed to receive enough votes to avoid a runoff election even called for the resignation of the Republican secretary of state, an action that appeared bizarre until considered in the context of what Trump was trying to do.[6] Trump even took the unprecedented step of calling the secretary to ask if he could "find some votes." The guardrails of democracy were under attack.

The Trump strategy was a long shot. It suffered not only from faulty legal arguments, which showed in the numerous lawsuits he lost contesting the results, but, more important, in the lack of public support. A Reuters/Ipsos poll conducted in the week after the election found that nearly 80 percent of Americans, including more than half of Republicans, believed Biden had won the contest.[7] And state legislative leaders showed little indication that they would seize control of the election. Trump continued to question the legitimacy of the election, failed to concede he had lost, and announced he would not appear at the inauguration. Throughout November and December, Trump's allies continued to assert their unsupported claims that fraud in the election was rampant. "Stop the Steal" became a rallying cry, and the constant criticism was beginning to change the views of many Republicans, some of whom were now coming to think that perhaps Trump was right.

On January 6, 2021, the implications of this narrative became clear. At the precise time that Congress and Vice President Mike Pence had assembled to perform the ministerial duty of certifying the results of the Electoral College, a mob, spurred to action after the president addressed them, stormed the Capitol, disrupted the proceedings, and occupied the House and Senate chambers. For the first time since 1814, the US Capitol had been attacked— and by Americans. Use of the word "insurrection" did not seem hyperbolic. The invasion was eventually repulsed, and on January 20, 2021, Joe Biden was inaugurated as the forty-sixth president of the United States. But the incident will not soon be forgotten and will forever influence how we view the challenges before us.

## Shocks to the System

As this is being written, our country is in the midst of three major challenges that will likely influence our politics for years if not decades. First, although Donald Trump is no longer president, the divisions that he exploited during his tenure are still with us, and will likely remain for years. Second, the COVID-19 pandemic has caused substantial disruption and a tragic loss of life from which recovery will not be easy. And finally, we are undergoing a much-needed racial reckoning following George Floyd's killing. Each of these challenges is huge individually; experiencing them all at once is a shock that will require patience and deliberative efforts to address.

The Trump presidency both exhausted the nation and left us more divided than at any time since the Civil War. It also had the effect of focusing the nation's attention on the drama occurring in Washington and the continuing gridlock at the federal level. After his election in 2016, Trump not only attempted to undo many changes enacted by his predecessors but appeared to be attacking the institutions and norms of democracy itself. Despite Robert Mueller's conclusion that the beneficiary of the "widespread and systematic" Russian interference in the 2016 election was Trump himself, the president persisted in his claims that it was all a hoax, and enlisted his third attorney general, William P. Barr, to frame the report as an exoneration of the commander-in-chief. Trump associates were indicted and convicted of numerous crimes, but instead of rebuking those convicted, he has dangled pardons in front of them.

Throughout his term, the president unceasingly stoked racial divisions, a continuation of the demagoguery evidenced over his lifetime, from his comments during the Central Park jogger case decades ago to his more recent insistence that President Obama was Kenyan, not American. In his response to the tragedy and outrage of the Unite the Right riot in Charlottesville in 2017, characterized by notable images of flaming tiki torches and chants of "Jews will not replace us," Trump downplayed the obvious antagonisms on display, saying only that some of the white nationalists present were "very fine people." He assailed basic American values when he told four members of Congress—all women of color and all American citizens—to go back to the countries they came from. When, following the killing of George Floyd in May 2020, police were used to violently clear peaceful protestors exercising their constitutional rights on a public plaza so that Trump could enjoy a photo opportunity in front of St. John's Church, across from the White House, even his supporters blanched. When to all this is added his continued diatribes against journalists and the media as "enemies of the people" and his reckless disregard of the rule of law, it brings to mind Benjamin Franklin's admonition in the aftermath of the Constitutional Convention in Philadelphia 250 years ago that the founders had created "a Republic . . . if you can keep it."[8]

While Trump's Ukrainian adventures brought him impeachment, they were not enough to sway Republican senators to remove him from office. His initial failure to engage with COVID-19 made the epidemic worse, and his seeming inability to marshal the forces of the federal government in a coordinated effort to halt viral transmission and aid the states in mitigating the effects of the pandemic undoubtedly played a role in his lackluster poll numbers. His attempt to convince state governors to send their National Guard troops to Washington, D.C., in late May 2020 to intimidate citizens peacefully protesting the killing of George Floyd was discarded only after it encountered significant resistance from many state chief executives—another clear example of why states matter.[9]

To his supporters, Trump is a hero, a crusader against political correctness and the power of the "deep state." To his detractors, his actions flouted the rule of law in a style unbecoming the most powerful person on Earth. But there is one thing on which both camps can agree—Trump focused the nation's attention on Washington and illuminated the challenges of a federal system paralyzed by continual gridlock. Trump is no longer president, but the divisions apparent in this country prior to his election and that he so adeptly exploited during his term will not soon dissipate. Addressing these problems productively may be the challenge of our generation.

## States Fill the Void

Supporters of the Trump presidency initially believed it might end the grid-lock in the nation's capital. It did not. But those four years continued a trend that has been apparent for years—states increasingly acting to fill the policy void. Time and time again, state lawmakers assert their independence from the federal government, if only in the form of a simple declarative statement, "We are not D.C." This has been occurring for years, but the COVID-19 pandemic brought it into clear focus. Governors of both parties, from Andrew Cuomo of New York and Gavin Newsom in California to Mike DeWine of Ohio and Larry Hogan in Maryland, exhibiting competency and steadiness during the crisis, provided a sharp contrast to the failure to mount a coherent federal response to the virus.

States today tackle some of the most vexing and complicated problems facing the nation—expanding health care access at a reasonable cost, reducing carbon emissions and expanding renewable energy, building an economy of the future while lessening inequality—problems that the federal government has not addressed in any meaningful way for years. Policy innovations are expanding throughout the states, whether they involve efforts to combat the opioid crisis, address the "school-to-prison pipeline," or devise a fairer and less partisan way to apportion representation by district.

This is not to downplay the critical importance of guidance and governance at the national level. But it is in the statehouses where change can occur faster, and with direct ramifications for the citizenry. State law and policy, it turns out, often influence what happens at the federal level. The classic example is the redistricting process. Many in the United States do not realize that the decisions that establish the boundaries of congressional districts are made by the states. State legislators have the authority to alter the party composition of the state's congressional delegation without any change in how the voters cast a single ballot. The states generally control who is qualified to vote; how, when, and where voters cast their ballots; and how electoral disputes are resolved. When it comes to who will represent you in Congress and how they are chosen, states truly matter.

The COVID-19 pandemic further clarified how the most important decisions that affect the lives of our friends and neighbors are made at the state level. Education is at the top of everyone's priority list; most decisions about schools are made in statehouses and during school board meetings. The shuttering of schools is a decision as impactful as it gets, and states not only made it during the pandemic but helped manage the challenge of reopening.

Educational policy and funding is largely the province of the states. In the criminal justice arena, states determine most crimes for which people can be arrested and the time they serve if they violate the law. What about health care? While the Affordable Care Act has established many of the rules, the delivery of health care through Medicaid is a major function of state policy and law. And as pressure mounts to repeal part or all of the ACA, more debates are taking place in statehouses about innovative policies that can deliver improved health care outcomes to US citizens for better value.

In other matters, states have different economic growth and labor policies that affect their citizens and the opportunities they seek. And there has been an explosion of new initiatives at the state level seeking to address the challenges of climate change. At a time when Washington has proved unable to move decisively on many of these issues, statehouses are beehives of activity and innovation, creating opportunities to move this nation in a positive direction.

## COVID-19

Even as the nation's attention was captured by the impeachment and subsequent trial in the Senate of President Trump in early 2020, an insidious threat was entering quietly from beyond our shores. The United States would soon be confronted by an unexpected challenge generated not by politics but by microbes. It was about to transform the nation, not simply because of the attendant loss of life and the shriveling of the economy but also because of the stepped-up role states played in mitigation. The federal administration's failure to grasp the severity of the crisis and its subsequent decision to downplay its catastrophic potential resulted in critical time lost, as the infection spread without any significant federal mobilization to combat it. In the absence of an effective federal response, state governors stepped up to lead the fight. Whether it involved stay-at-home orders, mobilizing hospital ICUs and ventilators, or purchasing protective equipment and test kits, governors took the lead—they had to. And although some federal assistance would eventually come, it was often in response to the solicitation of individual governors, who recognized that a personal ask of the president was the best way to access federal resources to protect their citizens. A massive coordinated national effort might well have been more effective than fifty states bidding up the cost of ventilators or struggling with how best to implement a testing regimen to contain the virus. A national policy that made aid to states contingent on enforcement of certain national standards for social distancing could have made a difference. But such a national policy or coordination at the federal level was not to be, and states were essentially forced to become, in Justice Brandeis's term, "laboratories of democracy," devising their own rules to slow the transmission of the virus and protect their citizens. The president left it up to the governors to combat COVID-19 as best they could.

In the spring of 2020, the states took the first steps toward reopening the economy, not really sure what that meant or what would eventuate. In so doing, they essentially pieced together a controlled scientific experiment at the national level. While the Biden administration rapidly built a federal response as vaccines became more widely available in early 2021, getting shots into arms remained primarily a state activity, and some places were more effective than others. Our experience with the pandemic proved that life itself can depend on the state in which you live.

## Why This Book at This Time?

Even before the COVID-19 crisis, the political guardrails within which we ordinarily conduct our public debate were being dismantled and destroyed, not just by a few highly placed elected officials but also by others who were growing increasingly angry and cynical about America's prospects as a nation. Repair is in order, and what better place to start than where government is closest to the people—in statehouses and council chambers around the country? Perhaps the most significant thing I have learned in twenty-five years of public service is the importance of educating the next generation of Americans about how their government works now, and could work better in the future. That means not just giving them basic facts about the three branches of government but letting citizens know, for example, that their participation, not just by voting but by engagement, really matters. The United States is a nation of laws, one where real people who hold positions at all levels of government make, interpret, and implement the rules. These people operate the gears of the wonderful machine called democracy. And understanding the institutions, norms, and values within which they operate, as well as their human capacities and liabilities, helps bring to life the policy decisions that affect all of our lives.

Events also have a way of influencing policy decisions and political discourse. One of those events incurred in a place I call home—Charlottesville, Virginia. The Unite the Right rally mayhem and tragedy of August 2017, when white supremacists from across the nation converged on our community, continues to affect our state and our nation. The city will forever more be known as the site where hatred and racism again reared their ugly heads and plunged the country into deep soul searching about both the nation's past and its future. Few emerged from those several days of disruption without being affected. And few anticipated that the spring and summer of 2020 would prompt yet another reckoning with America's history of racial oppression in the aftermath of the murder of George Floyd. These issues, however, have now become a major focus for state legislatures across the nation.

Charlottesville is not unique. It has many of the problems of other places its size. Poverty is present in the midst of plenty. Racism persists, though Charlottesville is not any more or less racist than many other places in America; if anything, it is more liberal and tolerant than most. It has many advantages that other places do not—a top-notch university, a good climate, a cosmopolitan atmosphere, access to beautiful countryside and the Blue Ridge Mountains. Yet it still illustrates the racial and economic fissures found in so much of America and is therefore instructive of the kinds of challenges we face as a country.

## The Road Map

Americans pay so much attention to national politics that they forget how much state policymaking affects their daily lives. Not only decisions affecting how we run our political system but matters of great significance to everyone residing in a state, from the quality of education available to our children and grandchildren to the nature of jobs in our communities, how roads are built and maintained, the degree to which criminals are punished for their wrongdoings, even our energy bills, are mostly decided at the state level. The difference between federal and state-level responses to the pandemic made that abundantly clear. Chapter 1 compares state responses to COVID-19 in the context of a national abnegation of leadership. At times, federalism appeared to be on trial, and the verdict remains unclear in the early days of 2021.

Chapter 2 analyzes states in light of US Supreme Court justice Louis Brandeis's observation that states are laboratories of democracy. Because different policies can be developed and tested at the state level without affecting the rest of the country, states have the maneuverability to develop innovative solutions to problems, which can then serve as models for other states to follow. Examples such as the unique health insurance reform adopted in Massachusetts, which subsequently served as the model for the ACA, and the numerous state initiatives to create "free college" underscore the importance of states in crafting policies to serve their residents.

Chapter 3 discusses state constitutions, the legal framework for state actions, and their impact on how policy is made and changed. As an example, most states are required by their constitution to produce a balanced budget, which has major consequences for state policy. But each state constitution is different, thereby creating opportunities for state action in some areas but not others. Virginia, for example, is unique because of its one-term governorship and in how it selects its judges. Many western states allow their citizens to revise their constitution simply by petitioning for a change and winning at the ballot box. Though most Americans know little about them, the provisions of state constitutions establish the parameters within which state policy is advanced.

Chapter 4 examines how a state's geographic location, demographic composition, and history and culture influence how it approaches problems and develops solutions. Policy gets made by people, however, and chapter 5 continues the theme by exploring how individuals and groups within states, from governors to legislators to advocates, decide which things get done, and how. Included in this chapter is a discussion of the role of state attorneys general, positions that have become both more partisan and more important in the last decade.

State law and policy can dramatically affect the control of the nation, particularly as manifested in the areas of redistricting and voting. Chapter 6 explores these distinctively state-run processes. How congressional districts are drawn dramatically affects state representation in the federal government and so affects policy decisions at the national level. Moreover, states generally determine the rules for voting, thereby influencing who gets elected. In the run-up to the November 2020 election, almost every state saw debates on voting, whether those debates involved the requirements for voting by mail (and how mailed ballots are counted) or other technical matters related to vote tabulation. These were state, not national, issues. Chapter 6 also examines how national interest groups view states as contested terrain and attempt to influence citizen legislators by providing them with "model legislation" designed to serve the interest groups' own needs. Interest groups attempt to get as many self-serving bills passed in as many statehouses as possible, in this way striving to change the character of the country one state at a time.

Chapter 7 explores what is arguably the most important state function, educating the citizenry. State governments provide much of the policy and many of the dollars that determine the strength of the US public school system and other public institutions such as libraries, museums, and cultural centers.

Chapters 8 through 10 serially address the discrete issues of criminal justice, the economy, and health care, where so much work is being done by states. Chapter 11 explores the culture wars ongoing at the state level, as exemplified by the debates around abortion, guns, and immigration. Chapter 12 reviews power relations between state and local governments and includes a discussion of the Dillon Rule, which holds that local governments are limited in their powers to those expressly granted them by the state; home rule, or the authority of local governments to exercise those powers within their administrative boundaries; and the legal concept known as preemption, which means that a higher authority takes precedence when two authorities come into conflict. Chapter 13 discusses energy and climate change as emerging areas of substantial state activity. A common theme throughout these chapters is Americans' tendency to place so much emphasis on what is happening in Washington that insufficient heed is paid to the activities of state government. Whoever controls the states has a huge impact on who controls the nation, and national interest groups are increasingly using states to carry out their agendas.

The conclusion to the book explores a question many believe is at the core of determining our future as a nation: How can we have a decision-making process that includes the broadest cross section of the public without tearing each other apart? Some call the underlying mental disposition civility, others call it respect. But whatever one calls it, it appears to be in increasingly short supply, not just in Washington but in state capitols and city halls. The conclusion explores some ways we can encourage respectful civil engagement in a democratic decision-making process. The future of our democratic experiment depends more on citizen engagement than perhaps any policy initiative adopted at any level of government. And it is here where we are in the fight of our lives.

## The Lens of Experience

People are psychologically predisposed to interpret events through the lens of their own experience, and so I want to say a bit about myself and my aims in writing the book. My intention throughout is to provide a balanced picture of state government to the reader. Nonetheless, my background and training have inevitably influenced how I interpret events. First, I am a progressive Democrat, and my views are influenced by that perspective. Second, because I am an attorney, my analyses tend to gravitate to the legal parameters within which states operate. Finally, my early training as a sociologist leads me to examine evidence from different perspectives, and to draw distinctions and conclusions based on facts instead of supposition. Transparency is important in the description and analysis of events. To the extent readers disagree with my perspective, they will understand the context in which it was developed.

Our views of politics and policy are also influenced by the places our policymakers call home. This happens both in Congress and in state legislatures: the perspectives of lawmakers are inevitably shaped by their places of origin and residence. People living in rural upstate New York, for example, may find it difficult to understand the poverty experienced by people living in some areas of New York City, and therefore may have difficulty engaging with the problem. Conditions in southern Illinois are very different from those in Chicago, some three hundred miles to the north. Many residents of Southwest Virginia have never quite grasped the nature of the economic engine of the northern part of the commonwealth, nor have residents of Northern Virginia fully understood the economic challenges faced by residents of the southwestern part of the state. And the residents of both areas are challenged to fully understand conditions in certain portions of Richmond, Virginia, and the difficulties faced by people of color, especially African Americans, throughout the state. The danger of separating ourselves based on ideological litmus tests, geographic sorting, or cultural identity is that we can easily forget that we interpret events, and even determine which facts to use, based on our own experiences.

The links between politics, policy, and personalities are discussed throughout this book for various reasons. First, whatever proposed policies are adopted or defeated determine the character of local communities, states, and the nation. Second, decisions about policies are made not simply on the basis of the ideas but through the mobilization of support or the organizing of resistance. This is the province of politics, not just in the legislative and executive arenas but also in the electoral process, where momentum can build toward policy enactment or lead to a proposal's eventual demise. And finally, there are the personalities that can either add grease to the wheels of change or throw sand in the gears. Decisions are never made in a vacuum or simply on the basis of rational discussion. A lot depends on who is in the room at the time.

# 1

# States of Emergency

I would leave it to the governors.
— PRESIDENT DONALD J. TRUMP, APRIL 3, 2020

The January 5, 2020, posting on the World Health Organization (WHO) website seemed relatively innocuous. Captioned "Pneumonia of unknown cause—China," it briefly reported about a number of cases of pneumonia detected in the city of Wuhan, a port city of 19 million inhabitants.[1] Few in the United States took note, with the exception of scientific specialists in the areas of infectious diseases and public health. Several days earlier, Li Wenliang, a Chinese ophthalmologist at Wuhan Central Hospital, had notified colleagues about a new illness that appeared highly contagious and resembled severe acute respiratory syndrome (SARS); the illness would later be named SARS-CoV-2, or, generically, coronavirus disease 2019—COVID-19 for short. He was criticized and sanctioned by Chinese authorities. A month later, Li died of the disease. America and the world were about to be plunged into one of the most challenging global crises since World War II. The nation was to learn important lessons about why states matter. And many of us would be left wondering whether our constitutional system of federalism provided an effective framework for addressing the crisis.[2]

## Legislatures Convene as the Storm Gathers

Halfway around the world, US governors and state legislators were preparing for their annual legislative sessions. Virginia was among the first states to convene, doing so on January 8. Major policy changes were projected for the state since the Democrats had just taken control of the legislature and held the governor's office as well. On the other side of the country, Washington State convened its own session on January 13. Both states were about to make history as each elected its first woman Speaker—Eileen Filler-Corn in Virginia and Laurie Jinkins in Washington. And Democratic governors Jay Inslee of Washington and Ralph Northam of Virginia were optimistic about leaving their marks on their states in light of a strong economy and Demo-cratic majorities. Within two months, they would join other governors across the nation in confronting the greatest challenge of their administrations.

Few state lawmakers noticed when the US Centers for Disease Control and Prevention (CDC) issued a travel warning advising against any nonessen-tial travel to China on January 6,[3] or even when the virus began to affect other countries. In Virginia, the new majority was focused on passing its agenda—gun safety legislation, raising the minimum wage, transforming the energy sector, and redistricting reform. And lawmakers in Washington State arrived in Olympia with priorities of their own: initiatives to address climate change, increase teachers' salaries, and enact greater workplace protections. Neither legislature seemed worried about COVID-19.

As legislatures in Virginia and other states focused on hundreds of new possible laws and state budgets in early January, the WHO was sending direc-tives to hospitals around the world suggesting immediate action to control the spread of the virus. Controlling its spread was especially important because there was no vaccine, and was significantly complicated by the fact that many carriers were asymptomatic and therefore did not realize they could transmit the virus to others. An emergency committee of international experts met on January 15 in Geneva to assess whether the outbreak constituted an inter-national emergency.[4] That same day, crowds cheered as the Virginia legisla-ture ratified the Equal Rights Amendment (ERA), becoming the thirty-eighth state to do so.[5]

## A Growing Concern

Most Americans were more focused on events taking place in Washington, D.C.—notably the first impeachment trial of President Trump—than on either their state legislature or a virus that was about to have a major impact on their lives. On February 5, the US Senate acquitted the president of the House impeachment charges. Meanwhile, a full-scale epidemic was under way in China, and cases were being reported in places as diverse as Iran and Italy. South Korea had initiated a massive testing program,[6] and Singapore was vigorously engaged in fighting the spread of the virus.

Washington State officials first became concerned when a thirty-five-year-old resident tested positive for COVID-19 after returning from Wuhan. Alarm spread as more and more deaths were reported in other countries, especially as the disease spread to Europe, and as additional cases were reported in the state. By the end of February, Washington had reported two deaths and was becoming a "hot spot" for the growing number of cases reported throughout the United States.[7] Johns Hopkins University, which had been monitoring cases, reported that the global death toll had surpassed 3,000 on four continents.[8] On February 29, 2020, Washington governor Jay Inslee, at the instigation of public health officials, declared a state of emergency.[9] COVID-19 had been unleashed on America.

Washington's new House Speaker, an attorney who had worked in health care for years, understood immediately the implications of the disease for her constituents and the state, and was an enthusiastic supporter of the governor's action. "When we looked at the data, it was clear that we had no choice but to get ahead of the curve by encouraging social distancing," she observed. "We also had to do some education; some of our members initially viewed this as a 'hoax.' Fortunately, our minority leader stepped up, stating that the data is there to support decisive action."[10]

Italy's spike in cases did not occur until early March, and, even with Inslee's emergency order, thoughts of a pandemic had not seriously crossed the minds of most US state lawmakers, especially in the Commonwealth of Virginia, which seemed so far away from China and even from Washington State. State public health officials across the nation, however, were growing increasingly concerned. In Virginia, Dr. M. Norman Oliver, the commissioner of public health, and Dr. Lilian Peake, the state epidemiologist, recognized the potential impact of COVID-19 in January as they watched its exponential growth in China and other nations; it would not be long until the United States—and Virginia—would face a similar challenge.[11] The state's pandemic work plan, developed several years earlier, was activated, and an incident command structure was established to respond to the threat; Peake, a twenty-year veteran of governmental experience in the public health arena, was placed in charge. "I had witnessed a number of close calls in the past—avian flu, SARS, H1N1; they were serious but could easily have become disasters," she explained. "It was important to us that we begin informing physicians and health departments about the developments without creating too much alarm."[12]

While there had not yet been an identified case in the commonwealth, Peake alerted the statewide network. The governor and his cabinet were briefed. On March 3, Governor Northam informed the public about the state's plan, attempting not to frighten citizens before the oncoming threat could be more easily communicated. It did not take long for the virus to hit the commonwealth. The legislature was largely focused on passing a two-year budget based on a rosy economic forecast and pushing various bills over the finish line for final passage. While most lawmakers were now aware of COVID-19,

few fully understood its implications, and they were up against the constitutional deadline for producing a budget.[13] The hope remained that "it can't
happen here."

On March 10, 2020, after COVID-19 had swept through at least 114 countries and killed more than four thousand people, the WHO formally labeled
it a pandemic, the first use of the term since the 2009 H1N1 swine flu outbreak.[14] On March 12, the same day Virginia legislators were scheduled to
vote on the budget and adjourn, Governor Northam announced a state of
emergency.[15] The legislature finished its work and adjourned until the next
scheduled session, slated for April 22, at which they expected to consider the
governor's vetoes and changes in the budget.

Over the course of the next month, the worlds of state governors and
policymakers would be turned upside down. Almost overnight, all state
actions became COVID related. As the virus slammed into local communities and the economy tanked, state legislatures watched as many new
initiatives passed during their sessions unraveled as a result of projected
budget shortfalls. Moreover, most lawmakers were now largely left on the
policy sidelines. It didn't matter whether you lived in a blue state or a red
state. Management of the crisis became quickly concentrated in the hands of
state executives. Even if they were briefed by their governors about numerous executive actions, legislators were largely left to calm constituents and
provide them with whatever information and services were available. Never
had so much power been concentrated so quickly in the hands of governors,
a dynamic that troubled policymakers genuinely concerned about the balance
and separation of power between the branches of government. State leaders
across the nation had begun to understand the implications of this rapidly
developing pandemic.

## Ignoring the Scientists

The initial response from Washington was less than salutary, with the administration ignoring both evidence of the spreading virus and the warnings of
epidemiologists, insisting instead there was not much to worry about. President Trump downplayed the extent of the spread, saying, "It's one person
coming in from China, and we have it under control. It's going to be just
fine."[16] Larry Kudlow, the president's chief economic adviser, stated in late
January that the virus would have "minimal impact" on the US economy.[17]
Other economists, however, were beginning to take notice. "The recent emergence of the coronavirus," the Federal Reserve Board said in its semiannual
report released on February 7, "could lead to disruptions in China that spill

over to the rest of the global economy." The administration remained skeptical, at least publicly. At a White House meeting on February 27, Trump sounded an optimistic note: "It's going to disappear. One day—it's like a miracle—it will disappear."[18] State governors knew better. They could wait no longer for a federal response.[19]

## Flattening the Curve

State governors possess extraordinary emergency powers. Emergency declarations permit governors to mobilize the National Guard, close schools, invoke curfews, and prevent gatherings. They allow states to redirect health care workers to where they are needed and organize hospitals to meet the demands of an outbreak. They can seize properties to create emergency medical centers if hospital beds are not available. They can transfer equipment and supplies from one hospital to another, based on the needs of the moment. They can impose quarantines. As the risks posed by the virus became clear, governors began using their powers in ways that we have rarely seen.[20]

Many citizens were focused on the federal response, but in the absence of a national plan to reduce the spread of the virus and mitigate its economic effects, it fell to the states to take action. Mobilization against the virus involved local and state health departments, state emergency preparedness offices, and state and local first responders, all of which are under the control of individual states. Most of the testing would be coordinated by the states, even if the federal government provided some of the kits. Once President Trump suggested that states should find their own ventilators and protective garb, states moved to obtain the needed supplies.[21] And finally, coordination of hospital beds, which were threatened to be overrun with virus cases, is largely a state responsibility.

From the first recognition of the crisis, most governors, regardless of party, knew that the best prospects for confronting the virus involved flattening the curve of transmission or slowing the spread of the virus over time, which would remove some of the excess burden from hospitals and caregivers. Social distancing became commonplace as state chief executives first implored, then compelled, citizens to limit their contact with others—a particularly important move, as individuals could harbor the virus and transmit it to others while remaining asymptomatic themselves. On March 4, Ohio's Republican governor, Mike DeWine, shut down a weekend fitness expo expected to draw 60,000 people a day to a Columbus convention center. This was a preemptive move based on the science of transmission: the state had no identified coronavirus cases at the time. The governor closed the state's schools three days later and issued a statewide stay-at-home order shortly thereafter. In early April, Ohio appeared to be realizing the benefits of the governor's efforts at early intervention. With about 5,100 COVID-19 cases, Ohio had fewer than a third the number of cases in three comparably sized states—Michigan, Pennsylvania, and Illinois.[22]

New York's Andrew Cuomo declared a state of emergency in his state on March 7, utilizing state law that allows the governor to "temporarily suspend any statute, local law, ordinance, or orders, rules or regulations" in an emergency.[23] Three days later, he deployed the state National Guard to New Rochelle, a small community north of New York City, to enforce a one-mile "containment zone" in response to a sharp uptick in cases.[24] On March 12, he effectively shuttered Broadway with his prohibition against gatherings above a certain number of people.[25] New York was about to overtake Washington State in the number of reported COVID-19 cases, and Cuomo was increasingly concerned. Cuomo and other governors were beginning to see exponential increases in the reported cases, a trajectory that appeared eerily similar to Italy's, and felt compelled to act. On March 17, Texas governor Gregg Abbott joined twenty other state governors, including in the governors of California, Florida, and Arizona, in mobilizing the National Guard.[26] By March 20, 2020, forty-five states had closed all or a portion of their schools; this meant that at least 118,000 US public and private schools were closed or were scheduled to close, affecting at least 53.7 million school students.[27] Several state governors canceled their presidential primaries, with Ohio governor Mike DeWine doing so the day before the vote was to take place.[28] Even state legislatures adjourned or suspended their sessions in response to the crisis. By March 20, twenty legislatures had either postponed, suspended, or adjourned their sessions due to the outbreak.[29] In these and myriad other ways, governors took up the task of managing the crisis.

## Few Good Options

Although orders designed to flatten the curve of transmission differed from state to state, most governors acted decisively in confronting this crisis.[30] And the public largely backed their efforts. A Kaiser tracking poll conducted in mid-April found that eight in ten Americans supported the stay-at-home initiatives. The same percentage said they could follow the restrictions for at least one more month.[31] The words "flatten the curve" were heard and seen everywhere, from internet sites to billboards to op-ed pieces in daily newspapers. But to say that it was an easy choice for states to curtail business with stay-at-home edicts would be simplistic at best.

Although governors and state lawmakers clearly understood the public health rationale for keeping citizens at home, they were also mindful of the negative economic impacts generated by such plans. When Nevada governor Steve Sisolak imposed a monthlong freeze on gambling in mid-March, he knew his action would affect an industry that fuels the state's tourism- and hospitality-powered economy.[32] It was a risk he was willing to take because the alternative appeared much worse. Similarly, Governor Cuomo, while outspoken in his statements that his state's economy was taking a hit, placed health concerns above all else. Announcing the shutdown of all nonessential services in the state on March 20, he explained, "I want to be able to say to the people of New York—I did everything we could do. . . . And if everything we do saves just one life, I'll be happy."[33] Gavin Newsom, the governor of California, agreed. On March 19, 2020, he "shut down" the most populous state in the nation by directing residents, with certain exceptions, to remain at home, an order affecting not only the state's 40 million inhabitants but an economy that is the sixth largest in the world.[34]

In March and April, the economy went into freefall. The national unemployment rate jumped to 14.7 percent in April, and the number of employees on firms' payrolls fell by 20.5 million, statistics unprecedented in terms of both size and speed. These numbers eclipsed the worst of the global financial crisis of 2008–9, when unemployment peaked at 10 percent. April 2020 brought the country the highest jobless rate since the 1930s.[35] In Washington State, Employment Security Department commissioner Suzan LeVine reported that "this week [the week of March 16], every day, the new claims we are receiving are at the level of the peak weeks during the 2008/2009 recession."[36] Virginia's unemployment claims in the week of March 16 were greater than for all of 2019,[37] and the governor's economic advisers were warning of a massive downtown in state revenues in the second quarter, a fact that would force major budget cuts.[38] The national Conference Board's Index of Leading Economic Indicators fell 6.7 percent in March, the largest monthly decrease in its sixty-year history.[39]

## Lives Take Precedence

Governors understood their dilemmas and choices: flattening the viral transmission curve would almost certainly make the economic losses more serious. They chose lives, heeding the advice of National Institutes of Health's

Dr. Anthony Fauci, who stated, "Some will look and say, well, maybe we've gone a little bit too far. . . . [But] when you're dealing with an emerging infectious diseases outbreak, you are always behind where you think you are if you think that today reflects where you really are."[40] Some governors were outspoken when confronted with the "good economy or good health" question. "Obviously we want a strong economy—who the hell doesn't?" responded Wisconsin governor Tony Evers. "But the fact of the matter is we put the value of human life at a higher level."[41] Mike DeWine of Ohio asserted, "When people are dying, when people don't feel safe, the economy is not gonna come back."[42] And they knew that the prohibitions would be needed for a while.

By March 28, the COVID-19 case reporting curve was exploding upward in New York and New Jersey. Washington State announced 627 new cases on March 27, bringing the state's total to 3,207, including 147 deaths.[43] By contrast, Virginia had reported only 739 cases and 17 deaths. Fortunately, the commonwealth's cases and death toll remained lower than those of many other states during the early days of the pandemic. With the social distancing and stay-at-home orders in place, Virginia's daily death numbers crested and began to decline in May and June. Without these measures, the case numbers and death toll would likely have been higher.

## State Confrontations with Washington

Throughout the month of March, the public was treated to daily press briefings from the White House highlighting frequent differences of opinion between President Trump and his scientific experts and foreshadowing a series of political and legal disputes between the president and state governors. By contrast, the daily press briefings of New York governor Cuomo, with their combination of empathy, scientific information, warnings, and encouragement, had become must-watch TV for those pining for some sort of leadership. Trump's predictions that the virus would just go away and the economy would soon reopen flummoxed governors as they witnessed exponential growth in numbers of cases and deaths in their states and heard dire forecasts from the scientific community of what might be coming.[44]

A bit of good news arrived in early April, when the University of Washington models projected that the apex of infection would likely hit earlier in most states than initially projected, and might cost fewer lives.[45] In New York, while the death toll was devastating, there was some evidence that state efforts were bending the curve of infection, and perhaps the health system would see some relief. State stay-at-home orders appeared to be working.

Governors nonetheless remained concerned about their state's resources being overtaxed and wondered whether federal help would be available in a coordinated fashion. They were also worried that relaxing regulations in other states might allow the virus to spread into theirs. "The patchwork remains a patchwork as long as the federal government doesn't step up and recognize this is a war," Illinois governor J. B. Pritzker argued. "The federal government needs to lead and until it does we will be a leader here in Illinois."[46] The president, nonetheless, kept pushing states to reopen.

Many observers began to speculate on what would occur if Trump attempted, as he had suggested in March, to "reopen America" sometime around Easter. But suddenly, at a press briefing of March 31, he abruptly changed course, and seemed to acknowledge the scientific projections at the time that more than 100,000 Americans might die from the pandemic. Instead of clinging to the "beautiful opening of the country by Easter," he extended federal social distancing guidelines until the end of April. Disputes remained between the White House and governors about the levels of assistance provided to state governments, but the president had avoided, for the moment, the possibility of a confrontation with governors and the public over whether or not people should largely remain at home.[47] Nonetheless, other administration officials periodically would threaten a showdown if states refused to relax restrictions. In an April 8 press briefing, Attorney General William Barr signaled such a conflict, referring to stay-in-place orders as "draconian" and promising that the federal government would be "very careful to make sure that the draconian measures that are being adopted are fully justified."[48]

In mid-April, the president reignited the debate about "reopening America," asserting, "The authority of the President of the United States having to do with the subject we are talking about"—rescinding stay-at-home orders—"is total."[49] Notwithstanding the president's claims, most legal observers believed that governors had the constitutional authority to impose these rules[50] and, other than the president withholding certain types of aid from states that failed to comply with his pronouncements, there was little he could do to override them. Moreover, Americans remained hesitant about resuming their normal daily activities amid the COVID-19 outbreak.[51] Finally, the public was clearly more enthusiastic about their individual governor's performance in the crisis than their president's. In California, Governor Newsom's approval rating in April went sky high; a stunning 85 percent approved of his handling of the crisis.[52] In the same month, a survey of

Virginians found that 76 percent approved of Governor Northam's handling of the public health crisis, while fewer than 50 percent believed that President Trump was doing a good job.[53]

## Politicizing the Crisis

It was almost inevitable that political considerations would enter the crisis. In some states, conservative governors attempted to define abortion as non-essential "elective surgery" to prevent the procedure from being carried out during the crisis.[54] In Virginia, business interests attempted to use the crisis to roll back progressive measures passed during the 2020 General Assembly session, arguing that these would impose additional costs on small businesses and local governments that were being hammered during the pandemic.[55] Finally, gun rights advocates chafed at the stay-at-home orders issued by eight states that defined gun stores as "nonessential services" and therefore subject to closure. The NRA sued in several of the states, thereby prompting the governors of Pennsylvania, New Jersey, and Delaware to relax their prohibitions to permit limited gun sales.[56]

Frustration generated by the extension of stay-at-home orders became the motivation for protest actions at capitals in Michigan, Kentucky, North Carolina, Idaho, Missouri, Washington State, and Virginia. Trump tweeted that citizens should "liberate Virginia" and other states. In Wisconsin, the state supreme court sided with the Republican-led legislature and blocked the efforts of Democratic governor Tony Evers to extend his state's executive order into late May.[57] Even the decision whether or not to wear a mask in public became a source of political division.[58] Trump made it a badge of honor to refuse wearing a mask, and many of his followers went along, even as the CDC kept arguing that mask wearing was one the most effective tools in limiting the spread of the virus.

## Testing Our Patience

As social distancing and stay-at-home orders began to bend the curve of infection, the next battle against the virus, and the key to a reopening of the economy, would focus on testing. Testing quickly became another "massive fail," primarily at the federal level, though there were logistical problems in the states as well. Trump continued to proclaim that "we are testing more people than anyone," which, while technically true, was misleading because of our lower per capita testing rate.[59] He repeatedly suggested that more testing simply identified more cases, and there were some suggestions that he had urged those in charge of the practice to "slow down." His comments did not stop the states. New York and New Jersey, the hardest hit by the pandemic in the spring, were ratcheting up their testing regimens, but it would take weeks to reach the level most epidemiologists thought was necessary. Governor Northam was roundly criticized[60] for Virginia's testing efforts, which ranked lower than many states and whose numbers were initially skewed by lumping different tests into its reports. The state's testing problems continued into the summer.[61]

When Trump insisted that it was not his responsibility to acquire the testing kits or build its infrastructure, states again filled the void. Republican governor Larry Hogan of Maryland enlisted his wife, Yumi Hogan, who was born in Korea, speaks Korean, and is the only Korean American first lady in the nation, to make a personal request to the South Korean government for test kits. By April 19, Maryland was able to secure 500,000 kits.[62] In the same week, Washington's Governor Inslee announced the purchase of roughly one million test swabs from China so it could rapidly scale up its testing network as a prerequisite to safely reopen parts of its economy.[63] And Cuomo was able to enlist former New York mayor Michael Bloomberg in funding a massive and unprecedented testing and contact tracing effort in the state and metro areas of New Jersey and Connecticut.[64] Without federal leadership and coordination, a patchwork of different testing regimens emerged in the states, thereby compromising efforts to control the virus.[65] In June 2020 the federal government said it was pulling its support for mobile testing sites around the country. The states were on their own.

## The Big Gamble

Early May brought an easing of stay-at-home orders in half the states, as a bewildering patchwork of openings and new distancing rules began to emerge. Georgia and its Republican governor Brian Kemp were initially the most aggressive, relaxing prohibitions against patronizing bowling alleys, hair salons, movie theaters, and even some restaurants. Mayors in Atlanta and Savannah expressed dismay, to no avail. South Carolina, Texas, and Tennessee soon followed with relaxations of their own. Scientists and public health officials warned against these actions, especially without good systems of testing, but that did not stop the governors, some of whom even acknowledged that COVID-19 cases would likely increase and deaths would rise.[66] Fauci and Dr. Thomas R. Frieden, a former director of the CDC during the Obama administration, expressed the concern of many scientists: "We're not reopening based on science," said Frieden. "We're reopening based on politics, ideology and public pressure. And I think it's going to end badly."[67]

Nonetheless, many states pushed ahead, and hoped for the best. In late June, such states as Arizona, Texas, and Florida, which had reopened the earliest, began to see major increases in cases and deaths. Houston quickly became a hot spot for the virus not seen by any other urban area with the exception of New York.

When the pandemic first hit, most states were fairly aggressive in trying to flatten the curve. They now appeared to be backsliding, and it was showing in the spike in cases. Governors who pushed for an early opening were severely criticized and faced difficult decisions about whether to reimpose restrictions. As Louisiana's Governor John Bel Edwards said in a Facebook post, "There's a lot of people out there saying they are done with this virus, but *the virus is not done with us.*" By July 4, 2020, 130,000 Americans were dead of the virus, and its first phase, which appeared to be waning in late May, was again on the increase.

## Summer Brings No Solution

By summer's end, no national plan had emerged, a vaccine appeared many months away, and President Trump was making matters more complicated by his approaches and pronouncements. He kept proclaiming that the virus was under control, refused to wear a mask, attempted to undermine Fauci through administration surrogates, and proclaimed that schools would reopen in the fall, while knowing that such a decision was the province of state and local governments. The CDC produced guidance for safety measures that were frequently contradictory and rarely reinforced by the actions of the president. As the number of cases soared, Trump's approval rating plummeted. And the states, many of which had taken similar approaches earlier in the crisis, were now struggling with rapidly increasing numbers and declining hospital space. Hot spots emerged in Texas, Florida, and Arizona, states with governors closely linked to Trump and which had relaxed restrictions earlier than scientists had advised. State legislators began contracting the virus as well and were forced into quarantine; in Mississippi, for example, the lieutenant governor, Senate majority leader, and as many as twelve House members had tested positive by mid-July.[68] Even governors became infected. The irony of Oklahoma governor Kevin Stitt, an ally of Trump who attended a generally mask-free political rally for the president in Tulsa that June, contracting the virus shortly thereafter, was not lost on many who argued that public gatherings ought to be discouraged.

By the end of September, at least four state chief executives had tested positive for the virus. Some places began to look more like "states of disarray" rather than "laboratories of democracy." With the notable exception of New York and some New England states, the nation was seeing higher numbers than ever before. Because of the failure of the federal government to develop a coordinated response, the governors of seven states—Virginia, Louisiana, Massachusetts, Michigan, North Carolina, Ohio, and Maryland— began a coordinated program to implement a rapid testing protocol for their citizens.[69] The start of the school year was rapidly approaching, and more and more communities delayed opening or began conducting classes virtually, concerned about infection.

## A Failure of Federalism?

The COVID-19 pandemic has forever transformed American society, and the ramifications will be felt for years. In a federalist system, there is a critical role for the national government to play in a national emergency as a mobilizer of resources and a coordinator of responses. In the absence of leadership and planning at the presidential level, the void was filled by individual states, each with its particular culture and approach to governing. Initially, this approach appeared to be working, but as the crisis continued and Trump urged relaxation of restrictions, the individual state approaches began to diverge, with some states retaining many restrictions and others fewer. This created significant challenges because state borders are porous, and without a national strategy and message, the virus could easily move from state to state, independent of restrictions. As voting in the presidential election began in the fall of 2020, the virus trend lines were again moving upward, and the president's approval ratings remained so low that pundits were speculating about a Biden landslide. The death toll had now passed 200,000, and the emergence of audiotapes in which the president acknowledged he had understood the risk as early as February further eroded the public's confidence in the federal response. Then, on October 1, 2020, the world discovered that the president had contracted coronavirus, and a seemingly serious case of it. This created more anxiety and confusion in the country as citizens struggled with what was true about the diagnosis and what was not. If anything, the president's sickness and his return to the White House sooner than his health seemed to justify further undermined the public's confidence in his handling of the crisis. Moreover, his statements that there was no reason to fear the virus merely made a coordinated response more difficult. All citizens had was their state governments, and those bodies were being undercut by pronouncements from Washington. On November 3, 2020, with over 225,000 Americans dead and daily infections in the United States hitting an all-time high, the electorate passed judgment on the Trump presidency, handing him and his administration a clear and convincing rebuke.

The virus, of course, did not care about the election, and cases continued to spike. As winter approached, some states were clearly doing better than others in combating the virus. As of November 1, 2020, for example, Vermont and Washington State had death ratios much lower than New Jersey or California.[70] But it was sometimes difficult to determine precisely why this was occurring because their policies focused on different priorities.[71] Vermont is more rural than Washington State, but both placed significant emphasis in curtailing the virus in nursing homes. The Green Mountain State also imposed a strong baseline of restrictions, including a mask requirement, but allowed its localities to enact stronger requirements if they desired. When OSHA, the federal agency charged with worker safety, failed to act, some fourteen states, including Virginia and Washington, enacted protections in workplaces.[72] In Michigan, significant efforts were made to combat the racial disparities evident in the pandemic, placing testing facilities in communities of color and testing every person incarcerated in the state's prison population. But whatever states were doing, case numbers once again began to explode, prompting one epidemiologist at the Boston University School of Public Health to exclaim, "The whole country is on fire."[73] The CDC counseled against traveling for the holidays. And states that had initially recoiled at statewide mandates—including Iowa, Oklahoma, North Dakota, New Hampshire, and Montana—imposed various forms of statewide mask requirements and hoped that a vaccine would arrive to save the day.[74] Perhaps the only thing that saved the public from total despair was the announcement in mid-November that two different vaccines with 95 percent efficacy would be available late in the year. And one of the most significant decisions loomed—how to prioritize the administration and distribution of a vaccine when it arrived.

However one judges the effectiveness of governors in the crisis, the pandemic experience made it absolutely clear that states have power, and they matter. The decisions of governors showed citizens the impact that state actions have on their daily lives. As vaccines became available, many decisions about how and to whom they were distributed were made at the state level. Almost every state prioritized health care workers, but variations emerged between state plans. Some, such as Colorado and Alabama, elevated university students above the general public, while others, such as Florida and Louisiana, prioritized correctional workers.[75] The new president improved the federal response, but the challenge of vaccinating 330 million was daunting, time-consuming, and again placed governors in the hot seat of decision-making.

As the nation seeks to recover from this major disruption, many of the consequential decisions will continue to be made by state executives and lawmakers. How will states respond to the budget challenges created by the economic slowdown? How will education at all levels return to some kind of normalcy? To what extent will regulatory patterns relaxed during the pandemic be restored? Will legislatures attempt to rein in the executive powers of the executive? Setting priorities in this environment will be more important than ever. Decisions in these areas will be affected by many factors, many of which are discussed in this book. They will be influenced by existing state law, including the state constitutions. They will be affected by the political culture of the state itself, and how it has responded to budgetary and other crises in the past. And finally, they will be determined by the elected and appointed persons who operate the institutions of state government in what are called the "laboratories of democracy."

# 2

# Laboratories of Democracy

[A] single courageous state may, if its citizens choose, serve as a laboratory;
and try novel social and economic experiments without risk to the rest of
the country.
—FORMER SUPREME COURT JUSTICE LOUIS D. BRANDEIS,
DISSENTING IN *New State Ice Co. v. Liebmann*

## Obsession with Washington

My city of Charlottesville, Virginia, is home to the Federal Executive Institute
(FEI), an offshoot of the Office of Management and Budget. Created in 1968
and housed in a renovated motel complex where Rock Hudson, James Dean,
and Elizabeth Taylor filmed portions of the film *Giant*, the FEI has provided
leadership training for thousands of senior federal executives. Since 2013, I
have been a guest lecturer at the institute, providing insights to career civil
servants about how best to work with legislators. I always begin the lecture
by asking how many participants live in Virginia. Many raise their hands in
response, reflecting the fact that many senior federal employees commute
to work in D.C. from the Virginia suburbs. I then ask participants whether
they can name the delegate or representative who represents them in their
state assembly. To the embarrassment of the group, only a few can do so.
Remember that these are seasoned, high-level government officials; they are
well educated, experienced, and have worked their way up through the system to their supervisory positions. Most are, by all accounts, successful, and
are valued for their understanding of how government works. And yet they
know little about the persons who represent them at the state level and who
make so many decisions that affect their lives and those of their families.
The reason for this may be understandable; as federal employees, their primary orientation is toward Washington. But this lack of knowledge extends
to citizens throughout the nation: the public knows little about their state
representatives and may understand even less about what they do and how
it affects their lives.

Countless studies have shown that many voters cannot identify their congressperson; a 2017 survey conducted by Haven Insights found that only 37 percent of those asked actually knew who represented them in Congress.[1] In 2015, only 23 percent of Americans between the ages of eighteen and thirty-four could name even one of their state's two US senators.[2] When it comes to knowledge about state government, the data are even more troubling. Not only do people vote in state elections less frequently than in federal ones, fewer still have much knowledge about state leaders. A 2018 Johns Hopkins University survey, for example, found that fewer than 20 percent of respondents could name their state legislator, and only one in three indicated they knew the name of their governor.[3]

There are many reasons for this lack of knowledge about state representatives, not the least being that media reporting on statehouses has declined in recent years. A 2014 Pew Research Center report found that the number of full-time statehouse reporters had fallen by more than a third since 2003.[4] In addition, American politics has become more nationalized. Not only do voters typically pay more attention to events in Washington, D.C., than to actions in their own state or locality but the two major parties have become much more homogeneous internally, offering largely the same ideological profile to voters in almost every state.[5] Thus, as media coverage of state and local politics declines, Americans have fewer options for considering local issues and are instead becoming more attuned to national concerns. As the political culture becomes more nationalized, the electorate is also becoming more divided in its political orientation and more polarized in how it views issues.[6]

These dynamics are affecting state and local elections and policy. While it was possible in the past for a candidate to be elected to a local office on the force of personality or character, party affiliation is more important than ever before. This "sorting" of political attitudes can simplify choices for voters, but it also intensifies partisanship and conflict. From a social psychological viewpoint, as group members identify more strongly with their group, they react more strongly to group threats. The debate over President Trump's first impeachment is a case in point. In late May 2019, about two months after the Mueller Report was submitted to the Department of Justice, an average of polling data compiled by Project FiveThirtyEight put the president's approval rating at 41.2 percent.[7] But Republicans nonetheless rallied to the president's side, with his approval rating among those partisans in a mid-May Gallup poll reaching 90 percent.[8]

Scholars like Alan I. Abramowitz argue that while many Americans are disillusioned by political parties and therefore call themselves independents, this label is somewhat artificial, and voters still tend to identify with one party or the other.[9] When they do, they often refer to the other group in very negative ways. At the same time, the notion of either party being a "big tent" capable of encompassing different views has fallen by the wayside as primaries essentially operate to purify the brand of the party and purge those who do not conform to certain tests of conservatism or liberalism, even if they are effective in bringing tangible benefits to their districts.

With less coverage of statehouses and a greater focus on Washington, voters lose track of issues that can have a great impact on their lives. Voter turnout typically falls off dramatically from presidential election years to midterm congressional elections—a recent exception being the 2018 midterms, when turnout was higher than for any midterm election since the early 1900s, clear evidence of the country's present state of polarization and voters' strong feelings for or against the then current administration.[10]

Voter turnout typically ebbs in years in which only statehouses are up for grabs. In Virginia and New Jersey, two states where statewide officeholders are elected in odd-numbered years and when there are no federal elections, the numbers are even more problematic. Virginia turnout numbers in years when the governorship is at the top of the ticket are consistently lower than when there is a presidential contest or US senators are running. For example, Virginia turnout was 47.6 percent in 2017, when the governorship was in play, but 59.5 percent in 2018, when only US Senate and House races were contested. And it has typically been even worse in "off-off" years, when only state Senate and House of Delegates elections are contested in Virginia; turnout percentages in those elections have fallen below 30 percent in recent cycles[11]—until 2019, when Virginia turnout hit 49 percent.

The lack of interest in statehouses is nothing new, but it is not to be celebrated. While we should always pay attention to the federal government's impact on issues, so many important decisions on matters that make a difference not only to the lives of citizens but also to the character of the country happen at the state level. In presidential, congressional, or senatorial debates, for example, candidates frequently seek to portray themselves as the "education candidate." But most of the action on education, in terms of both funding and policy, occurs at the state and local levels. Citizens rail against a political system that appears to be making it increasingly difficult to vote or, as a result of gerrymandering, for votes to count equally, but they forget that the decisions about voting and redistricting are made almost exclusively at the state level.

If you are worried about crime on the streets or rehabilitation for those who return to society after incarceration, you should focus on the states because that is where most criminal justice policy is made. States are actively involved in health policy, tax policy, and, increasingly, energy policy. And as Washington becomes less able to reach compromise on issues important to the citizenry, actions at the state level will assume greater prominence. Nonetheless, there remains a massive disconnect between citizens' perceptions of where the decisions that affect their lives are made and where those policies actually are enacted. As the news media place emphasis on Washington for political content and as reporting from statehouses and local government bodies declines, the risk increases that citizens will pass up their most immediate opportunities to exercise influence over legislation that affects their daily lives and their future.

## So Many States; So Many Differences!

Differences between states abound. If you live in Minnesota, with its extensive social safety net, the odds are that you will live six to seven years longer than your counterparts in Mississippi, perhaps the most conservative state in the nation.[12] Mainers are five times less likely to be imprisoned than residents of Louisiana.[13] In New York, where bargaining rights for workers are among the strongest in the nation and union membership totals about 25 percent of the labor force, the median household income for 2017 was $62,909. By comparison, in union-hostile South Carolina, where only 4 percent of workers carry a union card, median household income lags behind at $49,501.[14] If you are a teacher living in Mississippi and want to earn more money, move to New York! In the Empire State, teachers earn on average $40,000 more than the average teacher in Mississippi.[15] Stealing a neighbor's $500 iPad in North Carolina is a misdemeanor that might get you a fine or a short stint in county jail.[16] But, until 2020, if you took that same item next door in Virginia, you would have committed a felony that could have landed you in a state prison and cost you your right to vote.[17] With respect to violent crime, *USA Today* reports that the states with the highest rates are Alaska, New Mexico, and Tennessee. Maine, Vermont, and New Hampshire reported the lowest; Virginia was right behind them with the fourth-best rate nationally.[18]

Citizens rarely think about how laws can change every time they cross a state line. States have different laws on carrying firearms (in Virginia, unless you are a felon, you can carry a gun in plain view, and even carry a concealed weapon into a bar—but don't try that in California!). In Texas, you can drive 80 mph on some interstates. Vermont is the only state without a balanced budget requirement, and North Dakota is the only state that has its own bank.

When you cross the border from Delaware into New Jersey on the turnpike, forget about pumping your own gas at service stations; the state doesn't allow it. And if you move with your dog from Virginia to West Virginia, be ready to pay an additional tax; the state taxes dog ownership. Finally, you can smoke pot under certain circumstances in Colorado and Washington State, but be careful when crossing the line into Idaho. The Gem State has some of the toughest antipot laws in the country.[19]

One state, Delaware, is so friendly to large corporations that half the major firms in the United States are incorporated there. Many western states have provisions called "initiative and referendum," a form of direct democracy whereby the public can force issues that might otherwise be decided by legislatures onto the ballot for popular vote. And if you wish to truly enter the labyrinth of different state policies, you need only compare their alcohol and beverage laws.

In some places, most notably cities and towns that straddle state borders, the rules can change just by crossing the street. Small brass plaques embedded in the pavement on the center line of State Street in Bristol say "Tennessee" on one side and "Virginia" on the other. The twin cities appear very similar, but the rules in each are different, and one city is demonstrably more prosperous than the other. Bristol, Tennessee, has a population of 26,000, about 9,000 more than its Virginia counterpart. It has no income tax, and while its state has a higher sales tax (9.3 percent to 5.3 percent), Tennessee's state legislature has provided a special tax break to the city that effectively reduces the sales tax in the locality, thereby creating an incentive for more commercial development in the Volunteer State. The area has a huge NASCAR track, but it is in Tennessee. Bristol, Virginia, has a poverty rate five points higher and a lower median income than its Tennessee counterpart. As a result, Bristol, Virginia, which, ironically, is closer to the capital of Tennessee than it is to Richmond, has many more economic challenges than its Tennessee counterpart.[20] Where you live truly makes a difference.

## A Tale of Two States

Another example of differences across state lines can be found in the response of the adjacent states of Minnesota and Wisconsin to the Great Recession of 2007–8. Not only do Wisconsin and Minnesota share geographic proximity, their populations, culture, and industrial bases are similar, thereby making for useful comparisons between policy initiatives and results. Governors Scott Walker of Wisconsin and Mark Dayton of Minnesota took office in their respective states in 2011, at a time when both states were still scrambling to recover from the Great Recession. They took very different approaches. Walker, the Republican, focused on tax cuts for business and high-income citizens, deregulation, reducing aid to the poor, undermining safety net programs, and rejecting Medicaid expansion. He is best known, however, for his withering attacks on unions. He cut investments in higher education more dramatically than almost all other states.[21]

By contrast, Dayton, a Democrat, followed a different path. The legislature approved raising the minimum wage, raising taxes on the wealthy, and investing public monies in infrastructure, education, and aid to low-income families. Dayton allowed the unionization of new groups of state-funded workers and was an early proponent and adopter of Medicaid expansion under the Affordable Care Act. During Dayton's term, a pay equity law was passed to combat gender pay disparities, same-sex marriage was legalized, and the state made it easier to register to vote.

Although the economies of both states improved, data from the Bureau of Labor Statistics show that Minnesota has done markedly better. From 2010 to 2017, Minnesota's growth rate exceeded the Badger State's by 12.8 percent to 10.1 percent, and median household income in Minnesota grew by 7.2 percent, compared to Wisconsin's 5.1 percent rise during the same period.[22] Job growth between December 2010 and 2017 was markedly stronger in Minnesota than in Wisconsin—11.0 percent versus 7.9 percent—in nonfarm employment. From 2010 to 2017, wages grew faster in Minnesota than in Wisconsin in every decile of the wage distribution. Median household income in Minnesota also grew at a rate two percentage points higher during the period than in Wisconsin. Proving a causal relationship between the policies and the performance of the two states may be challenging. But the data clearly show that, at least on these measures, living in Minnesota provided, on average, more of a benefit than living in Wisconsin during this period.[23] In this case, state policies truly mattered.

Most recently, we have seen how different states have responded to the COVID-19 pandemic. A dramatic illustration is in the area of housing. When the pandemic hit and the economy collapsed, many were left without jobs and enough money to pay for necessities, including rent or mortgage. Some governors, legislatures, and even state court systems acted to prohibit mortgage foreclosures and impose moratoria on evictions to protect families from being removed from their homes.[24] These orders differed dramatically from state to state; Massachusetts had some of the strongest protections, while Missouri and Georgia had some of the weakest. Kentucky's governor initially instructed law enforcement not to carry out evictions during the state of emergency. The supreme courts of Virginia and South Carolina issued orders imposing a moratorium on evictions through the end of June 2020; in Virginia, this was extended into September. As stay-at-home orders were relaxed, however, so too were some of the housing protections.[25]

States would clearly matter to the thousands of tenants who had little income, could not pay rent, and had nowhere to go. Some states set aside monies to help. Virginia governor Northam, for example, reserved $50 million for rent relief, but projections suggested that the need was four times that amount. Illinois established a program to grant up to $5,000 per person for rent relief and $10,000 per person to help pay mortgages.[26] These actions would help, but they wouldn't end the crisis. By summer's end, the eviction moratoriums had expired in about half the states that had enacted them, and the courts were packed with tenants squeezed by loss of a job and landlords who could not service their commercial debt in the absence of rent payments.[27]

## State Rankings Are Everywhere

States today are compared on almost everything, and elected officials pick and choose rankings that show their state in the best light for whatever is the issue of the day. Governors and legislators celebrate their state being designated "best for business" or the "best place to raise a family"; it is a wonderful line in a campaign brochure. But in some ways, ranking states is a silly exercise. Depending on the criteria used for evaluation, state rankings can differ dramatically. Is the "best state for business" a function of lower tax rates or greater investments in education? Is the "best place to raise a child" dependent on finding quality health care at reasonable cost, access to playgrounds, or a clean environment? The Motley Fool financial website recently opined, based on data from the Bureau of Economic Analysis (BEA) on rental costs, where the average social security benefit would "go the farthest": Alabama, West Virginia, Arkansas, Mississippi, and Kentucky were ranked the best.[28] And *Kiplinger* recently concluded, based on tax burdens, that Wyoming is the best state for retirees.[29] Does that mean that older Americans should now flock to Alabama or Wyoming?

The problem with rankings is revealed in my home state of Virginia. The commonwealth ranks high in many surveys. A 2018 report published by *USA Today* ranked Virginia the eleventh "Best State to Live in America"; Massachusetts placed first and Mississippi last.[30] *U.S. News & World Report* ranked Virginia the "twentieth best" state in the nation for 2018 (Iowa was ranked number one), but in its 2019 ranking, Virginia had jumped to number seven (with Washington ranked first).[31] In 2019, CNBC moved Virginia from the fourth best state for business in 2018 to number one,[32] but when it came to "happiness," Virginia fared no better than fifteenth for 2018 (Hawaii was number one).[33] These comparisons underscore the seeming randomness of some rankings, but they also suggest that your life chances can be influenced by the state in which you live. A state's investment in education and access to health care are two main indicia of better life chances.

The Commonwealth of Virginia, to take one state, celebrates its educational rankings. The University of Virginia is traditionally ranked among the top five public universities in the nation,[34] and the Old Dominion's high schools also enjoy strong ratings; in the U.S. News & World Report's Best High Schools rankings for 2019, Virginia ranked eighth best among all the states, and almost one-third of its high schools rank in the top 25 percent nationwide.[35] In most national rankings, Virginia is consistently listed in the top half of all states.

In other rankings, however, Virginia has not fared so well. The 2015 report The Health of State Democracies, issued by the Center for American Progress Action Fund, rated Virginia the "least democratic state in the country,"[36] and Oxfam America ranked the commonwealth dead last among the states and the District of Columbia in its 2018 report The Best States to Work Index.[37] To illustrate how these rankings can become contested terrain when marshaled in support of policy change, the Oxfam study was frequently cited by Democrats who sought to change labor policies in Virginia in the 2020 legislative session. Business groups, however, pushed back, suggesting the Oxfam methodology was fundamentally flawed. The ratings so rankled the pro-business group, Virginia FREE, that its executive director, former Virginia delegate Chris Saxman, devoted an entire newsletter to building a case for how good Virginia was for workers.[38]

One should be careful before drawing too many conclusions based on rankings, and even more cautious in arguing that these can be attributed solely to policy and political differences. Although Oxfam gave low marks to Virginia, the state consistently ranks among the "best states to do business in in the nation." But why? Some, myself included, celebrate Virginia's state's highly educated workforce as the key factor, and employ this argument as a rationale for more state investment in higher education and workforce development. Others suggest that the high rankings are due to relatively low taxes or to the commonwealth being a "right to work" state; this leads to a different policy approach that emphasizes maintaining taxes at their present level or even cutting them.[39] Chapter 9 addresses in more detail the variety of ways states approach economic development, but suffice it to say, states matter both to those who rank them and to those who believe the rankings make a difference.

Each new day brings another set of comparative data on states, some with greater implications for policy development than others. In the health arena, comparative studies show wide differences between states. For the last thirty years, for example, the United Health Foundation has published a state-by-state report of health based on thirty measures.[40] Other studies provide a deeper dive into subsets of health outcomes. Analysts interested in infant mortality, for example, can cite recent data compiled by Child Trends, a national infant and child research and advocacy group. Its *State of Babies Yearbook: 2019* suggests that life chances are clearly related to the state in which you are born.[41] Although the national infant mortality rate in 2016 was 5.9 deaths per 1,000 births, the chances of surviving birth were much better in New Hampshire (infant mortality of 3.7 per 1,000 live births) than in Alabama, where the numbers were alarmingly high (9.1 per 1,000 live births).[42] If you wondered which state was ranked number one for "overall child well-being" in 2019, it was New Hampshire; New Mexico was last, and Virginia was ranked tenth, up four slots since 2015.[43] States also matter when it comes to life expectancy. There is a seven-year difference between the state ranked highest (Hawaii, at 81.5 years) and lowest-ranked Mississippi, where life expectancy was 74.5 years, about the same as in Vietnam. Virginia ranked sixteenth at 79.1 years.[44] These rankings depend on a number of factors, not the least of which are the policies enacted by the legislature and state government. And the Commonwealth of Virginia showed that policies can change very quickly with the arrival of new faces in the legislature.

## Redistricting and the REDMAP

Perhaps the best example of why states matter is found in the process of redistricting, a once per decade drawing of lines determining legislative districts for state and federal offices. Most citizens neither understand the process nor realize that it is done exclusively at the state level; congresspersons have no formal control of their district boundaries. This gives tremendous power to state lawmakers to influence the political composition of both the US Congress and their own legislative body. In this way, states have tremendous power over the nation. Though both parties have engaged in partisan redistricting in the past, only recently has it become part of a national political strategy to retain control of Congress. Such a national concerted effort began the day after Barack Obama was elected president in November

2008. Obama's victory, and the coalition it energized, did two things. First, it lulled Democrats into thinking they had won the country because they won the White House. Why focus on state legislatures if you control the presidency? Second, the Obama win not only concerned national Republicans, it energized them. They looked at the national electoral map and the changing demographics in the country and worried they might never again win a national election. Unless they developed a new approach, their national power would be gone.

While the Democrats remained complacent, it did not take long for Republicans to develop a plan to counter the Obama coalition. If the country was experiencing realignment at the presidential level, they reasoned, their only chance to exert power was to take control of Congress, and the best way to do this would be to gain control of statehouses so they could control redistricting. Led in part by two men with Virginia ties, lobbyist Chris Jankowski and former Republican National Committee head Ed Gillespie,[45] the party organized its donors and developed a strategy. Called REDMAP, the approach relied on redirecting the political spending of major Republican donors into state legislative races, with an eye toward flipping state chambers. It was wildly successful.[46] In 2008, Democrats controlled sixty-three of ninety-nine state legislative chambers; by 2017, they controlled only thirty-two, almost a complete reversal from ten years earlier.

The shift toward Republican control began with the 2010 midterm elections, a disaster for national Democrats as they lost their majority in Congress. But the losses were even more dramatic at the state level, where Republicans scored historic wins, gaining almost seven hundred seats and taking control of nineteen legislative chambers.[47]

Democrats made the mistake of viewing the election as only a temporary backlash to the passage of the Affordable Care Act; many did not grasp the significance of the state losses on national politics and redistricting. Obama continued to neglect state contests as he worked for his reelection in 2012. Republican control of state legislatures allowed the party to draw new congressional districts, and they did it with a hyperpartisan vengeance. Armed with incredibly sophisticated technology, they drew maps so effectively that while Democrats outpolled the Republican congressional candidates in 2012 by 1.4 million votes nationwide, the party of Lincoln still managed to retain a thirty-three-vote margin in the US House of Representatives.

In Virginia, Republicans used their power with ruthless precision. Just prior to redistricting in 2011, Republicans enjoyed a 54–44 majority in the Virginia House.[48] After new lines were drawn and the fall elections occurred,

Democratic strength fell to thirty-two out of one hundred total delegates. The power over redistricting is one reason why the 2019 and 2020 state elections were so important. In most states, it is the legislatures and the governors who are elected that will control this process and will have tremendous influence over the partisan composition of both the US Congress and the state legislatures for the next ten years, until the process of redistricting can start anew. Although Democrats took control of both the Virginia House and Senate in 2019, Republicans actually picked up 186 state legislative seats in 2020, and controlled at least fifty-nine of the ninety-nine state chambers as redistricting approached.

Nationally, Democrats, who had largely ignored the significance of state legislatures during the Obama years, eventually realized what was at stake, and began organizing to reverse Republican advances. The National Democratic Redistricting Committee (NDRC) was formed in 2016 as a response to the party's losses in state legislative races in the last decade. Chaired by Eric H. Holder Jr., US attorney general during the Obama administration, the group utilizes a variety of legal and political strategies designed to give Democrats a better chance at controlling state legislatures.[49] It has been instrumental in convincing courts to reverse various redistricting plans as unconstitutional, including the 2011 Virginia plan. The new Virginia redistricting map, imposed by a federal court in 2019 as a result of that decision, was one reason why Democrats gained control of the House and Senate in that fall's state election. To counter the NDRC, the Republicans formed a group of their own, the National Republican Redistricting Trust, led, in part, by former Wisconsin governor Scott Walker.[50]

All state legislatures are consumed with the redistricting process when it comes time to redraw maps. They understand that what they do not only affects their future and that of their colleagues. It can also determine which party will control the House of Representatives. In the last decade, there has been a major effort to reform the once-a-decade process, largely focused on creating independent redistricting commissions designed to take some of the politics out of it.[51] Independent redistricting commissions(IRCs) exist in some form in eighteen states; in the 2018 midterm election cycle, the formation of IRCs passed in Michigan, Colorado, Utah, Missouri, and Ohio.[52] For years, many Virginia Democrats had advocated for such a commission, which could only be enacted by adding an amendment to the state constitution, not an easy task.[53] In the final days of the 2019 session, both the Virginia House and the Senate adopted a proposed constitutional amendment that was not quite the independent commission that some advocates had envisaged but that nonetheless reformed part of the process. The vote on the amendment was strong and bipartisan. It was again approved in 2020 General Assembly session.[54] According to Virginia law, this proposal then had to go to the voters for final approval; this occurred in November 2020, when the proposed amendment was adopted by a convincing 66–34 percent margin.

## The Political, the Legal, and the Personal

Redistricting is an intensively political process; careers are both made and destroyed in the process. It is also a legal process, with different constitutional and statutory language guiding those who draw the lines. Finally, it is personal; the legislators in the room with the maps engage in a number of compromises that often are influenced by their interpersonal relationships and how they may feel about other colleagues, even those in their own party. That is why lines are sometimes drawn to protect a certain incumbent while placing two others into the same district. The next several chapters examine the context within which lawmakers work and some of the personalities that make our state governments function. We start with the legal terrain, the different constitutions in effect in different states and how those different documents influence how policy is made. We then move to a discussion of the unique advantages some states have over others in their physical and economic resources, their people, and their cultural traditions. And we then explore the players on the field of policymaking, from governors to state legislators to other elected and appointed officials. The interaction of these factors illustrates how various policies in different states come to life and explains the diversity in policy that can be seen across our nation.

# 3

# State Constitutions Matter

The Constitutions of most of our states assert that all power is inherent in the people.
—THOMAS JEFFERSON TO JOHN CARTWRIGHT, JUNE 5, 1824

When citizens talk about "the Constitution," they are typically referring the federal document developed at the Philadelphia Constitutional Convention in 1787 and ratified in 1789. National polls conducted thirty years apart, in 1988 and 2018, indicated that over 50 percent of Americans are not aware that each state has its own individual constitution.[1] But it is impossible to discuss state policy or to explain how it is made without understanding the fifty-one different constitutions that establish the operation of state government.[2] How many know that the Virginia governor cannot serve two consecutive terms, and how that limit affects the broad outlines of policy? Or that most state constitutions include the requirement that state budgets be balanced? Or that various state constitutions, unlike the federal one, include provisions for public education, even if the language of their commitments is very different? Or that they give different powers to their localities? Or include different ways by which the documents themselves can be changed? The state constitutions establish the guidelines for how states operate and are therefore critically important for understanding the decisions of our times.

The US federal Constitution has operated with relatively few amendments since its ratification in 1789. State constitutions, by contrast, were created at different times and differ dramatically from state to state; many have been fundamentally transformed multiple times since their initial approval. They are much more easily amended than the federal document, thereby giving states greater flexibility to include new rights for their citizens or new obligations for government.[3] The newest active state constitution is Georgia's, which took effect on July 1, 1983; the Commonwealth of Massachusetts, which adopted its present constitution on October 25, 1780, holds the distinction of having a state constitution that is not only the oldest one in the country but also the oldest functioning written constitution in continuous effect in the world.[4]

Some constitutions contain provisions that are no longer legal or make little sense in today's environment. Alabama's Constitution, adopted in 1901, still includes Section 256, which states: "Separate schools shall be provided for white and colored children, and no child of either race shall be permitted to attend a school of the other race."[5] Of course, this provision was rendered unenforceable by the US Supreme Court decision in *Brown v. Board of Education*, 347 U.S. 483 (1954). More than sixty years after *Brown*, this language remains in Alabama's Constitution because voters in the state rejected, in both 2004 and 2012, ballot measures that would have removed it.[6]

Each state's own constitution influences not only its policy development but also its politics. The California Constitution, for example, specifically includes an express right to privacy among its enumerated "inalienable rights"; this provision was added by a 1972 ballot initiative approved by state voters.[7] Since the right to privacy served as the primary rationale for the Supreme Court's decision in *Roe v. Wade*, the California provision creates an express right for its citizens that is only implied in the US Constitution.

Virginia's Constitution is unique from all others is that it prohibits the governor from seeking a consecutive second term.[8] While the commonwealth's constitution provides the office with extensive powers, many Virginia residents hold the view that a one-term governorship inhibits longer-term planning, especially in the area of economic development. Because governors are restricted to one term, they are sometimes perceived to be lame duck executives almost from the time they take office. And since Virginia does not have term limits for legislators, the lawmakers can develop an inflated view of their own influence on long-term policy; hence the saying, frequently heard in the halls of the capitol in Richmond, that "governors come and go, but the legislature is forever." This influences the politics of the state in substantial ways.

Although the Virginia Constitution is an outlier when it comes to the term of the governor, a number of its provisions are similar to arrangements in other states, which helps define the distinctions between federal and state government. Like the constitutions of forty-five other states, it includes a requirement for a balanced state budget.[9] Like thirty-nine other state constitutions, Virginia's contains a provision that requires a bill to address or contain a single subject.[10] These provisions generate a legislative dynamic very different from what is found in the US Congress, which has no such provisions. In most states, the budget bill is the one measure that "has to pass," thereby forcing compromise in a way not found in D.C. Second, the single object rule creates fewer opportunities for mischief and manipulation. Because it is nearly impossible to add an unrelated new provision to a piece of legislation, legislators tend to remain focused on the issue before them.

Although the contents of many state constitutions are relatively unknown to most citizens, their provisions can have impacts on citizens that are more direct than those generated by US constitutional provisions. The requirement that states produce a balanced budget is perhaps the most dramatic. The COVID-19 crisis illustrates the difficulties that states may confront when revenues dramatically decline at a time when demand for services rises and states do not have access to reserve funds or the ability to run deficits. A number of states were forced into major cuts simply to make their budgets balance as their tax revenues declined.

Constitutions that allow citizen-initiated petitions to circumvent the legislative process by enacting policy changes directly through the ballot box create very different dynamics in states that have them than in states that do not. And finally, there is increasing legal activity at the state level as interested parties attempt to use state constitutional provisions to compel elected officials to make changes in policy and budgeting that have traditionally been rejected. Efforts to increase school funding by arguing that the language of the state constitution requires it is the most prominent example, but advocates are also using language on environmental protection to bring change as well. These efforts are all being fought at the state level by advocates who see the conditions more hospitable there than in the federal courts.

## The Evolution of State Constitutions

On May 16, 1775, one month after the skirmishes at Lexington and Concord, the provincial congresses of several states, led by Massachusetts, wrote to the Continental Congress asking "your most explicit advice respecting the taking up and exercising the powers of civil government."[11] The Congress advised "to call a full and free representation of the people, and that the representatives if they think it necessary, establish such a form of government, as in their judgment, will best produce the happiness of the people, and most effectually secure peace and good order in the province, during the present dispute between G[reat] Britain and the colonies."[12] Shortly thereafter the Congress made a similar recommendation to all the colonies. Virginia, New Jersey, Delaware, Pennsylvania, Maryland, North Carolina, New Hampshire, and South Carolina soon followed the Bay State in forming provisional constitutions. The transition to new governmental forms was under way, and states were in the thick of it.

At the time of the American Revolution, colonial allegiances rested more with each state than with a national government. Hence it made sense that each state would develop its own set of rules for governance. These constitutions initially had features in common, but they were nonetheless unique, as they arose from the distinct political culture in their respective states at the time. And unlike the US Constitution, whose basic form has remained consistent for more than 230 years, most state constitutions have been totally rewritten over the years: Louisiana, for example, has replaced its document eleven times, and Georgia ten. While the US Constitution is a product of the late eighteenth century and the political thought of that era, only three current state constitutions—those of Massachusetts, New Hampshire, and Vermont—date from that time period. The majority of current state constitutions were adopted in the late nineteenth century, and nine, including those of states as diverse as Virginia and Montana, were adopted after 1960. In just twenty years, from 1963 to 1982, ten state constitutions were rewritten and adopted, and there would have been two more had voters in New York (1967) and Maryland (1968) not rejected efforts to create new documents.[13] Hence, while the federal constitution has changed very little since 1787, state constitutions have been altered with the times, and their most recent iterations can be very different from their original formulations and from each other.

Although most state constitutions include their own version of a bill of rights and a statement as to the separation of powers, other provisions are very different from those detailed in the US Constitution. The US Constitution is relatively brief compared to most state documents; it is generally viewed as a limited grant of power from the people to the government. The constitutional debate between express and implied powers in the US Constitution has been with us since the founding of the nation, but rarely has it been suggested that federal powers are anything but limited. Article I of the US Constitution grants only specific powers to Congress, such as the rights to borrow and coin money, regulate commerce, establish post offices, and even punish "piracies."

By contrast, while most state constitutions place certain constraints on state legislatures, they nonetheless empower state assemblies to enact a wider array of measures not specifically prohibited. This is often referred to as "plenary power," that is, the ability to act in ways that are not expressly prohibited in the state's constitution or the US Constitution. Because of this plenary power, states, especially their legislative branches, are often viewed as having more expansive powers than their counterparts in the federal system. State courts have historically been reluctant to overturn legislative actions, and countless state court opinions discuss deference either to the prerogatives of the legislature or to a strict reading of the words of its laws. For that reason, many state constitution-makers have found it necessary to elaborate, in considerable detail, the restrictions they seek to impose, either on legislative action or on court interpretation of statutes. (This is one reason why many state constitutions are lengthy documents. Today, thirty state constitutions each comprise more than 20,000 words; the longest is Alabama's, which stretches some six hundred pages, has over nine hundred amendments, and runs to 376,000 words, prompting one state constitutional scholar to quip, "State constitutions offer textualists a lot of text to interpret."[14]) In addition, this plenary power has the effect of legally making the power of states superior to that of localities.

James Madison, writing in *Federalist* No. 45, explained the distinction between state and federal constitutions by pointing out that the powers of the national government set out in the federal Constitution are enumerated and limited. By contrast, the powers "which are to remain in the State governments are numerous and indefinite . . . and will extend to all the objects which, in the ordinary course of affairs concern the lives, liberties, and properties of the people, and the internal order, improvement, and prosperity of the State."[15] States retain substantial power in determining the rules by which citizens live their lives and, as our federal government has become increasingly paralyzed by partisan gridlock, states have functioned as the laboratories within which wide varieties of social policies may be enacted.[16] For this reason, state constitutions are more important than ever. Since state constitutions include provisions not found in the US Constitution, they also may prove vehicles by which rights may be asserted independent of the federal document.

Beyond that, the arguments made in state court cases can influence the US Supreme Court as it considers whether and how to nationalize a right under the US Constitution. Some scholars suggest, for example, that the majority argument in *Obergefell v. Hodges*, the US Supreme Court case that established marriage equality in the United States in 2015, drew heavily from earlier state court decisions, particularly the Massachusetts decision in *Goodridge v. Department of Public Health*. By the time *Obergefell* was decided, nineteen states and the District of Columbia had legalized same-sex marriage.[17]

There is considerable variety among state constitutions in the provisions they include. Thirteen of these documents, for example, include statements about a state's obligations to public health, with six states explicitly including the requirement "to promote and protect the public health."[18] Several, including the constitutions of Hawaii, Missouri, and New York, explicitly grant collective bargaining rights to public employees.[19] The Oregon Constitution requires the presence of two-thirds of its legislative bodies to constitute a quorum for conducting business. This provision has led to several walkouts over the years, temporarily bringing legislative activity to a halt and providing the minority with substantial leverage and power in the legislature.[20] Understanding these differences helps make sense of why different policies are developed in different states at different times.

## Education Funding and Equity: A State Constitutional Requirement?

Among the provisions found in state constitutions that have no parallel in the US Constitution are those related to public education. Many state constitutions include language that not only addresses the need for a system of public education but also appears to impose obligations on state and local governments to provide it. The language differs widely from state to state, with the result that the enforcement of a particular article through court action can be very different.[21] For those who contemplate pushing policy change through court action, state constitutions can create opportunities—or deny them.

The Minnesota Constitution, for example, states that "it is the duty of the legislature to establish a general and uniform system of public schools." Pennsylvania's requires the General Assembly to "provide for the maintenance and support of a thorough and efficient system of public education to serve the needs of the Commonwealth," and the Colorado Constitution mandates "a thorough and uniform system of free public schools throughout the state."[22]

Using the words of a state constitution does not, however, translate into successful legal action to compel states to provide more resources. Article VIII, Section 1, of the Virginia Constitution, for example, states: "The General Assembly shall provide for a system of free public elementary and secondary schools for all children of school age throughout the Commonwealth, and shall seek to ensure that an educational program of high quality is established and continually maintained," while Section 2 requires that "each unit of local government shall provide its portion of such cost by local taxes or from other available funds." Despite the language, Virginia courts have been reluctant to impose directions to state or local government about financial resources necessary to meet this obligation. While the state constitution clearly states that education should be "free" and "of high quality," that language has not been sufficiently clear to permit court intervention to force a higher level of financial commitment by the state or localities.[23]

The education language of the Virginia Constitution was put to the test in 1992, when a coalition of school superintendents and school boards filed suit against the state, arguing that the General Assembly had violated Article VIII by failing to appropriate monies sufficient to provide "an educational program of high quality." The plaintiffs lost both in the trial court and on appeal to the Virginia Supreme Court, which held that the state constitution did not require equitable or near-equitable funding per student across districts.[24] No other major litigation on Virginia's school funding formula has occurred since the 1994 *Scott* decision.

By contrast, the state of Kansas has been embroiled in litigation for almost a decade to determine whether the legislature has met requirements to fund public education as set forth in Article VI of its constitution. "The legislature," states the article, "shall make suitable provision for finance of the educational interests of the state." In 2010, a citizens group called Schools for Fair Funding filed a suit alleging that the state was not meeting its requirements under Article VI to provide the same educational opportunity to all children in the state. The plaintiffs argued not only that a student's chance for a good education should be the same in a wealthy school district as in a poor one but also that all education should be adequately funded, and that recent state budget cuts were frustrating that objective.[25]

Kansas state courts issued a series of rulings holding that Article VI of the state constitution imposed a dual obligation on the state not only to equitably distribute monies for public education but also to ensure that the funding was adequate. Conservatives reacted negatively to almost every ruling. Former governor Sam Brownback, who had created much of the problem with massive tax cuts passed during his term, directly criticized the Kansas Supreme Court as "activist," and even began discussing changing the processes of judicial selection.[26] His allies, including Kris Kobach, the former secretary of state (Kansas) and unsuccessful candidate for governor in 2018, even tried to expand the legislature's ability to impeach justices based on decisions that might "usurp" the power of the legislature and executive.[27]

On June 25, 2018, the Kansas Supreme Court ruled that the state's school funding, while equitably distributed, was nonetheless inadequate, and gave the state another year to make changes.[28] The ruling gave impetus to many who were seeking an increase in school funding, including Laura Kelly, who proceeded to win the governorship in November 2018 and then shepherded a major school funding increase through the legislature in spring 2019.[29] In June 2019 the Kansas Supreme Court held that the $90 million in additional annual spending brought the state into compliance with its constitution. Rather than simply dismissing the decade-old lawsuit, the court retained jurisdiction in order to monitor spending in coming years.[30]

The intensity of litigation asserting that state constitutional language mandates larger state support of public schools has increased in recent years, and lawsuits are active in states as diverse as New York, Minnesota, New Mexico, and Arizona.[31] It is clear that localities and citizens are viewing state constitutional remedies as additional mechanisms for seeking change.

## State Constitutions and Environmental Protection

Though the US Constitution makes no mention of environmental protection, almost one-half of all state constitutions include a relevant provision.[32] Some, such as Pennsylvania's, Hawaii's, and Illinois's constitutions, explicitly use the term "right" in their documents; others, such as Florida's and Virginia's, are less direct in specific protections.

Illinois was among the first states to include environmental protections in its constitution. Article XI, Section 2, of its 1970 constitution even uses the word "right" to describe the "public policy of the State and the duty of each person . . . to provide and maintain a healthful environment for the benefit of this and future generations." The article continues: "The General Assembly shall provide by law for the implementation and enforcement of this public policy. Each person has the right to a healthful environment. Each person may enforce this right against any party, governmental or private, through appropriate legal proceedings subject to reasonable limitations and regulation as the General Assembly may provide by law." In contrast, Virginia's Article XII, Section 1, is less specific and never uses the word "right":

> To the end that the people have clean air, pure water, and the use and enjoyment for recreation of adequate public lands, waters, and other natural resources, it shall be the policy of the Commonwealth to conserve, develop, and utilize its natural resources, its public lands, and its historical sites and buildings. Further, it shall be the Commonwealth's policy to protect its atmosphere, lands, and waters from pollution, impairment, or destruction, for the benefit, enjoyment, and general welfare of the people of the Commonwealth.

Most state courts have historically been less than zealous in their interpretation of these constitutional measures to strike down legislation or to support initiatives supported by environmentalists. The Virginia Supreme Court, for example, has generally declined to give the environmental clause much substantive effect.[33] The court has held that the environmental protection provision in the Virginia constitution is not self-executing, that is, it requires supplemental legislation for the "right" to be anything other than an aspirational clause. To date, then, it is nearly impossible to assert a claim under this section of the constitution without reference to legislative enactment.

Similarly, Illinois courts, despite the use of the word "right" in the state's constitution, have rarely used this language to side with environmental petitioners. In his analysis of that state's case law, Jack R. Tuholske recently concluded that "in the forty years since the provision was enacted, Illinois courts have determined that the environmental rights are not 'fundamental,' that citizens lack standing to enforce them even when government actions threaten direct environmental harm, and that it is perfectly acceptable for the legislature to enact laws regulating the environment that immunize agencies from judicial review of their decisions, even when those decisions directly affect human health and the environment."[34]

State courts in Montana, Hawaii, and Pennsylvania, however, have taken a different approach to interpreting the precise meaning of a constitutional right to a "clean and healthful" environment. Montana's environmental rights are found in both Article II, the state's Bill of Rights, which grants a right to a "clean and healthful environment," and Article IX, which imposes a corresponding duty on the state and all citizens to maintain and improve the environmental efforts. The state's supreme court described the right to a clean environment as "inalienable" and ruled not only that the Montana Constitution granted the people the right to a clean and healthy environment but also that citizens had legal standing to enforce it. The court then applied a "strict scrutiny" test to overturn a state statute that exempted groundwater pump tests for new mines from environmental review.[35]

Similarly, the Pennsylvania Supreme Court relied on a 1971 amendment to its constitution that stated that "the people have a right to clean air, pure water, and to the preservation of the natural, scenic, historic and esthetic values of the environment" in striking down a state statute that would have prevented municipalities from regulating hydraulic fracturing to extract natural gas.[36] The environmental rights provisions of the Hawaii Constitution have likewise been found to support a liberalized view of the ability of private plaintiffs to file suit to support environmental laws.[37]

These differences make clear how important state courts are in interpreting state constitutions. How judges are chosen, then, can have a great impact on how statutes are interpreted and how law is made. Chapter 8 explores judicial selection in the states, an issue rarely discussed but critically important to how law is interpreted in the United States.

## The Amendment Process and Citizen Initiative

If the US Constitution is too hard to amend, state constitutions may be too easy, with Virginia serving as a notable exception. Alabama is, of course, the poster child for constitutional amendments, with more than nine hundred approved since 1901.[38] Some thirty-six states permit an amendment to be submitted to the state's voters after one passage through the legislature. Several states, such as Florida and New Hampshire, only allow amendments that are approved by supermajorities of each body of their assemblies. Delaware is the only state where a constitutional amendment does not require a popular vote of approval in some form to take effect; instead, the changes require a two-thirds majority vote of the assembly in two consecutive sessions.[39]

Eleven states, including Virginia, have more difficult processes. In the commonwealth, a proposed constitutional amendment must pass the legislature two years in a row, with an intervening House election, and then is put before the public in the next November election. Because of this challenging process, the Virginia Constitution has been amended only fifty-one times since its adoption in 1971.

The types of constitutional amendments considered by voters vary considerably, depending on the state and the politics of the day. In Florida, for example, a state with one quarter of the nation's disenfranchised former felons, citizens overwhelmingly voted in November 2018 to add Amendment 4 to the state's constitution, which restored voting eligibility to 1.4 million Florida citizens with a past felony conviction. Prior to passage, Florida was one of only four states in the country subjecting certain groups of people to a lifetime ban on voting.[40] In that same year, Florida voters also added the state's existing statutory ban on offshore drilling to their constitution. Alabama voters amended their constitution once again, in 2018 (the document is closing in on 930 amendments), this time authorizing the display of the Ten Commandments on state, public, and school grounds.[41] North Carolina voters recently amended their constitution to include the right to hunt and fish, something more than twenty states have done. Michigan and Colorado each created IRCs as an alternative to the state legislature's traditional prerogative of drawing district electoral maps.[42] Each state differs on how these constitutional amendments are placed before the voters for consideration. In some, the legislature must act first; in others, the measure is placed on the ballot because citizens have obtained the necessary signatures to do so.

In some cases, citizens themselves may initiate the process by which constitutions are amended.[43] The constitutions of twenty-six states plus Washington, D.C., for example, permit citizen-generated ballot initiatives as a way for voters to enact or change laws when their elected representatives are unwilling or unable to do so. These citizen initiative petitions can involve changes in state statutes or the constitution itself. These processes not only allow significant citizen participation in shaping the laws of their states, they may also engage powerful interest groups with substantial assets to try to influence public policy. The number of such citizen initiatives, which had fallen between 2006 and 2016, has recently seen an uptick; in 2018, voters in thirty-eight states decided on 154 separate ballot measures.[44]

Some of the 2018 ballot measures involved changes in state statutes, while others proposed altering state constitutions.[45] Voters in Idaho, Nebraska, and Utah elected to expand Medicaid, and Michigan became the first state in the Midwest to legalize and tax marijuana. Anticipating the possibility that the US Supreme Court might overturn *Roe v. Wade,* voters in Alabama and West Virginia preemptively criminalized the procedure. Washington passed a set of comprehensive gun control measures, while voters in Oregon rejected an effort to repeal the state's "sanctuary state" law, a provision in the state code that limits the use of state and local law enforcement resources to enforce federal immigration laws, including detecting and apprehending persons suspected of violating only immigration laws.

National interest groups have understood for years that state constitutional provisions matter, and have used citizen initiatives to implement policies that either were previously considered national or had been frustrated by state legislative action. In other words, states have become the battlegrounds for powerful interest groups to push certain issues. The most famous forerunner of this approach was California's Proposition 13. Its passage in 1978 ushered in what at the time was referred to as the "taxpayer revolt" and likely contributed to Ronald Reagan's winning the presidency. Prop 13 passed only because of special provisions in the California Constitution that allow citizens who gather enough signatures on petitions to place a proposed constitutional amendment before the voters. Passed with almost 65 percent of the vote, Prop 13 inserted property tax limitations into the California state constitution. National interest groups took notice: if they could not win a policy dispute at the federal level, perhaps they could change state constitutions to accomplish their goals. In the years that followed passage of Prop 13, the number of citizen initiatives increased dramatically, reaching a high-water mark in 1996: out of ninety-seven initiatives on statewide ballots that year, forty-four were adopted. Not all were constitutional amendments, but each initiative was possible because of provisions in state constitutions.[46] Today, major changes occur each year through citizen initiative. In 2020, for example, Floridians voted to increase the minimum wage in the state to $15 per hour by 2028, and the citizens of Nevada approved a constitutional amendment that requires the state to obtain at least half its electricity from renewable sources by 2030.[47]

Many western states, including California and Oregon, permit these citizen-initiated amendments, which originated largely during the Progressive era and sought to provide more power to the people. Most of these constitutional provisions were added between 1898, when South Dakota incorporated "initiative" into its constitution, and 1918; today, eighteen states permit citizens to directly change their state's constitution without first receiving the imprimatur of the legislature.[48]

Even in states without a citizen initiative mechanism, there are frequent debates involving constitutional amendments. In Virginia, for example, some of the most contentious constitutional amendments in the last several decades have involved national issues and have engaged constituencies from outside the state in the ballot measures that were considered. The most recent example of this occurred in 2016, when conservative legislators joined with business groups in a well-funded effort to enshrine Virginia's "right to work" statute, a law that had been in effect for fifty years and had never been seriously challenged, in the state's constitution. A majority of states have right-to-work laws on the books, but fewer than ten have included the concept in their constitution. The initiative was soundly defeated by the voters by a margin of 54 to 46 percent. Missouri voters rejected a similar proposal in 2018.[49]

Virginia also occupied a significant place in national efforts to amend state constitutions to ban same-sex marriage. In the commonwealth, the measure was before the voters in 2006. Dubbed the "Marshall-Newman amendment" in honor of its patrons, the provision stated that "only a union between one man and one woman may be a marriage valid in or recognized by this Commonwealth and its political subdivisions."[50] Virginia voters approved the measure by 57 to 43 percent.[51] In 2014, however, a federal court ruled the amendment unconstitutional, and the US Supreme Court refused to hear the appeal.[52] Between 1998 and 2014, thirty-one state constitutions had been amended to ban legal recognition of same-sex marriages, civil unions, or domestic marriage partnerships. With the Supreme Court's decision in

*Obergefell v. Hodges,*[53] all such bans throughout the United States are now unenforceable. In theory, they should be removed from all state constitutions, but it is not clear that either the legislatures or the voters could marshal the votes to do so. Consequently, just as the racial discriminatory provisions in the Alabama Constitution remain, so too do same-sex marriage prohibitions in many state constitutions.[54]

One recent example where ballot measures have been instrumental in advancing an issue on which the legislature is viewed as timid involves efforts to legalize or decriminalize marijuana. On November 6, 2012, voters in Colorado and Washington approved ballot initiatives to legalize marijuana for adult use.[55] Alaska, Oregon, and Washington, D.C., followed in 2014, and two years later, voters in four additional states—California, Massachusetts, Maine, and Nevada—also approved ballot measures legalizing the drug. In the 2018 midterm elections, Michigan joined the list,[56] and 2020 saw voters add another four states—New Jersey, Arizona, Montana, and South Dakota— to the fast-growing list.[57] This brought the total number of states that permit the recreational use of marijuana to fifteen and increased the number of states in which it can be used for medical purposes to twenty-five. That most of these changes occurred as a result of citizen initiatives underscores the importance of state constitutions. The success of these ballot initiatives has emboldened state legislators to look again at marijuana legalization,[58] including the job creation possibilities of a new industry, as well as the potential benefit to be derived from taxing sales of the drug.[59] In January 2018, Vermont became the first state to legalize marijuana by a vote of the state legislature, and now allows possession and cultivation at home. In 2019, Illinois's state legislature voted to do the same.[60]

One of the best examples of how activists have attempted—often successfully—to transform states through the constitutional amendment process can be found in the numerous antiabortion measures offered in the last several decades. For years, antichoice proponents have been active in state legislatures and have passed so-called trigger laws in such states as Louisiana, Mississippi, and the Dakotas that would automatically ban abortion in those states if *Roe vs. Wade* is overturned by the US Supreme Court. Concerned that these statutes might not pass constitutional muster, a complementary strategy has recently emerged, one that targets state constitutions themselves. In 2014, Tennessee voters approved a groundbreaking antiabortion constitutional amendment that states: "Nothing in this Constitution secures or protects a right to abortion or requires the funding of an abortion."[61] This language was largely replicated in the amendments approved by voters in

November 2018 in both Alabama and West Virginia.[62] These provisions are significant for two reasons. First, if the US Supreme Court overturns *Roe v. Wade*, abortion decisions would default to the states, and several now include provisions in their constitutions that impose major restrictions on the procedure. Second, once a provision is included in a constitution, it is very difficult to eliminate. The national movement against abortion understood clearly that the battle would have to be fought in the states, and that is what its proponents have been doing.

## Just the Beginning

Recent history suggests that when stalemate occurs in Washington, the burden will increasingly fall to the states to accomplish those things that the federal government cannot or will not do. The extent to which states can be successful in this effort is influenced by a number of factors, including what their constitutions will allow. States will likely continue to innovate, but the extent to which they will be successful could depend on how courts interpret the provisions of their unique state constitutions. But beyond that, other factors will play a role, from the political cultures that exist in different states to the personalities that steer the wheels of government. We turn next to a discussion of other elements that define states—their unique resources, whether they are geographic, demographic, or cultural—and the roles those attributes play in determining policy.

# 4

# The Cards You Are Dealt

There are checks and balances and there is a federal and state dynamic
tension that was written into the Constitution. But there has never been
a moment where state governments have been more instrumental in the
lives of the people of this country.
—New York governor Andrew Cuomo

Each state possesses certain structural strengths and weaknesses that are
derived from its population characteristics, geography and climate, natural
resources, proximity to transportation networks, and the nature of its workforce, as well as from its political structure and culture. To some extent, states
must play the cards they are dealt. In other instances, they can manufacture
a new hand by strategically investing in public infrastructure and certain
industries.

A state's geography and natural resources have always had an impact in
determining differences between them. Georgia, for example, is not suited
to grow wheat; Nebraska is. Mississippi does not possess the economic
resources of Virginia, and so it starts from a disadvantage when compared to
the commonwealth. The coastal states have access to oceans, thereby enhancing tourism. Some states have the geographic advantage of a good port, which
generates economic activity and brings visitors and trade from other nations
to our shores. Arizona and California have severe water constraints, while
many midwestern states enjoy an abundance of that natural resource. And
many western states have land that is rendered undevelopable either because
it is owned by the federal government or because its topography makes it
nearly impossible to cultivate.

Because these natural resources generate substantial revenues for state
and local governments, states come to depend on them and tend to promote
policies designed for their protection. In mineral-rich Alaska, North Dakota,
and Wyoming, government funding can rely on "severance taxes," fees

imposed on the extraction of mineral wealth and natural resources. Because they generate so much revenue from severance taxes, Alaska and Wyoming have no state income tax at all. The problem with this arrangement, of course, is that the value of minerals and resources can fluctuate dramatically from year to year, with the result that a state budget that looks flush one year can appear very different the next. North Dakota has experienced a boom-and-bust economic cycle related to the extraction of natural gas by new fracking technology. As the prices rose, the state made major investments in schools, but when demand fell, its budget became seriously constrained.

State action to protect these resources and the industries that rely on them can distract policymakers from addressing other concerns. In Kentucky, Pennsylvania, and West Virginia, the traditional view that coal is king has led lawmakers to pass measures to promote the viability of the coal industry, even though these policies do little to turn around a sector of the economy that the market is destroying.[1] Other states facing the same loss of market significance have attempted to reinvent themselves economically. Many that lost their traditional industrial base have transformed themselves into regional finance centers or hotbeds of technological innovation. States like North Carolina and Virginia, once centers of furniture making and tobacco production, have in this way experienced major changes in their economic trajectories and revenue base.

North Carolina placed a large bet on investments in its Research Triangle, originally anchored by three research institutions, and that decision brought large benefits to the state. Virginia, once viewed primarily as an agricultural state, is now quite different economically from what it was several decades ago. The role of the military and the federal government today is more significant. The state consistently ranks among the top five states in terms of federal spending and procurement. And with so much of the internet traffic originally passing through Virginia, it has developed a strong technology sector and is home to major data centers, especially in the northern part of the state. On the other hand, Virginia depends more on defense spending and consultancy related to federal employment than almost any other state. That is why the Virginia state budget took such a hit during federal sequestration, the process that began in 2013 and involved major automatic federal spending cuts.[2] As Department of Defense and other federal contracts dried up, so too did a major engine of the commonwealth's economy. It is estimated that sequestration cost the commonwealth $9 billion in curtailed contracts, affecting more than 150,000 persons. The impact on the state's budget during that time was substantial; the governor and General Assembly were forced not only to invade the Old Dominion's "rainy day" reserve fund held for fiscal emergencies but also to cut about $2 billion in spending.[3] This was a painful time for the commonwealth, and Virginia felt the impact of sequestration more than almost any other state.

The regulatory climate of states also reflects the role of the industries that dominate their economies. In Connecticut, for example, the state's treatment of insurance companies has been driven by a concern that overregulation may influence whether they remain in the state. Delaware's laws were designed to make it attractive for companies to incorporate there; imagine the controversy in the First State if lawmakers attempted to impose dramatically higher fees on this activity—or if Nevada were to pass bills or enact regulations that disadvantaged the gaming industry! It is natural to expect states to support their key industries and to develop policies to benefit their key constituencies.

## Demographics as Destiny?

In addition to a state's resources, its population size and character explain other differences in how they operate. California, for example, with a population approaching 40 million,[4] simply has a different level of demand for services than smaller states, such as Wyoming or Vermont. The number of public school students in California exceeds six million, more than the entire population of many other states, including Maryland, Wisconsin, and Colorado combined.[5] The fiscal burden of educating these students is significant. The absolute number of people in a state makes a difference, but so too does its age composition. In Florida, with 20.5 percent of its residents over the age of sixty-five, Medicare and social security programs are much more significant issues than they are in Utah, where only 11.1 percent of the population are over the age of sixty-five.[6] Because regulations concerning Medicare and social security programs are made at the federal level, it should surprise no one when Floridians focus more intently on federal than on state elections; in 2016, a presidential year, the voter turnout was 75 percent, about twenty percentage points higher than the national average and thirteen points higher than for the 2018 gubernatorial contest.[7] Other states have a similarly large representation of people over the age of sixty-five, most particularly West Virginia, with 19.9 percent of its population over the age of sixty-five, Pennsylvania, with 18.2 percent, and Maine, with 20.6 percent.[8] In some of these states, support for public education is not as high as in places where the age composition trends lower. This age differential can create serious political problems when legislators and citizens try to generate support for adequately funding public schools and other institutions.

Differences in the ethnic and racial composition of state populations are also significant and help explain variations in policies. Our nation's history has always been greatly affected by different waves of immigration, and we continue to experience these impacts today. The US foreign-born population reached nearly 11 percent in 2009, and 50 percent of those were from Latin America. By 2017, those hailing from foreign nations had increased to 13.6 percent of the US population, nearly triple the share (4.7 percent) as in 1970.[9] This is a major change, and some states are experiencing it more than others. Almost half of the nation's estimated 45.8 million immigrants live in just three states—California, Texas, and New York. The Golden State had the largest immigrant population of any state in 2017, at 10.6 million, followed by Texas and New York, each of which have more than 4.5 million immigrants.[10] States where substantial portions of the population are foreign-born include California (26.9 percent), New York (22.9 percent), New Jersey (22.8 percent), Florida (20.9 percent), and Nevada (19.9 percent). Virginia stands at 12.5 percent, up from 5 percent in 1990.[11] The presence of large numbers of foreign-born citizens creates dynamics that affect both elections and political decision-making.

The last several decades in Virginia serve to illustrate how these changes affect elections. The state's population has been increasing, especially in Northern Virginia. In 1970, only 12 percent of the population resided in the region; by 2010, it was home to one-third of the state's residents. This population was more ethnically diverse, wealthier, and better educated than residents in other parts of the state. Arlington, Loudoun, and Fairfax Counties were among the wealthiest jurisdictions in America. The Asian population grew rapidly;[12] by 2018, Asian Americans in Fairfax County constituted more than 20 percent of its population.[13] Fairfax now includes a House member of Korean descent and another who is a Vietnamese American. In another Northern Virginia county, Prince William, the total population grew from 402,000 in 2010 to 468,000 in 2018. The county's Asian population increased from 7.1 percent to 9.3 percent and its Hispanic population jumped from 20.3 percent to 24.2 percent.[14] This had a huge impact politically. Prince William County had mostly elected Republican legislators until 2017, when five Republican incumbents were defeated by Democratic challengers and two Latinas captured seats. The change in demographics heralded a change in the politics. Reliably Republican in national elections since 1968, Virginia voters suddenly chose not just a Democrat but an African American for president in 2008. And Hillary Clinton and Joe Biden both carried the state handily. As of January 1, 2021, Democrats held both US Senate seats and Republicans had not won a statewide election since 2009.

Slowly but surely, these demographic shifts are affecting elections all over the country, and with them, the political decisions being made by state governments. As an example, the issuance of driver's licenses is the province of the states, and each has its own rules by which such a license is acquired. Only a decade ago, the granting of driver's licenses for undocumented individuals was thought to be almost impossible. But by July 2020, seventeen states and the District of Columbia could issue licenses or a "driver's privilege" card to the undocumented.[15] Similarly, as rural areas lose population by comparison with urban and suburban areas of states, the balance of power shifts in statehouses. In Virginia, for example, fifty-three of the state's 133 cities and counties are projected to lose population by 2040. Most of this population loss will occur in southern, southwestern, and western Virginia, the areas of the state that are most challenged economically.[16] Seventy percent of the state's residents now live in the three largest metropolitan areas (Northern Virginia, Hampton Roads, and greater Richmond); only 12 percent live in rural environs. At the state level, a loss of population means a loss of political power; when redistricting occurs again in 2021, more seats will be allocated to rapidly growing areas at the same time that a diminishing tax base in many rural areas will negatively affect the funding for critical services for a population increasingly in need of them. This urban-rural divide exists in many states and is likely to become more acute in the next decade.

The United States is gradually evolving from a predominantly white society to an increasingly diverse one; in fact, it is projected that by 2044, minority populations in aggregate will surpass the white population.[17] This change is strongly evident in several states, most notably California, New Mexico, and Texas. Much of the change is being driven by an increase in Hispanic and Latino populations, but the Asian population in these states grew at a rapid pace from 2000 to 2010 as well, and Asians or Asian Americans make up an increasing proportion of the national population. As this demographic shift occurs, the power relationships will also shift, especially in states where diversity is increasing. Those who viewed Virginia as a conservative southern state find their perceptions being turned upside down as Democrats gain an advantage from the demographic shift. In the country's industrial heartland—say, Ohio—the same dynamics are not as pronounced, and Democrats face an uphill battle in capturing control of state government. The increasing nationalization of the electorate is undoubtedly playing a role;

in places throughout the country with high proportions of people of color and ethnic minorities, the tendency of these groups to vote Democratic is being evidenced in election results.[18]

Latinos have been concentrated primarily in the southwestern United States, but the 2010 census showed their numbers increasing in states such as Connecticut (16.5 percent), New Jersey (20.6 percent), and Rhode Island (15.9 percent).[19] In addition, Native Americans, though accounting for a relatively small part of the total population of the United States, are present in substantial numbers in New Mexico (10.9 percent), South Dakota (9 percent), Oklahoma (9.3 percent), and Alaska (15.4 percent).[20]

As the ethnic makeup of states has changed, so too have political and social attitudes. In Georgia, for example, the population explosion in the Atlanta suburbs, coupled with the African American population in the rest of the state, fueled Stacey Abrams's historic but ultimately unsuccessful run for the governorship in 2018 and was instrumental in Biden's win there in 2020. Texas, though still a red state, is increasingly urban and diverse, and the Democratic vote is increasing. In contrast, places such as Ohio, as they shed population, especially in cities, are providing Republicans greater electoral opportunities. In many states, dramatic divisions are emerging between urban and rural communities. A 2018 Pew Research Center study, for example, reported substantial political differences between urban areas and rural areas. The former were 62 percent Democratic-leaning and 31 percent GOP-leaning; the latter reported preferences of 54 percent Republican and 38 percent Democratic.[21] Just the year before, the center had found that divisions between Democrats and Republicans on fundamental values, already at a record high level during Barack Obama's presidency, had increased even more during Donald Trump's time in office.[22]

One of the additional by-products of this increasingly diverse ethnic and racial political landscape has been the emergence of new candidates from these different groups who are running for office—and winning. The 2010 Virginia House of Delegates, for example, was composed of 19 percent women, 12 percent African Americans, 2 percent Asians, and no Latinos.[23] By 2019, however, the composition had changed to be 27 percent women,[24] 4 percent Latinos, 14 percent African Americans, and 2 percent Asians.[25] Similar changes are occurring in state legislatures across the nation. Data compiled by the Center for American Women and Politics at Rutgers University found that the percentage of women legislators rose from 12 percent in 1981 to 22.4 percent in 2001 to 28.8 percent in 2019. Between 1971 and 2019, the number of women serving in state legislatures more than quintupled; in mid-2019, women made up 28.9 percent of all state legislators nationwide.[26] As of 2019, women of color constituted 24.3 percent of the 1,875 women state legislators serving nationwide and 6.2 percent of the total of 7,383 state legislators nationwide.[27] These changes alter the dynamic of legislating in statehouses around the country. Not only are different issues such as paid family leave and pre-K education more salient but the interpersonal relationships in legislatures have changed as well.

Some states have also experienced demographic change in the form of increases in the number of millennials. A recent study for the Brookings Institution finds the largest numbers of millennials are located in the most highly populated states—California, New York, and Texas—but the largest percentages are found in the District of Columbia, Alaska, North Dakota, and Utah.[28] In some cases, this group is drawn to urban areas, particularly those with jobs in the technology fields. Richard Florida predicted this trend in his celebrated book, *The Rise of the Creative Class*,[29] and the last decade has seen millennials gravitating to cities and small towns where the culture is cool and the atmosphere is hip—places like Austin, Texas; Boston, Massachusetts; Seattle, Washington; and San Francisco, California.[30] Millennials are the most racially and ethnically diverse adult generation in the nation's history. More than four in ten millennials (currently ages twenty-two to thirty-seven) are Hispanic (21 percent), African American (13 percent), Asian (7 percent), or another nonwhite race (3 percent). And their political attitudes are also dramatically different from their older counterparts'. Since 1994, the Pew Research Center has regularly tracked ten measures covering opinions on the role of government, the environment, societal acceptance of homosexuality, and race, immigration, and diplomacy. In its most recent survey of these attitudes, Pew found that millennials were the only generation in which a majority (57 percent) held consistently liberal (25 percent) or mostly liberal (32 percent) positions across these measures; they were also more likely to favor Democrats in congressional elections.[31]

In the federal 2018 midterm elections, young adult voter turnout surged by 188 percent in early voting when compared with the number in 2014.[32] When final turnout figures were determined, voter turnout was higher among adults of all ages in 2018 compared to 2014 but had increased the most among younger voters. Between 2014 and 2018, turnout among adults under twenty-five nearly doubled, from 17.1 percent to 32.4 percent. Turnout among adults ages twenty-five to thirty-four rose by more than fourteen percentage points (from 27.6 percent to 42.1 percent) and by more than thirteen points among those thirty-five to forty-four (from 37.8 percent to 51 percent).[33]

The trend continued in 2020; an analysis conducted immediately after the election estimated that youth voter turnout (ages eighteen to twenty-nine) increased by another 8 percent compared to 2016; a projected 53 percent of eligible youth voters cast votes in 2020.[34] Older voters continue to vote in much higher percentages, but this trend toward a higher turnout among younger age cohorts is already having an impact on the issues discussed during campaigns. In the 2020 presidential primaries, the Democrats sought to engage this demographic by promising free college tuition and a reduction of student debt, two issues rarely discussed in 2016.

## Political Culture

Resources and population mix are key elements in explaining why states differ and how their policy mixes are formulated. Yet there is another key if sometimes overlooked element that helps account for policy divergence, what observers call "political culture." The term encompasses a state's system of norms, values, and traditions, and it underpins how state policymakers attack problems and create solutions. This concept is nothing new to political scientists. Back in 1966, Daniel Elazar attempted to divide the cultures of states into three basic types—moralistic, individualistic, and traditional—based on settlement and migratory patterns of people.[35] Virginia was defined as having a "traditional" political culture, one in which the government's role involves protecting and preserving the status quo. While some individualistic cultural activity is prevalent within traditional political cultures, elites remain at the center of control, both in running the state and as the thought leaders guiding the process; it was no accident that historian V. O. Key Jr. proclaimed that "of all American states, Virginia can lay claim to the most thorough control by an oligarchy."[36] Reviewing Virginia's history helps explain the state's historical fiscal conservatism and prudence, an attitude that still prevails in the hallways of the capitol in Richmond. Virginia was left with substantial debt after its defeat in the Civil War, and elites experienced substantial economic loss. This affected the attitudes of citizens and lawmakers for decades and helps explain both the development of a generally conservative approach to budgeting and the state's "pay as you go" mentality. This attitude was central to the "Byrd machine" politics that prevailed through much of the twentieth century in the state, and candidates continue to celebrate this principle into the twenty-first century. It still influences the construction of state budgets and debates over their passage.

While many now consider the Elazar typology to be too simplistic and confining,[37] that has not prevented others from linking states or regions to certain cultural criteria.[38] And there is substantial evidence suggesting that cultural attributes have been at work in explaining differences in state policies. New York and many New England states were known as places where politics was dominated by old machine-style operations, particularly in urban areas. In the Midwest, a substantial populist strain still runs through state policy processes, and California is viewed almost as a nation in itself, with a GDP larger than that of all but the United States and three other nations in the world.[39] At the same time, it would be a mistake to view any state's political culture as monolithic. New York City residents view Westchester County, less than fifty miles to the north, as "upstate"; they have little understanding of actual upstate cities such as Syracuse, Rochester, or Buffalo, much less more rural locales such as Jamestown or Watertown. In Virginia, communities like Fairfax and Arlington in the north are separated from places like Bristol and Grundy in the southwestern portion of the state not only by hundreds of miles but occasionally by what can appear to be hundreds of years. The former's orientation is to Washington, D.C., and points north; the latter relates more to rural communities to the south and west running up the spine of the Appalachian Mountains. In fact, travel by car between Richmond and Bristol is 324 miles and takes about five hours. Traveling to D.C. would take another two hours. Bristol is actually *closer* to the capitals of six other states (West Virginia, Tennessee, Kentucky, North Carolina, South Carolina, and Georgia) than it is to Richmond.

In some cases the cultural divides are greater within states than between them. Most recently, the cultural divide became very apparent in Virginia as the state legislature debated a series of gun safety measures. This prompted many communities, mostly in rural areas of the state, to pass resolutions declaring themselves "Second Amendment sanctuaries" and to vow not to enforce any "unconstitutional laws" passed in Richmond. Beyond that, several toyed with the idea that they should secede from the commonwealth and join West Virginia.[40]

These cultural differences seem starker today than at any time in recent memory and in some places are breeding a resentment that affects policy-making at both the state and federal level.[41] They also help explain why citizens from poorer communities are often perceived to be voting against their economic self-interest. In fact, they may view their interests through a cultural lens rather than an economic one and come to believe that their world is collapsing around them. In an environment of low social mobility, poverty, and drug addiction, it is not difficult to feel pessimistic about the prospects for achieving what so many of their ancestors fought to attain—the American dream. This does not consign them to a "basket of deplorables" but instead traps them in a cultural crisis not easily addressed. Arlie Hochschild writes that these individuals perceive a "shifting" in the "moral qualifications for the American Dream." This dynamic has turned this culturally alienated group, already buffeted by an economy that does not appear to work for them, "into strangers in their own land, afraid, resentful, displaced, and dismissed" by people who do not look like them or think like them, and whom they perceive to be "cutting in line." This generates a large group of people "that is regularly convinced to vote against its collective self-interest."

The political culture of this group can be different from the one on display in statehouses. One reason for this is that lawmakers typically feel they can make a difference and are not mired in attitudes of pessimism and alienation. Another reason rests in the institutions of lawmaking themselves. When people are elected to the state legislature, they are socialized to act in certain ways within the body as they learn the values, norms, and culture of the institution. Cultures of institutions are always subject to change, of course: the actors within them can set a different tone and establish different procedures that then take root, for good or for bad. Virginia is presently experiencing a major turnover of representatives, especially in the House. Over the last two cycles, the body has added thirty-eight new delegates who were not serving in 2017. The sheer number of new people can change the place and is something to watch in the coming years.

Different legislative bodies have their own norms and practices, which can influence approaches to problem solving. Virginia, for example, prides itself on doing business "the Virginia way," a concept that has had different meanings over the years. To some, the Virginia way suggests support for a status quo that has not done enough to include diverse voices. But to many others, it reflects a desire for a collaborative approach to governing even as Virginia becomes more diverse.

## Private Troubles and Public Issues

Finally, policymaking at the state level is inevitably influenced by the interaction of private troubles and public issues. It is not unusual for a public controversy to emerge out of something that initially was perceived to be an individual trouble. Transportation issues are a good example. Most of us have had the experience of driving a car through a pothole. The car's front end becomes misaligned, we may blow a tire, and the bill for repairs can easily exceed $500. We often see this as a private trouble unique to us. But what happens when many of our friends and neighbors have the same experience, and we begin to see that there are just too many potholes in the roads? At some point, we conclude that hitting the pothole has less to do with luck and bad driving than it does with the lack of state maintenance of the roads. It is no longer a private trouble but instead a public issue that requires a political and policy response. We now demand that the government act, at either the state or the local level, to fill the potholes.

The sociologist C. Wright Mills was among the first to recognize how citizens can experience challenges differently depending on whether they are viewed as private troubles or public issues. In his classic book, *The Sociological Imagination,* Mills uses unemployment as a way to explain the distinction.[42] He argues that one person's unemployment can more easily be explained not as a crisis for society or as the basis for governmental intervention; in such instances, that person's problem can be more easily blamed on the individual himself, perhaps even as a failure of character or initiative. When 15 million people are unemployed, however, the public explanation of the challenge can change dramatically. No longer is it easy to place the blame on the individual. Other forces are at play that require a public response; the private trouble has become a public issue.

Some of the most powerful and sustainable policy ideas emerge when citizens come to view their private troubles as public issues that demand governmental action. Before the 1930s, problems of aging were largely viewed as a personal trouble: if you had not saved enough for retirement, too bad for you. And if you got sick, you had to rely on yourself or your family to help. The idea of social insurance, which eventually became known as social security, arose as citizens began to view this challenge as a social issue requiring a governmental response.[43]

In state legislatures, Mills's concept frequently helps to explain changes in policy. The opioid crisis, which was once viewed as a personal trouble faced by citizens who allegedly could not control their own pill consumption, is now viewed as a public health issue requiring state and federal intervention. With almost two hundred people dying every day in the United States from drug abuse, including almost fifty from overdoses involving prescription opioids, and with thirty-five states seeing statistically significant increases in drug abuse deaths between 2013 and 2017,[44] it is difficult to argue that this is a private trouble that should be ignored by government. Consequently, states are passing a wide variety of initiatives to tackle the issue.[45] Autism was once viewed as a challenge that families had to confront on their own—that is, until citizens became aware of how many people were actually affected. States stepped in with intervention programs and new rules that extended health benefits to more children.[46] And both of these examples are related to what is perhaps the biggest issue that has generated a change in perception over the last few decades: health care. Once thought to be a private responsibility, health care access at a reasonable cost is now viewed by the American public as a right, and both state and federal policymakers must respond to the demand.

## Policymaking as a Combination of Factors

Policymaking is conducted within the context of a number of factors. The legal underpinnings set forth in state constitutions and statutes provide a formal structure by which to compare states and their impacts on their citizens. The resources possessed by a state, its economy, and its demographic mix provide certain advantages and disadvantages to policymakers and can be key to the results of elections. Finally, the history and political culture of a state can create an environment that is conducive to some changes but not others. But of all of these factors, perhaps the most important are the players, those who, whether elected or appointed, help shape policy and determine what gets done and what doesn't. The next chapter looks at these agents of change, the roles they play, and how their actions determine the adoption and effectiveness of state policy.

# 5

# Players on the Stage

Legislation is like a game of poker. You are dealt a hand with strengths and weaknesses, but winning or losing depends a lot on how you play your cards.
—Anonymous legislator

## Governors Come and Go . . .

Andrew Cuomo sat again before the reporters, engaged in yet another of his daily briefings on the COVID-19 epidemic. Both empathic and combative, the New York governor did not hide his emotions as he explained the toll that the pandemic was extracting in his state. For many, he had become the national model for how to confront the challenge, and it was clear that he, like many other governors across the country, was prepared to act decisively to protect his constituents. He did not back down from the challenge. At a March 17, 2020, news conference called to explain why he had ordered businesses, restaurants and other operations to close, the governor asserted control. "Be upset at me," he said. "The buck stops on my desk. I assume full responsibility."[1]

Governors view themselves as the key agents of change in state government. These chief executives have constitutional powers to shape policy like few other actors in the American system of governance. Not only do they have the opportunity to appoint their own people to head major state agencies but, since most state legislatures are not full-time and meet for only limited periods during the year, governors are in a better position to capture the headlines and shape policy initiatives for their states. Most governors can exercise substantial power in setting the policy agenda. They prepare legislation through their cabinet and agency positions, and their ability to introduce budgets can set the agenda for the entire state. They are the commanders of military forces (the state National Guard), which they can mobilize in times of emergency. Since governors are also responsible for administering federal funds given to states, they can be creative within the law as to how such funds will be used. Their key to success, however, largely has to do with how they interact with legislators, many of whom think they are the most important actors within the three branches of government.

America's past includes a guarded mistrust of governors, a holdover from the period when the British Crown ruled its subjects by appointing various colonial governors. Many of the early US state constitutions initially designated legislatures to appoint governors. In only four of the thirteen original states were governors directly elected by the people; legislatures in the other nine made the selection themselves. All states entering the Union after the first thirteen required their governors to be directly elected by the people, and by the end of the nineteenth century, governors in every state were chosen by the voters. Over the years, the gubernatorial terms of office expanded, generally from two- to four-year periods, and provisions were made to allow governors to succeed themselves. This provided the chief executives with additional powers to set the agenda and ensure it was implemented. In 1960, fifteen states prohibited the governor from serving consecutive terms; by 2008, only one state remained—Virginia—where no consecutive terms were allowed.[2] Twelve states have four-year terms and no prohibitions as to how many successive terms can be served. Thirty-five states allow governors to serve two consecutive terms, but no longer.[3]

Governors are used to getting things done. They are also seen as prospective good candidates for president. In fact, seventeen US presidents served as state governors prior to their election to the presidency. Jimmy Carter, Ronald Reagan, and Bill Clinton are the most recent former governors to occupy the Oval Office, but there have been numerous others in US history, and in the recent presidential sweepstakes, many governors have occupied center stage in the debate. In 2016 the Republican field included Governors Scott Walker and Jeb Bush and the Democratic hopefuls included Maryland's Martin O'Malley. In 2018 the Democratic field included Governors Steve Bullock, John Hickenlooper, and Jay Inslee. Each governor has his or her unique personality, and many become well known both within their state and outside it, depending on their personalities and their signature initiatives. Jerry Brown, elected originally in California as a change agent and nicknamed "Governor Moonbeam" for his creative and challenging ideas, served the state for a total of sixteen years, with his two stints separated by a twenty-eight-year gap. Mitt Romney became identified by his Massachusetts initiative to provide health insurance to all state residents, a plan that served as the model for the Affordable Care Act (ACA).

Virginia has recently seen a succession of high-profile governors, several of whom have considered a run for national office, including the presidency. In fact, one of the jokes around Richmond is that as soon as a new Virginia governor is sworn in, they have visions of walking down Pennsylvania Avenue. George Allen was considered a strong contender until his infamous "Macaca moment" led to his defeat for reelection to the US Senate in 2006.[4] Jim Gilmore became a candidate for the top spot twice, in 2008 and 2016.[5] Mark Warner flirted with running for the presidency after completing a very successful term as governor from 2002 to 2006.[6] L. Douglas Wilder, the nation's first African American elected governor, made a brief attempt in 1992. Tim Kaine was chosen as Hillary Clinton's running mate in 2016. Bob McDonnell was touted as a candidate for national office until a major scandal led to his indictment on multiple counts of fraud. And Terry McAuliffe flirted with a presidential run in 2020.

Many state policy initiatives emanate from governors' offices and then are adopted, in one form or another, by other states. An example comes from Tennessee, where Governor Bill Haslam led an initiative to provide free community college tuition for all state residents. Passed in 2014, the "Tennessee Promise" was the first program of its kind in the country and now serves as a model for other states.[7] The program is a "last-dollar" scholarship, meaning it will cover tuition costs not met by federal aid or other scholarships. It gives high school graduates five consecutive semesters of free tuition at an eligible Tennessee community or technical college. There is no initial GPA requirement, but recipients must also complete community service. Other states embraced the concept, believing that if Tennessee could do it, so could they. While not all programs are structured in the same way, sixteen states now have at least one statewide Promise-type program.[8] An idea for how to provide greater access to college education was taking hold—and state leadership was making it happen.

The tremendous power of the office has occasionally been accompanied by officeholders who either attempted to exceed their powers or ran afoul of the law. Edwin Edwards, the previous four-time governor of Louisiana, once famously boasted that the only way that he could lose an election would be if he were "caught in bed with either a dead girl or a live boy." Edwards's bravado did not, however, allow him to escape the law, and a federal grand jury in 1998 indicted him on charges that he had extorted millions of dollars in exchange for granting lucrative casino licenses in the state. Edwards was convicted on seventeen counts and spent more than eight years in prison. Nonetheless, he had the audacity to attempt a political comeback at age eighty-seven and run for Congress. He lost.

Two Illinois governors also became famous for their failure to follow the law. George Ryan was convicted in 2006 of racketeering, mail fraud, and tax fraud, and served five years in prison. Rod Blagojevich was sentenced to fourteen years in prison for attempting to auction the US Senate seat vacated by Barack Obama after he won the presidency. Arch A. Moore Jr., the former Republican governor of West Virginia, received a prison sentence of six years and a $170,000 fine in connection with a vote-buying scheme, filing false tax returns, and a claim that he had extorted a $600,000 payment from a coal operator. Eliot Spitzer, the former governor of New York and previously celebrated as a fighter against white-collar crime and corruption, had to resign in 2008 after stories surfaced that he had paid high-priced prostitutes. In 2004, James E. McGreevy, former governor of New Jersey, resigned in the wake of sex scandals after two years in office. And Virginians witnessed former governor McDonnell's numerous fraud convictions, only to see them all reversed on appeal. Fortunately, such instances of malfeasance are the exception and not the rule.

Beyond the power to initiate policy, governors can also prevent legislation from becoming law through their veto powers. Unlike the federal system, in which the executive's veto generally applies only to entire bills, governors often have what is called a line-item veto, a power that provides them the ability to pick and choose provisions they like or dislike; in some instances they can even rewrite the entire piece of legislation.[9] The power of governors to exercise vetoes is largely found within the constitution of each individual state. According to the National Association of State Budget Officers, forty-four states allow their governors to veto individual line items of legislative budgets.[10]

It is very difficult for state legislatures to override a gubernatorial veto. In most cases, the override requires at least two-thirds of the members of each body. The power of the veto is one reason why political campaigns for governor are so contested. This power is even more apparent during the first legislative session following the census every ten years, when redistricting is to be determined. With the governor's veto power, he or she can either change new electoral districts that were approved by the legislature or veto the entire redistricting plan. This means that even if the legislature has a broad majority of one party, it cannot impose its will during the redistricting process to draw lines to advantage it for the next decade.

## "The Legislature Is Forever"

Of the thousands of people who have served in state legislatures around the country, perhaps the most famous is the prominent author John Grisham. Grisham grew up in the small town of South Haven, Mississippi, the second of five siblings. He eventually graduated from Mississippi State University and received his J.D. degree from the University of Mississippi School of Law. He won election as a Democrat to the 120-member Mississippi House of Representatives in 1984. His plan was to serve several terms in the House and then be elected to the state Senate, from where he thought he could land a judgeship (judges are elected in Mississippi, and their pay far exceeds that of legislators). Grisham also fancied himself a potential chair of the Judiciary Committee in the Mississippi House. Many legislators develop plans for their political future, and Grisham was no exception.

His blueprint for his future began to unravel, however, after he and several other Democrats made two unsuccessful efforts to dislodge the Speaker of the Mississippi House. Not unexpectedly, Grisham was then relegated to minor committee assignments and given very little work in the House. Without much committee work, he tired of the pace of legislative action and wanted something new. He found it in the written word. Grisham's writing took most of his free time while the House was in session. He finished his first novel, *A Time to Kill,* and completed much of his second, *The Firm,* while still a legislator. Upon receiving a contract for the movie rights to *The Firm,* he decided that his time in the legislature was over and he would instead dedicate his life to writing. It was a great decision; since September 1990, his books have sold over 300 million copies worldwide. Now living in Charlottesville, he is a forceful advocate for equal rights and a generous financial supporter of those efforts. "Serving," he said, "made me very cynical about politics. . . . It was very frustrating—a microcosm of what you see in Washington these days."[11] Fortunately for me, this was not my experience. While I would frequently be frustrated by the politics of the Virginia legislature, I was always busy, and remained convinced that we were not D.C. and that positive things were being accomplished, including a major transportation bill passed in 2013, the expansion of Medicaid in 2018, and major gun safety legislation in 2020.

Most of us learn in third grade civics classes that there are three co-equal branches of government: the executive, the legislative, and the judicial. In many cases, legislators do not really subscribe to this view; instead, they believe they are the superior of the three branches, thereby giving rise to jokes such as "Governors come and go, but the legislature is forever." Governors are elected in statewide votes to represent all the people of the state, but legislators can sometimes have much more parochial interests, given the nature of their constituents. And with many serving for decades, their institutional knowledge and accumulated power can sometimes frustrate the goals of governors.

In all but one state (Nebraska), legislative representation is organized into two chambers, with the numbers of legislators in each body varying widely by state. In New Hampshire, for example, there are four hundred representatives in the House, while in Alaska the number is only forty. In highly populated states, state representatives and senators typically represent an average number of constituents that is larger than in states with low populations. California Assembly Districts average nearly 475,000 residents, while Virginia Delegate Districts are about 40,000. In one of the smallest states, New Hampshire, House districts average about 3,300 residents.[12]

The dynamic between governors and state legislators is illustrated each legislative session with various bills and the state budget. The legislature is terribly protective of its prerogatives, to the point of sometimes excluding the executive from discussions on legislation until it has been completed. For example, Virginia leaders had been struggling unsuccessfully with finding additional monies to address transportation challenges for two decades when Bob McDonnell decided to make it a major initiative in 2013. McDonnell's initial proposal raised little revenue compared to the need, primarily because his party was reluctant to raise taxes. But, as is the case with many policy proposals, the legislative process leads to interesting results. During weeks of committee meetings on the bill, the attitude of the legislature changed; a majority were finally ready to raise revenue for roads, rail, and transit. The plan that emerged involved imposing regional taxes that would help regional needs, and more taxes than McDonnell initially desired. The package totaled several billion dollars. When the bill got to the legislative conference committee to work out final details, the governor offered his assistance. The response of the conferees was "Thanks a lot, Governor, we've got this covered." When the multimillion-dollar bill passed, the governor received much of the credit. But it was the legislature that did the heavy lifting.

## Growing Impacts of State Attorneys General

State attorneys general (AGs) are not typically recognized by the American public. While there have been some famous ones—Bill Clinton in Arkansas, Eliot Spitzer in New York, and Earl Warren, Jerry Brown, and Kamala Harris in California—many citizens do not understand precisely what they do.

In fact, when people campaign for the job, they have to spend much of their time explaining they will not be the J. Edgar Hoover of state government, and they have many powers and responsibilities outside the criminal law. This has changed dramatically in the last decade, and the offices of state AGs have become very sophisticated operations, where the priorities are more reflective of national issues than ever before. For many who occupy the office, it is viewed as a stepping-stone to the governorship and beyond, prompting some to say the term "AG" refers to "aspiring governor." In forty-three states and Washington, D.C, state AGs are directly elected. In Maine the AG is selected by the state legislature; in Alaska, Hawaii, New Hampshire, New Jersey, and Wyoming, the AG is appointed by the governor. The Tennessee AG is appointed by the state supreme court.

Bill Clinton was twenty-nine years old when he was elected AG of Arkansas; two years later, he became governor. In New York, Eliot Spitzer used his two-term stint as AG to build a reputation for fighting corruption in the financial services industry.[13] He was also actively engaged in suing gun manufacturers, the Bush administration over acid rain, and large corporations. In recent Virginia history, both Jim Gilmore and Bob McDonnell served terms as AG before becoming governor.

Of the recent AGs across the nation, Spitzer epitomized the newly emerging activist model. When elected in 1999, he is reported to have said, "I suddenly became a fan of the new federalism. . . . States' rights are a beautiful thing. States' rights are the future, and we want to do everything we can to support them."[14] Beginning with tobacco litigation in the early 1990s[15] and continuing with drug and environmental actions of recent years, state AGs have been actively engaged in the transformation of social policy in the states and nation, without the passage of any legislation or even the involvement of the institutions typically viewed as those that initiate change in the country—the executive and the legislature. It is one of the untold stories of why states matter.

In Virginia, recent experience has shown how national politics can shape the efforts of state AGs. When Bob McDonnell was elected AG in 2005, he viewed the job primarily as being the chief lawyer for the executive and state agencies, from universities to the Department of Transportation. He nonetheless held strong views that differed from those of the governor. As one of his first actions of his new administration, Governor Tim Kaine signed an executive order adding sexual orientation to the state's antidiscrimination policy, something that Mark Warner had done at the end of his term. At the request of Delegate Bob Marshall, McDonnell issued a very public AG's opinion suggesting that the new governor had exceeded his authority. Kaine's office fired back, stating that he was "flabbergasted"; around Capitol Square, those who took issue with the AG's view were frequently heard to say, "It is his opinion, and worth nothing more."[16]

McDonnell's term as AG began at a time when the role of statewide AGs was being reinvented and taking on a decidedly more political character. Prior to 1999, there had been only one national association for AGs, and Republicans and Democrats frequently worked together on major initiatives; the litigation leading to the Tobacco Master Settlement is the best example of this cooperation. Bipartisanship declined dramatically with the creation of the Republican Attorneys General Association (RAGA) in 1999. Not to be outdone, the Democrats created their own group several years later, called DAGA. Prior to 2017, each group operated under an informal incumbent rule; both partisan national AG groups agreed not to help fund campaigns to oust the incumbents of the other party. Republicans did away with that rule in 2017 in their unsuccessful challenge to Democrat Mark Herring in Virginia; Democrats followed suit.[17] And offices became more political. Conservative AGs joined together to seek to overturn the ACA and attacked the efforts of the Environmental Protection Agency (EPA) to combat climate change. Democratic AGs filed numerous lawsuits opposing a wide array of Trump administration policies.[18] They can occasionally work together, however, as evidenced by collaborative efforts to make inroads into the opioid epidemic.[19]

Scott Pruitt provides a good example of the conservative approach. Elected Oklahoma's AG in 2010, Pruitt made headlines by questioning the established science of human-caused climate change. He sued the federal government to push a wide variety of socially conservative initiatives, from attacking the EPA to advocating against undocumented immigrants. He became chair of RAGA in 2012 and proceeded to launch the Rule of Law campaign, an initiative designed to promote state autonomy and federalism. When Donald Trump became president, Pruitt was appointed head of the EPA.[20]

On the other face of the coin, progressive AGs aggressively confronted a number of President Trump's initiatives during his term. In Trump's first two years, AGs filed or joined sixty-one lawsuits against the administration, including challenges to both the Clean Power Plan rollback and the separation of migrant children from their parents at the US-Mexican border.[21] AG Maura Healey of Massachusetts helped form AGs United For Clean Power,[22] a group committed to using various litigation tools to discover whether major energy companies have misrepresented their knowledge of climate change to investors. In the months before the 2020 presidential election, AGs from each party organized efforts to further the interests of their respective candidates. Democrats such as Bob Ferguson of Washington State and Dana Nessel of Michigan mounted efforts to ensure polling places would remain safe from intimidation by poll watchers and that mail-in votes would be counted properly,[23] while twenty Republican AGs joined to dispute a federal court ruling that allowed Arizona voters five days after the election to correct certain errors made in their absentee ballots.[24]

Both conservative and progressive AGs, however, share one thing in common. "Our major task is to change behavior," said Betty Montgomery, a longtime AG in Ohio. Monies collected through settlements, she argues, were "incidental."[25] Litigation involving over half of the nation's AGs, once an unusual event, now represents more than 40 percent of all the multistate cases filed since 2000.[26] The last two decades have elevated the impact of state AGs, and their offices pursue more overtly political agendas than ever before.[27]

Virginia was one of the notable states where this occurred. One prominent proponent of this approach was Ken Cuccinelli, McDonnell's successor, who took office in 2010 and eventually became Trump's acting deputy secretary of the Department of Homeland Security in 2019. When Cuccinelli took office as AG, both national and state Republicans had aligned themselves against President Obama, and Virginia became a major source of litigation against the president's policies. Cuccinelli was cut from right-wing cloth, and it showed in just about everything he did while he was in office. He was the first state AG to file a lawsuit challenging the constitutionality of the ACA, doing so on the day the bill was signed into law in 2010.[28] He attempted to utilize a relatively unknown statutory provision called a civil investigative demand to attack leading climate scientist Michael Mann. He was a point person for conservative legal advocates concerned about gay rights and immigration. In early 2010, Cuccinelli wrote to his clients, the state's public colleges and universities, and requested that they rescind their policies banning discrimination based on sexual orientation.[29] One month later, he issued a legal opinion stating that state and local law enforcement officials were permitted to investigate the immigration status of anyone they stopped.[30]

While Cuccinelli used his AG office to push conservative lawsuits, his successor, Mark Herring, took a different approach. In November 2019, for example, he joined a coalition of AGs and local governments in a lawsuit opposing Trump's EPA's efforts to block actions by states designed to reduce air pollution.[31] And shortly after Virginia became the thirty-eighth state to ratify the Equal Rights Amendment (ERA), Herring and state AGs from Nevada and Illinois filed a federal lawsuit to compel the measure's inclusion in the

US Constitution when the national archivist, who certifies the ratification of amendments, indicated that, on the guidance of the Justice Department, the measure would not be added to the US Constitution as its twenty-eighth amendment.[32] In response, AGs from five states who had first approved and then rescinded support for the amendment—Tennessee, Alabama, Louisiana, Nebraska, and South Dakota—intervened in the lawsuit to express their opposition to the amendment's inclusion.[33] For years, we knew that states mattered in the fight for the ERA, if only because thirty-eight of them would need to ratify the amendment for it to become part of the US Constitution. Now we are witnessing how the legal arguments of different state AGs will influence whether the ERA will become the law of the land.[34]

## Interest Groups

Players in state policy involve more than elected officials. Largely unknown to the American public are the efforts of powerful interest groups to control state legislatures not only through campaign contributions but also by writing actual legislation that is considered and passed. In that way, they hope to develop consistent policies that cross state lines, all designed to serve some narrow self-interest or ideological position. In the last several decades, these groups have come to believe that it is much easier to pass legislation at the state level than to negotiate the increasingly cumbersome congressional process. And they are right. A 2019 investigation by *USA Today*, the *Arizona Republic*, and the Center for Public Integrity reported that in an eight-year period commencing in 2011, more than 10,000 bills were introduced in state legislatures that were essentially written by special interest groups.[35] More of these model bills were generated by conservative organizations such as the American Legislative Exchange Council (ALEC), the Goldwater Institute, or the Heartland Institute than by their progressive counterparts, such as the State Innovation Exchange, State Voices, or Future Now.[36]

The investigation examined nearly one million bills proposed in all fifty states using a computer algorithm developed to detect similarities in language. Sometimes referred to as "model legislation," these bills were and are often introduced, almost word for word, in multiple statehouses at the same time. The report found that 2,100 of the 10,000 bills were signed into law. Some states copied far more model bills than others; the study listed Mississippi as offering the most model bills, with some 744 such measures copied and introduced. New Jersey was next, with 564, followed by Illinois. A report on this activity in Minnesota using the *USA Today* data found groups on the right proposing copycat bills on abortion and right to work and groups on the left introducing measures to tax and regulate marijuana and to implement paid family leave.[37]

Special interests have funded think tanks and lobbying focused on federal legislation for years. Countless think tanks were spawned on the right in the 1970s and 1980s, and the left has struggled to keep up ever since. Similar efforts to change the states, however, are a more recent development. Although founded in 1973, ALEC's influence was not that apparent until the late 2000s, after the involvement of such major donors as David and Charles Koch became clear, and the organization's name kept popping up as the impetus for a host of conservative legislation in the states.[38]

ALEC, Americans for Prosperity (AFP), and the State Policy Network (SPN) have engaged conservative legislators in numerous states, providing them with model bills and legislative drafts they could introduce and attempt to pass, all in an effort to solidify the conservative agenda.[39] Their plans were and are broad and audacious, and involve a wide variety of issues. One clear target was the ACA and how it might be undermined in the states. Another effort sought to undermine unions; as a publication of the SPN put it, "The only way to curb union influence is through systematic reform efforts targeting multiple states."[40] ALEC was also active in promoting the so-called castle doctrine, a principle that supports the use of lethal force by private citizens in self-defense of their property. And, of course, there is climate change, thought to be a hoax perpetrated by globalists, liberals, and perhaps even polar bears.

One of the most significant efforts of ALEC involved voter ID bills. As early as 2009, it drafted model legislation to require voters to produce special identification at the polls; within several years, thirty-seven states had introduced replicas of ALEC bills, more than half sponsored by legislators who were actual members of the group.[41] Chapter 6 of this book explains how laws like this had the effect of making it more difficult to vote. This strategy was widespread and effective; in 2011 alone, nineteen states passed twenty-five laws of this kind, including seven of the eleven states with the highest African American turnout in 2008.[42]

Most citizens believe that their legislators develop ideas for legislation on their own to reflect the interests of their constituents. ALEC's approach is dramatically different. The group realized that the citizen legislators who populate state capitals are overworked, underpaid, and frequently challenged for ideas on legislation and the assistance necessary to pass their proposals. Hence, ALEC would develop bills that could and would be introduced in any state, and would fund legislators to attend regional and national conferences to sell them on their product. The headline of one news story, "Pssst . . . Wanna Buy a Law?," aptly captured the process.[43]

The efforts went farther than just legislation. The AFP was actively engaged in elections, mobilizing several million conservative volunteers and spending millions of dollars for ads targeting not just Democrats but also Republican lawmakers who might depart from the party line and vote against the organization's positions.[44] When coupled with the activity of the tea party, Republican legislators became deathly afraid of challenges, not so much from Democrats but from Republicans on their right flank. In Virginia, two well-respected and relatively conservative Republican delegates, Beverly Sherwood of Winchester and Joe May of Loudoun, were defeated by right-wing insurgents shortly after they voted to raise taxes for transportation in 2013. And when Eric Cantor, the US House majority leader representing the Seventh Congressional District in Virginia, was unceremoniously ousted by insurgent "tea party patriot" Dave Brat in his 2016 primary, fear swept through Republican caucuses throughout the country about possible primary challenges from the right.

## A Complex Interplay

Social policy does not emerge in a vacuum. It is shaped by the historical and political context within which a state finds itself, its constitution, the institutions, norms, values, and culture of its citizens, and the people who are in the room at the time. This complex panoply of influencing factors is at work every day, whether it is during each legislative session, within the bureaucracies of state government, or through the words and actions of officeholders. It is through this interplay that power is sought and exercised and policy is passed and implemented. It is for that reason that policy development, passage, and implementation cannot be explained formulaically. There are no stages that, if followed, get you to the desired result. There are constant twists and turns as the players in the chess game of politics exercise their skill, filtered through that state's culture and traditions. The public also plays a key role in the process. It elects leaders to implement what they have promised. And once legislation is passed and policy enacted, the public can decide whether the changes it got were what it wanted, and whether more or less change is justified. Citizens of a state do this through elections and by voting, a process itself controlled by the states. The next chapter argues that when it comes to voting and elections, states make a critical difference. Those who control this process control the nation.

# 6

# Controlling the Nation One State at a Time

The future of this republic is in the hands of the American voter.
—DWIGHT D. EISENHOWER

While few Americans remember the name of Judge Robert A. Rosenberg, many would recognize the photo of him staring incredulously from behind his eyeglasses at a rectangular dimpled card perforated with numerous punch holes. Rosenberg, a judge appointed by then governor Jeb Bush in 1999 to the civil division of Florida's Seventeenth Judicial Circuit, became the person of "hanging chad" fame and one of the key players in determining who would become president of the United States. The judge and his assistants labored for days examining ballots in Broward County, attempting to discern the intent of thousands of voters based on the nature of punch card perforations. During this process, he frequently received instructions from Florida's secretary of state, Katherine Harris, who had been elected only two years earlier on the same ticket as Jeb Bush. Using Florida law with the skill of a zealous partisan, Harris eventually halted the recount and certified George Bush as the winner in Florida. Court filings ensued, and the case eventually went to the US Supreme Court, which refused to permit the recount to resume, thereby determining the presidency.[1] In a different state and at a different time, the results might have changed, and so too might the history of the nation. States matter!

## States Control the Vote—and Therefore Rule the Nation

Many Americans focus solely on the justices of US Supreme Court in *Bush v. Gore*, neglecting to consider how Florida's election laws, as well as the persons who controlled the levers of power in the state at the time, influenced the ultimate result.[2] They do so at their peril. The Supreme Court's decision was largely determined by the election laws of the state and the certification of the election results by Harris. This is not as unusual as one might think; absent a direct and clear constitutional problem, courts are generally loath to interfere with state policies in the voting and electoral realm. And so we are left to live with fifty different states, each having different and complicated ways of determining everything from the lines of state legislative and congressional districts to remedies for weird occurrences such as elections where there is an absolute tie in the vote.

Virginia had its own mini-version of *Bush v. Gore* in the 2017 state elections. By election night's end, Democrats had won fifteen new seats and were on the brink of winning a sixteenth, which would have brought them to parity in the House of Delegates. They were poised to win perhaps a seventeenth and eighteenth, depending on recounts and court challenges. In the House district located primarily in Newport News, the Democratic candidate, school board member Shelly Simonds, was within ten votes at the end of the evening, and Democrats firmly believed she would be ahead after a recount. They were right—at least for twenty-four hours. The recount gave her a one-vote margin, and the Republican candidate had even conceded. But before the three-judge panel reconvened the next morning to certify the results, as they are required to do by law, the Republicans "discovered" another ballot, which they claimed was a vote for them. Despite the irregularity of that ballot, which included different marks in different places that could suggest different things, the judges accepted the ballot, counted the vote for the Republican, and the race became a tie. Under Virginia law, that meant the election would be determined by lot. Several days later, lots were drawn; Democrats "lost" the election, and with it, a chance at parity or even the majority.

As the 2020 presidential election approached, pundits were worried about litigation much as in Florida in 2000. But the nightmare scenario in 2020 could involve six or seven states—not just one. And those states could hold the key to the election. Because of the COVID-19 pandemic, many Americans decided to vote by mail. But each state had different requirements for voters who sought to cast their ballot in this way. Some required witnesses to sign certifications indicating that the voter had signed the ballot before mailing it in. Others, most notably Pennsylvania, required the absentee ballot to be inserted into a separate envelope before it was mailed.[3] And the counting process in many states was also different. Interpretation of the language of state law would make all the difference. In Pennsylvania, one of the states thought likely to determine the election, Donald Trump's 2016 vote total exceeded his opponent's by 44,292. Absentee ballots rejected that year totaled more than 37,000.[4] Imagine that number of mail-in ballots multiplied fiftyfold, and one can understand the concerns of the pundits. Trump spent much of the summer and fall railing against mail-in voting and bringing lawsuits in numerous states. His primary targets were Arizona, Florida, Wisconsin, Pennsylvania, Michigan, Ohio, and Georgia, all swing states and all permitting mail-in voting. To make it more complicated, four of those states—Florida, Pennsylvania, Michigan, and Wisconsin—have state laws that prevent acceptance of mail-in ballots if received after Election Day, *even if postmarked weeks in advance*. And in all but Florida, these states could not begin processing, much less counting, absentee ballots until Election Day.[5] No wonder so many were skeptical that the results would be known on November 3!

The pundits were correct. Despite Biden's ultimate seven million vote margin in the popular vote and his substantial victory in the Electoral College, these results were not clear on the evening of November 3. Since many more Democrats had voted by mail, their ballots were counted later in those states that would determine the election. Consequently, Trump initially took the lead in several of these states, particularly Pennsylvania, only to be overtaken when the substantial mail-in vote was counted. And while Biden lost Florida, his margins in Pennsylvania, Michigan, Wisconsin, Arizona, and (shockingly) Georgia were large enough to prevent any reasonable observer from concluding that Trump had won. Despite numerous lawsuits that the president's team brought both before the election and after, and despite the more than $20 million spent on the effort, there was little evidence of fraud, and litigation could not overcome the victory margins for Biden in these key states.[6] Nonetheless, observers could not ignore the broad differences in voting procedures across the states, which can contribute to a public perception of irregularities. Understanding these differences helps us evaluate the effectiveness of what is arguably this nation's more important right—the right to vote. States make a difference in how, when, and whether different citizens in different situations can exercise the franchise.

## State Policy and Voter Participation

Historical voting patterns simply confirm what we already know—that there is a dramatic drop-off in voter participation depending on the nature of the seat being contested and whether it is federal or state. For example, voter participation rates are substantially higher in federal presidential races than in congressional races; the turnout in presidential elections, while not great, usually tops 60 percent, while the turnout in midterm congressional races can hover in the 30 percent range. Virginia elections dramatically show this differential: the turnout of the voting-age population in the 2016 presidential election was 67.2 percent, but it was only about 40 percent for the 2014 midterm elections. In 2018 this number jumped dramatically to over 50 percent nationally, the highest figure in one hundred years but still below the turnout in most presidential years.[7] Virginia's 59.5 percent turnout in 2018 exceeded that national average but remained well behind Minnesota's (64.2 percent), Colorado's (63 percent), and Montana's (62 percent), the national pacesetters in this category that year.[8]

Voter participation in state legislative races is even worse; Virginia's 2019 number was only 42.4 percent.[9] In some instances, contested state races occurring when there are no federal contests on the ballot consistently report turnout levels in the high 20 percent range.

Pundits rail against American voters' relatively low participation rates everywhere, but state policies matter when it comes to voting: some states simply make voting easier. For example, Nonprofit VOTE, a public advocacy group, recently listed the highest voter participation rates in the 2016 presidential election. They included Minnesota (74.8 percent), Maine (72.8 percent), New Hampshire (72.5 percent), Colorado (72.1 percent), Wisconsin (70.5 percent), and Iowa (69 percent); several of these states are among the highest performing in each election. One policy common to them all is same-day voter registration, which allows a voter to register and vote on the same day; as of 2020, a total of twenty-one states plus the District of Columbia had such policies, some of which were adopted in response to the pandemic.[10] A 2020 study ranked states with robust mail-in programs—Oregon, Washington, and Utah—as the easiest states in which to vote; Texas had the lowest ranking.[11] The study further showed how changes in individual legislatures can make a tremendous difference in ease of voting. In 2020, Virginia Democrats took control of both the Senate and the House and implemented substantial reforms designed to make voting easier. As a result, Virginia's ranking in the study jumped from forty-ninth in 2016 to thirteenth in 2020.[12]

Colorado even mails out a ballot to every eligible voter, and the ID necessary for in-person balloting does not require a photo. Nine of the ten states with the highest 2018 turnouts offer same-day voter registration or vote-at-home (vote by mail) policies.[13]

By contrast, the lower-performing states make voting more difficult, whether by limiting absentee voting or by imposing significant advance lead times for registration prior to an election. Of the ten lowest-turnout states, eight have four-week-in-advance registration deadlines.[14] A recent study of state election laws concluded that voting is hardest in Mississippi, which requires a photo ID at the polls and allows neither early voting nor no-excuse absentee voting.[15] The state is joined at the bottom of the list by Tennessee, Indiana, and Texas.[16]

In Virginia, the voter participation challenge is exacerbated by the fact that the state has off-year elections. Virginia's voter participation rate has been higher than the national average in presidential years. In 2012, the state had the eighth-highest voter turnout rate, and voter participation in the state recently has been increasing, from 67.2 percent in 2016[17] to an estimated 73.9 percent in 2020.[18] But participation drops dramatically in gubernatorial election years. Virginia is only one of two states—New Jersey is the other—that elect a governor in odd-numbered years. That means that no federal contests occur at that time. Critics of Virginia's schedule argue that the politicians who built this system decades ago wanted it that way. They hoped to discourage large numbers from voting in state and local elections, thereby enhancing the ability of small cadres of political elites to control the statewide levers of power, to the detriment of the mass population. But whatever the reason, the numbers are clear: the last three Virginia gubernatorial elections saw voter turnouts of 47.6 percent (2017), 43 percent (2013), and 40.4 percent (2009).[19] Turnouts for legislative races are even lower. In 2015, for example, when only the one hundred House of Delegates and forty state Senate seats were up for election, turnout was a dismal 29.1 percent.[20] In 2017, there was an uptick in turnout compared to other off-year elections, but many have attributed this to the energy generated in response to the Trump presidency. Virginia's turnout in 2019 also dramatically exceeded expectations, again largely due to the antipathy toward the person in the White House.

## Voter Suppression and the 2018 Midterms

Voter suppression, usually directed toward groups about which the powerful are most worried, has a long and troubling history in the United States. Pulitzer Prize winner Alexander Keyssar's *The Right to Vote* provides a detailed history of how states in the late 1800s and early 1900s restricted the voting rights of Catholics and other working-class immigrants, concerned about the "invasion of peasants, misfits, and radicals," "those pledging allegiance to the Pope," and others of the "loafer element," which, some politicians feared, could eventually outnumber "hardworking good citizens."[21] Women, of course, were not extended the right to vote in all states and nationally until the ratification of the Nineteenth Amendment in 1920. Of all groups, African Americans were the most effectively targeted, with everything from Jim Crow–era constitutions to literacy tests and poll taxes. The impact of voter suppression efforts was felt most in the southern states. In Mississippi, for example, 66.7 percent of the black population was registered to vote in 1867; by 1955, that number had fallen to 4.3 percent.[22]

Today, efforts at voter suppression are much more sophisticated. The proponents of many so-called reforms such as voter ID and voter purges often frame their arguments in the guise of protecting the integrity of the system. While most Americans believe voting should be made easier, a powerful minority prefers just the opposite. And some state legislatures have been more than willing to oblige, frequently disguising their efforts as attempts to address "voter fraud" and to "protect the sanctity of the vote."[23] A 2014 study by Justin Levitt of the Loyola University of Chicago School of Law, however, found only thirty-one reported instances of in-person voter impersonation between 2000 and 2014, certainly not enough to swing an election.[24] In fact, the odds are one in 32 million that an actual vote is fraudulent.

Some strategists are open in their disdain for participation. Conservative columnist Matthew Vadum has written, for example, that "registering the poor to vote . . . is like handing out burglary tools to criminals."[25] And Ted Yoho, prominent tea party activist and Republican congressman, recently stated that "property owners have a little bit more of a vested interest in the community than non-property owners."[26] Paul Weyrich, a major conservative strategist and Republican until his death in 2008, was extremely direct in his reasoning: "I don't want everybody to vote," he said. "Our leverage in elections, quite candidly, goes up as the voting populace goes down."[27] And the best way to reduce the voting populace is to suppress the vote through state policies, whether they involve draconian ID schemes, massive purges of state voting rolls, or artificial ways of restricting voter registration.

The 2018 midterm elections were viewed by many as a testing ground for whether the recent round of voter suppression initiatives would work. After Trump's upset win in 2016 and the colossal failure of polling predictions, few knew how many voters would turn out in 2018, or how they might vote. In the weeks before the election, Democrats had been heartened by the numbers of absentee ballots cast in Democratic areas and the level of energy felt on the ground, but a general discomfort prevailed. After all, most had felt Hillary Clinton was sure to win in 2016. In some ways, the feelings were similar to those felt by Virginia House Democrats in the weeks just before the 2017 elections: we could sense a shift in the electorate, and our polling told us we would pick up seats, but the extent of the energy in the base remained cloudy until the "blue wave" washed over the state on election night.

In 2018, Democrats were also concerned that the massive efforts at voter suppression in individual states would dampen turnout. In yet another example of why states matter, policies throughout the country that had been enacted in the ten years since Obama's victory had the potential to effectively disenfranchise millions of voters, with dramatic implications for election results. Of the eleven states with the highest African American turnout in Obama's 2008 race, seven had enacted laws by 2011 that made it harder to vote. And new voting restrictions were enacted in nine of the twelve states with the largest increase in the Hispanic vote during this period.[28] The result, at least in 2016, was diminished African American turnout. Nationally, black turnout dropped 7 percent, and in some states the lower turnout might have been enough to transfer that state's electoral votes to Trump.[29] In Wisconsin, for example, the percentage of registered African Americans dropped from 78 percent to 50 percent.[30]

In many instances, these so-called reforms, implemented under the guise of "combating voter fraud" or "strengthening election integrity," appear relatively benign. But closer examination makes it clear that the impacts would be felt primarily among minority groups and the poor and marginalized—and that those who favored the changes often knew exactly what they were doing.[31] Some of these policies were designed to maintain certain elites in power and lessen the impact of groups seeking change (for example, New Hampshire passed a measure making it more difficult for students to vote).[32] State legislatures continue to be very active in this area because so much is at stake.

Some states have been more blatant than others. In Georgia, for example, former secretary of state (now governor) Brian Kemp administratively implemented a practice of "explicit matching " of voter names on their IDs to the names on the voter rolls.[33] If there was even a slight difference, the person would be denied the ability to vote. The courts initially struck down this provision, which disproportionately affected African American voters, but Kemp simply convinced the legislature to make the process a state law. As a result, heading into the 2018 election, the state had refused to accept some 53,000 applications for registration, 70 percent of which were from African Americans (who make up 32 percent of the state's population). While campaigning as the Republican nominee for governor, Kemp remained in his position as secretary of state, supervising the office that operates the elections even as he campaigned against his formidable African American opponent, former state House minority leader Stacey Abrams.[34] On Election Day, reports surfaced about irregularities, including the rejection of provisional and absentee ballots and accounts of citizens being turned away at the polls. Abrams came within 18,000 votes of forcing a runoff and within 55,000 votes of direct victory, an incredible accomplishment given the recent failures of Democrats seeking statewide office. Whether voter suppression was essential in getting Kemp elected or, alternatively, served to mobilize a voting population angered by the policies is up for debate. The 2020 turnout data in Georgia merely added to the discussion. Voter participation in the state was higher than ever, partly because of the mobilization efforts undertaken by both parties, but the African American turnout percentage was lower, and this group's percentage of the total electorate declined.[35] Many factors contribute to turnout, of which voting laws are but one.

The more celebrated cases of voter suppression involve laws requiring voters to produce a picture ID at the polls. On their face, these policies may seem reasonable—until you realize that over three million Americans do not have a government-issued picture ID. Even more troubling, a voter may simply forget to bring their ID to the polls and therefore be prevented from casting an actual vote as a result. My now deceased law partner was a victim of this several years ago when he arrived at his polling place without his ID. A decorated Vietnam veteran and well known not only in his community but also specifically to the precinct election officials, he was told that he would have to cast a "provisional ballot" and return later to "prove" who he was. This strikes most observers as outrageous, but it is the product of numerous state voting systems that are making it increasingly difficult for Americans to exercise the franchise. Even more insidious, in 2018, North Dakota passed a law requiring voters to produce an ID that includes an actual street address—a post office box would not suffice—in order to cast a ballot.[36] This might seem reasonable until it was revealed that many residents of Native American tribal lands, who are primarily Democratic voters, do not have actual street addresses.

Another arena where state policies may appear on their face to be designed to improve the system but operate instead to disenfranchise voters is the "voter purge" efforts initiated by various states. A 2018 report of the Brennan Center for Justice at New York University's School of Law found that states removed almost 16 million voters from their rolls between 2014 and 2016, almost four million more than were removed between 2006 and 2008.[37] The greatest numbers of purges occurred following the US Supreme Court's decision in *Shelby County v. Holder*, 570 U.S. 2 (2013), which effectively ended the previous requirement under the federal Voting Rights Act that election procedures in jurisdictions with a history of racial discrimination undergo a "preclearance" by the Justice Department before changes are implemented. In Texas, a state formerly subject to Voting Rights Act preclearance, 363,000 more voters were purged from the rolls in the first cycle following *Shelby* than in the comparable midterm election preceding it.[38] Similarly, in Georgia, 1.4 million registrations were canceled between 2012 and 2018, including 670,000 in 2017 alone.[39]

To be sure, election rolls require constant revision to ensure they are accurate and up to date (as an example, a Pew Charitable Trusts issue brief in 2012 estimated that voter rolls nationwide included 1.8 million deceased persons).[40] But researchers are finding that the databases used to generate purges are replete with errors and that some states do not provide citizens with enough time to correct inaccuracies. And when states either do not take appropriate precautions or do not care, problems emerge. In 2013 the Virginia State Board of Elections (SBE) under Republican governor Bob McDonnell joined the Interstate Voter Registration Crosscheck (IVRC), an operation created and maintained by the State of Kansas since 2005. The IVRC had thirteen states as members in 2010, but, under a push from then secretary of state and "voter fraud" crusader Kris Kobach, it was able to extend its network to twenty-nine states by 2014. In August 2013, less than three months before that year's Virginia gubernatorial election, the Virginia SBE, using data provided by the IVRC, gave instructions to local jurisdictions to purge 57,000 designated voters. Although the localities discovered huge errors in the information, some 40,000 were removed before the election. No one is quite sure about the extent that it affected the results; Democrats won all three statewide offices, but the margin of victory for Attorney General Mark Herring in 2013 was only 165 votes.[41] Today, Virginia, though still nominally a member of the IVRC, uses the Electronic Registration Information Center (ERIC) as a superior way to assist in maintaining reliable voter lists.

Another way to potentially suppress voting is by closing polling places. This is occurring throughout the nation, but especially in the South since the Supreme Court decision in Shelby. A study by the Leadership Conference Education Fund found that 868 polling places were closed in the aftermath of Shelby in Alabama, Arizona, Louisiana, North Carolina, South Carolina, and Texas. Between the 2013 Shelby decision and the 2016 election, Texas reduced its polling places by 403.[42] Another study, just of Georgia, found that between 2012 and 2018, 214 voting precincts were closed, about 8 percent of the state's total.[43] Again, some of these initiatives can be benign, either in reality or appearance. To be sure, there can be good financial reasons for closing or moving the location of a voting precinct, but the easy ability to do so creates yet another opportunity for mischief and justifies the additional scrutiny originally contemplated by the Voting Rights Act. The US Commission on Civil Rights recently concluded, based on extensive statistical data, that in a number of states, cuts in the number of polling places resulted in decreased minority voter access and influence.[44]

Setting Election Day during the workweek is not normally viewed as voter suppression, but it certainly can make participation more difficult. To compensate and make it easier for citizens with challenging work schedules or child-care demands to vote, five states—Washington, Hawaii, Utah, Oregon, and Colorado—conduct their elections almost exclusively by mail. Many others have instituted early voting, opening the polls days or weeks prior to the actual Election Day. In recent years, however, several states have attempted to curtail these initiatives. North Carolina, following the takeover of the legislature by Republicans, reduced the time periods for early voting.[45] In Florida, former Republican governor Rick Scott attempted to stop early voting on college campuses, but the courts halted the initiative before it was implemented.[46] Politicians generally love Election Days; it gives them a target for their messaging and one day on which they can work their constituents. But it should not be about them; it should be about maximizing participation, and the data indicate that the more options you provide voters, the more likely they are to cast their ballots.

Efforts to make voting easier continues in states across the nation. Consider Florida, for example. In November 2018, state voters approved, by a 65–35 percent margin, a ballot measure to restore voting rights to up to 1.4 million people with felony convictions who had served their sentences.[47] The Republican-led legislature immediately responded with legislation that would condition this restoration on a requirement that outstanding court fees and costs be paid before those previously convicted were placed on the voter rolls. Democrats immediately analogized this to the constitutionally invalid poll tax, but proponents remained committed to its enactment. The Republicans pushed the measure through the legislature, and the governor signed it.[48] It is now being challenged in the courts.

## State Efforts to Increase Participation

One of the most promising approaches to increasing participation is called automatic voter registration (AVR).[49] According to the National Conference of State Legislatures, eighteen states and the District of Columbia have now adopted some form of AVR.[50] Various states embrace different approaches to AVR, but the purpose is always the same—to increase registration and participation.[51] In Oregon and Vermont, enactment of the policy led to a dramatic spike in registrations. Some states permit citizens to register at DMV offices, but it is not automatic, and many citizens fail to take advantage of this option.

The other value of automatic registration is that it is an easy way to update the system, ensuring accuracy without the downside of voter purges, which are often accompanied by errors.

Some states allow voters to register and vote on the same day. According to the National Conference of State Legislatures, twenty states and the District of Columbia currently offer this practice, including Election Day registration.[52] Although the costs of moving to such an arrangement may be high for some states, seven of the ten highest-turnout states have this system.[53] By comparison, eight of the ten lowest-turnout states require voters to register four weeks before the election.[54]

Colorado, Washington, and Oregon, three states with some of highest participation rates, automatically mail ballots to all registrants. The public likes the mail-in option; in 2016, over one-third of all votes cast were by mail.[55] And when more states provided voters with this option in the face of COVID-19 challenges, the public responded enthusiastically. In nine states, ballots were mailed to each registrant. Utah reported that more than 90 percent of its 2020 votes were cast by mail.[56] More than 103 million votes nationwide had been cast prior to Election Day in a contest that saw voting participation at levels not witnessed since William McKinley defeated Williams Jennings Bryan in 1900.[57] The COVID-19 pandemic prompted other states to explore other options as well. For example, twenty-three states permit mobile voting, whereby bipartisan teams can be sent to residential care centers to aid residents in completing the absentee voting process prior to an election.[58] And some permitted localities to set up drop-off boxes so that voters could return an absentee ballot without concern that it would be lost in the mail. These initiatives are exclusively the responsibilities of the states.

As of August 2020, a majority of states had some provision for absentee voting, but some required voters to provide a reason why they would have to vote early. This became a huge issue during the COVID-19 pandemic, when some states took the position that the pandemic provided a legitimate excuse, even though the word was not actually in the state code. Some advocates were worried about legal challenges to this view, especially if the word "pandemic" was not listed specifically in the state code as a reason for casting an absentee ballot.[59]

Election officials braced for a huge increase in mail-in votes as November 2020 approached. And proponents of voter participation became increasingly concerned by the efforts of the Trump administration to make cuts in the postal service, which some argued was a direct attempt either to discourage mail-in voting or to cause votes to arrive after the deadline.[60] In the months prior to the 2020 election, attorneys for each party prepared either to file or to oppose lawsuits contesting the votes of citizens cast by mail. Since elections are run by the states, attorneys general also intervened to protect the rights of citizens to have their votes counted. In many of these cases, the arguments centered on state law and the extent to which vote counters applied it properly. The biggest worry was that lawsuits in several swing states might prolong the outcome of the 2020 election for weeks, if not months, and cause the public to doubt the legitimacy of the electoral outcome. Since the election was not that close, the litigation strategy designed to contest various categories of votes gained little traction in the courts.

Ultimately, to be invested in the system, citizens must feel that their vote makes a difference. State policies can establish the rules to make it easier to fairly exercise the franchise with minimal challenge, thereby increasing the participation of citizens in the selection of their leaders.

## Redistricting: Representatives Choosing Their Constituents

States matter in determining who can vote, what ID you need at the polls, whether you can vote by mail, how much time prior to the election you need to register, the hours of voting, the number of polling places, the types of voting machines used, the logistical support for the voting process, and whether and how a felon can get voting rights back. But of all the issues where states make a difference, by far the most significant is redistricting. State legislatures draw district lines for both congressional and state representative races, and in so doing they dramatically influence who runs, who wins, who loses, and who controls the US Congress and the state legislatures.

Under the US Constitution, there is a requirement that congressional and state legislative maps be redrawn every ten years to reflect changes in population, under the general principle of one person, one vote.[61] But how the lines are drawn is determined by the states. The US Supreme Court has established certain criteria for drawing lines, such as compactness of districts and nondiscrimination, but there is no prohibition against incumbent legislators drawing lines to protect their own seats or the seats of their colleagues from the same party. And that is what they frequently do. The process is called "gerrymandering" after the famous Massachusetts politician Elbridge Gerry, who, as governor, signed a redistricting plan with strange-looking districts drawn by the majority party in the state Senate in order to add to their numbers.[62]

Today, with the use of sophisticated computer software, politicians and their consultants can slice and dice voters with the precision of a surgeon and construct districts where they are truly choosing their voters rather than the other way around. The stakes in redistricting are extremely high because drawing lines that last for a decade can create a partisan advantage that can be difficult if not impossible to overcome at the polls.

A partisan redistricting process can be particularly insidious for a number of reasons. First, districts can be drawn in ways to artificially maximize the influence of the party in power. This occurs in both blue and red states. Maryland's 2011 redistricting clearly moved lines designed to create a more Democratic congressional delegation in the state.[63] In Virginia, Republicans controlled the redistricting process in 2011 and constructed maps that concentrated Democratic votes into a small number of districts in order to maximize the Republican vote in many more. Democrats continued to win statewide elections during the decade as Virginia moved from a red to a purple state, but the House lines were so beneficial to Republicans that Democrats never held more than thirty-nine out of one hundred seats until 2017, when the blue wave hit and the party won fifteen seats. Between 2005 and 2018, Democrats were successful in capturing ten of fifteen statewide elections, with Obama winning the state twice, Clinton outpolling Trump by a healthy margin, Mark Warner and Tim Kaine each twice capturing US Senate seats, and the party winning four out of five gubernatorial races between 2001 and 2017. Yet until 2016, and a successful court case that required a redrawing of the congressional maps, the Virginia congressional delegation included only three Democrats out of eleven.

The Republican control of map drawing had an even greater impact on the Virginia House of Delegates. Prior to the 2009 election, Democratic strength in the House of Delegates had risen to forty-four, and the party was feeling the momentum. Democrats knew that the gubernatorial election that year would be critical because redistricting was on the horizon and a Democratic governor could protect the party from hyperpartisan redistricting. In 2009 the Democratic candidate, Creigh Deeds, was demolished in the election by former delegate Bob McDonnell, and the coattail effect took out several other Democratic incumbents, reducing the party's numbers to thirty-nine. After that election, the House was firmly controlled by Republicans, and while Democrats enjoyed a small margin in the Senate, Governor McDonnell was in a position to veto any redistricting bill he didn't like. Democrats' worst fears were realized: the 2011 redistricting was tailored to ensure Republican control for the coming decade. In the fall of 2011, Democrats lost more seats, and their numbers declined to thirty-two.

Another problem with hyperpartisan redistricting is that it tends to magnify the power of those at the extremes of the political spectrum. When so many safe seats are created for both parties, the decision of who will represent a district is often made during a primary, when turnout is low and only the most motivated and partisan voters appear at the polls. This tends to create a legislature in which so many representatives are drawn from opposite ends of the political spectrum that it is difficult to achieve compromise and get things done. Polarization and partisanship have become more pronounced than ever before. Many argue that this hyperpartisan redistricting is taking its toll on the US House of Representatives as well. Few seats remain competitive, and there is more polarization, as representatives are elected from either safe Democratic or Republican districts, often representing the ideological extremes in both parties. When they arrive in Washington, they have little in common with most of their new colleagues, thereby making compromise increasingly difficult.

Over the last decade, fights over redistricting at the legislative level have largely been won by Republicans. In the courts, the results have been more mixed. Proponents of redistricting reform have developed new arguments that have won court approval and marshaled some older ones in ways that Republicans had not anticipated.[64] In Pennsylvania, for example, the League of Women Voters brought a lawsuit that overturned a partisan redistricting, with the result that a new congressional map was installed for the 2018 election. The composition of the Pennsylvania congressional delegation went from a 13–5 Republican majority to a 9–9 division.[65] A federal court ruled that a Republican-drawn congressional map for North Carolina was unconstitutional but delayed the implementation of a new map because of the approaching 2018 election. As a result, though Republicans won only 51 percent of all votes cast for Congress in the state, they won ten of thirteen seats.[66] In Michigan, a sweeping federal court judgment issued in April 2019 held that Republicans in 2011 conducted an unconstitutional gerrymander and that new state legislative and congressional maps would need to be drawn for the 2020 election.[67] Litigants brought lawsuits in Wisconsin and Maryland alleging that their state's gerrymanders were so partisan as to be unconstitutional under the equal protection clause and the First Amendment to the US Constitution.[68] Reformers seemed to be on a roll.

In June 2019 the US Supreme Court dealt a serious blow to litigation attempting to overturn maps drawn simply for partisan advantage. A sharply divided 5–4 decision issued in June 2019 held that redistricting based on partisan considerations was constitutional. Justice Elena Kagan wrote the dissenting opinion, joined by Justices Ginsburg, Breyer, and Sotomayor. In it, she stated, "Of all times to abandon the Court's duty to declare the law, this was not the one. The practices challenged in these cases imperil our system of government. Part of the Court's role in that system is to defend its foundations. None is more important than free and fair elections. With respect but deep sadness, I dissent."[69] The legal efforts to challenge partisan redistricting have been fundamentally undercut.

The Supreme Court ruling discouraged many critics of partisan redistricting, but it has not prevented other efforts, particularly those focused on using state constitutions to overturn unfair maps. In September 2019, plaintiffs were able to convince a three-judge panel of the North Carolina Supreme Court to rule a Republican-drawn state legislative map unconstitutional based on state rather than federal law.[70] The ruling did not apply to congressional districts. As a result of the tendency of state justices to be even more conservative than the US Supreme Court, these attacks will continue to be challenging, but the North Carolina result portends more litigation on this issue in state courts in the coming years.

The most fruitful argument for overturning redistricting maps has focused on the improper use of race in drawing district lines. In Virginia, for example, Democrats successfully challenged how congressional maps were drawn in 2011 as an unconstitutional racial gerrymander.[71] After the legislature failed to redraw the maps in 2015 in response to judicial mandate, new districts were created by the courts, and Democrats gained another congressional seat in the next election. In June 2018 the US District Court for the Eastern District of Virginia applied the same analysis in finding that eleven House of Delegates districts were racially gerrymandered and therefore unconstitutional.[72] When the legislature was unable to agree on new maps, district lines were drawn by the court. Not surprisingly in a state that was trending Democratic, the new maps created many more districts that were competitive. In the next election, Democrats won fifty-five of the one hundred seats and gained the majority in the House of Delegates.

## The Need for Redistricting Reform

Largely as a result of hyperpartisan redistricting, there is growing support for reform, pushed with great enthusiasm by citizen advocacy groups such as OneVirginia2021.[73] Much of this takes the form of demands for nonpartisan independent redistricting commissions (IRCs). The structure, design, and operation of these commissions vary greatly, ranging from commissions that include direct political appointees and, in some cases, even elected officials (as in New Jersey) to commissions (California's) created with the goal of having ordinary citizens serve as members. The commissions also differ in size, their map-approval processes, and their substantive rules.

Redistricting reform has been accomplished in numerous ways and looks different depending on the state. In Virginia and many other states, major redistricting reform requires a constitutional amendment, a process that is neither easy nor fast. In other states, the process has been driven by citizen ballot initiatives. Voters passed redistricting reforms in Arizona in 2000 and in California in 2008 and 2010. More recently, voters in Colorado, Michigan, Missouri, New York, Ohio, and Utah have also adopted changes to improve the redistricting process.[74]

The most dramatic departure from the typical redistricting process is found in states with IRCs. Truly independent commissions are composed of members who are neither public officials nor elected officials and who are selected in a process that is conducted by an independent entity. With these arrangements, the commissioners determine the final maps. As of January 2019, four states—California, Arizona, Colorado, and Michigan—had IRCs that will draw both congressional and state legislative districts.[75]

Some states depart only partially from legislative control of redistricting. In these states, advisory commissions are created, which may consist of legislators, nonlegislators, or a mix, that then recommend redistricting plans to the legislature. In these instances the advisory commission draws the maps and the legislature has final approval, usually by an up-or-down vote. Connecticut and Maine require a plan to be passed by a two-thirds majority of the legislature, and in Connecticut the plan is not subject to gubernatorial veto. As of December 2018, four states—Utah, Iowa, New York, and Connecticut—were utilizing this type of commission to determine congressional plans, and another two, Vermont and Maine, were developing maps for state legislative districts in this way.[76] In these cases, however, the legislature still votes on the plan and thereby exercises effective control over it.

A third variation involves commissions whose members are directly appointed by elected officials, party leadership, or political party committees. The membership of such "political appointee commissions" may be evenly divided between parties, or members of one party may be permitted to hold more seats on the commission than members of the other. Four states—Hawaii, Washington, New Jersey, and Idaho—utilize these commissions to draw congressional maps, and five others—Alaska, Montana, Missouri, Ohio, and Pennsylvania—use them to draw state representative districts.[77]

In November 2020, voters in Virginia approved a constitutional amendment that combines elements of these three variations on redistricting commissions.[78] While the makeup of Virginia's commission is not totally independent, in that legislators would serve on the commission, it does remove some elements of partisanship. The commission would include eight citizen representatives and eight legislative members and would require a majority vote of each member category for a redistricting plan to be approved. If no plan is approved, the process would then move to the Virginia Supreme Court for final action. This approach will be unique among the states, in part because a state court rather than a federal one could be the final arbiter. It is also significant because a state legislature, controlled by two separate parties in two separate years, voted to take away the traditional legislative prerogative to draw their own districts.

With the recent decision of the US Supreme Court in *Rucho* providing legal cover to partisan redistricting, states matter more than ever before; the fight over drawing lines will only be resolved by individual legislatures in individual states, even if that resolution finds its form in the status quo or independent commissions. And there will likely be more legal challenges in state courts interpreting the provisions of differing state constitutions. In other words, the states will determine the rules by which we exercise the most fundamental of rights affecting the future of our democracy—the right to vote.

# 7

# States of Knowledge

Education remains the key to both economic and political empowerment.
—Former US congressperson Barbara Jordan

It was a relatively quiet day in the Virginia State Senate when HB 516, a bill that would give parents the right to object to explicit reading materials in their children's classrooms, came before the forty-member body. After twenty minutes of spirited debate, Tom Garrett, a Republican legislator from Buckingham County, took the discussion to another level by reading aloud sexually explicit passages from Toni Morrison's Pulitzer Prize–winning novel, *Beloved*, that included graphic descriptions of rape, sex, and bestiality. The senators listened in shock, as did several dozen adolescent pages, boys and girls who occupied the chamber on a daily basis to assist senators with everything from photocopying to obtaining lunch.

Morrison's graphic words held the body transfixed, and senators, pages, and Senate staff listened open-mouthed as the shocking descriptions flowed over the assembly. At several points, other senators attempted to intervene and point out to Garrett the youngsters in the room. Senator Stephen Newman of Lynchburg interrupted Garrett and asked him to stop reading, and Senate Majority Leader Tommy Norment made a "humble request" for Garrett to cease. At one point, Senator Garrett claimed, in the presence of the pages, that no student should have to listen to these words "without the consent of their parents." The Senate, by a 22–17 vote, adopted the measure, which was later vetoed by the governor.

Events of this sort occur more frequently in statehouses than one might think, and reflect the strong feelings and high stakes that are involved in educational policymaking in the states. At the time of Garrett's speech, about one-half of Virginia's school districts already provided parental notification when these materials were to be used in class, but lawmakers who supported the bill said it should be codified in state law. The bill's opponents were concerned that the measure would remove discretion from local school boards and create a culture of censorship in the public schools.[1] This bill, seemingly innocuous at the time it was introduced, became yet another flashpoint in the culture wars that are now playing out in states all over the country. Garrett went on to be elected to the US Congress but resigned after one term following revelation of a wide variety of personal issues.

Few would argue that Virginia's decision on parental notification might determine the fate of the Western world, but the debate illustrates that so much of what happens in educational policy emanates from the states. And so much is at stake. For years, commentators have argued that America's ability to compete in the world depends on the quality of our educational system. Many have focused on the differences in test scores between American youngsters and those in other nations, or on our ability to properly train the twenty-first-century workforce. Countless tomes have been written decrying the so-called decline of our public university system and what this means for the nation. These concerns are legitimate, so much so that candidates for federal office often build their campaigns around their support for education. But most decisions about the direction of public education, and certainly decisions on its funding, whether they concern grades K–12 or higher education, are made at the state level.

## Differences in School Funding

Most families are concerned about their children's and grandchildren's ability to gain the skills needed to succeed. Families tend to pay more attention to what is happening in their local schools—whether there are enough teachers and they are paid properly, classroom safety, and how the achievement gap is being addressed—than with how American schoolchildren compare on test scores with Finnish youngsters. They pay little attention to the source of school funding, and many do not realize that, on average, federal money accounts for less than 10 percent of K–12 education funding;[2] the rest of the responsibility falls to state and local governments.

States differ dramatically when it comes to the mix of state and local funding. In Vermont, for example, about 90 percent of school funding that does not come from the federal government is provided by the state; by contrast, state government in Nebraska, New Hampshire, and South Dakota accounts for only about a third of school funding.[3] When we talk about the schools, some argue that it should not be about the money; quality, they suggest, does not directly correlate with funding. Yet inadequate state investment in schools means that buildings are not maintained, programs and positions are eliminated, and teachers suffer. Larger financial burdens are imposed on localities, some of which are not in a position to tax their citizens to make up the difference. It is not surprising, therefore, that the most vigorous debates in state legislatures center on funds for education.

In all but five states, statewide formulas determine most school funding.[4] These formulas are designed to ensure adequate funding across schools; some, such as Virginia's, also seek to promote equity by providing additional monies to divisions that are poorer. But assessing differences in state funding for education is very difficult. Advocacy groups and the federal government assemble enormous amounts of data, and almost every state has budget staffs that are ready, willing, and able to celebrate reports lauding their state or to dispute data that may be interpreted as reflecting negatively on what they are doing to support public education. Comparing states, then, often requires a review of numerous data sources. Recent reports consistently indicate wide discrepancies in state spending per K–12 student. A 2020 study using census data showed dramatic differences, from a low of $7,628 per student in Utah to a high of more than $24,040 in New York.[5] This is consistent with the 2018 report of the National Center for Education Statistics (NCES), the primary federal entity charged with collecting and analyzing data related to education in the United States and other nations, which ranked Utah the lowest and New York the highest. Other states with large investments were Connecticut, New Jersey, Vermont, Alaska, and Massachusetts.[6]

Comparing aggregate data between two states is difficult enough; determining the impact of state investment in different school divisions is even more challenging. Two school districts may spend the same amount per pupil, pay the same salaries to teachers, and provide the same level of additional resources, but may not achieve the same level of student performance. The primary reason for this discrepancy is that no two school districts are alike. If one is located in an area where costs are higher because of market pressures or if it serves a higher percentage of students with special needs or a school body with greater ethnic diversity, it may need to spend more to ensure that the educational inputs are the same as in a district with more homogeneity and where costs are lower.[7]

Numerous other factors can affect both spending and the state rankings. In rural states, per capita spending may be increased by transportation costs, even though those monies do not show up in the classroom. Other states have higher labor and operating costs, which generate higher spending; in fact, the top overall spenders tend to be states with a higher cost of living.

Some jurisdictions may have higher administrative expenses, while others, such as Utah, have a population mix that includes a larger number of students, thereby driving down their per capita expenses.[8]

## School Funding Formulas: Opportunities by Zip Code?

Comparing states is made more complicated by monies that localities provide, either voluntarily or as required by state statute. In Virginia, for example, localities must match state funding up to a certain amount. To do this, the state uses what are called the Standards of Quality (SOQ), a concept that harks back to the state's 1971 Constitution and efforts to address school funding in the aftermath of massive resistance. The SOQ are used to determine what is needed to provide basic education, including staffing standards and other resources associated with projected student enrollment. The state then estimates the total cost of the SOQ, allocates a portion of this funding in its budget, and requires local governments to contribute the rest. Each year there are efforts to add additional requirements to the SOQ—for example, making school nurses available in every elementary school. If this happens, state spending increases—and so does the local match.

To further complicate matters, the commonwealth then employs an additional calculation, called the "composite index," to determine the proportionate mix between state and local funding. This formula is designed to reflect a local school division's ability to pay, factoring in each district's aggregate property wealth, adjusted gross income, and taxable retail sales. This figure determines the share of funding for a school division that the state must provide. In Virginia, this creates a funding dynamic whereby wealthier communities subsidize poorer regions of the commonwealth with additional state funds. Local divisions are not prevented from contributing more than their share. In fact, most do so, and in some cases, considerable extra funds are provided. Smaller and poorer school divisions, however, find it more difficult to invest money above what is needed to meet the standards, if only because their tax base is depressed compared with that of the richer and larger jurisdictions.[9] Virginia is not the only state that attempts to achieve some equity in funding based on a jurisdiction's ability to pay.[10] But even in states that embrace this approach, debates continue about the fairness of the formula and whether it accounts sufficiently for levels of poverty found in some localities.

These formulas create some interesting funding patterns. In wealthier jurisdictions such as Fairfax County, Virginia, the locality invests substantial monies in excess of what the state projects to be necessary to fund the Virginia SOQ; with these monies, the locality is able to buy down student-

teacher ratios, provide more school counseling, and fund efforts at remedi-
ation designed to boost student achievement. Poorer districts, however, find
making these investments more problematic. An apt contrast can be found
by comparing Arlington County, in wealthier Northern Virginia, to Norton,
in the poorer southwestern part of the state. In Arlington County, local taxpayers pay $17,193 per student for education and the state provides $1,676.
This is nearly twice as much as the total amount of money spent per student
in Norton, even after all the local, state, and federal money ($9,219) is added
in.[11] Hence, while the state may be providing proportionally more dollars
per student to Norton, greater real investments are being made in Arlington
County.[12] Similar dynamics occur in most other states that provide only base
levels of funding and can create different educational opportunities for students based on nothing more than their zip code.

States struggle with how to address these funding disparities. Lawmakers
constantly talk about addressing their state's school funding formula, but
adjustments are very difficult to make without at the same time injecting
a large amount of additional funding; otherwise, the process becomes one
that simply divides the funding pie in a different fashion, creating winners
and losers in so doing. While Virginia has not altered its funding formula,
recent budgets have provided additional funding to at-risk divisions based
on the numbers of students who qualify for the federal free or reduced-price
lunch program. That funding has a cap attached to it, but it provides extra
monies over and above the school funding formula. In Idaho, which has the
dubious distinction of having both low per pupil expenditures *and* equity
problems, the legislature recently considered moving to an enrollment-based
funding formula that would provide additional funding for economically disadvantaged students and other at-risk student groups, but then rejected any
change.[13] In New York, similar efforts to change the state's education funding
formula have failed.[14]

Before state budgets contracted during the COVID-19 crisis, some states
were engaged in significant debates over modifications to the school funding
formula in light of changing demographics and needs. Several states, most
notably Massachusetts and Maryland, have major initiatives under way to
determine possible changes to their school funding formula, in part to assist
school divisions with larger populations living with poverty. And the Virginia
Department of Education is considering major changes to its SOQ, which, if
enacted by the legislature, would add about $1.2 billion to K–12 funding while
addressing many of the needs of divisions with large populations living with
poverty.[15] The success of these efforts will rest with lawmakers who are will-

ing to invest substantially more; otherwise, the debate will be about redistributing the existing pot, thereby creating winners and losers and making it difficult to assemble coalitions necessary to effect the change.

It is no surprise that the poorest states economically tend to spend the least on education. Moreover, most of the top spenders, including Massachusetts, New Jersey, Connecticut, New York, and California, are not only considered to have the best educational systems but typically have higher state GDPs than most other states that spend less. They can afford more, and choose to invest it. Massachusetts, a leader in educational quality, consistently reports among the highest GDP per capita each year, and Mississippi ranks near the bottom in both categories.[16] New York, Connecticut, and California also rank high on both school spending and GDP per capita. One must be cautious, however, before concluding that higher school spending spurs more economic activity; in fact, it can be argued that a state's economic wealth permits it to invest greater amounts in education. Nonetheless, there is clearly a relationship between educational quality and state GDP.

When it comes to the quality of a state's schools, per pupil spending matters but is not determinative. *Education Week* attempts a more involved analysis, and compiles an annual ranking of school system quality based on a number of factors.[17] Called "Quality Counts," the criteria include high school graduation rates, per pupil public school spending, math and reading proficiency, the percentage of adults with bachelor's degrees, and adults with incomes over the median national average. State rankings based on these criteria have not changed much in a decade.[18] The top four for 2020—New Jersey, Massachusetts, Connecticut, and Maryland—have ranked consistently in the top ten, even if their per pupil spending is not always the highest. In the 2018 rankings, of the eight highest-spending states, six were rated the highest in terms of the overall quality of their systems. The lowest spenders—Nevada, New Mexico, Mississippi, Idaho, and Louisiana—ranked between fifty-one and forty in terms of systems quality.[19] Virginia ranked twelfth highest in the 2020 Quality Counts survey but was the fifteenth lowest-rated state in terms of per pupil spending.[20]

## It's Not Just about the Money

Education policy is more than just about spending. Early childhood education, charter school policy, testing regimens, sex education, teacher evaluation, and school discipline are some examples where the contested terrain of school policy is often found at the state rather than the federal level. Even the No Child Left Behind act, arguably the largest federal attempt ever to assert a national governmental role, left the standards for judging educational systems up to the states. And during the COVID pandemic, while local divisions remained largely responsible for the conditions under which schools would open, their actions could always be short-circuited by executive action at the state level.

The state role applies to everything from student-teacher ratios to the content of textbooks. A prominent example is the use of different textbooks by different states to explain and study the Civil War. In most southern states, the conflict was frequently referred to as the War between the States, the War of Northern Aggression, or the Lost Cause, thereby reducing the significance of slavery as the rationale for secession and elevating the "noble character" of those who fought to destroy the United States.[21] Over the years, some states have relinquished the exclusive power to choose texts, but the problems remain. The portrayal of African Americans in history books, to take another example, has become so salient in Virginia that Governor Northam created a commission to address it.[22]

Much racially offensive language has been eliminated from textbooks, but debates continue over what topics to discuss and how they should be addressed. Recently, Texas bureaucrats and the state's Department of Education debated removing Helen Keller and Hillary Clinton as persons worthy of discussion in civics classes; ultimately the state's Board of Education voted to keep both in the social studies curriculum, but the vote was not unanimous.[23] With the advocacy of the Florida Citizens' Alliance, an umbrella conservative group, Florida passed a law in 2017 that permits anyone to object to textbook content and establishes a process by which those objections can be heard and decided by each school district. Though final decisions rest with the school board, some are concerned that this process will become overly political and could prevent schools from tackling controversial issues.[24]

The same historical event may be described differently in textbooks from the same publisher, depending on the state to which the book is targeted. A recent analysis comparing history textbooks in California and Texas revealed a number of areas where explanations of events differed.[25] For example, white resistance to black progress was covered differently in the two states. The California textbooks included criticism of wealth inequality and the impact of companies like Standard Oil on the environment; by contrast, textbooks intended for Texas, which passed a law in 1995 that requires high school economics courses to emphasize "the free enterprise system and its benefits," included celebrations of such entrepreneurs as Andrew Carnegie and Republican criticisms of President Obama's environmental policies.

And in almost every state, there are ongoing disputes over the content of the family life curriculum as educators attempt to respond to changing mores at a time of tremendous cultural conflict. These curricula, which are designed to provide a comprehensive, sequential K–12 program that includes everything from age-appropriate instruction in family living and community relationships to information about human sexuality and reproduction, have often served as a source of local and state educational conflict as policymakers and parents struggle to determine the best information to convey and the means to do so during times of rapid change.

Learning materials in schools generate constant disputes that are argued by state boards of education, and sometimes in the halls of legislatures. Among the most celebrated topics of debate in the educational arena is school choice. Arguments around this topic occur largely at the state level and usually involve school vouchers, which grant parents who opt out of public schooling a certain sum of money to help pay tuition at private schools. A recent initiative that is getting substantial attention is legislation to create what are called Education Savings Accounts (ESAs), a big favorite of the Koch brothers and Betsy DeVos, the secretary of education in the Trump administration. These are not the typical education savings accounts with which many Americans are familiar, the 529s or Coverdell accounts, which allow families to receive a tax break if they deposit their own money into savings vehicles. Instead, ESAs use public dollars and channel them to private schools. Parents join the program by pledging not to enroll their son or daughter in a public school or a charter school. In exchange, most of the monies that the public school would have spent on the pupil (usually 90 percent) are placed on a debit card or into an account. The remaining 10 percent is used to fund program administration. Those monies can then be used to cover private school tuition and fees, online learning programs, private tutoring, and other approved customized learning services and materials. Unlike many of the recent school choice initiatives, which have focused on educational services and options for low-income families or persons with disabilities, ESAs are more far-reaching; in most cases, there is no means testing, and, since the schools attended are private, there is no state accountability. Instead, the programs amount to the transfer of public dollars for private purposes.

Florida has perhaps the largest school voucher program in the country, and its governor, Ron DeSantis, recently signed a Republican-crafted bill to create yet another program using taxpayer dollars traditionally spent on public schools. More than 140,000 students currently attend private schools using Florida's existing scholarship programs, and more than 80 percent of them attend religious schools.[26] Numerous lawsuits challenging these programs have failed.[27] According to the American Federation for Children, there are fifty-six publicly funded private school choice programs in twenty-six states, the District of Columbia, and Puerto Rico.[28]

For many policymakers, the success of their systems derives from outcomes—how students perform and whether their schooling prepares them for the world they are about to enter. The impact of COVID-19 has only accelerated these concerns. Preliminary studies suggest that a $1,000 reduction in per capita spending is associated with a drop in average test scores in math and reading and expands the achievement gap between black and white students.[29] School divisions have placed faith in online education, but even acknowledging the challenges of the digital divide between households, researchers have shown that as many as one in five teenage students frequently miss homework assignments because of a lack of technology or internet access.[30] Students from rural and poor areas are finding it more difficult to learn in this environment.[31] As the pandemic subsides, state educational policy will enter a phase of evaluating the full impacts of the virus and what, if any, remedial measures will need to be taken to address the disruption.

## Higher Education: Engine of Opportunity or Driver of Inequality?

Like so many of my generation, I enrolled in college, and my life was fundamentally changed. Part of the American dream has always included the prospect that higher education would propel citizens to greater opportunity and a better life. While Americans remain convinced that higher education is a good investment,[32] the country has recently expressed concern about the role of universities in our society.

In a 2018 poll conducted by the Pew Research Center, 61 percent of Americans surveyed said the higher education system in the United States was going in the wrong direction.[33] A 2018 Gallup poll found that confidence in higher education had dropped from 57 percent in 2015 to 48 percent in 2018.[34] Various reasons have been cited for these findings. At the top of the list are the increasing cost of tuition and whether what students are learning today can help them gain a footing in the marketplace. But the concerns also carry a political tinge, with some critics suggesting that colleges are merely "liberal breeding grounds."[35] Other Americans increasingly view higher education as a private benefit consumed by the individual rather than as a public good underwritten by the state for the benefit of society. Some are concerned about the degree to which the academy is simply reinforcing the inequality that exists in American society.[36] They cite increasing evidence of the sorting of students who attend different schools, with the wealthy tending to attend elite universities,[37] thereby feeding the inequality that already exists in the country. And the explosion of student debt is creating large numbers of former college students, including both those who graduate with a degree and those who do not, who face formidable economic challenges that limit opportunities.[38] These concerns have only intensified in the aftermath of the COVID-19 pandemic. Of all the institutions whose business model has been disrupted by the pandemic, higher education is perhaps the most prominent. Serious questions are being asked about the effectiveness of virtual versus face-to-face learning and the value of the degree itself. Whether these debates will subside after an effective vaccine allows colleges to reopen remains to be seen.

For many US educational institutions, years of financial strain are only making these challenges more difficult to address. While much of the political debate has focused on state investments in K–12 education, the financial challenges of higher education are perhaps even more significant. Several years ago, Sweet Briar College, a small institution in Virginia, almost closed its doors in the face of declining enrollment and fiscal challenges. It was saved only by a major outpouring of financial support from its alumnae.[39] Hampshire College in Amherst, Massachusetts, recently contemplated merging with another institution for the same reason.[40] Admittedly, these are private universities, but public institutions are experiencing similar challenges. Faced with falling tax revenues and the need to balance budgets in the wake of the Great Recession, many states reduced their higher education spending dramatically. And when the pandemic shuttered college campuses, their business model, based not only on tuition and fees but also on room and board, was thrown into disarray. Some private schools and elite public institutions such as the University of California, Berkeley, and the University of Virginia had substantial endowments that could fill the financial gaps, but many smaller state colleges did not have that resource. To meet their bottom line would require an influx of public monies, and few could see from where those monies might come.

Even before the COVID-19-related contraction, funding challenges existed. The economics of higher education continue to generate discussions about closing the doors of some institutions and merging others. The University of Wisconsin system plans to consolidate thirteen two-year colleges into seven four-year colleges.[41] The University of Georgia system has been consolidating campuses for several years, and the Alabama and Connecticut community college systems are developing plans for administration consolidation.[42] But beyond that, the COVID-19 pandemic has shaken the academy and forced some deep thinking about how to deliver the educational product effectively at lower cost. The online experience, whose promise seemed so bright a decade ago but lost steam in recent years, has enjoyed a resurgence as colleges have coped with the need to slow the transmission of the virus.

Higher education receives a small percentage of overall federal spending but is the third-largest category in state budgets.[43] Depending on how the data are analyzed, there has been either a subtle but clear disinvestment in higher education in many states in the last decade[44] or simply substantial volatility brought on by ebbs and flows in the economy.[45] Whether it is the former or the later explanation, thoughtful observers are concerned about the long-term state support of public university education. As public funding has declined or remain stagnant, public universities have become increasingly reliant on tuition and private donations, with all their attendant strings, to fund their operations. With fewer state dollars available, public universities have increased tuition and fees above the rate of inflation, placing a greater burden on students, many of whom have taken on substantial debt to obtain their education. It has also made observers of American higher educational institutions increasingly concerned that the lack of public investment in education may diminish the technological innovation that flows from American universities and has contributed so dramatically to the success of the US economy over the past fifty years.

State legislators always talk a good game about investing in higher education, but the record over the past decade shows that their deeds rarely match their words. A study by the Center on Budget and Policy Priorities found that funding for two- and four-year institutions in 2017 was nearly $9 billion below that in 2008, after adjusting for inflation. Forty-four states actually spent less per student in 2017 than in 2008. Only Indiana, Montana, Nebraska, North Carolina, and Wyoming spent more. Tuition was up more by than 35 percent during the same period.[46] This has left many young people with substantial debt at the end of four years, thereby limiting their ability to buy a home or take the risk of starting a business.[47]

## Building a Talent Pool for the Future

Until the pandemic hit, college enrollments had remained fairly steady for the last decade. Recent numbers, however, are sparking concern. The impact was most felt at the nation's community colleges, institutions that provide key certificate and associate degree programs that train for critical jobs from nurse to electrician. In 2020, community colleges reported an enrollment

decline of first-time students of nearly 23 percent, and a 9.4 percent enrollment drop overall.[48] According to experts in workforce development, these
institutions are a key source of talent to help solve the country's skilled tech
talent shortage.[49] Consequently, continuation of this trend could greatly compromise the creation of the talent pool that will take the United States to the
next level economically. Prior to COVID-19, most states were hoping to make
college more accessible and affordable, if only to meet the needs of a future
workforce. They are now reexamining what they do and how they do it.

Funding, of course, will be key. Many states now rely primarily on tuition
revenue from students and their families rather than on state support to
fund public higher education. Nationally, tuition dollars collected by public
universities jumped 43 percent per student from 2008 to 2018 after adjust-
ing for inflation.[50] In fiscal year 2008, nationwide state financial support
peaked at $9,248 per full-time-equivalent student, but fell by about a quar-
ter, to $6,888, in fiscal year 2012. By 2018, state support had partially recov-
ered, but still remained 13 percent below fiscal year 2008 levels in that year,
at $8,073 per student, and total and aggregate spending was, after adjust-
ing for inflation, 7 percent less in 2018 than in 2008. Total state support for
higher education increased in 2019 for the seventh year in a row, but so too
did costs.[51] And potential economic slowdowns pose future risks to continued
increases in funding.

States differ dramatically in what they charge students to attend public
colleges and universities. In 2018–19, the College Board reported that average
tuition and fee prices for in-state students at public four-year institutions
ranged from $5,400 in Wyoming and $6,360 in Florida to $16,460 in New
Hampshire and $16,610 in Vermont.[52]

As budgetary challenges increase at the state level, the area of higher education may pose the most dramatic example of why states matter. Rising
tuition could undoubtedly affect the talent pool in the years ahead as future
students consider options other than higher education. Stagnant levels of
funding will affect how and whether researchers are recruited to, and retained
by, which institutions. The traditional powerhouse state universities such as
the University of Virginia, the University of California, Berkeley, and the University of Michigan will likely continue to thrive, but others could languish
or even decline, with damaging consequences to the communities and states
in which they are located. Leadership at the state level will likely make the
difference in how this story eventually unfolds. Success or failure could rest
on two things—money invested in the process, and leadership in policy development and implementation.

There are many ways to evaluate and compare state expenditures on public higher education. One analysis is issued by the State Higher Education Executive Officers Association (SHEEO), which conducts an examination each year of the costs of higher education and state investments in it.[53] Its 2018 report indicates that per student higher education appropriations in the United States have only partially recovered since the Great Recession. In SHEEO's data, Virginia's tuition and fees were at the higher end, ranking among the top ten highest in the country. For 2017, SHEEO found Wyoming was the highest-ranked state in per capita spending on higher education and New Hampshire was the lowest; Virginia ranked below the national average in per capita financial support.

Several other of the report's conclusions are striking. First, beginning in 2016, and in contrast to the states' financial commitments to their universities and colleges in decades past, more than one-half of the states relied more on tuition revenues to fund higher education than on government appropriations; in 2018, tuition accounted for more than 50 percent of total revenue available for public universities and colleges in twenty-seven states. Virginia crossed this line several years ago. Despite its public pronouncements (and language in the state budget) that it seeks to fund 67 percent of public higher education, tuition and fees make up more than 50 percent of the cost of public education in the commonwealth. A study by the Southern Regional Education Board analyzed the changes in the decade between 2006 and 2016. In 2005–6, Virginia appropriations provided 47 percent of total funds available for operations of the state's public institutions. By 2015–16, the state's share had dropped to 31 percent, with the remaining 69 percent made up from net tuition and fees.[54]

Second, despite five years of increased support, states have not yet returned to their prerecession level of funding. Virginia has increased its public investments substantially in the last few years, but it still lags slightly its prerecession levels.

With all these challenges, some states are taking action to reinvest in their public institutions, even if the appropriations are not as large as many would desire. In the 2019 legislative session, the Virginia General Assembly enacted an incentive plan by which it offered its public institutions additional sums of money on the condition that tuition would not be raised. It worked: each institution announced that tuition would not increase in the following academic year, the first time there was a statewide tuition freeze in twenty years.[55] The budget problems created by COVID-19 have made the extension of this freeze extremely problematic, however. And with many state universities choosing to employ virtual learning, an economic model based on revenue from room and board becomes very challenging. The degree to which this is a long-term issue will be determined in part by how quickly the population can achieve immunity through a vaccine.

## Affordability Brings Access

The ability to attend a community college or university is often a function of affordability, and state policies and funding can make a huge difference. Since the early 2010s, affordability has been more of a challenge. When the Southern Regional Education Board examined the affordability issue, it found increasing challenges for students and their families to finance a degree. In Virginia, for example, the ten-year period between 2006 and 2016 saw household income decline by 2 percent. At the same time, tuition and fees at four-year institutions in Virginia increased by 116 percent, and by 124 percent at two-year colleges. The impact was felt more by those with lower incomes. In 2015, families earning less than $30,000 per year who sought to attend top-tier universities, such as the University of Virginia or the College of William and Mary, needed 70 percent of their income for educational expenses. In 2010, that percentage was only 44 percent.[56] In part because of these increasing burdens, for "several straight years, more talented young Virginians have left the state than have migrated here."[57]

Across the nation, there is increasing interest in free college tuition, and some level of tuition-free college now exists in twenty states.[58] Indiana touts its 21st Century Scholars program, a thirty-year-old initiative that offers four years of tuition to students who qualify for free or reduced-price lunch programs and who meet certain academic standards. The Tennessee Promise, New York's Excelsior program, and Oregon's Promise program are frequently celebrated as state efforts to provide tuition-free college.[59] Washington State recently enacted a similar program for free tuition at its community colleges.[60] In 2020, Virginia created a similar program to make community college free for low- and middle-income residents seeking jobs in such fields as cybersecurity and early childhood education.[61] It will likely remain inadequately funded until the economy recovers.

These tuition-grant programs can be expensive, and their different structures determines their costs. Many free college and free tuition programs take a "last-dollar" approach, meaning they cover only the amount of tuition left over after a student's grants, scholarships and other financial aid money are applied. Last-dollar initiatives are often less expensive to the state since they pay only after other monies, such Pell and other grants, are applied to student costs. New Mexico's proposed Opportunity Scholarship program is one such last-dollar initiative. If passed, the state will join New York in covering tuition for residents over four years at all in-state public institutions.[62] The scholarship would cover tuition and fees for New Mexico students, but only after they have exhausted federal and state aid.

These last-dollar approaches have been criticized by some as disadvantaging low-income students; critics argue that since these programs provide money to students regardless of their family's income, they are unfair. As the advocacy group Third Way described it, "If two students attend college—one a low-income student receiving a Pell Grant and the other a wealthy student not receiving any other financial aid—tax dollars from the free college plan would flow to the wealthy student (who is already more likely to go to college in the first place and be able to afford it) because they will have greater tuition expenses not already covered by existing aid."[63] By contrast, first-dollar programs pay for tuition and fees up front, thereby allowing students to use Pell grants and other aid to cover expenses such as housing, food, and books. Whatever program is embraced by an individual state, its usefulness will rise and fall with the appropriations reserved to it, an increasingly challenging task until the economy recovers from the pandemic.

## Will COVID Bring a New Normal?

Of all the items that state policymakers consider, education usually occupies the most attention. States have always faced a suite of dramatically new challenges to educating youth and preparing the next generation to take its place in society. These complexities have only been exacerbated during COVID-19 and its aftermath. Public schools have done their best to cobble together an alternative delivery system for their curricula that combines in-person and virtual learning, and jury is still out on how effective it has been.[64] It has not helped that almost 16 million students, mostly those from low-income and rural households, do not have adequate internet access or digital devices at home to support online learning.[65] At the same time, several states have been innovative in their use of federal dollars to create or expand broadband and internet services to those most in need. Several states that did not have broadband grant programs before the COVID-19 emergency, including Delaware, Idaho, Kansas, Mississippi, New Hampshire, and South Carolina, have used Coronavirus Relief Fund dollars to establish emergency initiatives.[66] Beyond that, the challenges in reopening schools and universities are immense, and a "new normal" in the aftermath of COVID-19 will probably involve much experimentation and, hopefully, successful innovation. Most of this will occur at the state level as policymakers establish guidelines for learning in a new environment. Not only will these state decisions make a difference to the health and success of young people today, they will have a huge impact on how the US economy functions in the future. During this period of rapid social and technological change, decisions made in legislatures about curriculum, training programs, and incentives will determine whether the nation has enough workers in the right position to generate economic vitality. The country's quality of life is at stake, and it is in state government where it will largely be determined.

# 8

# Crime, Punishment, and Justice

> One of the problems in America is that everybody focuses on their
> own narrow little bit of the problem without connecting punishment
> and prevention together, without connecting the schools and the police
> together, without connecting the pediatricians and the social workers
> together.
> —FORMER US ATTORNEY GENERAL JANET RENO

The United States has a higher level of incarceration per capita than any
other nation in the world, and the vast majority of the incarcerated are held
in state, not federal, prisons. Recent figures from the US Department of Justice reveal that about 2.2 million Americans were incarcerated in federal and
state prisons at the end of 2017. Only a small percentage of these individuals
were in federal penitentiaries for committing federal crimes; about 1.3 million of those incarcerated were housed in individual state facilities,[1] with an
additional 745,200 people (two-thirds of whom had not been convicted) held
in county or city jails.[2] Most of those behind bars had been charged with violating a state law, tried and convicted in a state court, sentenced under rules
made by a state, and were serving time either in a state facility or in a local
jail partially funded by a state. States matter when it comes to incarceration.

National incarceration numbers and rates have fallen over the last decade.[3]
Yet the incarceration rate remains high compared to that of other nations: for
every 100,000 people residing in the United States in 2017, approximately
440 of them were behind bars.[4] The US incarceration rate has been higher
than other nations' for decades. And there are wide variations among states.
Data from 2018 reveal that seven states had reduced their prison populations
by over 30 percent since reaching peak levels in 1999. Those states included
New Jersey, which saw a 38.5 percent decline between 1999 and 2018, and
New York, which saw a 36.1 percent decline. However, six states recorded
their highest-ever prison populations in 2018: Wyoming, Nebraska, Iowa,
Wisconsin, Kansas, and Oregon.[5] Between 1985 and 1995, Virginia's prison

population more than doubled, largely driven by the abolition of parole. In the next two decades it continued to rise, but not as much.[6] In recent years the prison population in the commonwealth has dropped by about 4.5 percent.[7]

These changes in incarceration rates have been driven largely by state policy. Not only do states play the major role in generating these national numbers, they also have very different policies that produce very different results. According to the Prison Policy Institute, thirty-one states, including the Commonwealth of Virginia, have incarceration rates higher than any nation other than the United States. In 2018, Oklahoma and Louisiana had the highest rates, followed closely by Mississippi.[8] Even states like New York and Massachusetts, thought to be more liberal in their approaches to criminal justice, jail people at higher rates than nearly every other country on Earth.[9]

Fifty years ago, the US prison system and jails looked very different. In the 1950s and 1960s, the federal and state combined prison population never exceeded 225,000. The incarceration rate actually dropped into the early 1970s, reaching its lowest figure—93 per 100,000 population—in 1972; that year the US Justice Department reported that the number of Americans behind bars was 196,092.[10] Over the next four decades, incarceration rates steadily rose, mostly as a function of mandatory sentencing policies and the end of parole in many states. More people are serving life sentences today (206,000) than the entire prison population in 1970 (196,000). In 2016, twenty-four states reported more people serving life sentences than the state's entire prison population in 1970.[11] Yet US crime rates during the increases in incarceration rates showed no clear trend; the rate of violent crime rose, then fell, rose again, then declined sharply.

In the view of many analysts, the best single explanation for the rise in incarceration over the decades was not an increase in crime rates but policy choices made by state legislators that greatly increased the use of imprisonment as a response to lawbreaking.[12]

## New Laws and More Criminals

In the last several decades, states became increasingly aggressive in changing how crimes were charged and punished. The "war on drugs" and other sentencing changes increased the likelihood of incarceration and criminal justice supervision. New laws were passed to require mandatory prison sentences. In twenty states, parole was abolished, with the effect that felons spent more time in jail.[13] Drug laws were increasingly enforced with longer sentences. Initiatives such as enhanced punishments for repeat offenses and so-called truth-in-sentencing laws that limited the amount of time that inmates could earn off nonlife sentences contributed not only to overall high rates of incarceration but also had disproportionate effects on black and Latino communities. While the incarceration rates for sentenced black adults declined by 31 percent from 2007 to 2017, their imprisonment rate was still almost six times that of white males. The Bureau of Justice Statistics (BJS) reports that, as of mid-2017, 50 percent of prisoners in jail were white, 34 percent were black, and 15 percent were Hispanic.[14] And patterns differ from state to state. BJS data showed that in eleven states, one of every twenty adult black males was in prison, while in twelve, over 50 percent of the prison population was African American.[15]

State policymakers justify incarceration in several ways. First, a prison sentence is viewed as retribution or punishment, a way for society to enforce its norms by depriving someone of liberty based on the severity of the crime. Second, imprisonment operates as a deterrent, either to show others that a crime will not be tolerated or to discourage the wrongdoer from transgressing again. Third, incarceration takes a transgressor off the streets. If a person is behind bars, that person simply cannot commit a crime. Finally, a prison sentence may be justified as a vehicle of rehabilitation, that is, of preventing future crimes by reforming the criminal wrongdoer. This justification is found more frequently in a state's treatment of juvenile offenders.

State criminal law typically differentiates between misdemeanor and felony offenses. Misdemeanor crimes include lower-level theft offenses, simple assault, impaired driving, disorderly conduct, and criminal trespass. Conviction for those offenses may bring fines or time in the local or county jail not exceeding one year. If someone is convicted of a felony, such as grand larceny, malicious wounding, manslaughter, or murder, the punishment can be confinement in a state penitentiary, with sentences ranging from one year to life.[16] But some definitions of the crimes, especially grand larceny, appear especially draconian. In 2017, Virginia punished theft of property in excess of $200 as a felony, a provision that had not been changed since the 1980s. Many other states had thresholds of $500. These low thresholds had the effect of creating more felons and prison inmates.

When people are convicted, they can serve longer periods in jail or prison, depending on the method of sentencing. Juries are notorious for imposing longer sentences than judges, and in six states, including Virginia, when a case is tried by a jury, the jury determines both guilt or innocence and the length of sentence.[17] In addition, almost twenty states use what are called sentencing guidelines, which impose a range of time judges should assign to those convicted of the same type of crime.[18] Ostensibly designed to provide for the equal administration of justice, they can restrict judges from constructing unique and perhaps more lenient sentences, if only because the judges are aware that their conformity with the sentencing guidelines is often the topic of discussion during their reappointment hearings or in re-election campaigns.

Throughout US history, there has always been a significant emphasis on rehabilitation as one purpose of incarceration. But that began to change in the mid-1980s as American society became increasingly concerned about rampant drug use and violent crimes associated with it. Sentences became harsher and their imposition more certain. Notable policies adopted during this period included not just antidrug bills but new offenses and initia-tives, including the registration of sex offenders and a lowering of the age at which juveniles could be tried as adults. A number of states passed truth-in-sentencing laws requiring people to serve a greater percentage of their nominal sentences. To much fanfare, Virginia abolished parole in 1995. By the end of 2000, sixteen states had abolished discretionary release from prison by a parole board for all offenders, and another four had eliminated discretionary parole for certain violent offenses.[19] The movement toward a more punitive system was under way, and the result brought both higher rates of incarceration and higher numbers of inmates.[20]

During this period, states also began incarcerating more of their citizens for nonviolent crimes such as petit larceny, driving without a license, posses-sion of marijuana, and failure to pay child support. The Virginia Department of Corrections, for example, reported that in 2014, 9,000 offenders, repre-senting 24 percent of its prison population, had no violent crimes on their records. At $27,000 per inmate per year, the state was spending approxi-mately $243 million annually to house nonviolent offenders.[21]

Academic research suggests that the incarceration of nonviolent offend-ers is actually counterproductive; a review of the literature found incarcer-ating more nonviolent offenders did not reduce the crime rate but actually increased criminal behavior.[22] As further evidence, when a number of states began raising felony theft thresholds at the beginning of the twenty-first cen-tury, causing fewer people to be imprisoned for nonviolent crimes, there was no spike in criminal activity. Instead, the general downward trend in criminal behavior continued. A 2017 report by the Pew Charitable Trusts found that in twenty-four of the thirty states that raised their felony larceny thresholds between 2000 and 2012, downward trends in property crime or larceny rates, which began in the early 1990s, continued without interruption. The same trends were evident in states that did not change their theft laws. No statistically significant differences were noted.[23] This study supports the analysis of earlier detailed studies conducted in three states, Florida, Maryland, and Michigan, all of which had longer prison terms for nonviolent offenders than many other states. The research found little or no evidence that longer prison terms for many nonviolent offenders either affected the crime rate or kept offenders from committing crimes once they had been released.[24]

The impact of harsher sentences is felt most acutely in minority communities and is coming under increasing scrutiny in the aftermath of George Floyd's killing in 2020. Aggressive policing in communities of color has led not just to well-publicized examples of brutality but to more arrests and convictions. For drug crimes, the racial disparities are especially striking. Data show that whites and African Americans use drugs at roughly the same rate, but blacks have been nearly four times as likely to be arrested for drug offenses and 2.5 times as likely to be arrested for drug possession.[25] The racial element involved in higher incarceration rates has prompted some observers to argue that our criminal justice system has become the functional equivalent of the Jim Crow laws of the past.[26] The monetary costs of incarceration are also high: according to the Prison Policy Institute, over $80 billion is spent each year on correctional facilities and almost another $30 billion on the judicial and legal apparatus of the criminal justice system, dwarfing the entire discretionary budget of the US Department of Education.[27]

## The Public Switches Direction

A cursory look at recent polling data suggests that Americans are paying attention. A 2016 Gallup poll revealed a significant shift in Americans' views of the criminal justice system.[28] It reported a drop in the percentage of those who responded that the system is "not tough enough" from 65 percent in 2003 to 45 percent in 2016. Support for tough drug crimes sentencing also dropped, with only 34 percent asserting that sentencing for drug crimes was "not tough enough." More recently, a Public Opinion Strategies poll conducted for the Justice Action Network reported that 76 percent of those polled think the criminal justice system needs significant improvement, and another 73 percent say the United States spends too much money on prisons.[29]

The murder of George Floyd further accelerated this change in public opinion. A 2019 Pew study found that 87 percent of African Americans and 61 percent of whites believe that blacks are generally treated less fairly by the criminal justice system than whites.[30] After Floyd's death, a CNN survey reported a big shift in attitudes about criminal justice from a few years earlier. In June 2020, 67 percent of those surveyed believed that nation's criminal

justice system favors "whites over blacks," an increase from 52 percent holding that view in 2016.[31] State lawmakers felt compelled to act. Within a month
of Floyd's death, the Minnesota state legislature passed several police reform
measures, Iowa governor Kim Reynolds signed a new bill restricting police
chokeholds, Colorado became the first state in the nation to allow victims of
police violence to sue officers under state law,[32] New York passed a measure
making it easier for the public to access police disciplinary records,[33] and Virginia enacted a series of police reforms, from a required code of conduct to
incentives for localities to create civilian review boards.

Determining the proper role of police is one of the most divisive debates
in the area of criminal justice. Though more of a local than a state issue,
the calls for state action have been loud and persistent. And state policymakers are considering a wide variety of measures that could not even be
discussed just a year ago. Many states, for example, are debating whether to
allow citizens either to sue police directly or to take away some of the automatic immunities previously used to prevent verdicts from being rendered
against officers and departments. "Defund the police" has been the rallying
cry for some in this debate. Although it is a slogan that creates consterna-
tion not only within police departments across the country but also among
citizens in poor neighborhoods who want an officer to show up if they call
911, the idea that a policing system should include greater accountability and
emphasizes approaches that rely more on mental health intervention than
unjustified force is widely accepted, and policymakers will struggle with how
best to make this happen.

## Strange Bedfellows

Interesting coalitions are forming among conservatives and liberals at the
state and federal levels to push reform.[34] The American Legislative Exchange
Committee (ALEC) and the Prison Policy Institute (PPI), two entities associated with Charles and David Koch, known for their support of conservative
causes, are actively engaged with the American Civil Liberties Union (ACLU)
and progressive groups such as the Center for American Progress to build
political pressure to reform the system. Watching these groups cooperate
may seem incongruous, but their association forms a potent coalition that
may bring about needed changes at the state level. For conservatives, the
reform initiatives are being driven by two factors. First, there is concern,
especially regarding juvenile incarceration, that there is too much reliance
on the state to solve problems that might better be addressed by families or
communities. Second, incarceration has significant budgetary impacts. For

liberals, the racial inequities of mass incarceration are prompting desires for reform. Prisoner reentry and reducing recidivism are critical elements of these efforts; after all, more than 95 percent of all individuals serving a prison sentence will eventually be released.[35] Promoting reentry into the workforce after prison has been a large part of these initiatives; in 2018, this advocacy prompted such states as Arizona, Indiana, Kansas, Tennessee, and Wyoming to enact legislation relaxing their occupational licensing restrictions to make it easier for ex-offenders to obtain jobs.[36]

Some states have modified their statutes for possession of certain drugs by reducing them from felonies to misdemeanors. Alaska, Delaware, Mississippi, and Utah have changed the possession of certain drugs from felonies to misdemeanors. As of January 2020, eleven states had legalized recreational marijuana use and twenty-seven had decriminalized possession of small amounts. Critics of this approach suggest this change is too much, too soon, but public support for both decriminalization and legalization is strengthening. The results of three major polls conducted by the National Opinion Research Center at the University of Chicago, the Gallup organization, and Pew show rapid shifts in public opinion supporting legalization, with more than 60 percent of Americans favoring such an approach, an increase from the 30 percent that supported the proposal in 2000.[37]

This is not just a criminal justice issue but a fiscal one as well. States that have legalized pot are raising substantial monies from taxing the product. Washington State and Colorado each raised over $300 million in 2018 from taxing pot, and California was not far behind.[38] Public opinion is moving very quickly on this issue, and we can expect more states to embrace either decriminalization or legalization in the coming years.

States are also paying attention to diversion programs such as drug treatment courts. In the 1990s there was an explosion of arrests and convictions for drug offenses, many of which involved possession but no violence. The National Center for State Courts reported that 31 percent of the 870,000 felony convictions in state trial courts in 1994 were for drug offenses (possession or trafficking).[39] Rather than incarcerate offenders for nonviolent possession, states are funding drug courts, which operate to address underlying problems and keep people out of jail.

Of all the states, California is perhaps most active in reforms. In 2014, voters passed Proposition 47, a citizen-initiated ballot measure designed to reduce the prison population, save money, and reduce recidivism. Prop 47 reduced the penalties associated with a set of lower-level drug and property offenses and used budget savings to fund mental health and other rehabilitative services. A recent study of the reform's impact concluded that prison and jail incarceration levels declined substantially after passage of the law, and there were also decreases in arrests and jail bookings.[40] The researchers reported that while there has been a slight increase in violent crime and some petit larceny offenses, they found no convincing evidence that violent crime increased as a result of the measure; instead, recidivism declined.[41]

And the Golden State is not the only place where reform is under way. In 2016, Kansas began major reforms to its juvenile justice system designed to reduce recidivism. Within two years the state's youth prison population fell 31 percent, allowing the shift of $30 million in savings to community-based programs designed to keep youngsters out of jail.[42] Similarly, a bipartisan group of Louisiana leaders recently decided that the state should no longer be recognized for having the nation's highest incarceration rate. They proceeded to pass numerous bipartisan bills and invest substantial dollars to support diversion programs and reduce recidivism. Almost immediately, the prison population began to drop (by 7.8 percent in the first year), and the state began saving money. The hope is that the state will be safer as recidivism is reduced and that more state funds become available for other programs that state residents consider important.[43]

The pressure for criminal justice reform is likely to accelerate in the states over the next decade, if only because the social and economic costs of the present levels of incarceration are placing increasingly unsustainable burdens on state budgets. Nonetheless, many of the policy considerations will rest on the politics in statehouses and the personalities of those who propose change. Elected officials remember the Willie Horton ads that doomed presidential hopeful Michael Dukakis in 1988 and can be extremely skittish about loosening criminal sanctions and as a result being branded "soft on crime."[44] To many, it takes only one bad occurrence to doom a political career, and it is for that reason that one can never predict precisely how these reform measures will fare in the years ahead.

## Who Controls the Judges?

Justice—criminal or civil—cannot be discussed without considering those who sit in judgment, our judges. Here again, states matter, if only because approximately 95 percent of all cases initiated in the United States are filed in state courts.[45] At the time of our nation's founding, most states appointed judges in a fashion similar to the mechanism established in the US Constitution for the selection of federal judges: life tenure, with nomination by the executive followed by legislative confirmation. That began to change in 1832, when Mississippi became the first state to authorize judicial selection by the direct election of the voters. New York followed suit in 1846, and by the time the Civil War began, twenty-four of the thirty-four states were electing judges by popular vote.

Today, states employ a dizzying assortment of methods for the selection and reappointment of judges at various levels, from trial court judges, who preside over most criminal trials, to appellate court judges, who decide whether the proper law has been applied to the facts in a case. In twenty-nine states, judges are elected. In twenty, these elections are purportedly "nonpartisan"; the other nine allow parties to nominate judicial candidates. In nine states—all in the Northeast—the governor nominates or appoints judges. When it comes to the supreme courts of the states, some twenty-two states rely on contested elections.[46] In most cases, justices are elected for a specified term. But even if justices are chosen by a method other than popular election, some states require them to gain voter approval to be retained.[47] In thirty-eight of fifty states, then, state supreme court justices have to face the voters for confirmation or retention.[48] Because of this, some court observers have argued that state supreme court justices act strategically to limit electoral opposition.[49] And we know that the voters will act to defeat incumbent state supreme court justices with whom they disagree. Following the 2009 landmark decision of the Iowa Supreme Court that held same-sex marriage legal in the state,[50] three judges who voted in favor were subsequently defeated in their retention elections.

Fourteen states use a "merit selection" system, by which judicial selection commissions screen and evaluate prospective justices for their supreme courts and then present a slate to the governor, who must choose from that list.[51] These selections are often subject to legislative confirmation. In Virginia and South Carolina, judicial appointments to most courts are the province of the legislature, though the Virginia governor can appoint appellate court justices if the legislature is not in session.[52]

There is little doubt that the popular election of judges is replete with problems, most of which involve the extent to which those on the bench are able to exercise independent judgment free from political influence. First, there is the issue of the role of campaign contributions. Spending on judicial elections has been rising dramatically, and much of the money is coming from outside groups with specific agendas. In 2013–14, state supreme court election spending took place in nineteen states and exceeded $34.5 million—

much of it coming from special interests.[53] The 2015 Pennsylvania Supreme Court elections, where Democrats scored victories in all three contests, cost about $21 million, a record at the time.[54] As of January 2017, one-third of all elected state supreme court justices sitting on the bench had run in at least one $1 million-plus election.[55] In the April 2, 2019, "nonpartisan" election for the Wisconsin Supreme Court, Appeals Court judge Brian Hagedorn and his opponent, fellow Appeals Court judge Lisa Neubauer, together spent almost $8.2 million on the race; of that amount, more than $4.5 million came from special interest groups.[56] Although outspent by his opponent, Hagedorn, known as a conservative allied with Republican interests, bested Neubauer by just under six thousand votes, fewer than 1 percent of the more than 1.2 million votes cast.[57]

To say that judicial selection is important is an understatement. Moreover, different selection processes in states can have an important impact on governmental action. An example can be found in the responses of three different state supreme courts during the COVID-19 crisis. Minnesota, Wisconsin, and Michigan are all midwestern states that have similar appointment processes. All have nonpartisan elections with candidates who have partisan affiliations. All permit their governors to make appointments on the retirement of a justice, with the appointee remaining in place until the next election. In 2020 the majority of judges in Wisconsin and Michigan were considered Republicans; in Minnesota, the opposite. In the Badger and Wolverine States, the state supreme court denied their governors continuing executive orders enacted to combat COVID without legislative affirmation. In Minnesota, where five of the seven justices had been appointed by Democrats, litigation designed to curtail the power of the governor was rebuffed.[58]

Once elected, numerous conflicts of interest can emerge for judges who decide cases affecting their campaign supporters.[59] One would expect judges to recuse themselves in cases of clear conflict, but what about the closer calls, and is justice always served in that environment? Finally, some evidence exists to suggest that judges change their behavior on the bench to avoid being targets in future elections.[60] For example, in an examination of 2,100 death penalty appeals to state courts in thirty-seven states over fifteen years, researchers from the American Constitution Society and Reuters found differences between the fifteen states where the judges were directly elected and the seven states where they were appointed. Elected judges overturned death sentences in 11 percent of appeals. By contrast, judges who were appointed overturned death sentences in 26 percent of appeals—more than twice as many.[61] There are, of course, many variables to consider in these decisions, but the results raise questions about whether future election contests are influencing judicial decisions.

When they can, legislators and state policymakers frequently attempt to influence the judiciary and the judicial selection process. In 2018, the Pennsylvania and West Virginia legislatures sought to impeach justices, and in North Carolina, Republican lawmakers, stinging over the loss of the governorship in the fall election, proposed legislation to undermine the governor's ability to make appointments to judicial vacancies when the legislature is not in session.[62] And policymakers are not averse to expanding the judiciary so that they may install judges more attuned to their philosophy. In 2016, for example, Republicans in Georgia added two seats to the state supreme court in an effort to solidify a conservative majority. In that same year, Republicans in Arizona took similar action, adding two high court seats so that GOP governor Doug Ducey could use appointments to create a new conservative majority.[63]

Legislative appointment, an approach used only in South Carolina and Virginia, avoids some issues associated with popular election but nonetheless has problems of its own.[64] In some cases, legislators appoint their former colleagues after they retire. In others, they appoint relatives. Appointments tend to be controlled by the party in power, and decisions are frequently made behind closed doors with little input from local bar associations, which would better know the applicants. But perhaps the most troubling is the effort by lawmakers to create a judiciary based not on the abilities of the applicants but on their politics or personal connections. When Republicans controlled both chambers of the Virginia General Assembly, there was a tendency to fill vacancies with conservative judges, many of whom came from prosecutorial backgrounds. This injected a subtle bias into the judiciary. Not only does the legislature write the laws; it attempts to appoint a judiciary that shares its worldview and therefore its interpretation of the state constitution and state statutes. In this way, legislators can influence the administration of justice even though they may no longer control the legislative branch. As Justice Judith French of Ohio candidly admitted, the judiciary can serve as a "backstop" to protect against the political leanings of the new party in power.[65] Moreover, as openings emerge for higher courts, the selection pool is stocked with judges appointed by legislators in earlier years.[66] Reform of the judicial selection process is not much more than a blip on the consciousness of the voting public. Political operatives, however, understand exactly what is at stake, and it is for that reason that they remain active in attempting to shape how states choose the judiciary.

Of the core services of government, keeping citizens safe and secure is among the most important. To do so, we enact laws that proscribe certain behavior and determine punishment. These goals are embodied in a criminal justice system. We develop rules—what we call "due process"—by which justice is rendered. These mechanisms apply to the police who enforce the laws and to the courts that determine guilt or innocence. We determine how judges are selected, and the role of juries in determining guilt or innocence, as well as punishment. And while there is a large federal system to hold people accountable for their transgressions, most of the criminal justice system operates at the state level. The consequences of this system can be severe, not just in the denial of a person's liberty but in limiting former inmates' ability to get a job, access public benefits, or even vote. The public can—and does—judge the degree to which these policies keep us safe. But there is little doubt that the expansion of convictions in last several decades has generated millions who carry the stigma of felon.[67] The criminal justice system in the states is more than about defining crime and dispensing justice; it can dictate the trajectory of lives. And it is in the states where this system is constructed and maintained.

# 9

# Building State Economies

The economy, stupid.
—Posted on wall by chief strategist James Carville in
  Bill Clinton's presidential campaign headquarters, 1992

Many people complain about the weather, but there is little we can do about it. The economy, however, is another matter. State officials believe that policies can make a difference in the economic health of communities, and citizens demand that officials act with this in mind. As a result, states have elaborate plans to build wealth and economic opportunity, and are engaged in high-stakes competition with neighboring states to land the next big project that will generate jobs and tax revenues. Winning these sweepstakes generates major publicity for lawmakers and can have huge impacts on states and communities within them.

## Virginia Wins Amazon HQ2

When Amazon announced its intention to create another major US headquarters in September 2017, a number of states took immediate notice. The grand prize in the HQ2 sweepstakes would be huge: as many as 50,000 high-paying jobs and $5 billion in capital investment. Over the next thirteen months, development teams were assembled, strategies were worked out, and pitches were prepared. Many states understood the significance of bringing major capital investment to their communities and knew that to have a chance, they would need an elaborate package, one that would likely include significant subsidies for the corporation. The company received bids from 238 sources. On November 13, 2018, Amazon announced its decision: it would build two new headquarters, one in New York City and one in Northern Virginia. The investment in Virginia was projected at $2.5 billion.

Many observers believed that Virginia could not compete in the bidding war for Amazon. The state had never been especially aggressive in offering incentives, and the legislature, while increasingly more generous over the last decade, was fairly conservative in its approach to business recruitment. If the commonwealth was going to land the company, it would be with a package that was unique. Then governor Terry McAuliffe instructed his team to move forward aggressively, and that is what it did. It recruited prominent economist Enrico Moretti to assist the effort. Moretti argued to state leaders such as Stephen Moret, president and CEO of the Virginia Economic Development Corporation, the commonwealth's economic development arm, that the way to pitch to Amazon was to focus on an emerging dynamic involving highly educated workers that the company needed. The jobs of tomorrow, he argued, are headed not to markets offering lucrative subsidies but instead to dynamic cities and regions that already had concentrations of this new labor.[1] It would not be tax breaks that would seal the deal with Amazon but a commitment to invest in education and build a tech pipeline to service the company's future labor needs.[2]

Moret's team, working with key legislators on the General Assembly's money committees, proposed three major initiatives totaling about $1.1 billion that caught Amazon's interest and differentiated its proposal from those of other regions that offered only subsidies. First, the state would direct more resources toward tech education from kindergarten through twelfth grade. Second, it would expand university offerings to produce up to 17,500 new bachelor's degrees in computer science and related fields. Finally, it would fund the building of a tech campus that could produce the same number of master's degrees. According to Holly Sullivan, Amazon's director of worldwide economic development, the key factor in choosing Virginia was its commitment to invest in talent development: "The primary driver of this entire project was talent," she said, "not just day-one talent, but the opportunity to evaluate a talent pipeline."[3] In addition, the state's universities stepped up in a major way, especially Virginia Tech and George Mason, and helped distinguish Virginia's offer from more lucrative bids made in neighboring Maryland, whose package was higher than the commonwealth's.[4]

Virginia offered state subsidies in the amount of $550 million, but they would be paid only after the Amazon campus was built and the jobs were created. Finally, the state committed $195 million additional for transportation improvements, an investment that was needed independent of the Amazon decision. Since the capital investment would pay tax dividends many months before the job subsidies would be due, the financial analysts concluded that the project would generate a positive revenue flow from day one. Two months after the announcement, the state funding approval necessary to make it happen sailed through the Virginia General Assembly. By contrast, after considerable public criticism of the subsidies offered to Amazon in New York, the company withdrew its plans to locate a headquarters in the Big Apple.[5] Later that year, and without the public subsidies, they eventually decided on some expansion in that location, thereby rekindling the entire debate about whether incentives were needed in the first place, but the number of jobs to be created was only 1,500 (as compared to the initial 25,000), and the capital investment was substantially less.[6]

## Debates over Economic Subsidies

What is the best state in which to do business? In 2018, CNBC said it was Texas, followed by Washington, Utah, and Virginia; by 2019, Virginia had moved back into first place, having reclaimed its top ranking from several years prior.[7] Rankings, of course, are great talking points, but a business hoping to expand or seeking to relocate to a state will be looking at a variety of factors before making a decision. Some elements, such as the cost of money or the overall condition of the economy, are largely beyond the control of state governments. But in other areas, state policy can make a major difference. Several areas that draw major public attention involve tax and regulatory policies, state subsidies, education initiatives, transportation networks, and efforts to improve a state's workforce.

States employ a wide variety of targeted tax and monetary incentives designed to recruit and expand businesses. They take many forms, from job development and retraining tax credits to tax abatements or infrastructure financing. In some instances, they involve grants and loans of public funds. There are tax credits to encourage motion pictures, new technology, job creation, and even coal production. Studies show that these credits can be expensive for taxpayers and have mixed results, but states continue to enact them, largely out of the belief that to attract a private firm to a new location, help support or expand an existing business, or prevent a company from relocating to another city or state, it is sometimes necessary to provide incentives.

Competition for jobs and tax revenue among the states has never been as intense as it is today. Witness the recent competition as to which state would capture the new headquarters for Amazon. Before Virginia and New York were picked as the new headquarters locations, the competition took on a character similar to the competition among sports for free agents, as each state tried to outbid each other for the best opportunity. But much like dabbling in the free agent market, states can engage in expensive bidding wars for new companies or expansions with no assurances that they will either land the deal or, if they do, whether it will pay dividends over time.

About 90 percent of business incentives are tax incentives. In many cases, once they are granted, they are either spent immediately or become baked into state and local budgets through statutory credits. In the latter case, these tax credits, unlike other appropriations, are not typically reviewed every year. Hence future legislators become bound to the actions, bad or good, of previous ones. In other cases, however, one state administration can negotiate incentives that are unwound when there is a change in governors. As an example, Governor Scott Walker committed the State of Wisconsin to $3 billion in refundable tax credits to lure Foxconn, the Taiwanese electronics supplier, to build a new factory in the state. Projections placed the budgetary cost to the state at between $200 and $250 million per year, and estimated the cost per job created at about $19,000.[8] Tony Evers criticized the deal in his successful run for governor, and the arrangement was canceled in late 2020, after it had become apparent that the firm was not meeting the criteria necessary for the award of the incentives.[9]

While most states include incentives in their economic development arsenal, they can be controversial. Proponents of incentives argue that they create new jobs that pay higher wages and better benefits. More jobs at higher pay raises all incomes and generates increased tax revenues. Greater economic activity can increase property values. Some detractors suggest that not only do incentives inefficiently disrupt the functioning of the market, they also inappropriately choose economic "winners and losers."[10] Critics also focus on the potentially large costs of incentives and how they may redirect funds from needed public services, such as K–12 education, and argue that investing in the skills of local residents might be a better strategy to promote local prosperity.[11]

Finally, some argue that firms would expand or locate in a certain area even without the incentive; in such cases, the state or locality is simply providing a benefit to a company that is not needed. There is some empirical evidence in support of that argument. Timothy Bartik reviewed the literature on the relationship between incentives and locational and expansion decisions, asking what percentage of incented firms would not have made a particular decision "but for" the incentive. After reviewing thirty different studies, he concluded that at least 75 percent of incented firms would have made a similar decision to expand or relocate without the incentive.[12] In reviewing incentives offered by thirty-two states from 1990 to 2015, researchers at North Carolina State University concluded that they hurt the overall fiscal health of the jurisdiction that enacted them more than helped it.[13]

When they work as intended, tax incentives can be useful components of a successful economic development strategy. They can also be costly disappointments. In some cases, firms make promises to create new jobs, receive their subsidy, and then nothing happens. In others, the incentive does not generate the level of economic activity that was projected. In these situations, taxpayer cynicism about corporate giveaways is heightened, and subsequent state economic initiatives that could increase revenue and bring jobs are further complicated by the lack of public trust.

Even in states with strong controls over the award process, failures occur. Terry McAuliffe's term as Virginia governor was marked by a level of economic activity not seen in many years. The McAuliffe record was strong; during his tenure, Virginia brought in more than $20 billion in new capital investment, $7 billion more than under any previous governor, from nearly 1,100 economic development projects.[14] Nonetheless, McAuliffe's administration experienced a major disappointment when a prospective deal with Chinese investors to build a new $113 million ceramics factory and bring 349 new jobs to rural Appomattox County fell apart, leaving the commonwealth with nothing to show for providing a $1.4 million grant that remains unpaid by the Chinese firm promoting the expansion.[15] The one positive development from this experience was a tightening of the criteria for the awarding of grants and incentives, also enacted on McAuliffe's watch.

Assessing the quality of these deals can be very difficult for citizen legislators. Unlike a state's governor, legislators have very little staff and sometimes insufficient financial background to make quality assessments. In many cases they defer to the experts, many of whom come armed with all kinds of studies showing the value of the transaction. It is even more challenging when legislators do not have adequate time to review these deals or to seek meaningful independent analysis of their expected economic and fiscal impact before actual decisions are made. A state's economic development office may have worked on a deal for months, keeping the specifics secret for fear of losing the transaction. After the deal is struck, time may be of the essence, in which case legislators have little time to reflect on the proposal. For instance, the incentives of up to $330 million that Mississippi approved for a tire plant in 2013 were so secret that most legislators weren't even told the name of the company—Yokohama Tire Corp.—until the day they voted.[16]

Fortunately, more than thirty states now require periodic review of their incentive programs.[17] Virginia, for example, requires the reauthorization of most tax credit programs every five years and requires periodic evaluation of its economic development incentives by the state's Joint Legislative Audit and Review Commission (JLARC).[18] The state even has a legislative commission charged with reviewing tax credits for their effectiveness in order to recommend elimination of those that have outlived their usefulness. In the last fifteen years the commission has failed to recommend any for elimination, yet another example of how difficult it is to remove these incentives once they are placed into state law. Pennsylvania recently joined thirty other states in requiring detailed examinations of whether the tax credits in their codes are producing desired results.[19]

Despite the efforts to professionalize the evaluation of tax preferences, many decisions on reauthorization of preferences remain extremely political.[20] The Virginia coal tax credits are a good example. Enacted in the mid-1980s, these credits provided tax breaks to coal companies and the utilities that utilized the fuel, ostensibly to increase coal production and create jobs. When an audit was conducted of the credits, however, the conclusion was that they had done little except to provide a large tax break to the companies.[21] Between 1988 and 2015 the state transferred $610 million in taxpayer monies to coal mine operators, electricity generators, and other coal-related companies through the operation of the credit. Yet during that time, the number of Virginia coal miners fell from 11,106 to 2,946, and coal production fell by over 67 percent.[22] The incentive was not working. Beginning in 2012, a number of House members attempted to end the credits, but rural Republican legislators continually blocked the effort. In 2018, the size of the credits was reduced, but they remain among the subsidies Virginia grants to companies.

In recent years, states have become more cognizant of the need to have accountable incentive programs that can prove their effectiveness. They have become more sophisticated in how they model progress, measure success, and how they can recover taxpayer dollars if initiatives fail.[23] The National Conference of State Legislatures maintains a "state tax incentive evaluations database" that can be accessed to compare and evaluate states and the types of incentives and their effectiveness.[24]

Another set of controversial incentives involves the film industry. State film tax credits are almost always refundable or transferable, and exist even in states that have no income tax, such as Wyoming and Nevada. Consequently, many film tax credits are essentially spending programs run through the state tax code. Film incentives are controversial, sparking a debate about how to evaluate tax credits and economic activity associated with them. A recent independent study conducted by Michael Thom of the University of Southern California found that state film incentive programs have *no impact* on their states' economies or industries, and states are increasingly reviewing their approach to these incentives.[25] As a result, thirteen states have ended their film incentive programs since 2009, and others have capped the amount that could be awarded.[26] Most recently, state auditors in Georgia reported that any additional revenue coming into the state as the result of the credits was not enough to offset its cost to the taxpayer.[27]

These incentives can be difficult to justify financially, even when specific state studies suggest their limited benefit. Virginia has two film incentives written into law, one a credit and the other a grant, which, taken together, totaled some $55 million between 2014 and 2019, an amount that pales in comparison to the incentives provided by such states as Georgia and New York.[28] Nonetheless, they have been touted as instrumental in bringing productions like Spielberg's *Lincoln* and *Homeland* to the state. Virginia's incentives were examined in 2017 study by the state's audit commission, JLARC, which found that both incentives provided a low return in revenue to the state (20 cents per dollar invested for the tax credit and 30 cents per dollar for the grant).[29] Despite the report, legislative efforts to cut or eliminate the programs have consistently failed; in fact, the 2020 session increased both the grants and the caps on tax credits.

The issue of tax credits and subsidies sometimes unites the left and the right of the political spectrum. Conservatives occasionally argue that implementation of tax credits disrupts the marketplace and has the effect of picking winners and losers. Progressive critics suggest that these credits can be mere corporate giveaways.

Among the few credits that seem to have broad-based support are those dedicated to historic preservation. These credits are written into state law to increase the benefits already available to developers through the federal tax code. They have proved to be effective in revitalizing urban areas and protecting critical historic elements of local culture. More than thirty states have historic tax credit programs that provide some assistance over and above the federal effort. States that have attempted to withdraw or reduce the credit have encountered stiff resistance. When North Carolina lawmakers, for example, let a robust 20 percent state historic tax credit program sunset in 2015, pressure from developers, historic preservationists, and the governor led them to reverse their position.

Virginia has its own historic rehabilitation tax credit (HRTC), which it works alongside the federal initiative to provide extensive breaks to investors for renovation and historic preservation. Virginia's credit, which offers builders a 25 percent tax credit for construction costs on top of the 20 percent federal tax credit, has been in place since 1997. It is estimated to have stimulated $4.5 billion in private investment since that time.[30] Other studies of Maryland, Ohio, and Wisconsin's HRTC programs show rates of return on dollars invested of between 30 and 40 percent.[31]

Of all the incentives states can provide, one of the best is also the least sexy—infrastructure improvement. Monies to prepare sites for development, such as utility right-of-way acquisition, power line extension, and road and rail access, can make a huge difference and have healthy spinoffs as well. Such investments usually create good jobs right away, often employing local labor to make the changes. Moreover, even if the expanding industry were to fail, the investments would remain on site rather than finding their way to the bottom line of a company whose shareholders may or may not reside in the state. It is for that reason that some states are reemphasizing this approach as a catalyst for corporate investment.[32]

## Wage and Labor Policies

Statehouses are also the sites of substantial debates about the role that wage rates and labor policies have on economic growth. Historically, the federal government has set the minimum wage. But since the federal government shows little interest in expanding it, states are increasingly setting their own wage floors. The national Fight for $15 movement, for example, has become a rallying point for efforts to raise the minimum wage in states across the country. And it has been effective. Twenty-one states began 2020 with higher minimum wages than the federal floor of $7.25 per hour.[33]

The other labor issue that has drawn controversy is the so-called right to work. Business interests continue to celebrate right to work as essential for maintaining a sound business climate. "Right to work" refers to the concept that every person has the right to be employed without being compelled to belong to, or pay dues or fees to, a union. Right-to-work opponents and labor advocacy groups frequently characterize right-to-work laws as "right-to-work-for-less" laws. One such organization, the Economic Policy Institute, concluded, based on comparisons between states where right to work (without joining unions) is the law and states where it is not, that "workers in 'right-to-work' states have lower wages."[34] As of the beginning of 2019, twenty-seven states, mostly in the South and West, have right-to-work provisions in their state law.[35]

Until very recently, support for right-to-work laws was viewed as a litmus test for many politicians seeking to burnish their bona fides as supporters of business. But that may be changing. In Missouri, for example, voters, by a 67 to 33 percent margin, rejected a 2017 statewide ballot initiative to insert right-to-work clauses into the state code. In 2016, Virginia voters defeated an effort to include a right-to-work requirement in its constitution. And many observers believe that former Wisconsin governor Scott Walker lost his reelection bid in 2018 because he pushed passage of right-to-work and other antilabor initiatives.[36] In 2020, the newly elected Democratic majority in Virginia considered, but ultimately tabled, a full repeal of its right-to-work statute, which had been part of state law for seventy years.

The actual effects of right-to-work laws are widely debated, and the data are frequently conflicting. One study found that "private sector employment grew by 27 percent in RTW states between 2001 and 2016, compared to 15 percent in non-RTW states,"[37] and another suggested positive impacts on manufacturing growth as the result of right-to-work laws.[38] Other studies disagree. After reviewing much of the scholarly literature in the field, labor economists Ozkan Eren and Serkan Ozbeklik concluded that "some studies find significant effects of RTW laws on various state outcomes, while others find no effect."[39] The authors did their own study of the implementation of right-to-work statutes in Oklahoma and found no effect on employment; another study of three midwestern states drew a similar conclusion,[40] Other scholars argue that right-to-work jurisdictions have lower rates of political participation and tend to drive state policies in a more conservative direction.[41]

Many researchers acknowledge the inability to prove a causal relation between right-to-work laws and the outcomes they desire.[42] For example, of the five states that rank highest in gross state product (GSP) per capita—Massachusetts, New York, Connecticut, Delaware, and Alaska—only Alaska has a right-to-work statute,[43] and only three of the top ten GSP states ranked in 2018 have such provisions.[44]

While labor and certain business interests may dispute the implications of the scholarly research, they agree on one thing: right-to-work provisions hurt unions.[45] If unions are prevented from obtaining dues from employees to pay the cost of representation, there is little incentive for an individual to join.[46] Individual employees can instead become "free riders," benefiting from labor's bargaining efforts without paying for them. The problem emerges later, when unions are drained of funds and cannot mobilize to help those they represent as zealously as they had previously. They lose influence and become even less useful to the rank and file. Fewer people join, and the union may simply wither away. This is one reason why many supporters of organized labor were concerned by the 2018 US Supreme Court decision in *Janus v. AFSCME, Council 31, et al.,*[47] which held that the laws of twenty-two states that obliged public workers who were not union members to pay "agency fees" to these organizations violated the First Amendment. The court found that such arrangements unconstitutionally compelled public employees "to subsidize private speech on matters of substantial public concern." The 5–4 decision applied to 5.9 million state and local public employees covered by union contracts and overturned a forty-one-year-old precedent.[48] No longer can a state or local government employee be forced, as a condition of employment, to pay union dues unless he or she "affirmatively consents" to do so.

The impact was dramatic. One analysis suggested that following *Janus*, the National Education Association lost 88,000 nonmember agency fee payers it had in 2017, and the American Federation of State, County and Municipal Employees union lost 110,000 agency fee payers.[49] In response, some states took action. California, Maryland, and Washington State, for example, passed bills to ensure unions' access to new employees so that they can make the case for union membership.[50] And Oregon and Illinois made it more difficult for persons to leave a public employee union after they had joined.

In some ways, the *Janus* case simply resurrected the fight over public employee unions in the states. Until Wisconsin created a framework for municipal collective bargaining in 1959, labor legislation in the United States had largely excluded public employees from any legal framework for collective bargaining. Today, most states provide some protections for public employee negotiations with states or municipalities [51]

## State Tax Policies—Who Pays, Who Benefits

Former Supreme Court justice Oliver Wendell Holmes Jr. is frequently quoted as saying "Taxes are the price we pay for civilization,"[52] but the type and amount of taxes imposed by states make a tremendous difference in what kind of civilization is created, as well as who bears the greatest burden in building it. Tax policies and rates differ tremendously between states, and while citizens and company executives would rather pay fewer taxes than more, there are very divergent views about the extent to which low tax rates play a role in corporate retention and relocation. It becomes further complicated because a state may have a higher tax in one category and a lower tax in another. Bristol, Virginia, and Bristol, Tennessee, are separated by a line down State Street and a brass marker. Though Virginia's income taxes are not high (the top bracket is roughly 5.75 percent), Tennessee has none. Because of this, and because Virginia's sales tax is 5.3 percent while Tennessee's is

9.25 percent, there is an incentive for people to live in Tennessee and shop in Virginia.

Most of the debate over state tax policy focuses on the burden on the individual and business taxpayer. This discussion can neglect consideration of the fairness of various taxes, their impact on different income groups, and what many suggest may be the most important principle of all, the extent to which state taxes generate the revenue necessary to fund services needed and desired by citizens.[53]

Each year, countless analyses of the highest- and lowest-tax states appear. The Tax Foundation publishes yearly information comparing tax rates throughout the nation. In 2019 the five states with the highest average combined state and local sales tax rates were Tennessee (9.47 percent), Louisiana (9.45 percent), Arkansas (9.43 percent), Washington (9.17 percent), and Alabama (9.14 percent); Virginia ranked forty-first. On a comparison of sales taxes, California had the highest rate, at 7.25 percent, while five states—Alaska, Delaware, Montana, New Hampshire, and Oregon—have no state sales tax at all; Virginia ranked thirty-first, with a rate of 5.30 percent.[54] In their 2019 rankings for state business tax climate, New York, California, and New Jersey were ranked lowest on the list, while South Dakota, Alaska, and Wyoming were ranked the best. These rankings did not change from the previous year's rankings.[55] It is very difficult to compare tax systems between states. Nonetheless, there is a growing concern among lawmakers about the fairness of the state tax systems. In support of this view, lawmakers frequently cite the nonpartisan Institute on Taxation and Economic Policy (ITEP), which recently conducted an elaborate analysis of the distributional aspects of the tax systems of all fifty states and the District of Columbia.[56] What ITEP found is troubling to those concerned about the tax burden on individuals and families least able to pay. The report found the following:

1. The vast majority of state and local tax systems are inequitable, taking a greater share of income from lower- and middle-income families than from the wealthy. This inequity arises from several factors. First, many states collect much of their revenue from the sales tax and other flat taxes, where the same percentage is applied no matter one's income. Second, in the thirty-two states where graduated income tax rates apply, there is not a substantial difference between the highest rate and the lowest rate. In Virginia, for example, there are two rates, and the highest (5.75 percent of income) begins at $17,000 per year.

2. The lower a person's income, the higher are the overall effective state and local tax rates. The lowest-income 20 percent of taxpayers experience rates that are 50 percent higher than rates paid by the top 1 percent of households.

3. Tax structures in forty-five states exacerbate income inequality. Much of this inequity results from flat-rate consumption taxes, such as the gasoline tax and the sales tax: a wealthy person and a poor person pay the same consumption tax rate regardless of their income.

4. Washington State is the most regressive of all the states in its tax structure, followed by Texas, Florida, South Dakota, Nevada, and Tennessee.

5. Some states that are viewed as "low-tax" states have tax structures that place high burdens on their lower-income residents. The ITEP report singled out Arizona, Florida, Hawaii, and Illinois as leveling the highest taxes against the poor.

Assessing total tax burden can be very complex. Texas, for example, is usually considered a low-tax state; it has no personal income tax, no estate tax, and no corporate tax. Nonetheless, the state is ranked forty-third among all the states in terms of state and local tax collections as a percentage of personal income. And its tax budget hits different segments of the public in different ways. It is the ninth-lowest state in terms of taxes on the richest top wage earners. The top 1 percent pay 3.1 percent of their income in state and local taxes while the poorest 20 percent devote 13 percent of their income to paying state and local taxes.[57] In addition to Texas, six other states have no income tax at all: Alaska, Florida, Nevada, South Dakota, Washington, and Wyoming. They prefer to raise revenue by taxing energy (Alaska and South Dakota), gambling (Nevada), or tourists (Florida). In certain cases, however, the lack of an income tax can create higher tax rates for state citizens, either in the form of higher state sales taxes or higher local property taxes.[58]

Changing tax rates can also affect the ability of a state to fund critical services. In Kansas, for example, Republican governor Sam Brownback and his legislative allies pushed through massive tax cuts in 2012 and 2013. Proponents of this change argued that the action would stimulate capital formation and provide more revenue to the state by generating more economic activity, and Brownback asserted that the cuts "will be like a shot of adrenaline into the heart of the Kansas economy." The cuts backfired. By early 2017, Kansas had experienced nine rounds of state budget cuts and three credit downgrades, and the legislature was forced to curtail critical services. State lawmakers eventually reversed course and raised taxes to restore funding to education and other initiatives supported by state residents. Brownback did not serve out his full second term as governor; in 2018, he was appointed by President Trump to be the US ambassador-at-large for international religious freedom. That fall, Brownback's policies were repudiated at the polls as Democrat Laura Kelly defeated the governor's handpicked successor, former secretary of state Kris Kobach.[59] Kobach went on to head Trump's controversial and now defunct Presidential Advisory Commission on Election Integrity, and Kelly pushed through additional funding for education in the state.

## Still an Open Question

An examination of most political campaign literature will disclose countless promises about candidates' commitments to creating jobs. Moreover, public officials are famous for celebrating new companies opening and businesses expanding, making frequent public appearances to cut ribbons and touting their efforts to make these happen. While states, with the exception of public employment, do not directly create jobs, they can be a catalyst for economic activity, whether it involves building the infrastructure that encourages investment, creating an educational system that provides the trained workers that employers need, or providing targeted subsidies that will make the difference in a business's decision to expand or relocate. As we have seen, the subsidy issue is often the most controversial. Amazon's expansion into Virginia is a classic example of how carefully developed subsidies can be effective, but there are other cases that raise serious questions about whether financial incentives are the best use of the limited resources states have. States are presently in serious competition with each other in the economic development arena, and absent some regional cooperative efforts designed to limit it, this will continue in the years ahead. In addition, state tax policies can have an impact on corporate and individual behavior. This is frequently difficult to judge. An individual may choose to move from New York to Florida to escape income tax, but some companies may actually prefer to locate in a state that raises monies sufficient to fund a good educational system.

The COVID-19 pandemic affected state economies in ways not experienced in decades. And there was little states could do except to reopen as soon as they could and hope the virus did not return. Unlike the federal government, states are not permitted to run deficits and therefore could not pump money into the economy to reignite it. What became clear during the crisis was that states would need to be extremely focused in the policies they embrace to stoke the recovery. Beyond that, efforts to mitigate the effects of COVID-19 again exposed the key link between health care and the economy. As we will see in the next chapter, states are searching for new ways to provide their citizens with options for accessible and reasonably priced health care, in part so that they may become or remain productive members of the workforce.

# 10
# Don't Forget Health Care!

Nobody knew health care could be so complicated.
—PRESIDENT DONALD J. TRUMP, FEBRUARY 27, 2017

Tonia Large and her grandchildren had just made their way to the annual remote medical access clinic in Wise County, Virginia, in hopes of receiving treatment for severe dental and other medical problems. Like many others in Southwest Virginia, she had voted for Donald Trump in 2016, largely because of his promise to make health care better and more affordable. Unemployed and lacking insurance, she saw attending the clinic as the only option available to her and her family to secure medical services. "Unless people come up with something with premiums that people can afford," said Large, "people are still going to be doing without."[1] With no income and no insurance, most of those who attend the clinic have few choices for accessing health care.

Though the clinic changed its name to Move Mountains Medical Mission in 2020, its goal since 1985 has been the same—to serve the poor and uninsured throughout the region. It does so by marshalling volunteer service providers—dentists, physicians, nurses—from all over the country to come to this poorest part of Virginia one weekend in late summer each year.[2] The needy pour out of the mountains to seek help because they cannot pay for insurance or for services.[3]

The unemployment rate in the area is usually double or triple the rate in the rest of Virginia. It is also among the most Republican areas in the nation. Trump received about 80 percent of the vote here, and the area has consistently elected Republicans to office for the last two decades. As the coal industry declined, so too did the fortunes of the Democratic Party, which just thirty years earlier had enjoyed great support in the region. Despite the extensive health challenges of Wise County, the high poverty rates, and the high percentages of the uninsured, former president Obama and the Affordable Care Act (ACA) were viewed unfavorably. Elected representatives from Southwest Virginia in both Congress and the Virginia statehouse railed for years against

Obamacare and any efforts to expand Medicaid coverage to the thousands who could use it. When Virginia voted to expand Medicaid in 2018, however, it was a clear example of how state action could change the lives of thousands. If those without health insurance wanted an example of why states matter, this was it.

## State Challenges and Innovation in Health Care

Most of the recent public debate in the health care arena has focused on national politics and policy, specifically the ACA. But states have been tremendously active in this area, and the innovation that some hoped the ACA might spur has actually been occurring. State lawmakers realize their policies can make a tremendous difference in health care access and outcomes. For example, Massachusetts, because of its decision in 2006 to dramatically expand insurance to its citizens, reduced the level of uninsured in the state to the lowest in the nation; in 2018, only 2.8 percent of the state's population lacked insurance. At the time, Texas and Oklahoma had the highest percentages of uninsured residents in the nation.[4]

Access to insurance and health is often linked to positive health outcomes. And not only do states differ in these rankings, their performance can also change dramatically over time. One can see this by looking at statistics on life expectancy and infant mortality. In 1970, for example, Virginia ranked fortieth among the states in life expectancy, at 70.08 years—just under the national average but, interestingly, worse than some southern states such as Florida, Arkansas, Tennessee, and Kentucky. By 2014, however, life expectancy in Virginia had risen to 79 years, exceeding the national average (78.9 years) and moving it up in the rankings to twenty-fourth place. In those forty-four years, Virginia had moved far beyond most of its southern counterparts in this ranking. Hawaii has consistently ranked number one in life expectancy, and Mississippi, West Virginia, and Alabama consistently rank at or near the bottom.[5] A similar change has occurred in infant mortality. In 1967, Virginia ranked fortieth among the states, at 24.3 deaths for every 1,000 live births.[6] By 2017, however, the state had improved, not just in its national ranking, which saw it rise to the twenty-sixth spot, but in its actual numbers (5.9 deaths per 1,000), a tremendous accomplishment during a period in which its southern counterparts, such as North Carolina, continued to be ranked in the forties.[7]

Much of the change in health outcomes is related to improvements in state economies. Virginia's improvement in rankings corresponds to an improved economy during this period and an accompanying increase in the wealth of its citizens. In 1960, the state was thirty-third among all the states in per capita personal income, not much improved from its ranking in the 1930s, when it was thirty-sixth among the fifty states. But between 1960 and 1980, the commonwealth's economy and social conditions changed. By 1980, Virginia's income ranking had moved to number sixteen, and by 2010, it had moved into ninth place, far outpacing its neighbors to the south and many states in the rest of the nation. Virginia in this respect stands in contrast to conditions in the rust belt of the Midwest. As Virginia was improving its ranking in per capita income, Michigan was moving in the opposite direction. In 1950 the state ranked twelfth in per capita income; by 2017 it had fallen to thirty-first place, largely due to deindustrialization and the challenges facing the American auto industry. Clearly, the state in which you live can make a difference to the income you earn. For Michiganders, the decline in the union-oriented auto industry also meant that thousands lost generous employer-based health insurance. That state's decision in 2013 to expand Medicaid provided insurance access to 300,000 who did not have it previously. To those families, states clearly mattered.

The fight over expanding access to affordable health care has been conducted almost entirely in Washington for decades, and major efforts were made during the Truman and Clinton administrations to increase access. But the principles underlying the ACA came not from the federal government but from a state. In 2006, Massachusetts became one of the "laboratories of democracy" described by Justice Brandeis by enacting an innovative state-based health insurance system that promised universal coverage. Under then governor Mitt Romney, it was the first such plan passed in the nation and became the model for the ACA. The initiative was based on a simple idea generated by the Heritage Foundation, a Republican think tank, in 1989. Proponents of this approach reasoned that if individuals were compelled to assume personal responsibility for their own health care by having coverage (the so-called individual mandate), the increased numbers entering the pool of the insured would spread the risk and lower the cost of insurance. The individual mandate became the fundamental feature underpinning the Massachusetts plan and ultimately the ACA. It was dramatically successful in the Bay State. Massachusetts was able to lower the number of citizens who remained uninsured from 9.6 percent in 2004 to 2.8 percent in 2018. The state's life expectancy now approaches eighty-one years and its infant mortality rate is 4.4 deaths per 1,000, down from 5.2 per 1,000 in 2000, one of the lowest rates in the nation.[8] Obama made the decision early in his first term that this model would be the best fit of all the options for expanding coverage in the entire country, but by the time the ACA was introduced, politics had taken over, and an idea first embraced by the GOP could not garner a single Republican supporter. The ACA passed with no Republican votes in support and was signed by President Obama on March 23, 2010. It would become a political flashpoint for the next decade.

While the individual mandate was at the core of how the ACA would work, much of the heavy lifting for the expansion of health care access would be done by the states. A key provision of the initial legislation was the requirement that states expand Medicaid—the health care insurance program that helps the poor, elderly, and disabled—to larger numbers of citizens in individual states. This program, often confused with Medicare, the insurance program for seniors, is administered exclusively by the states, each of which determines its own eligibility criteria. Unlike Medicare, which is both administered and paid for by the federal government, Medicaid is a partnership between the states and federal government, with the costs shared between them. The federal share of Medicaid, called the Federal Medical Assistance Percentage (FMAP), varies, depending largely on the state's per capita income. State contributions range from about 22 percent for Mississippi to 50 percent for California, New York, and eleven other states, including Virginia. The federal government pays the rest.[9] Under the original ACA, however, the federal government would assume almost the entirety of the costs of new participants in Medicaid. It was designed to be a financial offer that states could not refuse.

Before states had the opportunity to proceed with expansion, however, the entire act, including the mandatory Medicaid expansion, was challenged in court. In a landmark decision, the US Supreme Court upheld the constitutionality of the individual mandate as a "tax" that the government could impose on citizens but, surprisingly, struck down the requirement that states expand Medicaid.[10] The states would now have only the option, not the requirement, to expand Medicaid coverage. The financial incentives for expansion were not struck down, so states like Virginia, where the traditional Medicaid match was 50 percent of every dollar spent, would receive more funding from federal reimbursement with expansion than it had been receiving under its traditional Medicaid program. Nonetheless, when expansion was first considered by the Virginia state legislature in 2013, the Republicans were in control, and anything remotely linked to Barack Obama was politically toxic. Expansion did not pass until 2018, after the Democratic "blue wave" election of 2017 brought the party to within a vote of the majority. By August 1, 2020, thirty-nine states (and the District of Columbia), many of which had Republican governors, had voted to expand Medicaid.[11] Most of these expansions were approved by legislative votes. More recently, however, voters themselves have approved these measures. Three states—Utah, Nebraska, and Idaho—passed ballot initiatives in 2018; Oklahoma and Missouri, over the objections of their Republican governors, did the same in mid-2020.[12] As Phil Cox, former head of the Republican Governors Association, recently put it, "The battle has been fought and lost on Medicaid expansion."[13]

Medicaid serves many people—and costs a lot. About one in every five Americans is enrolled in the program, and total Medicaid spending was $593 billion in FY 2018, with 62.5 percent paid by the federal government and 37.5 percent financed by states.[14] And increasing amounts of state spending are being allocated to Medicaid. A recent survey by Pew showed New York and Rhode Island leading the nation in the percentage of state-generated dollars allocated to Medicaid, at 28.7 percent and 23.4 percent, respectively.[15] Moreover, the growth of state spending on Medicaid has outpaced overall state general fund growth because health care expenses have been rising faster than inflation. In Virginia, for example, Medicaid general fund spending grew by an average of 8.9 percent annually in the decade between 2007 and 2016, while total general fund spending increased by just 1.3 percent.

Medicaid budget increases have moderated in the last few years but remain substantial, and are likely to rise dramatically as the full impact of the COVID-19 pandemic is felt. Economic downturns typically lead to upticks in Medicaid numbers, and the COVID-19-induced recession was worse than the Great Recession of 2008, when enrollment increased by 7.8 percent.[16] State budgets at the time felt the pain as they struggled to fund an entitlement program that was difficult if not impossible to cut, and will likely incur additional challenges as the full impact of the pandemic is felt.

Even before the pandemic, lawmakers were concerned that if Medicaid spending continued to rise faster than the increase in state revenues, other funding needs, such as education, might suffer. And, as US society ages, there will be even more pressure on costs because long-term residential care and end-of-life care are very expensive. In fact, the major driver of costs is increased enrollment, brought on not just by Medicaid expansion but by the aging of the population. In addition, the program has seen higher costs for prescription drugs; increasing expenses for long-term services, family support, and behavioral health; and provider rate increases.[17]

States will continue to be concerned about Medicaid costs, even with the increase in federal reimbursement for expansion. Nonetheless, expansion is increasingly being viewed positively in states where it has been enacted. Recent research indicates that it has improved access to care, increased insurance coverage, brought greater financial security to individuals and economic benefits for states and providers, and improved health outcomes.[18]

## Addressing New Challenges

Independent of Medicaid, states face great challenges responding to constituents who continue to feel the effect of market dislocations brought on by the uncertainty in Washington, D.C. President Trump and the conservatives in Congress were not able to repeal the ACA directly, so the administration attempted to undermine it by disrupting the marketplace. First, Trump threatened to withhold the subsidies authorized by the act to be paid to the insurance companies so they could hold down premiums. He then removed the requirement that each individual American have insurance. As a result, more and more healthy citizens are expected to leave the health care marketplace, so that the pool of persons remaining will be older and less healthy. At the same time, fewer persons will contribute to the system. Insurance companies, seeking to lower their risk and respond to market signals, will then hike their rates or withdraw from the market altogether. Virginia is one of those states where this occurred.

In the summer of 2017, Anthem Blue Cross Blue Shield of Virginia, the state's largest insurer, announced it would withdraw from the individual marketplace in the commonwealth, potentially leaving more than 206,000 Virginians to lose their insurance. Pointing to the instability of the ACA under the Trump administration, the company said its business model no longer worked, and that it would no longer offer these policies in Virginia. Aetna followed shortly thereafter, and its departure meant that many other state residents would have no insurance options at all, other than those they may have secured through their employer. Governor McAuliffe and Senators Kaine and Warner immediately intervened and were able to convince Anthem to reverse its decision to completely abandon the commonwealth. The company agreed to participate in the marketplace in some but not all localities; Charlottesville, Virginia, however, was not included, and residents faced the prospect of having no access at all. When Optima, a smaller company with ties to a group that operates a number of hospitals in Virginia, including one in Charlottesville, entered the marketplace, its rates proved to be higher than for any other place in the country.[19] Similar developments occurred elsewhere across the United States. In many places, consumers could not rely on competition to keep rates down because only one company offered a product; in other communities, there was no choice at all. Even in 2020, a number of areas in the country had only one exchange insurer, and about 10 percent of enrollees (living in 25 percent of counties) had access to just one insurer in the marketplace.[20] At one time, the entire state of Colorado had only one provider offering insurance on the exchange.

Continuing frustration with federal efforts to undermine the ACA, coupled with renewed concerns about the increasing costs of medical service and insurance, has generated sharp debates in statehouses about the best policy options for consumers. Conservative lawmakers have generally focused on creating cheaper insurance options in state markets by proposing that companies be permitted to offer plans that do not include the coverage requirements of the ACA. Sometimes referred to as "skinny plans" because they typically offer fewer services and require higher deductibles and copays than products in the ACA marketplace, their projected premiums are typically lower than what consumers could find on the exchanges. Because of the lower premiums, the talking point arguments for these initiatives are attractive. Proponents of these plans fail to realize, however, the impact on the insurance market created when younger and healthier consumers leave the ACA insurance pools to buy cheaper insurance.

There is little doubt that rates will rise for those who remain in the ACA insurance pools, and it is also likely that consumers who purchased the skinny plans might not have the level of coverage needed to avoid exorbitant out-of-pocket costs in the event of illness. If they need to go to the hospital and are unable to pay for the services necessary to address their condition, the financial burden often falls on the taxpayer. This creates a dynamic by which the public ends up paying the costs for the services rendered that are not covered by the cheaper plan.

One side sees these skinny plans as commonsense solutions; the other side argues that they simply amplify problems in the marketplace. For those who oppose the conservative approaches, pooling is viewed as a way to spread risks and limit cost increases. On the opposing side, freedom is the guidepost, and no one should be required to purchase insurance or a certain level of coverage. Some of this debate is subject to data collection and empirical assessment. For example, to what extent are people opting out of the insurance pools because the costs are too high, choosing instead to go without insurance altogether? Second, in the states that do permit skinny plans, how is the marketplace affected?

An Urban Institute report in 2018 predicted that the combined effect of eliminating the individual mandate penalties and expanding short-term limited-duration policies would be to increase 2019 ACA-compliant nongroup insurance premiums by 18.2 percent on average in the forty-three states that did not prohibit or limit short-term plans, and would increase the number of people without minimum essential coverage by 2.5 million in 2019.[21]

Similarly, the Kaiser Family Foundation predicted that 2019 premiums would average 6 percent higher, as a direct result of Trump's intention not to enforce the individual mandate and of the expansion of more loosely regulated plans, than would otherwise be the case.[22] The data on these issues are scant, and, independent of the politics, policymakers have a hard time determining the best course without assessing the actual impacts.

With the political swirl in Washington, and in the aftermath of COVID-19, the coming years will doubtless see more innovation and policy development at the state level. State leaders and officials are, for example, exploring proposals such as reinsurance and state public options as ways to stabilize markets, provide access, and cut costs. California has developed its own version of an individual mandate, coupled with tax subsidies for consumers, all designed to reduce costs and make the market more attractive to insurers who want to enter. Preliminary data suggest it is working. Covered California, as the plan is called, projects average premium increases of just 0.8 percent in 2020, far below 2019's hike of nearly 9 percent and the lowest since enrollment began in October 2013.[23]

Reinsurance is designed to lower the risk to insurance companies from catastrophic claims. Prior to enactment of the ACA, insurers could charge premiums based on several factors, including preexisting health conditions, thereby shielding themselves somewhat from unexpectedly high costs for serious illnesses such as cancer. When a company determines that it is too risky to remain in the insurance pool, it may choose simply to withdraw. With reinsurance, the state government intervenes, either by setting aside a reserve or by purchasing another insurance product that can pay to cover claims exceeding a certain amount. In other words, state reinsurance helps pick up where the health plan left off, thereby helping protect the primary insurer from the additional claims of high-cost members.

Reinsurance, when it is used, covers some of the costs that the insurance company would otherwise have to pay itself once the total claim reached a certain amount, or when enrollees experienced certain high-cost medical conditions. States can set those parameters wherever they desire; the more generous the subsidy, the higher the state cost. A robust reinsurance program can bring lower premiums since the insurers know that some of their high-cost claims will be covered by the state subsidy, with the result that premiums in the state's individual market are lower than they would otherwise have been, and more people can afford coverage.

To initiate a reinsurance program that uses federal funds under the ACA, a state must first apply to the federal government for a Section 1332 innovation waiver. Several states have already received such a waiver or are considering applying for one.[24] The Oregon Reinsurance Program, which took effect in 2018, pays 50 percent of individual market claims between $95,000 and $1 million, and Minnesota's reinsurance effort, also in effect since 2018, covers 80 percent of individual market claims between $50,000 and $250,000. The Oregon program is said to have reduced premiums by 6 percent in 2018.[25] According to the Urban Institute, 2018 premiums offered on Minnesota's exchange fell by 15 percent.[26] Delaware and Rhode Island had Section 1332 waivers approved for state-based reinsurance in 2019; thirteen states now are authorized to adopt such an approach.[27]

The data show that reinsurance works. But it is also expensive.[28] Minnesota's reinsurance pool will start with an infusion of $271 million in the first year, about one-half of which will ultimately be derived from state money. Oregon initially committed to $1.1 billion over 10 years, $356 million of which it hopes to receive in federal money. Maryland is considering a similar arrangement partially funded by a tax on providers; the projected costs of such an initiative were $462 million for 2019.[29] A recent program in Colorado is expected to cost $500,000 over two years, part of which will be funded by a tax on hospitals.[30] When Virginia looked at a plan, the costs were projected at $155 million per year.

Debates are also occurring in states about the possible creation of a "public option." This could take the form of a new state-sponsored health insurance plan or marketplace that citizens could join, or by allowing the public the ability to "buy in" to the state's existing Medicaid system. Washington State is leading the way on the public option; its plan was approved in early 2019 for implementation in 2021. Under what is known as Cascade Care, the state will offer different plans that cover standard health services and are projected to cost up to 10 percent less than private insurance.[31] The state will not be operating its own health plan. Instead, it will contract with a private carrier—or several—to oversee its public option, and the system will rely on insurance companies and the private sector to operate. Prompted by increases in health care costs, legislators in New Mexico are studying a Medicaid buy-in, and Colorado has approved a public option study bill.[32] Connecticut, Illinois, and

Nevada have also considered some version of the idea.[33] Pennsylvania and New Jersey are transitioning to state-based exchanges and reinsurance programs as a way to make insurance more affordable.[34] Virginia is considering doing the same.[35] Change is alive in the states.

Like reinsurance, these approaches are controversial and complex. Putting aside the opposition from those who fundamentally believe that government's role should not include providing health insurance for citizens, the marketplace is complex. Hospitals and health care providers seek adequate compensation for their services and often feel that the reimbursement rates from state and the federal government are neither fair nor adequate. One reason why some doctors no longer take Medicaid patients, for example, is that the fees they receive for the same services provided to a private payer are dramatically lower. Some insurance companies have been skeptical, wanting to ensure that the premiums they charge reflect the risk they accept. Cigna, for example, helped torpedo a public option proposal in Connecticut based on those concerns.[36]

As the Trump administration continued attempts to unravel the ACA, some states returned to one idea that was originally central to the ACA: state-operated marketplace exchanges. In the years following the ACA's adoption, only twelve states enacted state-run exchanges. That is now changing. In the summer of 2019, Maine announced its intention to join four more states that had recently announced their intention to create their own exchanges in the next several years.[37] "By pursuing a state-based marketplace," Maine governor Janet Mills explained, "we will be putting ourselves—not the federal government—in the driver's seat when it comes to helping consumers and small employers understand their options for affordable coverage, and we will better insulate ourselves from the attacks on healthcare that are coming out of Washington."[38]

## COVID-19 Exposes the Weaknesses

The COVID-19 pandemic not only exposed significant weaknesses in our health care system, it derailed many of the state initiatives designed to expand access. The United States is viewed as having the best health care system in the world, but suddenly it experienced a challenge for which it did not appear prepared—a projected lack of hospital beds for COVID-19 patients, especially in intensive care. This seemed unthinkable in a nation that touts itself as being the most medically advanced in the world, but it was true. The pandemic also revealed problems in our public health systems. Since

2010, per capita spending for state public health departments has fallen by 16 percent, and more than 38,000 state and local public health jobs have disappeared since 2008. Fewer than ten states increased their spending in this category between 2010 and 2018.[39] And this was at a time when the demand was exploding. Burgeoning opioid addiction, climbing obesity rates, contaminated water, and easily preventable diseases from measles to gonorrhea were overwhelming public health programs even before the pandemic set in.

When the pandemic hit, the differences between state health capacity became more apparent. States like Nevada and Texas were judged to have the lowest capacity for addressing COVID-19 as measured by facility capacity, clinician capacity, and state public health funding.[40] New York and Texas would experience problems with ICU hospital bed and ventilator availability. In New York City, these deficits became so acute that makeshift field hospitals were built at the Javits Center and in Central Park, and Governor Cuomo, using his emergency powers, developed a plan to commandeer ventilators from other parts of the state for use in New York City.

Because of stay-at-home orders and the flattening of the curve in the spring of 2020, hospital bed availability was preserved, but the deficiency had been exposed, and when cases spiked in early winter, the situation became more dire. And the economic impact of the pandemic on state budgets fundamentally altered the prospects for making other health care and health insurance reforms. Kansas tabled an initiative to expand Medicaid for about 150,000 people. California abandoned plans to extend coverage to 27,000 undocumented immigrant seniors. Washington State delayed its launch of a state public option, and Colorado nixed it altogether. California, Ohio, and New York began looking at Medicaid cutbacks. As one health care expert put it, "When your house is on fire, you're not focused on building another wing."[41]

As the economy languished, more Americans lost their health insurance along with their jobs. The Economic Policy Institute estimated that in the first four months of the pandemic, approximately 12 million people lost the health insurance they had previously received through an employer.[42] In Texas alone, the largest state that declined to expand Medicaid, an estimated 1.6 million individuals had lost their employer-provided health insurance by June 2020.[43] Many of those citizens would end up relying on Medicaid. The safety net provided by Medicaid would, of course, differ dramatically based on residency. People who lived in states with Medicaid expansion fared much better than those who did not. And the benefits provided would also differ depending on the state.

## States Continue to Innovate

The COVID-19 pandemic prompted the states to innovate.[44] When the federal government showed neither the ability nor the competence to fully act, states had to. Because governors had extensive power over the hospitals and health care systems in their states, they could, and would, suspend elective surgeries. In some states, scope-of-practice regulations were relaxed to permit nurse practitioners to perform services formerly reserved solely to doctors.[45] Governor Cuomo in New York forced some private nursing homes to accept COVID-19 patients with lesser symptoms, a decision that came to be criticized later. New Jersey, Connecticut, and New York attempted to impose quarantine requirements on visitors to their states coming from certain hot spots in the country.[46] These were executive powers reserved to the states that most had not considered using prior to the crisis.

Technological innovation was also spurred by the virus. Telehealth, which has been expanding in recent years, literally exploded during the pandemic. And Virginia and Maryland pioneered the use of special smart-phone technology produced by Apple and Google that provides notice to citizens that they have come into contact with someone who tested positive. These initiatives will likely remain after the pandemic subsides.

Our health care system was complex and challenged even before the COVID-19 pandemic. While citizens in the poorer areas of our nation are affected the most by our failures, the problems affect everyone, if only because we are all paying for health care, in some form or another. The pandemic engaged states in health care issues more than ever before. As the nation struggles to emerge from the crisis, states will continue to lead the way in developing policies that respond to a changing environment. The ultimate test will come in the form of health outcomes, that is, which program or combination of programs provides the best health outcomes for citizens. Some combination of private sector innovation and public sector programming will undoubtedly be needed. Marshalling data as to what works, what doesn't, and the costs inherent in the various initiatives can be brought to the process. Whether these innovations can overcome the political divisions that can prevent good policymaking remains to be seen. Some of those divisions are outlined in the next chapter.

# 11

# Flashpoints in the Culture Wars of States
## Abortion, Guns, and Immigration

> As the culture war is about irreconcilable beliefs about God and man, right
> and wrong, good and evil, and is at root a religious war, it will be with us
> so long as men are free to act on their beliefs.
> —PAT BUCHANAN, *New York Daily News* COLUMN, FEBRUARY 26, 2017

## Abortion and Reproductive Choice

When citizens discuss abortion, they typically focus on the US Supreme
Court and critical decisions like *Roe v. Wade*[1] and *Planned Parenthood v. Casey*.[2]
But many of the major debates have occurred in statehouses; and it has been,
and will continue to be, state law that often sets the parameters of women's
health care access in this arena. For those who seek to restrict abortion, their
focus is not just on state regulations that would make the procedure less accessible but on overturning *Roe* itself.[3] An Alabama state representative proposing one of the so-called "heartbeat bills" that would deny abortions after
six weeks of pregnancy articulated the purpose of these measures: "What
I'm trying to do here," Representative Terri Collins told the *Washington Post*,
"is get this case in front of the Supreme Court so *Roe v. Wade* can be overturned."[4] The Guttmacher Institute, a Washington, D.C.-based research
group that supports reproductive choice, reports that as of July 1, 2019, eighteen states had passed laws to restrict abortion if *Roe* is reversed.[5]

Abortions in the United States have decreased in recent years, and those
that occur are less dangerous.[6] The Centers for Disease Control and Prevention found that between 2006 and 2015, the American abortion rate declined
26 percent, to the lowest level on record since data have been collected on
the topic.[7]

Legislators hold very strong views on these issues. For many conservatives,
abortion is *the* major issue; for some, it was the reason they became involved

in politics and helped get them elected. They cite estimates from the National Right to Life Committee that 60.9 million abortions have been performed between 1973, the year that *Roe* was decided, and 2018, and are resolute in their efforts to make abortions more difficult to obtain.[8] And for political progressives, particularly women, reproductive rights are one of their key issues. There is no reason to doubt the sincerity of either set of these legislators, and they would probably take these positions even if their constituents did not support them.

In many state legislatures around the country, the conservatives are in the majority, and continue to press for more laws and regulations to prevent abortion. State legislators have been especially active in this arena in the last several years. In 2019, Georgia, Kentucky, Louisiana, Mississippi, and Ohio passed bans on abortions after six weeks of pregnancy, even though many women may not even know they are pregnant at that time.[9] Pitched by anti-abortion groups as "heartbeat bills" because movements can be detected in the area of the fetus where the heart would form at that time in the pregnancy, the initiatives have drawn fire from physicians, who face felony prosecution under some of these laws, and from other medical providers, who claim this is a serious misrepresentation of the physiology of pregnancy. Courts have typically declared these laws unconstitutional, but the six-week bans keep coming.[10]

During the COVID-19 crisis, conservative governors attempted to restrict abortion by characterizing it as a "nonessential" service that would be precluded by various orders designed to prevent the spread of the virus. Planned Parenthood, the ACLU, and other groups immediately filed lawsuits against such actions in Ohio, Texas, Oklahoma, Iowa, and Alabama, and obtained preliminary injunctions against the states' actions. The "Supreme Court has spoken clearly" on a woman's right to abortion, said a federal judge in striking down Texas's prohibition. "There can be no outright ban on such a procedure."[11] A day later, a federal three-judge panel reversed the Texas decision and reinstated the prohibition.

In some states, ballot referenda have been passed to restrict abortion. On November 7, 2018, voters in Alabama and West Virginia approved amendments to their constitutions that would make it easier for state lawmakers to ban abortion if *Roe* was overturned. Both amendments included the language "Nothing in this Constitution secures or protects a right to abortion or requires the funding of abortion," a provision similar to Tennessee's constitutional amendment approved by voters in 2014.[12] The West Virginia amendment passed with 52 percent of the vote, while Alabama's received 59 percent.

The Alabama Constitution now states that it is "the public policy of this state to ensure the protection of the rights of the unborn child" and to "support the sanctity of unborn life."[13] Consistent with the constitutional provision, the state recently passed a law that could charge a doctor who performs an abortion with a Class A felony—punishable by life or ten to ninety-nine years in prison. That is more prison time than convicted rapists face in the state. The stated intent of the proponents of these measures is to get a case to the US Supreme Court in order to overturn *Roe,* and hopefully return all abortion decisions to the states.

While antiabortion forces have engineered much legislation in the last decade, some states have recently seen a resurgence of efforts to expand reproductive choice. Illinois recently passed a law that establishes the "fundamental right" of a woman to have an abortion and states that a "fertilized egg, embryo or fetus does not have independent rights." It further eliminates felony penalties for doctors that perform abortions, removes previous waiting period requirements, and requires that an abortion be treated as any other medical procedure for insurance purposes.[14] Vermont recently enacted a similar measure.[15]

According to the Pew Research Center, Americans' views on abortion have changed little over the past twenty years, with 58 percent saying the procedure should be legal in all or most cases in 2018, compared to 60 percent in 1995. A 2018 Gallup poll agreed. Among survey respondents, those who think abortion should be illegal "under any circumstances" has hovered at around 18 percent for decades. About 50 percent believe it should be legal "under certain circumstances," a figure only slightly lower than twenty years ago, and there has been a slight uptick (to 29 percent) in the percentage of those who believe it should be legal "under any circumstances."[16] In other words, few voters are persuadable on this issue. Nonetheless, it is a hot-button issue to base voters and a litmus test issue for activists on both the left and the right. It is almost impossible to receive a Republican nomination for any seat without proclaiming support "for the unborn," and some advocacy groups supporting reproductive rights have threatened to withhold endorsements from Democratic candidates who assert, in a nod to Bill Clinton's pronouncement on this issue, that "abortion should be safe, legal, and rare."[17] They have objected to the inclusion of the word "rare," arguing that it imposes a stigma on women who may have need for the procedure. This view seems jarring to those who strongly support preventing abortion through education, contraception, and reproductive health care and embrace adoption as an option to provide children with good homes.

## Guns

Abortion activates one group of voters who make political decisions based solely on this single issue. The guns issue energizes other, and sometimes complementary, groups. Political fault lines in statehouses have always existed around this issue, but in recent years, increasing numbers of mass shootings, especially those that have occurred in and around schools or are animated by racial, ethnic, or religious bigotry, have drawn more citizens into the debate. State lawmakers have grown increasingly frustrated by the lack of federal action on gun safety and have generated their own change. In the aftermath of the mass shooting in Virginia Beach in 2018, Governor Northam called a special session on gun safety, knowing in advance that the Republican majority would kill all his proposals. He predicted correctly; the GOP adjourned the session in less than ninety minutes. The Democrats then used this inaction in the 2019 state races to flip the legislature. In 2020, the commonwealth passed major gun safety legislation.[18]

Until very recently, the results of gun safety efforts in the states have been mixed, partly because of deep cultural divisions that go beyond party. In many rural areas, gun ownership is a way of life, and any efforts to limit access to them is perceived to be a direct assault on norms and customs held dear by those who live there. During the Obama years, the manufacture and purchase of firearms increased dramatically.[19] For some, these purchases were motivated by the fear that "he's coming to take our guns away." But with every new mass shooting, the clamor increases for reasonable gun safety measures, if only because a growing number of citizens now believe they could fall victim to such an attack.[20]

Mass shootings have received most of the headlines, but the death counts are far higher for gun deaths in our homes, neighborhoods, and communities. One simple reason for this is that there are large numbers of guns in the country. Per capita gun ownership is much higher in the United States than in any other country; according to the US Bureau of Alcohol, Tobacco, Firearms and Explosives (ATF), there are more civilian-owned guns in our country today than there are people.[21] Determining gun ownership on a state-by-state basis is very difficult, largely because of the lack of national standards for licensing and registering firearms, but one group used ATF data on sales to conclude that Texas had the highest number of guns and Wyoming had the most per capita.[22]

The good news about gun violence in the country is that the national rate of firearm-related homicide has actually decreased over the last two decades, from 6.64 per 100,000 in 1991 (17,746 deaths) to 4.13 per 100,000 in 2015 (12,979 deaths). In contrast, firearm-related suicide deaths actually rose from 18,526 in 1991 to 22,018 in 2015.[23] What has energized the public recently is not the incidence of homicide or suicide, however, but the increasing frequency of mass shootings across the United States. Although much has been written about the failure of Congress to act, significant debate about gun policy is occurring in the states.

Gun regulation is an area where states have actively prohibited localities from taking their own independent action. Forty-three states have laws that preempt or preclude cities and municipal governments from creating their own gun control ordinances; New Mexico even prohibits it in its constitution.[24] Consequently, when Pittsburgh ignored state preemption laws to pass three local gun control ordinances after a white nationalist gunned down eleven people in the Tree of Life synagogue, the city was immediately met with lawsuits, and enforcement of the new laws was put on hold by the courts.[25] Only a small number of states—Connecticut, Hawaii, Massachusetts, New Jersey, and New York—have no state laws expressly preempting local authority from regulating firearms or ammunition.

There is some evidence suggesting a link between gun violence and incidents of either mental health challenges or previous trauma. A recent study by the US Secret Service on mass attacks, for example, provides support for the assertion that signals often precede attacks. It found that one-third of the perpetrators of these attacks in 2018 had a history of serious domestic violence. Almost all of the attackers had made threatening comments prior to their action, and more than three quarters had acted in a way that worried others before their attack.[26]

Eight out of ten people considering suicide give some sign of their intentions.[27] Not surprisingly, data exist that suggest extreme risk protection orders (ERPOs) can be effective in reducing suicides with guns. In Connecticut and Indiana, which enacted laws in 1999 and 2005, respectively, the vast majority of firearms seizures in both states have been to prevent possible suicides. A 2018 study of the two programs reported reductions in gun suicides as a result of the law.[28] Following the Parkland tragedy, Florida passed an ERPO statute in 2018,and New Mexico and Virginia followed in early 2020.[29]

Many state lawmakers struggle with the extent to which empirical data and studies can and will be utilized to create new policy in this area. In recent years, additional scholarship has emerged that attempts to determine the impact of policy change on gun violence. In 2018 the Rand Corporation examined more than sixty studies that addressed the link between policy and gun violence. While concluding that much additional research is needed, the study argued that certain safety measures had proven effective, most notably waiting periods for gun purchases and provisions that can remove guns from those who are adjudged a risk to themselves or others.[30] More recently, Dr. Michael Siegel, a physician at the Boston University School of Public Health, has assembled data linking the presence of universal background checks to reduced gun violence.[31] And a study by the Violence Prevention Research Program at the University of California at Davis concluded that "red flag" laws, now enacted in seventeen states and the District of Columbia, reduce gun violence.[32] Siegel and his colleagues have also created a compendium of state gun laws to assist policymakers as they consider numerous options for their states.[33]

Opponents of gun safety measures typically wrap themselves in both the Second Amendment and the view that "laws will not solve the problems because people will find their way around them." And gun safety advocates sometimes forget that policies enthusiastically supported in suburban and urban areas may create resistance in rural areas. In the last several years, gun rights advocates in some of these rural areas have gone so far as to declare themselves "Second Amendment sanctuaries," with sheriffs and local governments stating that they will refuse to enforce gun safety measures they consider unconstitutional.[34] After newly elected Illinois governor J. B. Pritzker pledged to pass gun safety measures in 2019, 64 of the state's 102 counties passed sanctuary resolutions.[35] When New Mexico expanded background checks, twenty-five of its thirty-three counties declared themselves Second Amendment sanctuaries. Similar actions have either been taken or are under consideration in Colorado, Oregon, and Washington State.

The rhetoric around the Second Amendment sanctuary movement is disturbing. Words like "nullification" and "interposition," common at the time of massive resistance to desegregation and even harking back to the secessionist arguments prior to the Civil War, are being heard once again in many rural areas of the nation.[36] Following passage of an ERPO law in New Mexico, for example, a representative of the state Sheriffs' Association said a large majority of sheriffs would refuse to confiscate a person's firearms if given a court order to do so. "We don't work for the governor. We don't work for the Legislature," Cibola County sheriff Tony Mace told the *Santa Fe New Mexican*. "We have discretion to use whichever laws we want."[37] Many of the sanctuary resolutions, while they may provide solace to opponents of gun safety legislation, are legally problematic. The sanctuary movement is yet another manifestation of the cultural alienation present in the more traditional, rural areas of the country, where some citizens feel that they are losing their way of life as a result of actions at the national and state level.[38] And it has the potential to create substantial challenges to the state and local power relationships, some of which are discussed in chapter 12.

## Immigration

Immigration is yet another hot-button issue for state legislators. It is actually a series of issues, but the "culture wars" always seem to serve as the backdrop for the debates. An estimated 45.1 million immigrants were living in the United States in 2016, accounting for 13.9 percent of the nation's population. Most (76 percent) are in the country legally.[39] There are nearly 11 million undocumented immigrants living the United States today. Among those immigrants, roughly 800,000 are classified as Dreamers, those who had been protected under the Deferred Action for Childhood Arrivals (DACA) program since its implementation in 2012. With the federal government seemingly paralyzed to address issues related to immigration, many of the debates have found their way into statehouses and state elections.[40] As the United States becomes more diverse ethnically, states are facing increasing pressure to guaranty greater opportunity to both documented and undocumented immigrants. At the same time, many groups remain worried about how these changes will affect them and their children. For many, the fast pace of change in the world is concerning, and appears to be out of their control. Polling data on white working-class Americans paint a picture of anxiety fueled by perceptions of immigrants posing a threat to their culture and way of life; nearly one-half say that "things have changed so much" that they "feel like strangers" in their own country.[41] To this group, academic studies suggesting that undocumented immigrants actually pay more in taxes than they receive in services are irrelevant.[42] As in so many cases, they feel as if they are losing control and status, and anger is the result.

Despite worry in some segments of the population, the public's view of immigration's impact on the country remains largely positive. A 2019 survey by the Pew Research Center found that 62 percent of respondents believed that immigrants strengthen the country because of their hard work and talents; only 28 percent said they were a burden on the country. These results were largely the reverse of what was found in a similar study done in 1994.[43] The largest differences in attitudes were between self-described Democrats and Republicans; immigration is much more troubling to the latter group.

Each year, hundreds of bills are introduced in states that force localities in the states either to take action against illegal immigrants or to provide some additional rights to those people who are loosely referred to as "new Americans." For conservatives, the bills attacking "illegals" provide red meat to their base, even if states can do little when dealing with federal law. For progressives, measures that provide more assistance to "new Americans" are a response to their growing constituencies and their activist base. The National Conference of State Legislatures provides an update each year of state laws and resolutions enacted in this area.[44]

Legislatures have recently seen an uptick in debates over immigration at the state level, driven largely by statements from President Donald Trump about everything from "the wall" to so-called sanctuary cities. Some of the discussions involve the proper role of local and state law enforcement. In Virginia and other states, efforts have been made recently to force localities to report to Immigration and Customs Enforcement (ICE) the presence of illegal immigrants in local jails and to make those persons available for arrest by federal authorities when they are released. This creates a local fiscal impact that is being resisted by a number of states and localities. States and localities often cooperate with federal law enforcement, particularly in the area of criminal investigations, under voluntary agreements permitted under federal law. When someone who is undocumented is arrested and detained in local jails, ICE may be informed so that ICE officers potentially can pick up the detainee.

Issues arise, of course, as to what to do at the end of the detention: if ICE has not arrived, how can the locality constitutionally continue the detention? Some states or localities balk at having to take responsibility for enforcing federal law on their own; there are costs involved in detaining people, as well as constitutional issues. Section 287(g) of the Federal Immigration Act, passed in 2002, allows local law enforcement to perform certain functions under the supervision of ICE officers, but there is no requirement that they do so. Some states and localities are pushing back, going so far as to refuse cooperation with ICE. These jurisdictions have been labeled "sanctuary jurisdictions," and a number of bills have been introduced targeted at localities that do not voluntarily comply with ICE. In a technical sense, there are few sanctuary jurisdictions in the United States, and presently none in Virginia, but that has not prevented legislators from offering bills that either penalize these localities or force them to act in certain ways against their will.

In Virginia, a number of bills prohibiting sanctuary cities were introduced and passed in 2017 and 2018, only to be vetoed by Democratic governors.[45] Most recently, Tennessee and Iowa enacted state laws requiring law enforcement personnel to comply with federal immigration requests and barring local governments from adopting sanctuary policies. The debates on these bills have generated ample political heat and little light, as one side decries "lawlessness" in the country while the other says these measures are examples of "dog whistle politics." In contrast to those states that have attempted to enhance the ability of ICE to take action against undocumented migrants, such states as Vermont actually prohibit state and local governments from sharing information with the federal government related to the immigration status of residents of that state. Similar legislation had been passed in ten states and the District of Columbia as of April 2019.[46]

One of the most emotional debates related to immigration involves states granting permission for undocumented students born in this country (the Dreamers) to attend college at in-state tuition rates. While states are required to provide all students, including undocumented ones, with a K–12 public education,[47] there are differences between the states as to whether in-state tuition should be extended to the undocumented. At present, Arizona, Georgia, and Indiana specifically prohibit these students from receiving in-state college tuition, and Alabama and South Carolina prohibit undocumented students from enrolling at all. Seventeen states have extended in-state tuition rates to undocumented students who meet specific criteria.[48]

Many of the Dreamers arrived in the United States with their parents as young children and have built relationships and contributed to their community as they grew up. Why, they ask, should we be deprived of higher education because of a choice our parents made over which we had no control? And why, they ask, should we not have access to public institutions that have been partially funded by taxes paid by our families? Some business groups support states granting such a benefit because of critical worker shortages that require specialized training. They cite studies like the one conducted by the Cato Institute that argues against changing DACA because of tangible evidence of the economic benefit derived from the participation of DACA recipients in the workforce. In a recent report, the institute estimates that policies reversing DACA would cost the US economy $351 billion from 2019 to 2028 in lost income and that the US Treasury would lose $92.9 billion in revenue, including payroll taxes.[49]

In at least one state, Texas, business leaders got actively involved in this issue. In 2019, a business coalition formed by Rupert Murdoch and Michael Bloomberg and calling itself Texans for Economic Growth was launched to oppose "harmful effects of anti-immigrant legislation," including efforts by the legislature to "increase public college and university tuition for certain long-term Texas resident students." To date, they have been successful, and all students who have lived in the state for three years and who graduate from a Texas high school continue to be eligible for in-state tuition rates at public colleges and universities.[50]

Disputes over immigration policy also find their way into statehouses on issues related to public safety. The issuance of driver's licenses, a state responsibility, is an example. The public hears countless stories of undocumented immigrants who commit traffic offenses or cause accidents without having a driver's licenses. This is largely because most states prevent them from acquiring licenses. As of February 2020, fifteen states and the District of Columbia had enacted laws to allow certain categories of unauthorized immigrants to obtain driver's licenses or a driver's privilege card.[51] Virginia was added to the list in July of that year.[52]

Many of these states provide only limited-purpose licenses and identification documents for qualified undocumented residents. Individuals are typically required to complete a driver's education class, pass a written exam, and take a behind-the-wheel driving test before obtaining a license to drive. During this time, the person learns to properly operate a vehicle, to interpret various traffic signs, and to exhibit practical knowledge of the rules of the road that make driving a safe activity. This sort of training can improve traffic safety; studies in California and Connecticut found declines in hit-and-run accidents and auto property damage following enactment of these measures.[53] Nonetheless, these approaches have their detractors. Critics argue that expanding driving privileges to undocumented residents reduces the incentive to follow immigration laws[54] and could lead to increased voter fraud, ID fraud, and bank fraud.[55]

## Debates Continue

Our national culture wars are not likely to end any time soon; in fact, they may be intensifying. With legislators in Washington seemingly unable to grapple with their responsibility in the area of immigration, states will be debating and determining many more policies with impacts on an increasingly diverse population. Abortion is an issue in state capitals that continues to generate substantial debate. And debates surrounding gun rights show few signs of abating. These issues often involve the relationship between state and local power, the subject of the next chapter.

# 12
# Tip O'Neill Is Still Dead

All politics is local.
—FORMER SPEAKER OF THE HOUSE THOMAS "TIP" O'NEILL

When former Speaker of the House Tip O'Neill wrote *All Politics Is Local*,[1] many political decisions came down to the local level; indeed, local contacts and unique local issues were the bases on which people were elected to office, not their political affiliation. That is no longer the case, as even local elections can turn on how candidates feel about a national issue or the party to which they belong.[2] Perhaps even more important, however, localities are not always able to decide social policy on their own. In fact, localities in the vast majority of states are constrained in their actions, either by what is known as the Dillon Rule or by other forms of state preemption.

The US Constitution does not discuss local government power, instead reserving all powers apart from those granted to the federal government to the states, or to the people.[3] If you ever wanted an argument to support the principle that states matter, this is it.

States and localities across the nation continue to struggle and debate their relative powers to act. In some places, states are determined to reassert their legal dominance over cities and local governments. Part of this dynamic can be traced to demographic change in the country and to what political scientists refer to as "sorting."[4] Over the last decade, more liberal elements of the populace have tended to gravitate to urban areas, bringing with them a set of values often at odds with those of the population in the rest of the state. Responding to their electorate, urban leaders often have passed ordinances—from banning plastics to increasing the minimum wage to LGBTQ+ non-discrimination measures—that the public in the rest of the state has found objectionable. State lawmakers then attempt to nullify these local measures.[5] During the COVID-19 pandemic, efforts by some cities to implement more stringent restrictions than those of state government prompted threats and lawsuits as governors and legislatures sought to assert their prerogatives.

Governors in both red states and blue states bristled when big-city mayors attempted to make independent efforts to protect their constituents. "We would like for federalism to operate smoothly, so we don't have to think about it," explained federalism expert Tim Conlan to *Governing* magazine, but "the coronavirus response is actually sort of a perfect measuring stick of our transition to our contemporary, very polarized model of federalism."[6]

## The Firestorm over HB2

In February 2016, the city of Charlotte, North Carolina, by a 7–4 vote, expanded its nondiscrimination ordinance to include gay, lesbian, and transgender citizens, applying it to places of public accommodation such as bars, restaurants, and stores. Included in the ordinance was a provision that allowed transgender residents to use either a men's or a women's bathroom, depending on the gender with which they identified.[7] The North Carolina legislature wasted no time attacking the measure. In a specially convened session on March 23, 2016, state lawmakers passed the Public Facilities Privacy & Security Act, also known as HB2, a measure that not only reversed the city's recent action but also nullified all local ordinances around the state that included protections for the LGBTQ+ community.[8] The action thrust North Carolina into the epicenter of the nation's culture wars over protections for the LGBTQ+ community and is a dramatic example of the ongoing legal wrangling over the relative powers of state and local governments. The ACLU and other civil rights organizations immediately sued. Major business groups, including Apple, General Electric, IBM, Ikea, Levi Strauss & Co., Marriott, Nike, PayPal, Red Hat, and United Airlines, protested the legislation. The NBA and NCAA moved major events to other states, and boycotts of the state were organized. One commentator estimated North Carolina lost $400 million from the cancellation of events and projects.[9]

In 2017 the North Carolina legislature partially relented and passed a substitute measure that asserted the state government's control over transgender bathroom access and sunset the nullification of local antidiscrimination rules at the end of 2020. Critics asserted that partial repeal was not enough. The lawsuit continued until a legal settlement was reached in July 2019 whereby the city would repeal its ordinance and the state was permanently barred from using current state law to "prevent transgender people from lawfully using public facilities in accordance with their gender identity" in state government buildings.[10] Throughout it all, the North Carolina legislature continued to assert its powers to preempt local legislation not granted to municipalities under the state's constitution.

The North Carolina case is the most celebrated, but disputes around these issues have occurred in many other states, predominantly those in which the political character of the legislature differs dramatically from that of the state's cities.[11] In several states, legislatures have passed explicit measures to protect LGBTQ+ rights, even if localities object.[12] Illinois, for example, recently passed a measure requiring all single-occupancy public bathrooms to be labeled gender-neutral beginning January 1, 2020, a clear assertion of state over local powers.[13] As of January 28, 2018, some 225 cities and counties had passed ordinances prohibiting employment discrimination on the basis of gender identity in all public and private employment.[14] These types of disputes between state and local governmental authority, especially in the cultural arena, will likely remain salient for years. Understanding the legal origins of these discussions requires some history and constitutional explanation.

## The Dillon Rule

If citizens saw a picture of John Forrest Dillon today, they might mistake him for Andrew Smith, the famous bearded gentleman pictured with his brother on the packages of Smith Brothers cough drops, an American institution since 1847. Smith and Dillon both sported long beards, and were born in the 1830s, but the comparison ends there. While the Smith Brothers are arguably more famous and certainly more recognizable than Judge John Forrest Dillon, it is the latter who defined the relationship between states and localities, perhaps more than any other American.

Embraced in some form by thirty-nine states, the Dillon Rule, named for the jurist, describes a legal concept that local governments have only limited authority, which they derive from the state and which can only be exercised upon a grant of approval from the state. Dillon, who was the chief justice of the Iowa Supreme Court in the 1860s, later rising to the federal bench, developed this legal principle at a time when cities were attracting population and municipal reformers were concerned about growing interconnections between governmental officials and private enterprise. In Dillon's view, improving the operation of government meant reining in the power of localities, which he believed were less competent and more corrupt than state governments.[15] In his legal treatise, *Commentaries on the Law of Municipal Corporations,* Dillon advanced the principle that local jurisdictions have no inherent powers granted by the people; rather, any and all local authority flows from the state.[16] Dillon explained the concept this way: "Municipal corporations owe their origin to, and derive their powers and rights wholly from the legislature. It breathes into them the breath of life, without which they cannot exist. As it creates, so may it destroy. If it may destroy, it may abridge and control."[17] In Dillon's view, municipalities possess only those powers indispensable to the purposes of their incorporation and others expressly granted to them by the state. The US Supreme Court upheld the Dillon Rule in 1907,[18] holding that "municipal corporations are political subdivisions of the state, created as convenient agencies for exercising such governmental powers of the state as may be entrusted to them. . . . The number, nature, and duration of the powers conferred upon these corporations and the territory over which they shall be exercised rests in the absolute discretion of the state."[19] Under the Dillon Rule, then, if there is a reasonable doubt whether a power has been granted to a local government, the power has not been conferred.

State supreme courts have expressed their support for the Dillon Rule in many ways. Virginia is merely one: "A municipal corporation has no powers except those conferred upon it expressly or by fair implication by its charter, or the general laws of the State, and such other powers as are essential to the attainment and maintenance of its declared objects and purposes. It can do no act, make no contract, nor incur any liability that is not thus authorized. If it is even doubtful whether a given power has been conferred, the doubt must be resolved against the power."[20] Ask a city councilor or a county supervisor what they think of the Dillon Rule and they are likely to unleash a long diatribe about how they could fix every local problem if not constrained by the concept. Local governments complain every time it is necessary to seek "enabling legislation" from the state to take actions that are precluded because they have not been given explicit permission. Each legislative session, a number of bills are introduced that seek to amend the charter of a city or a county or to give that jurisdiction authority to do what would otherwise be prohibited.

In Virginia and many other states, these "enabling bills" require supermajorities to be enacted. Nonetheless, most are adopted without much controversy. Legislators refer to this practice as "home cookin'," that is, doing what your locality needs to help govern its citizens. In some cases, however, what might seem to be reasonable ends up being complex. The most common examples involve any time a locality seeks permission to impose certain taxes within its jurisdiction. A number of legislators have taken the "no-tax" pledge promoted by Americans for Tax Reform and its founder, Grover Norquist, and therefore always vote no, even if it does not affect their constituents. In Virginia, counties are prevented from enacting so-called transient occupancy taxes without enabling legislation from the state. These taxes are imposed by localities on people who use hotels, inns, and other temporary lodging and can be very useful in supplementing local tax revenues. Almost every legislative session includes bills from one locality or another requesting the ability to impose the tax. Even with the supermajority vote requirement and the block of legislators who have taken the no-tax pledge, the measures usually pass, which suggests that the Dillon Rule is not as rigid as some would argue.

For local governments, the Dillon Rule has restricted their ability to do many things that some of their citizens might desire. In many states, for example, localities are precluded from requiring developers to build to more energy-efficient standards because a statewide building code imposes regulations from the capital. While some cities would like more flexibility in these matters, their efforts have largely been rebuffed by state legislatures. In fact, state legislators and business leaders will occasionally argue for the Dillon Rule because it imposes similar statewide regulations and certainties across jurisdictional boundaries. In Virginia, for example, debates have raged about whether local governments should and can impose a minimum wage that is higher than what the state has approved. Independent of the legal prohibitions against doing do, many state business leaders feel that imposing higher local wages would put businesses in some localities at a comparative disadvantage. In contrast, a number of localities, many located in urban areas where the cost of living is higher, believe higher local minimum wages not only are fairer but also provide them with an opportunity to employ more people with higher skills.

Support for the rule is not found solely among business interests in the states. Some environmentalists have been concerned that transferring too much control to localities may permit them to loosen clean drinking water initiatives being pushed at the state level. Similarly, when localities attempted to create so-called Second Amendment sanctuary jurisdictions to allow them to escape control of state-imposed gun regulations, proponents of gun safety measures argued that these were precluded by the Dillon Rule and state preemption. The issues are complex and varied. And some of the debates around this issue can appear absurd. As an example, for years, Virginia legislators would debate and pass enabling legislation each session that permitted one jurisdiction or another the ability to cut weeds and grass on private property if the owner failed to do so after notice (it is hard to believe that this would require state legislative approval). After seeing these bills year after year, the legislature recently passed a measure giving all localities this "power."[21]

Of the states that embrace some form of the Dillon Rule, thirty-one apply it to all municipalities, eight (including California, Illinois, and Tennessee) use the rule only for certain municipalities, and one state (Florida) applies the concept only to taxation.[22] Ten states do not adhere to the Dillon Rule at all. And yet Dillon Rule and home rule states are not polar opposites. No state reserves all power to itself, and none devolves all of its authority to localities. Virtually every local government possesses some degree of local autonomy and every state legislature retains some degree of control over local governments.[23] In some instances, larger cities in Dillon Rule states are granted home rule authority; New York and Baltimore are prominent examples.

## Home Rule

The inflexibility of Dillon Rule systems was one of several reasons why many states began either passing home rule laws or included those provisions in their new or revised constitutions. A second reason for the expansion of home rule involved a growing view in the 1880s that state legislators had become too susceptible to corporate corruption and that shifting power to localities would provide them some insulation against state efforts to extract economic wealth created by cities. Finally, municipalities became more professionalized during this period, largely in response to progressive reformers at the local level.

Under home rule, local communities are able to exercise some authority and local autonomy without state interference. In home rule states, some or all powers are delegated to smaller units of governments, such as cities, counties, and towns. The nature and type of delegation differ from state to state, but in home rule states, localities need not ask permission before taking action on a wide variety of issues. The first state to pass a home rule charter was Missouri in 1875. Shortly thereafter, California, Minnesota, and Washington State enacted similar measures.

When Virginia was rewriting its constitution in the late 1960s and early 1970s, it flirted briefly with transforming itself into a home rule state. The Commission on Constitutional Revision, the group empowered by the General Assembly to develop recommendations for the new constitution, initially proposed that the commonwealth switch from being a Dillon Rule state to one based in home rule for all localities with a population of more than 25,000.[24] Changing the doctrine could have been as simple as including language in the proposed constitution, the entirety of which would then have been submitted to the voters for approval. By the time the recommendation was considered by the General Assembly, however, resistance had emerged from an unexpected source, the Virginia Municipal League, usually the strongest advocate for empowering localities. Concerned that passage of home rule provisions would simply mean that the General Assembly would pass a series of general laws preempting the ability of localities from exercising real power, the group lobbied against the change, and it was not included in the proposed new constitution.[25]

The debate over the merits of the Dillon Rule versus home rule has intensified recently as the political differences between rural and urban localities have increased. Urbanites see their communities as having problems very different from those of other areas within their states and not only want to address them but frequently are willing to levy additional taxes or pass special measures to do so. When they discover that certain state laws prevent them from acting, their opposition to the Dillon Rule only intensifies. At the same time, not only are legislators reluctant to cede their authority to local government but argue that laws ought to be relatively uniform throughout their state. And when localities attempt to pass measures that trouble a state legislature, efforts arise to stop that legislation from taking effect, a process known as preemption.

## Preemption of Local Initiative

Local elected officials frequently describe the Dillon Rule versus home rule debate as an either/or choice, without realizing that it is much larger than that. The real issue is the degree to which a state will act to preempt local control, either before or after a locality adopts a certain policy. Preemption is permitted in most state constitutions, including states with home rule, and is used to restrain localities from adopting or enforcing changes desired by their constituents.[26] Dillon saw the need to assert the power of states over localities to address what reformers saw as incompetence, waste, extravagance, and corruption in local bodies. But today's local governments are much more professional today, and bear little resemblance to those that existed in the 1860s.

Most local versus state disputes presently have more to do with the nationalization of state and local politics. The more typical situations have involved Democratic-controlled cities within Republican-controlled states attempting to adopt policies that states and the federal government refuse to consider, only to be met by state legislative action designed to restrict them from enacting ordinances that contradict the dominant ideology of Republican lawmakers. More recently, we have seen some conservative jurisdictions assert local authority to pass regulations to counter what they judge to be unconstitutional overreach by their states. The Second Amendment sanctuary initiative, an effort by some localities to prevent states from imposing gun regulations, is among the most prominent recent example.

The Local Solutions Support Center (LSSC), a national coalition of legal scholars and activists, chronicles the efforts of state legislatures to consolidate power and prevent unilateral local action. The LSSC reported that, as of May 2017, twenty-four states had passed laws to preempt local minimum wage ordinances, eighteen had banned local laws guaranteeing paid sick days, and three had passed measures to prevent the adoption of local LGBTQ+ antidiscrimination ordinances. Another six states prohibited local fracking bans, and thirty-seven states have passed measures limiting local authority to regulate ride-sharing services such as Uber.[27] At least five states (Arizona, Idaho, Michigan, Missouri, and Wisconsin) have barred local governments from regulating the use of plastic bags.[28] According to the National League of Cities, Madison, Wisconsin, was subject to thirty-seven instances of state preemption between 2011 and 2018.[29]

One of the most prominent examples of state preemption involves action to prevent, even in home rule states, efforts by cities to act either as legal or de facto "sanctuary cities" to protect illegal immigrants against legal processes initiated by the federal government.[30] In Virginia, preemption bills on this issue have been proposed every year since 2016; until Democrats gained control of the legislature in 2020, these bills passed the legislature, only to be vetoed by the governor.[31] And there is increasing contention surrounding the efforts by cities to develop climate goals, with accompanying ordinances that may be at odds with state policy.

Much of the recent push to end the Dillon Rule has emanated from progressives, who argue that if they only had home rule, key problems could be solved. What many forget, however, is that state initiatives applying to all localities will occasionally require recalcitrant local officials to act more progressively than they otherwise would have. Environmental protection is one example. Some of the strongest resistance to strong state-mandated stormwater protections has come from local governments. In such cases, if localities were permitted to adopt their own less stringent regulations, they could undercut statewide initiatives designed to make water cleaner and protect the Chesapeake Bay. The same could be argued for having statewide standards for education. If each independent school division could control the textbooks that were used or the subject matter that was taught, dramatic differences could emerge throughout the state as to what children learn. In short, there are strong arguments to be made for some consistency of laws across an individual state.

Preemption activity can occur even in states that purportedly are governed by home rule principles. In 2010, the Ohio Supreme Court, for example, rejected the City of Cleveland's home rule challenge to Ohio's broad preemption statute on gun control.[32] In 2019, Missouri and Idaho, two states that permit some degree of local home rule, joined at least twelve other states that had preempted localities from adopting ordinances to ban plastic bag use.[33] In Arizona, another home rule state, when state lawmakers heard reports that Phoenix was considering the passage of certain climate change initiatives, they passed a law preempting it.[34] Kansas, where cities have home rule by constitution and counties have it by statute, blocked local efforts to require restaurants to list calories on their menus.[35] And partial or complete home rule states such as Oregon, New Jersey, and Rhode Island have state laws that specifically prevent localities from adopting inclusionary zoning ordinances.[36]

In December 2018, Miami passed an ordinance mandating the inclusion of affordable housing in new developments in certain neighborhoods. It did not take long for the state legislature to act. In June 2019, Florida, ostensibly a home rule state, approved a law prohibiting municipalities from passing mandatory inclusionary zoning ordinances, thereby rendering the city's action a nullity.[37] As one scholar keenly observed, "Home rule has been far more effective in enabling local governments to take the initiative and adopt new measures without having to wait for specific or express authority from the state—in other words, undoing Dillon's Rule of limited delegation of power—than in protecting those local actions from state displacement."[38]

For proponents of local control, however, being in a home rule state, especially one in which the provision is embedded in the state's constitution, can make a difference. The Colorado Supreme Court, for example, while invalidating Denver's ordinances that prevented juvenile possession of firearms and carrying concealed firearms with a permit into a public park because they conflicted with state law, nonetheless held that state law expressly preempting localities from regulating firearms unconstitutionally infringed on the city's home rule authority.[39] It seems that localities in Colorado may enact some, but not any, regulation of firearms or ammunition.

Preemption is a challenging legal concept, if only because there are several different types. Preemption may be explicit, as when states, by constitution, statute, or law, reserve a given function for themselves, or implicit, as when state laws so completely control a governmental function that there is no room for local authorities to do so.[40] And it has become a critical field for inquiry because cities have been much more innovative in addressing problems even as states have become more assertive in claiming their prerogatives.

The preemption debate is now one of the hottest issues in the panoply of discussion surrounding why states matter.[41] And while many of the debates in state capitols have focused on specific issues, some state leaders would go much farther than issue-by-issue preemption. In March 2017, for example, Governor Greg Abbott of Texas stated: "As opposed to the state having to take multiple rifle-shot approaches at overriding local regulations, I think a broad-based law by the state of Texas that says across the board, the state is going to pre-empt local regulations, is a superior approach."[42]

Some lawmakers would prefer not only to enact broad preemption statutes but also to engage in "punitive preemption," so called because it attaches penalties to localities and even local elected officials who seek to go beyond what state law allows. A 2019 Florida law, for example, allows the governor to remove individuals from local office if they pass regulations that violate the state preemption laws.[43] Even more draconian is a 2016 measure passed in Arizona whereby legislators can submit a form to the state's attorney general if they believe that a local "ordinance, regulation, order or other official action" is in violation of state law or the Arizona Constitution.[44] If the Arizona attorney general believes the local ordinance violates state law, the local government has thirty days to either change or withdraw the local ordinance or lose *all* state funding. Not only that; the attorney general can then submit the case for review by the state supreme court. If the locality contests, it must "post a bond equal to the amount of state shared revenue paid to the county, city or town" in order to challenge the decision in court. Whether these laws can pass constitutional muster has yet to be determined.

Punitive preemption is also occurring in unexpected places. California is typically viewed as a strong home rule state where municipalities have great flexibility to be innovative in their local policies. But when the California Supreme Court declared, in a case where a locality sought to pay a contractor *less* than the state's prevailing wage, that the payment of wages was entirely "exempt from state regulation," the state legislature intervened. It passed a law that not only prohibited state funding for public construction projects for which a locality refuses to pay the prevailing wage but also denied state funding for construction projects to any jurisdiction that had not paid the prevailing wage for a public contract "within the *prior two years*."[45] In this instance, California joined a number of conservative states to diminish the power of the local government. If this attitude were to become the predominant one in the country, the ability of localities to respond to uniquely different problems with innovative local solutions would be seriously compromised. And states would become even more important than they are today.

## Activism and State Backlash:
## Disputes over a Local Minimum Wage

Over the past decade, the nation has witnessed increased progressive activism in localities, primarily in larger cities controlled by Democratic majorities. While a majority of states were controlled by Republicans heading into the fall 2019 election, thirty-six of the mayors of the fifty largest cities were Democrats.[46] Many of these cities are adopting new local policies designed to attack difficult problems, from gun regulation and housing to environmental protection and wage regulation. In response, states have not hesitated to confront this independence directly, by passing a wide range of measures designed to preempt local authority and overturn initiatives not to their liking. It does not seem to matter whether these cities exist in Dillon Rule states or in those guided by home rule. When states decide that the localities are going too far, they act to rein them in.

The federal government has not raised the minimum wage beyond $7.25 per hour since 2009. Because the federal government failed to act, states and localities did. In the process, they created an interesting discussion not just about federalism and federal-state relations but also about the proper role of policymaking at the local level.[47] Twenty-one states began 2020 with higher minimum wages than the federal floor of $7.25 per hour.[48] In most parts of New York in 2020, the minimum was $11.80; in New York City, it is $15 for most businesses. California's wage floor in 2020 was $13 per hour; in San Francisco, it's $15.59. Many of these states and localities include cost-of-living adjustments in their statutes and ordinances.[49]

A 2019 analysis of state preemption of local wage ordinances found that "25 states have statutes preempting local minimum wage laws" and "12 cities and counties in six states (Alabama, Iowa, Florida, Kentucky, Missouri and Wisconsin) have approved local minimum wage laws only to see them invalidated by state statute."[50] Birmingham, Alabama, provides an example of how states can react to assertions of independence by cities. When the Iron City voted in 2016 to increase the local minimum wage to $10.10, in phases, the state legislature and governor acted to stop it with breathtaking swiftness. Within one hour of the city's action, and despite objection from all African

American members of both chambers, Alabama quickly voted to preempt the increase.[51] The city took no legal action to assert its authority to make the change, but citizens did. A group of fast-food workers and the NAACP filed suit, claiming that the state's majority white legislature discriminated against the majority black city by preempting the minimum wage increase.[52]

Similarly, proposed minimum wage increases in St. Louis and Kansas City were blocked before they could be implemented, as courts ruled that the state minimum wage law preempted cities from enacting their own.[53] In 2014, Louisville, Kentucky, passed an ordinance that would have gradually raised the minimum wage to $9 per hour by July 2017. However, in 2016 the Kentucky Supreme Court struck down Louisville's minimum wage ordinance, ruling that the city did not have the authority to set a minimum wage above the level set by the state.[54] Courts also blocked an ordinance in St. Louis and a ballot initiative in Kansas City on the grounds that the state minimum wage law preempts cities from enacting their own.[55] In many cases, states feel compelled to pass preemption measures only after the localities have acted. In Ohio, however, the state acted before the City of Cleveland could vote to increase the minimum wage. Six months before the city council was to hold a public vote on whether or not to increase the minimum wage to $15, the state passed legislation banning local governments from doing so.[56]

Advocates supporting increases in the minimum wage struggle with how best to do it. There are strong arguments against a patchwork of wage ordinances across each state; such arrangements can place localities in the position of competing against each other. If the argument is that the minimum wage should increase with the cost of living, however, perhaps differentials should be permitted within states that are reflective of the preferences of citizens and the particular needs of communities. Oregon and New York presently have different minimum wages for different parts of the state.[57] California has different wage rates depending on the size of the employer.[58]

In May 2019, Colorado became the first state to legislatively repeal its minimum wage preemption law, and advocates in Louisiana have launched a campaign calling for the state to grant local authority to raise the minimum wage.[59] Colorado was one of the first legislatures to adopt a minimum wage preemption law in 1999, but, because of a constitutional provision allowing legislation by citizen initiative, voters have twice raised the state minimum wage via the ballot. Legislation introduced in many states, including Virginia,[60] designed to repeal preemption of local ordinances that would increase the minimum wage,[61] have largely failed.

## COVID-19 Tests the Boundaries

The COVID-19 pandemic of 2020 not only reinforced the power of the states to issue restrictive emergency orders to protect their citizens but brought many of these preemption issues into sharp contrast.[62] Arguments for stay-at-home orders and the suspension of nonessential business activities were initially raised in places of urban density, most notably the cities of Seattle, San Francisco, and New York. Many cities issued emergency orders limiting local activity early in the crisis. In most states, governors followed by issuing their own orders, which were generally farther-reaching than those of the localities. In some cases, mostly in southern states, cities were actually more aggressive in their restrictions, but the interests of the governors and the localities aligned: everyone was seeking to "flatten the curve." Preemption, as an issue, was only raised, if at all, in the context of whether President Trump, his assertions of "absolute authority" to the contrary, had the power to overrule the stay-at-home emergency orders of the states. There was little discussion of whether state actions could overrule those of localities.

This began to change as pressure emerged to reopen the economy. The debates took on different forms in different states. And it did not much matter whether you were a Dillon Rule state or a home rule state—or a red state or a blue state; localities and their officials generally wanted more control over how they would operate in service of their citizens. In some cases, this involved assertions by localities that they could reopen their local economies despite state orders to the contrary. In Snohomish County, Washington, home to the first identified US case of coronavirus and a county that was generating among the highest number of deaths in the entire state, some local representatives began to argue that the governor should relax the prohibitions, and Sheriff Adam Fortney even said he would not enforce the state orders, claiming they were unconstitutional.[63] In other instances, cities sought to impose regulations that went beyond state orders. Boston mayor Marty Walsh, for example, issued an emergency order in March 2020 that shut down all construction sites in the city. Seven days later, however, Governor Charlie Baker issued his own emergency order that explicitly contradicted the mayor's. In it, he specifically stated that construction workers "perform an essential service," and made clear that state law superseded and made "inoperative" any local order that "will or might in any way impede or interfere with" the provisions of his order. This was a clear attempt to preempt the actions of Mayor Walsh and Boston.[64]

Massachusetts was not the only state where governors explicitly asserted the state's power to preempt local emergency ordinances. Emergency orders in Wisconsin, Mississippi, and New York all contained precise language asserting the state's right to issue orders "superseding" all conflicting local orders.[65] When Tennessee governor Bill Lee relaxed restrictions, Chattanooga mayor Andy Berke complained, but there was little he could do in the face of the state's preemption of the city's local ordinance.[66] Mississippi governor Tate Reaves specifically preempted any social-distancing restrictions or guidelines passed by local jurisdictions.[67] Arizona governor Doug Ducey issued an executive order prohibiting any county, city, or town from "restricting persons from leaving their home due to the COVID-19 public health emergency" or closing the long list of businesses he deemed "essential."[68]

And in Texas, a state with some elements of local home rule, Governor Gregg Abbott's initial emergency order made clear that local efforts by Dallas to implement its new sick leave ordinance would not be enforceable, regardless of the history of home rule in that city. When the state began to reopen, the attorney general sent letters to the cities of Austin, San Antonio, and Dallas stating that their more stringent regulations were "unlawful."[69] And when public health officials continued to urge the wearing of masks to curtail the virus spread, Abbott invoked the preemption argument in denying major Texas cities the ability to impose their own restrictions.

Other southern governors like Brian Kemp of Georgia (a home rule state) and Henry McMaster of South Carolina unleashed preemption issues of their own as they addressed the COVID-19 pandemic.[70] When Kemp, a political ally of President Trump, moved to reopen some of the state's businesses, including gyms, tattoo parlors, bowling alleys, nail and hair salons, and some movie theaters and restaurants, he specifically preempted localities from adopting their own ordinances.[71] Atlanta had previously issued its own stay-at-home order, and the mayor was not pleased with Kemp's actions. But the state not only had the power to overrule the locality but sued to do so, and the mayor was left largely to "encourage" people to stay at home. They clashed again months later when the mayor imposed a mask requirement in her city.

Similarly, mayors in Columbia and Charleston, South Carolina, balked when Governor McMaster relaxed some coronavirus-related restrictions to permit certain businesses, including bookstores, department stores, flea markets, florists, and music shops, to reopen.[72] South Carolina's Constitution grants greater authority to localities than do the constitutions of some other states, including the ability to "adopt emergency ordinances" to "meet public emergencies affecting life, health, safety or the property of the people," thereby setting up a potential legal conflict between the state and some localities.[73] In this instance, most observers were betting on the state and its power to preempt local ordinances.[74] An uneasy truce between localities and state governments emerged over the spring and summer as to how and when to lessen earlier restrictions or to reimpose them. Few really wanted to test the issues of preemption in the context of the pandemic. Nonetheless, as COVID-19 infections began to break daily records in the fall of 2020, conflicts continued between states and localities. When Florida governor Ron DeSantis issued an order allowing restaurants and bars to open at full capacity and prohibiting local governments from collecting fines to enforce local rules requiring masking inside establishments, Miami-Dade mayor Carlos Giménez complained, but had few remedies in the face of the state's action.[75] And Texas attorney general Ken Paxton threatened legal action against localities that sought to impose regulations more stringent than those adopted by the state.[76]

Governmental policies in the COVID-19 environment illustrate problems with bright-line rules involving preemption. It makes good sense for localities to be able to respond to what is occurring in their communities, and combating the virus in one locality may require more prohibitions than in another. But what about the recalcitrant locality that refused to adopt regulations to protect its neighbors? Isn't it reasonable for the state to preempt decisions in such cases? This struggle over the prerogatives of power will undoubtedly continue in the years ahead. Cities will keep pushing, if only because of the character of their electorates. But, in the present legal environment, much of the power will remain with states if they attempt to assert it.

# 13
## Saving the Planet

Suddenly, everything went dark.
—ANONYMOUS, 1965

On November 9, 1965, I was a naive fifteen-year-old high school sophomore in Syracuse, New York, who studied hard but also played on the basketball team. We practiced every afternoon until about 5:00 p.m., when we boarded the bus home. It was an era when after-school buses did not deliver you to a destination near your house. Instead, the driver would drop us 200 yards from the top of a steep hill and we would negotiate the next quarter mile, without sidewalks, to reach our neighborhood. From the top of that hill, though, we could look out over the glimmering expanse of the entire city of 200,000 people.

That November night was like any late fall evening in upstate New York—clear and crisp, with a trace of snow on the ground. My buddies and I jumped off the bus and proceeded to the crest of the hill, where we could see the lights of the university in the far distance and the illumination of Manley Field House, the glow stretching into the hills on the other side of the valley. It was about 5:20 p.m., and the view was breathtaking. And then everything went dark! As we crested the hill, we were dumbfounded by the sight. No more sparkle or shimmering, no streetlights or stoplights, only the sight of the stars in the heavens, their faint glimmering now fully revealed by the elimination of the artificial light on the ground below. Unbeknownst to us, we were witnessing the largest electrical blackout the world had ever experienced.

Perhaps it was that night that people began to develop some idea of how much we depend on an elaborate transmission network known as "the grid" to provide our basic electricity needs. This November event would come to be called "the Great Blackout of 1965," and it began at the Adam Beck hydro station in Ontario, Canada, where the failure of a somewhat minor protective circuit set off a chain reaction and electricity began overloading portions of the connected networks throughout parts of Canada and the northeastern United States (a portion of the grid). The surge rushed through upstate New York, overloading circuits on its way east and south. By 5:21 p.m., Boston was in the dark, followed seven minutes later by the Big Apple. It took less than fifteen minutes to depower 80,000 square miles, portions of nine states, and as many as 30 million persons.

## New Terrain and Old Concerns

States have always been active in the area of energy policy, if only because their regulatory powers affect some 3,500 utilities across the nation. Although the grid remains a constant as the mechanism by which electricity is transmitted throughout the nation,[1] the world of energy, electricity, and utilities today is much different today from what it was in 1965. Yet most Americans remain primarily focused on the same two issues as they were in 1965. First, they want to be confident that when the switch is flipped, the lights will go on—and stay on. Second, they hope that the electricity bill can be paid when it arrives. We expect these two things to occur, and if they don't, people get angry. That is why state policy is so important. If a policy mistake is made that leads to a decline in production, electricity to consumers or businesses can be disrupted. And if a change leads to a spike in prices, legislators will certainly hear about it.

In addition to concerns about availability and pricing, a new issue has arisen for state regulators and policymakers during the last several decades—the problem of climate change. As with so many other issues, Congress has largely been unwilling or unable to address this challenge, with the result that states are exploding with activity, charting paths that few could have imagined a decade ago. Between 2013 and 2017, 16,000 energy-related bills were introduced in statehouses across the country, and 2,800 of them passed.[2] In 2019 alone, governors from Wisconsin, North Carolina, Virginia, and Maryland issued far-reaching executive orders designed to accelerate efforts to expand renewable sources of energy and reduce carbon emissions in their states. Colorado passed legislation pushed by the new governor, Jared Polis, that established a green bank and dramatic new goals for renewable energy sources. And in 2020, Nevada voters adopted a constitutional amendment to compel the state to use 50 percent renewable energy by 2030.[3]

As of September 2020, the five largest utilities in the nation were committed to zero carbon emissions by 2050, even though one of them, Xcel Energy, acknowledged that doing so would require use of "technologies that are not cost-effective or commercially available today."[4] By 2020, twenty-nine states and the District of Columbia had set ambitious energy targets,[5] in some cases announcing a transition to 100 percent clean energy by mid-century.[6] In Washington State, Governor Jay Inslee signed cutting-edge legislation to improve the energy performance of thousands of large commercial buildings.[7] California passed a bill that set a statewide goal of carbon neutrality by 2045.[8] In response to legislation passed in 2018, Dominion Energy announced plans to build the nation's largest offshore wind farm off the coast of Virginia, a 220-turbine installation that will produce 2,600 megawatts by 2026 and power 650,000 homes at peak wind.[9] At the beginning of 2020, ten states in the Northeast and mid-Atlantic states had joined an interstate compact called the Regional Greenhouse Gas Initiative (RGGI), a cap-and-trade regimen by which participating states sell emission "allowances" through auctions and invest the proceeds in energy efficiency, renewable energy, and other consumer benefit programs.[10] In 2020, not only did Virginia join RGGI, it also passed one of the most comprehensive renewable energy bills in the country.[11]

States are also actively engaged in creating policies to build the electricity grid of the future. Some of these policies have originated with governors or legislators, others have been generated by public utility commissioners, relatively unknown to citizens but critically important to the structure of energy generation and distribution in the country. New York was among the first to attempt a disruption of the regulatory paradigm. In April 2014, Governor Cuomo pushed the Empire State, which already allows consumers and businesses to choose their own electricity supplier, to embark on a project called New York REV (Reforming the Energy Vision).[12] Billed at the time as a major transformation in the state's energy policy, REV and state goals now include generating 70 percent of the state's electricity from renewable sources by 2030 and reducing greenhouse gas emissions by 80 percent by 2050.[13]

Building the future energy infrastructure is an issue that many Americans overlook, but policymakers working in this space realize the importance of grid modernization and resiliency to the future of the country. In 2018, Massachusetts governor Charlie Baker signed bipartisan legislation authorizing more than $2.4 billion in capital allocations for investments in safeguarding residents, municipalities, and businesses from the impacts of climate change.[14] Governors in Louisiana, North Carolina, Florida, and Rhode Island have appointed their states' first-ever chief resilience officers. Almost everyone understands the immense damage flooding, wildfires, and hurricanes can cause, even if they are unwilling to accept that some of these disasters are related to changes in the climate. The future of the grid and of energy is being transformed into a significant public issue that demands policy responses from governmental officials. And while Washington remains paralyzed, major policy initiatives on energy proceed in the states.

## Disruption in the Marketplace

Change in the energy arena is being driven by several factors. First, the marketplace and advances in technology are generating change that few would have dreamed possible two decades ago. Twenty years ago, coal was king. Today it has largely been replaced by natural gas as the lowest-cost generator of electricity. [15] And the costs of solar and wind power have fallen so much that they not only have undercut coal but are increasingly competitive with natural gas.[16] As recently as the beginning of the twenty-first century, few would have predicted that individual homes could generate more electricity than they actually use, and feed the excess into the grid. Or that smart meters and the internet of things would allow businesses and residences to be controlled remotely and provide instantaneous data so that electricity could be dispatched more efficiently. Or that the electrification of vehicles would proceed so quickly. Or that new storage technology would allow consumers to contemplate a day when their needs could be met almost exclusively by energy from renewable sources.[17]

A second factor driving change is businesses' demand for renewables. Major corporations such as Walmart and Starbucks have established target dates by which they will be powered by renewable energy and have negotiated contracts with utilities and independent power producers to implement their plans.[18] In Virginia, for example, companies like Salesforce, Microsoft, LinkedIn, Apple, and others that own data centers want their operations powered by solar, wind, and other renewable energy sources, not by fossil fuels.[19] This has prompted the major utility in the state, Dominion Energy, to develop special bilateral contracts to respond to this need. Other companies, such as Costco, are requesting authority to purchase solar energy from generators outside the state. For those who believe that commerce is the engine of change, these actions provide daily confirmation of the power of business to drive progress in the energy field.

A third factor is the creative leadership emerging in statehouses as governors and lawmakers attempt to respond to the public's demand for more renewables and its insistence that states address the challenges of climate change. Capitols are abuzz with new proposals and legislation, and every week brings breaking news of yet another state developing a new timeline for how quickly it will transition to fossil-fuel-free electrical power generation.

A fourth factor is the resurgent activity of state utility commissions, many of which had previously viewed their roles as merely administrative. Now they are charting new directions in this arena and can no longer be viewed as mere rubber stamps by utilities. In coal-heavy Indiana, for example, the state utility commission recently questioned the future of the natural gas boom and decided to reject a proposal to build a $780 million natural gas plant.[20] Similarly, commissioners in Arizona rejected a utility company's proposal to build a major new natural gas plant so that they could review more carefully the cost-effectiveness of solar and wind as alternative sources of power.[21] The North Carolina Utilities Commission rejected Duke Energy's original ten-year, $7.8 billion grid modernization plan in 2018, and Virginia's State Corporation Commission refused to approve several of Dominion Energy's modernization efforts.[22] Even more significant, many state commissions have initiated proceedings to determine the best ways to modernize the grids that serve their states.[23]

And finally, the public is pushing lawmakers to do more. A 2020 national survey by Pew Research found that almost two-thirds (65 percent) of Americans say the federal government is doing too little to reduce the effects of climate change and 79 percent believe the nation should be developing alternative sources of energy, such as wind and solar.[24] They are resistant to building fossil fuel infrastructure, with many celebrating the cancellation of the Atlantic Coast Pipeline and opposing offshore drilling and coal power generation. While not always conversant with the economic impacts of these approaches, those holding these views nonetheless represent a powerful force that is manifesting itself in statehouses across the nation.

## PUCs—the Unknown Policymakers

Few citizens know much about state public utility commissions (PUCs). Most were created in the early 1900s as lawmakers sought to gain control over the burgeoning utility industry. The principle behind regulation was simple: consumers would receive reliable service and protection against monopoly pricing, while utilities would gain market stability and guaranteed rates of return (to ensure infrastructure capital costs could be recouped).[25] And lawmakers saw it as a way to meet two goals for their constituents—system reliability and reasonable cost. Much of this framework was established when Congress passed the Federal Power Act in 1935. The Federal Energy Regulatory Commission was charged with responsibility for interstate transmission and wholesale sales of electricity, and individual states, typically acting through their public utility commissions, regulated the generation and distribution of energy to consumers in their respective states. Regulation, then, made sense to numerous actors, and the utility commissions would serve as the watch-dogs of the system.

The subject matters before these commissions are dense, complex, and involve areas of analysis that can be difficult for nonexperts to understand. Commission deliberations and decisions typically involve the interplay of law, economics, and technology, and understanding the rationale for any decision can mire the analyst in a bottomless pit of jargon and technicalities. But deci-sions now being made by these commissions, and the legislatures that often instruct them, are increasingly important in determining the quality of life in our states and nation. Decisions made by PUCs influence $100 billion per year in utility infrastructure investment expected through 2020 across the nation, whether it involves new power plants, transmission lines, or smart meters.[26] In states like Virginia, with vertically integrated electric utilities, PUCs regulate generation, transmission, and distribution to customers. In states where generation is deregulated, PUCs regulate only distribution, and an independent system operator (ISO) or a regional transmission organiza-tion (RTO) regulates the generation markets and transmission systems. The rulings of these state commissioners affect the electric and natural gas bills paid by every consumer in the country. States matter!

The selection of these guardians of the grid is important, but is not uni-form across the states. Commissioners in thirty-five states are appointed to their positions by the governor. In thirteen states, however, commission-ers are elected by the voters in statewide elections. Commissioners in the remaining two jurisdictions, South Carolina and Virginia, are selected by legislators.[27]

Commissions are granted different responsibilities and powers depend-ing on how they were established and the degree to which the state legisla-tures exercise oversight of the regulatory process, but most were designed to be relatively independent bodies that could exercise their authority free of political pressure. In reviewing the history of these various commissions, as well as the legislative actions involving utility regulation, however, politics frequently intervenes, in some places more than others.

Most commissions continuously face a major dilemma. On the one hand, they have either a constitutional or a statutory responsibility to keep rates low for consumers. On the other, they are being told by legislatures that they must approve certain infrastructure projects, no matter how costly (or how much more costly than other alternatives), and without considering how those costs may increase the base rates. This dilemma is only intensifying

with the increasing pace of worldwide climate change and the accompanying public demand to replace fossil-fuel-powered plants with plants powered
by energy from renewable sources—quickly. It will remain a central policy
debate for lawmakers and regulators in the coming decades.

The interplay between these bodies and the legislative and executive
branches of state government is increasingly important. With the substantial
interest in renewable energy come more initiatives on the legislative front.
Yet state lawmakers by themselves still find it difficult to bend the utilities
to their will. Giant utilities still enjoy considerable power, partly because of
the financial resource gap between them and the offices of individual legislators. Most states have part-time legislatures composed of citizen lawmakers, who are only able to hire one staffer to assist in deciphering hundreds
(sometimes thousands) of bills filed on many diverse subjects each session.
Until very recently, most energy bills were written by the industry. Independent of the drafter, the legislation remains extremely complex and difficult
to understand. The lobbyists for the utilities are smart, engaging, savvy, and
numerous, and the companies recognize that it is often easier to influence
citizen legislators who must be elected periodically than appointed utility
commissioners and the experienced staff who advise them.[28] In states where
commissioners are directly elected, a slightly different dynamic is present,
but utility lobbyists are nonetheless well equipped to engage on various fronts
to protect their clients' interests.

## What's Next

While polls show increasing support for renewable energy across partisan
lines,[29] the public is also mindful of costs, and policymakers neglect those
at their peril.[30] The costs of energy in a state are a function of many things,
policy being one of them. But geography and infrastructure also play a role.
Virginia has several nuclear power plants that produce relatively cheap
energy. It also has a network of good pipelines, so access to natural gas is not
difficult. The state now ranks eighteenth in installed solar capacity,[31] but that
could soon change, as the state passed a major energy bill in 2020. As solar
and wind become more prominent energy sources, the geographic advantage
may shift to sunnier or windier areas. Iowa and Texas are already trendsetters
in wind energy generation, and California, Arizona, and Nevada will continue
to expand their leadership portfolios in solar energy.[32] A number of northeastern states are hoping to capitalize on offshore wind for energy and job
creation in supporting industries. And, of course, when the energy storage
challenge is resolved so that electrons can be stored for later use when the

wind doesn't blow and the sun doesn't shine, different comparative advantages will emerge based on how this disruptive technology is dispatched.[33]

Key questions remain. While much of the public's attention is focused on renewables, the nation has major infrastructure problems. Sixty percent of US distribution lines have surpassed their fifty-year life expectancy, and the Department of Energy projects that between $1.5 trillion and $2 trillion will be needed by 2030 to modernize the grid just to maintain reliability.[34] How will we create infrastructure to electrify our transportation network, a key element in the transition? What policies do we need to enact to increase energy efficiency, a valuable "source" of power? Can we inject more competition into the generation field without exposing utilities to risks that may compromise their ability to transmit and distribute electrons to consumers? How do we handle "stranded capital assets" of fossil-fuel-burning plants and the employees who work there? How can we protect the privacy and data of consumers who utilize smart meters to manage energy demand at their homes and businesses? How do legislators balance the trade-offs among short-term costs to consumers, long-term benefits, and other social values such as decarbonizing the economy? What incentives need to be in place to modernize the grid? And when do policymakers know they have been successful: is 100 percent clean energy (however defined) the measure, or should success be defined by another metric?

The next decade will likely be a time of significant state action in the energy arena. There is little that will depress the positive trajectory of clean energy. Wind is now the largest single source of electricity in Iowa and Kansas and continues to expand on land and off the coasts.[35] Solar energy has had a series of economic banner years. In the coming years, some of the policy areas in states to watch include the following:

1. A renewed emphasis on energy efficiency through what is called "plugging the leaks." Energy savings targets are not a new concept. More than one-half of states have energy efficiency resource standards, and the American Council for an Energy Efficient Economy considers the tool "one of the most effective ways for a state to guarantee long-term energy savings."[36] Tremendous waste is built into the US energy system. New building codes for residential and commercial buildings are likely to be adopted, and new incentives to reward utilities that save energy. Virginia residents, for example, use more electricity per household than most other states in the nation; in fact, the state's energy use has been rising, not falling. Data centers consume

much electricity even as they demand more energy from renewable sources. Lawmakers will likely see new policies to reward efficiency in the next decade.

2. A move to "electrify everything." States are already purchasing more electric vehicles for their fleets; California, Ohio, New York, Utah, and Colorado have major transitions under way. These include efforts designed to electrify school buses in a number of states, including Virginia, where the utility plans to use the vehicles' batteries to feed power back into the grid.[37]

3. A push to remove incentives that reward utilities for selling more energy. Under the present rate structure in many US energy markets, revenues for utilities depend on the amount of energy they produce and sell to consumers. "Decoupling" is a regulatory mechanism that eliminates the relationship between revenues and sales volume. In decoupled systems, utilities' earnings are based on factors other than the amount of energy sold, which allows utilities to recapture their costs while providing an incentive to conserve energy. In 2015, twenty-three states had decoupling policies for gas utilities and fourteen had policies for electric utilities.[38]

4. A quest for more vigorous renewable energy portfolios and carbon reduction standards. Many of the Renewable Portfolio Standards (RPS) enacted in the last decade are under review, and more aggressive targets are already emerging. Energy storage goals will likely be part of the new targets.

5. A greater emphasis on letting market forces work. Unreasonable regulatory or statutory barriers to players entering the market should be removed. Most states allow private companies to contract with such institutions as schools and businesses to build, own, and operate solar facilities on site and essentially sell the generated power directly to the consumer through power purchase agreements (PPAs). PPAs allow institutions to procure on-site solar energy at no upfront capital cost while leveraging federal tax credits to support the investment. The savings are then passed on to the institution in the form of lower prices for the electricity.

## Policy and Politics

State policies in the next decade will either accelerate or depress the rapid changes already occurring in the market. Policymakers must understand the existing system of energy generation, transmission, and distribution lest they make changes that stymie progress rather than support it. For those who question climate change, it is time to finally acknowledge that the fossil fuel sector will not rebound; coal is not being destroyed by the federal government or by environmental activists but by the all-powerful market. And for those who believe that climate change is an existential threat, it will no longer be sufficient simply to say "I support the Green New Deal." The complexities are so great that they need to be attacked using both the heart and the head. Expertise can be built in state PUCs, committee staff in the energy field, the executive branch, or among the legislators themselves, but in its absence, lawmakers are at the mercy of lobbyists or so-called experts, who may or may not share their values. The stakes are high, and the role of lawmakers will be significant.[39] Much of our future is in the balance, and states will be key players in shaping it.

# CONCLUSION
## Reimagining Civic Engagement

We are not enemies, but friends. We must not be enemies. Though
passion may have strained, it must not break the bonds of our affection.
The mystic chords of memory will swell when again touched as surely as
they will be, by the better angels of our nature.
—ABRAHAM LINCOLN, FROM HIS FIRST INAUGURAL ADDRESS

The elderly but still optimistic Benjamin Franklin left Carpenters Hall in
Philadelphia on the steamy afternoon of September 17, 1787, the last day of
the almost four-month-long Constitutional Convention convened to ensure
the survival of the fledgling United States of America. The eighty-one-year-
old was in poor health. His energy had been so sapped by the long hours and
contentious debates that his major speech, written to close the convention,
had to be delivered by James Warren, a colleague from Massachusetts. After
the speech, recommending compromise and adoption of the Constitution,
was read, Franklin labored to leave the building. He was met outside by a
woman who inquired about the results of the extremely secretive and closed-
door deliberations. "Well, Doctor," she asked, "what have we got, a republic
or a monarchy?" Franklin's purported response was immediate and direct: "A
republic," he exclaimed, "if you can keep it."[1]

Those seven words summarize all we need to know about our country
and its fragility. They underscore, first, that the founders deliberately chose
a representative republic rather than a direct democracy. Madison and his
colleagues were concerned, ironically, about too much democracy, and the
potential for what they termed "factions" to undermine common goals and
overwhelm the operation of government. This concern helped generate the
unique system of checks and balances embodied in the US Constitution and
the state constitutions that followed it.

Second, Franklin's words intimate that our nation's survival is always an
open question, with the answer provided not simply by our leaders and our

founding documents but by the actions of all of us. Today the United States appears to be coming apart at the seams. The public views many elected officials with suspicion if not with outright antagonism. We appear to have lost productive ways of communicating with each other. In some cases, we are prisoners of the political tribes and ideologies we ourselves created. We appear to be slowly but relentlessly squeezing the optimism out of us all.[2] The uncertainty of the COVID-19 pandemic did not make it any easier. And the killing of George Floyd in May 2020 further crystallized the deep racial divisions in the nation.

States play an important role in a country where national consensus and action appear increasingly problematic. Partisanship and polarization at the federal level have been significant factors in this increasing state activity: if the federal government is gridlocked or lacks the leadership to act, leaders in states attempt to fill the void. But the future of the nation will be influenced not simply by the policies states embrace but also by the process by which they enact them. Otherwise the states will become merely smaller versions of the federal government, where agreements are difficult to forge and efforts to construct policy are submerged in a sea of mistrust and political antagonism.

Many observers believe that some of the nation's answers will be found in civic engagement, though there are disputes about the actual meaning of the term. But one thing appears clear: some of the greatest opportunities we have for rejuvenation will involve governments closest to the people. The answers are more likely to be found in our localities and our states than at the federal level. And a key leadership challenge of our time involves lighting the spark and fueling the flame of productive engagement with the representatives who serve us at those levels.

Doing so will mean recognizing that democracy constantly demands renewal, and US citizens must summon the will and marshal the forces to protect and enhance it. There will always be authoritarian challenges from leaders who reject the democratic rules of the game, the unwritten norms on which we rely to make the political system work. Frequently demagogues, they deny the legitimacy of their political opponents, using extreme language to vilify and disqualify their perspectives and degrade them as people. They tolerate or even encourage violence as a way to advance their goals or silence their opponents, often labeling those with whom they disagree "enemies of the people."[3] In such an environment, many citizens disengage, experiencing a paralysis of pessimism that simply makes the situation more difficult. When this occurs, the institutions of our democracy are easily captured and exploited to benefit the few at the expense of the many.

States and their leaders play an important role in encouraging a robust civic engagement that is the basis of a strong democracy. We are now seeing increasing openness to new approaches in this area, even as there are sharp differences over the proper measures to embrace. And in the process, we are being forced to examine the practices of the past to determine how they can be adapted to the challenges we now face. One of the areas inspiring the greatest debate involves the function of civil discourse in generating change.

## Civility as Contested Terrain

Civility and civil discourse are qualities that Americans formerly held in high esteem. Today they frequently appear to be under attack—from both the right and the left. Remember the infamous interruption of President Obama during his 2009 address to a joint session of Congress by Republican congressman Joe Wilson, who shouted "You lie"? Or the spectacle of newly elected Democratic representative to Congress Rashida Tlaib, proclaiming to her supporters that "we're gonna impeach the motherfucker [Trump]!"?[4]

Every week brings yet another example of behavior that, depending on your viewpoint, violates conventional norms, threatens our sense of order, or potentially poses risks for democracy itself. How do we judge, for example, a restaurateur's refusal to serve Trump's former press secretary Sarah Huckabee Sanders?[5] Is it acceptable for my former colleague, Delegate Ibraheem Samirah, to disrupt a presidential speech on the four-hundredth anniversary of the Virginia House of Delegates by displaying placards of opposition immediately in front of the podium?[6] How about the shouting down of opposing points of view, however repugnant to American values, either during speeches or on college campuses?[7] Or doing the same at public hearings in the chambers of the Charlottesville City Council merely because the speaker has a different view?[8] How do we respond to "Antifa activists" who appear at alt-right rallies ready to engage in violent confrontations to vanquish their opponents?[9] Or to religious leaders who engage in the traditional civil disobedience that, while disruptive, does not involve either violence or disrespect of those with whom there is disagreement?[10] What is the proper reaction to sheriffs and local governmental officials who proclaim they will not enforce gun safety legislation they deem unconstitutional?[11] There is certainly no consensus about whether these actions are justified; there may be even less agreement about whether they are civil.

Most Americans know there is a problem with how we conduct our political business, even if they may differ on the cause.[12] A 2019 study by Powell Tate and KFC Research, for example, found that the vast majority of

Americans—93 percent—identify incivility as a problem, with most classifying it as "major" one (68 percent).[13] Yet there is little consensus on what civility actually means. "When people talk about a crisis in civility," argues Keith Bybee, "they usually are reporting their sense that there is not a shared understanding of what that baseline of respect ought to be."[14] No matter your definition, however, one thing is clear. Civility in public life is completely optional; there is no law compelling it.

As the philosopher John Rawls explains, "The idea of citizenship imposes a moral, not a legal, duty—the duty of civility—to be able to explain to one another on those fundamental questions how the principles and policies they advocate and vote for can be supported by the political values of public reason."[15] Rawls reminds us that obedience to the laws in our society is required and typically enforced by a coercive threat embedded in the legal system. The rule of law typically emanates from an external source, such as a statute or judicial opinions. But civil behavior is quite different. It emerges instead from something internal to the individual. Civility is powerful precisely because it is not coerced; people are not required by law to act that way. Because of this, it can enhance social cohesion. Without it, life can become a battlefield filled with conflict and uncertainty.

While civility has been associated with the avoidance of unpleasantries, a broader conception of the term is probably justified.[16] In this view, civility requires the courage to speak your mind to an opponent in an open fashion. It does not mean we should respect the position of the adversary, only that we engage our opponents, speaking our truth to them while remaining in the room to hear theirs. This last point is key, for this broader concept of civility implies the willingness to listen to the response despite its abhorrence, to generate the moral toughness necessary to resist our opponent's incivility. We can acknowledge the opponent as a person without agreeing with their viewpoint.

While Americans believe that President Trump shoulders great responsibility for the most recent decline in public civil discourse, it has been developing for years and is becoming more pervasive in our political culture.[17] But the critique of civility has also come from some on the left. In this view, civility has merely been a tool to oppress people, to "keep them in their place" and to prevent change. These critics argue that civility is not a call to virtue and respect but instead a subtle demand for conformity that delegitimizes dissent and reinforces a status quo of white privilege and male supremacy.[18] Ben Franklin's admonition that we should be "civil to all; sociable to many, familiar with few; friend to one; enemy to none" would gain few adherents among the many who suggest that taking or exploring "the other side" on a divisive political issue is "giving in," a betrayal of moral or political principles. Michelangelo Signorile's 2018 missive "F*** Civility" was given that specific title for a reason.[19]

A broader concept of civility will never be the solution to our political divisions, but it may be a helpful prerequisite to establishing personal connections and relationships necessary for the political system to operate without coercion serving as its base. Is it easier to solve problems when people are talking with, rather than at, each other? Probably. Should that be an end in and of itself? No. Should it remain a principle to which we should aspire? Yes. The broader concept of civility challenges us not to disagree less but to *disagree better*. In that way, we can hopefully avoid holding in contempt those with whom we merely differ.

## Principles of Civic Engagement

The eight-minute-and-forty-six-second knee-on-the-throat asphyxiation of George Floyd by a Minneapolis police officer in May 2020 gave new urgency to issues of civic engagement. Large protests, often generated by loose social media networks, immediately appeared in US cities, large and small. Though some of the protests disintegrated into looting and mayhem, the vast majority were nonviolent. Many Americans realized that we had to change.

Elected officials can have a difficult time with disruption and protest. Their world is one of structured argument. They propose a bill or certain spending; it gets debated, and there is a vote. If successful, the initiative moves forward. If not, the proponents determine whether and when to try again. There is normalcy—and presumably rationality—to the process. That is not necessarily the experience of many Americans who are alienated and even oppressed by a political process and a system that do not work for them.

Engaging Americans who feel left out of the political and economic decisions that affect their lives is among the most significant challenges of our time. And many believe that the best place for this engagement is in state and local government. Fifty-seven percent of respondents in a recent study agreed that "state and local governments should play a larger role" in building an atmosphere of civility.[20] Despite this view, evidence exists that the polarization in Washington is moving into the states; in my fourteen years in the Virginia House of Delegates, I have certainly felt this, and recent academic work provides empirical support for it.[21] So what is to be done? Fortunately, there are many ideas that both state leaders and citizens can embrace. [22] Here are a few:

## 1. Employ Empathy, Humility, and Respect for Disagreement as the Basis of Civility

Civility and politeness should not be confused. While white racial segregationists in the South were frequently polite to African Americans, most were
anything but civil. Beneath their velvet gloves of gentility were often iron fists
ready to compel obedience. When Rosa Parks refused to sit at the back of the
bus, her protest did not bring out the civility of the powerful in Montgomery.
Instead, the white establishment moved to shut her and others down.

Advocates of change can learn from actions that, while not polite, contain elements of empathy and respect that can disrupt the status quo. Martin Luther King Jr., for example, was both angry at injustice and civil in his
protest. In his "Letter from a Birmingham Jail," King decried black minis-
ters who he claimed were more concerned with civility than with justice, and
famously chastised the "white moderate," who, King asserted, preferred "a
negative peace which is the absence of tension" over "a positive peace which
is the presence of justice."[23]

Americans, King said, should not fear tension; they should fear its
absence. The intent of the nonviolent protests was to "create such a crisis
and foster such a tension" that Americans would be forced to confront racial
oppression in America. But while he was disruptive and anything but polite,
he insisted that the confrontations be nonviolent. While he may have person-
ally believed that nonviolence was "morally superior" to other approaches,
his use of this strategy was designed primarily to expose the violence of the
system he was confronting. King always gave his opponents a way to move
away from their established position. Civil disobedience, while not necessarily polite, would be that vehicle.

Treating people with contempt, even if we believe they deserve it, can
make persuasion impossible.[24] Our political health and the strength of our
institutions should not and cannot be measured on whether we agree; rather,
they should be judged on whether we can channel ferocious argument into
periodic resolution that reflects a substantial portion of public support and
trust in the process. This is the essence of a strong political system, one that
accommodates different views and melds them into solutions that work.

## 2. Embrace the Truth; Reconciliation Will Follow

It is more important than ever for Americans to understand the nation's past,
in its glory and its oppression, its idealism and cynicism, the times when we
have been truly "exceptional" and the instances that revealed anything but the
better angels of our nature. Without understanding our complex history, dis-

covering the proper road ahead will prove impossible. This will require penetrating the multiple "competing realities" swirling around the nation that are exacerbated by social media and the twenty-four-hour news cycle, but the task is essential for the success of the democratic experiment.

Elected officials may need to approach this effort in ways unfamiliar and uncomfortable to them. In our present political environment, admitting an error or apologizing for a mistake is often viewed as a sign of weakness or something that can be used by an opponent in the next campaign. Nonetheless, the sincere acknowledgment of imperfection and errors of the past can be powerful; it can both build trust and encourage civic engagement. Trust is an attribute that is in short supply, and it is one of the most powerful elements that an elected official can use to build support.

Fortunately, we have a number of good examples from our recent past that illustrate the power of apology. In Virginia, Governor Mark R. Warner formally apologized in 2002 for the state's role in eugenics, stating that it "was a shameful effort in which state government never should have been involved."[25] The commonwealth was the first state to issue such an apology, and in 2015 the legislature authorized compensation of up to $25,000 per claim to individuals sterilized "pursuant to the Virginia Eugenical Sterilization Act."[26] Virginia was also the first state to apologize for slavery, passing such a resolution in 2007.[27] In the aftermath of the George Floyd murder, political leaders from across the country acknowledged what so many had known for years—that police brutality, especially in communities of color, is an extremely serious problem. Alabama's Governor Kay Ivey extended a "sincere, heartfelt apology" to a survivor of the 1963 Ku Klux Klan bombing of the 16th Street Baptist Church in Birmingham, arguing that then governor George Wallace "and other leaders at the time played an undisputed role in encouraging its citizens to engage in racial violence."[28]

Words, of course, are cheap, and state lawmakers will have to follow up with concrete action if things are to change. By the end of 2020, major steps toward police reform had found their way into state law. Colorado passed a new law that eliminated the qualified immunity defense that generally protects police officers from misconduct lawsuits. Minnesota passed a broad slate of police accountability measures that included a ban on chokeholds like the one used on Floyd. Pennsylvania and Oregon passed police oversight bills. Virginia even included police reform as part of a major special session that convened for two months, and passed a package of major reforms, including support for local citizen review panels to investigate brutality claims.[29] These actions were occurring at the state, not the national, level.

One public official who has been deeply involved in the racial reconciliation process is Governor Ralph Northam of Virginia. In early 2019, Virginia politics was rocked by the publication of Northam's 1984 yearbook page purporting to show the governor dressed in blackface and posing next to another person in KKK garb. Northam and his political team fumbled his response, and demands for his resignation exploded from across the nation. Northam resisted resignation and instead attempted to rebuild a political reputation that had collapsed in shambles.[30] The governor quickly recognized the power of earnest apologies. Slowly, softly, and sincerely, he made efforts at reconciliation. He made a regular practice of attending significant events involving African Americans, frequently just sitting in the crowd and rarely asking to speak. He appointed African Americans to key leadership positions and created a director of diversity, equity, and inclusion, an entirely new position in state government.[31] He initiated the Commission on African American History Education to ensure that Virginia's education standards would be "inclusive of African American history."[32] The governor's 2020 budget included new funding to attack maternal mortality among people of color and new investments in historically black colleges.[33]

Northam also began the process of replacing a statue of Robert E. Lee at the US Capitol that had been installed there in 1909, eliminated the Lee-Jackson state holiday,[34] and, following George Floyd's murder in Minneapolis in May 2020, authorized the removal of the massive statue of Lee that has stood at the entrance of Monument Avenue in the former Capital of the Confederacy for more than one hundred years. Finally, he pushed significant reforms to address police brutality in the commonwealth. Northam not only became a leader on racial reconciliation but won substantial public approval in the process.[35] Significant examples of cultural insensitivity and racial discrimination remain in the state, but Virginia is a very different place from what it was before the Northam scandal hit.

### 3. Reinforce the Political Guardrails to Guide Our Path

Understanding and empathy are not enough to ensure all voices in a democracy are effectively heard. There must be rules to guide the way. Some of these will be written and more formalized, while others will exist as norms and customs that reflect our values. Without some shared semblance of commonality about how to treat each other fairly, the social compact disintegrates, with the result that decisions are no longer based on debate and deliberation but instead on the marshalling of raw political force.

These formal rules and informal norms are tantamount to guardrails that allow citizens to negotiate the highways of democracy without fear of running off the road. A good example of buttressing the political guardrails of democracy comes from the 2008 presidential campaign. During a public forum, a participant alleged that Barack Obama was "an Arab." John McCain interrupted the woman who made the claim and shook his head. "No ma'am," McCain said. "He's a decent family man, a citizen that I just happen to have disagreements with on fundamental issues, and that's what this campaign is all about. . . . I admire Senator Obama and his accomplishments; I will respect him. I want everyone to be respectful, and let's make sure we are. Because that's the way politics should be conducted in America."[36] One rarely hears such acknowledgments these days, especially in presidential contests. McCain's comments provide an example of how to reinforce the informal norms that help democracies operate.

A recent study of ten legislative bodies found that the keys to success in reducing partisan divides were interpersonal relations, traditions that foster interparty trust, and rules to respect the minority.[37] This can often take the form of small gestures extended to colleagues. In Virginia, for example, there are formal rules against introducing some types of legislation after certain deadlines "without unanimous consent." A lawmaker making such a request, however, is rarely denied the courtesy; breaching this protocol would be viewed as violating the informal norms of the body.[38] Similarly, embracing an informal norm or a formal rule that "every bill should receive a hearing" cultivates the idea that the minority has a right to be heard. Respect for the minority should involve a simple but sometimes neglected practice in statehouses—the principle of proportional representation on committees. In the Virginia House of Delegates, this approach had largely been ignored until Republicans took control of the body in the early 2000s; when Democrats resumed control in 2020, they retained the rule.[39] Finally, there are traditions in statehouses across the country about cutting off debate. Virginia, for example, does not use cloture or the filibuster, but debate can be ended by voting "on the pending question." During my time, the Speaker played the key role in determining when debate would cease. He even had a designated person on whom he would call, who would then dutifully rise and move to end debate. Finding the right time to end debate is an informal practice, and involves a delicate balance between the majority's control of the body and the right of the minority to make its case in a public forum. In my time, it was rare for debate to be prematurely terminated, and a "motion to call the pending question" would frequently bring cheers from both sides because we had all heard enough debate and were ready to vote.[40]

There are some instances, however, that go beyond mere courtesies. In these situations, how the rules are enforced can have major consequences for the dynamics of the body itself. Like many other states, Virginia utilizes a concept known as "germaneness": any amendment to a bill must not go beyond the measure's original purpose or outside its general scope. One could not amend a bill on animal control, for example, by adding language to fund a new road. This rule ensures some structure and fairness to lawmaking by preventing amendments that have little relevance to an original bill from being added to it. But even such rules require interpretation and enforcement, usually by the Speaker of the House or the chair of a legislative body, who may choose, for convenience or politics, to ignore precedent and adopt a certain position simply to support the majority. The Virginia House of Delegates has traditionally been very supportive of its rules, and in 2013 it proved once again why it celebrates itself as the oldest legislative body in the Western world. The Virginia House had just passed and sent to the Senate an innocuous bill that made minor technical adjustments in several electoral districts for the upcoming elections. At the time, the Senate consisted of an equal number of Democrats and Republicans—until one day, when one Senate Democrat took leave to attend Obama's second inauguration. Republicans realized they were in the majority, and pushed through a thirty-six-page amendment to the bill that made massive changes in districts across the state. The amended legislation, which would likely ensure a Republican legislative majority for a decade, passed 20–19.

Senate Republicans were betting that the House, where the GOP far outnumbered the Democrats, would support the brazen power grab. Since the Senate had made changes to a House measure, the bill had to return to the other chamber for approval. Under the rules, the changes were not germane to the original legislation and so should be ruled out of order. The Republican Speaker of the House, William J. Howell, faced a dilemma. If he ruled the amendments out of order, he would anger Senate Republicans and frustrate their power play. If he allowed the amendments to remain, he would violate both the informal norms and formal rules of the House, and inject a higher level of partisanship into the body. A lot was at stake. After delaying for almost two weeks, the Speaker docketed the bill for debate and a vote. When it was finally considered, a Republican moved to strike the amendments as nongermane; it was then clear that Howell had decided to rule the amendments out of order.[41] "I have the responsibility and obligation," he explained from the dais, "to uphold the honor, dignity and integrity of both this office and the institution as a whole," and proceeded to find the amendments out of order.[42] Senate Republicans were not pleased, but Howell had reinforced the guardrails within which transactional governing can occur.

Contrast Howell's actions with the tactics Republicans in North Carolina used to override Democratic governor Roy Cooper's veto of the state budget in 2019. Press reports suggest that Republican leadership misled Democrats into thinking that no vote would be taken on whether to sustain the governor's veto of the budget; based on this assurance, several Democrats were absent when the measure was brought up on the House floor. With a number of Democrats out of the room, the Republicans had enough votes to override the veto. Chaos ensued, as the small number of Democrats vocally protested, so much so that the police had to be called. For some observers, those actions further destroyed the guardrails of trust in the state, already weakened as the result of the political hardball that had been played for years in Raleigh. What elected officials frequently forget in these battles is that they may win significant victories but the hard feelings will remain for years, and the other party may act the same way if given the opportunity.[43]

### 4. Cultivate the Disruption of Dynamic Listening

Using the word "disruption" and "civility" in the same sentence may seem an oxymoron, but there is value in embracing both concepts as leaders listen to their constituents. Elected officials frequently make two mistakes as they solicit input from the public. First, they have a tendency to hear only the positives about their performance. Many constituents are more than willing to indulge their representatives with plaudits on what they are doing well; they tell them only what they think they want to hear.

The second risk flows from an unwillingness to engage in discussion where there is discomfort, disagreement, or argument. True listening should be about disruption, not in the destructive sense but in a constructive way that encourages both the speaker and the listener to consider approaches, perspectives, and ideas in a new light. This dynamic listening does not mean embracing ideas that one finds abhorrent. It is merely a set of rhetorical techniques that invite the *other* person to talk. It does not mean remaining quiet while someone launches into a diatribe of one kind or another. Quite the opposite! Dynamic listening is about how you respond, the degree to which the clear expression of another person's thoughts is encouraged, and, in the process, the extent to which this interactive process clarifies your own. This may be as simple as saying "I don't see the world through your lens. Explain to me how you got there."

There is so much focus today on our disagreements that it is hard to accept that Americans are less divided on issues than we sometimes believe. A 2019 study from the group More in Common reported on what they call "the perception gap," the difference between the actual views of a political group and what opponents believe those views to be.[44] In their study, they found that the proportion of Republicans who denied that "racism exists" (21 percent) was actually much less than the percentage of the GOP that Democrats *thought* held that view (49 percent). Similar perception gaps existed for Republicans in their beliefs about the numbers of Democrats who support "completely open borders" or think that "most police are bad people." To be sure, some data from this study are troubling. There are strong extremes in both political perspectives: 30 percent of identified Republicans do not accept the statement that "many Muslims are good Americans," and 29 percent of self-identified Democrats believe in "completely open borders." Those strong views fuel a group polarization effect whereby people engage only with like-minded others, sometimes generating a more extreme version of what they previously believed.[45] Dynamic listening has the potential to disrupt these tendencies and explode the various political bubbles in which many elected leaders presently reside.

## 5. Reject the Paralysis of Guilt and the Straitjacket of Saintliness

Effective political work is often frustrated by a paralysis of guilt, a belief that things are so bad that no amount of effort will change them. Guilt also has a way of inhibiting real communication. People become afraid of what others may think of them, or whether their expression of a point of view will hurt others' feelings. We see this most acutely when discussing issues of race. It is a difficult topic, but feeling guilty about events over which you had no control can inhibit the ability to develop good policy. Similarly, more productive civil discourse might occur if citizens realized there are few saints in our midst, and probably many fewer in the political realm. During the 2020 presidential primaries, Joe Biden drew fire from his opponents because of statements he had made about his ability to work with ardent segregationists while in the US Senate.[46] But as Bryan Stevenson, a civil rights attorney and founder of the Equal Justice Initiative located in Montgomery, Alabama, once said, "Each of us is more than the worst thing we've ever done. . . . We all need mercy, we all need justice, and—perhaps—we all need some measure of unmerited grace."[47] He is certainly not implying that we simply overlook positions people have taken in the past or views with which we may strenuously disagree, especially when it comes to basic human rights. But if we wait for everyone to become saints, or condemn leaders because they aren't, we may be missing opportunities to help bend the arc of the universe toward justice.

There are countless examples of this in the political realm, where people surprise us with what they are willing to do. Lyndon Johnson held very insensitive racial views when he entered public life, and they continued throughout much of his career. But few can fault his efforts on behalf of civil rights while he was president. The Koch brothers and their conservative allies in the American Legislative Exchange Council (ALEC) have been aggressive in attacking many liberal proposals for years. But their recent positions on criminal justice strike many as progressive, and their efforts in this area are helping states move away from policies that have led to the mass incarceration of African Americans. The point is to recognize the transactional character of politics. People need not be saints to work together, and there are ways whereby people with very divergent views can find common ground.

Former president Obama spoke recently about applying too many political litmus tests. "This idea of purity," he said, "and [that] you're never compromised and you're always politically woke and all that stuff—you should get over that quickly. . . . The world is messy. . . . There are ambiguities. People who do really good stuff have flaws. People who you are fighting may love their kids and share certain things with you."[48] In politics, not only can the perfect be the enemy of the good, but your worst enemy today may be your best friend tomorrow.

## A Rebirth of Constructive Engagement?

Voter participation data clearly indicate a recent uptick in political engagement, at least at the polls. But what precisely does this mean? It certainly appears to be reflective of more division and polarization, and the tendency of people to vote "against the other"—the "negative polarization" about which so many political observers have written.[49] Under this theory, more people are participating because they are angry—at the other side, as they perceive it.[50] We are seeing this increasingly with primary contests indicating that "the other" resides not only in the opposing party but in one's own as well. Legislating in this environment becomes extremely difficult. Now a lawmaker has to worry not only about a challenger from the other party but also about a contest from within. One example of this is found in the failure of most

Republican US senators to say anything in the aftermath of the 2020 election to dispute Trump's unsupported claims that the election was stolen from him through widespread fraud. Since key members of Trump's administration reported that "the November 3rd election was the most secure in American history,"[51] and even the US attorney general William P. Barr, a Trump appointee, acknowledged that he had "not seen fraud on a scale that could have effected a different outcome in the election,"[52] the only reasonable explanation is that the GOP leaders are afraid of Trump, his base, and how they might extract revenge in a future primary. While some argue that primary contests breed more accountability, experience suggests a more complex picture. Legislators are pressured to embrace more ideological positions, thereby making compromise more difficult.

With all the challenges, there remain reasons for hope. First, many elected officials in the states, unlike their counterparts at the federal level, have not given up on the idea that common ground can be reached on many issues. Second, most elected officials still believe that facts matter and reject the assertion attributed to former Republican strategist Lee Atwater that "politics and facts don't belong in the same room."[53] Third, despite the recent assault on logic and reason, Americans remain convinced that rational discourse can lead to positive change. Without this belief, public service is merely a pursuit of economic and social advantage in a cynical struggle for power that may or may not help other Americans. Finally, the COVID-19 pandemic, at least in its initial phase, brought some sense of unity to the country. Ninety percent of respondents in a poll released at the height of the crisis in April 2020 agreed that "we're all in it together," a dramatic increase from the 63 percent who agreed with the statement in the fall of 2018.[54]

When Arizona senator Jeff Flake announced his retirement from the US Senate in October 2017, he decried "the state of our disunion . . . the disrepair and destructiveness of our politics . . . [and] the compromise of our moral authority." "When the next generation asks us," he inquired; "'Why didn't you do something? Why didn't you speak up?' What are we going to say?"[55] Similarly, at the close of Michael Cohen's testimony before the House Oversight Committee in February 2019, Baltimore congressman Elijah Cummings issued a comparable challenge: "When we're dancing with the angels, the question will be asked, . . . . what did we do to make sure we kept our democracy intact?"[56] Here were two leaders from two different parties and dramatically different backgrounds and political perspectives. That they were both pleading for things to change illustrates the crisis in which we find ourselves.

But they are merely stating what so many elected officials think. This recognition is key, because the first step toward solving any problem is to acknowledge that there is one. Critical events in 2020, from COVID-19 to George Floyd's murder, illustrate more than ever before why states matter. The economic, political, and social implications of these events will be felt for years, and many of the solutions to the challenges generated by them will be found in our states. So much of our future will depend on what happens there, both in terms of policy and, perhaps even more critically, in terms of our political process. We have entered one of the most challenging periods of our democracy, and the extent to which we are civically engaged will largely determine how our nation will look in the decades ahead.

We remain in the fight of our lives.

# Notes

## Introduction

1.  National Conference of State Legislatures, "Absentee and Mail Voting Policies in Effect for the 2020 Election," November 3, 2020, https://www.ncsl.org/research /elections-and-campaigns/absentee-and-mail-voting-policies-in-effect-for-the -2020-election.aspx.

2.  Brennan Center for Justice, "Preparing Your State for an Election under Pandemic Conditions," New York University School of Law, October 26, 2020, https://www.brennancenter.org/our-work/research-reports/preparing-your -state-election-under-pandemic-conditions#t4.

3.  US Elections Project, "Pennsylvania Early Voting Statistics," November 5, 2020, https://electproject.github.io/Early-Vote-2020G/PA.html.

4.  Mark Niesse, "Early Voting Brought Record Turnout in Georgia Ahead of Election Day," *Atlanta Journal-Constitution*, October 31, 2020.

5.  Dan Lamothe, Missy Ryan, Josh Dawsey, and Paul Sonne, "Trump Administration Upends Senior Pentagon Ranks, Installing Loyalists," *Washington Post*, November 10, 2020.

6.  Jim Galloway, Patricia Murphy, Greg Bluestein, and Tia Mitchell, "The Jolt: The 'Orchestrated' Push to Discredit Georgia's Election Sparks More GOP Infighting," *Atlanta Journal-Constitution*, November 10, 2020.

7.  Chris Kahn, "Nearly 80% of Americans Say Biden Won White House, Ignoring Trump's Refusal to Concede—Reuters/Ipsos Poll," Reuters, November 10, 2020, https://uk.reuters.com/article/uk-usa-election-poll-idUKKBN27Q3DW.

8.  Attributed to Benjamin Franklin in the notes of Dr. James McHenry of Maryland, delegate to the Constitutional Convention, in Max Farrand, ed., *The Records of the Federal Convention of 1787*, vol. 3, appendix A (New Haven, CT: Yale University Press, 1911), 85 (https://memory.loc.gov/cgi-bin/query/r?ammem/hlaw :@field(DOCID+@lit(fr003131))#N0089-141).

9.  Aaron Davis, "How Trump Amassed a Red-State Army in the Nation's Capital— and Could Do So Again," *Washington Post*, October 1, 2020.

## 1. States of Emergency

1. World Health Organization, "Pneumonia of Unknown Cause—China," January 5, 2020, https://www.who.int/csr/don/05-january-2020-pneumonia-of-unkown-cause-china/en/.

2. Jennifer Selin, "How the Constitution's Federalist Framework Is Being Tested by Covid-19," *FixGov* (blog), Brookings Institution, June 8, 2020, https://www.brookings.edu/blog/fixgov/2020/06/08/how-the-constitutions-federalist-framework-is-being-tested-by-covid-19/.

3. Centers for Disease Control and Prevention, "COVID-19 in China" (update of August 6, 2020), https://wwwnc.cdc.gov/travel/notices/warning/novel-corona virus-china.

4. "Factbox: What We Know about the New Coronavirus Spreading in China and Beyond," Reuters, January 19, 2020, https://www.reuters.com/article/us-china-health-pneumonia-factbox/factbox-what-we-know-about-the-new-coronavirus-spreading-in-china-and-beyond-idUSKBN1ZJ039.

5. Maureen Groppe and Ledyard King, "Virginia Becomes 38th State to Pass ERA for Women, Likely Setting up Issue for Courts," *USA Today*, January 15, 2020.

6. Stephen Engelberg, Lisa Song, and Lydia DePillis, "How South Korea Scaled Coronavirus Testing While the U.S. Fell Dangerously Behind," *ProPublica*, March 15, 2020.

7. Kim Bellware, Joel Achenbach, Katie Mettler, Alex Horton, and Meryl Kornfield, "Washington State Reports Second Death; First Case Confirmed in New York," *Washington Post*, March 1, 2020.

8. Johns Hopkins University, Center for Systems Science and Engineering, Coronavirus COVID-19 Dashboard, "Global Cases," https://www.arcgis.com/apps/opsdashboard/index.html#/bda7594740fd40299423467b48e9ecf6.

9. Doug Stanglin and Grace Hauck, "Washington State Declares Emergency after First Patient Dies from Coronavirus in US," *USA Today*, February 29, 2020.

10. Author's telephone interview with Hon. Laurie Jinkins, March 21, 2020.

11. In early February, Oliver sent a memo to the state's school superintendent suggesting that "schools should be prepared to meet the challenges the novel coronavirus may create" (http://www.doe.virginia.gov/administrators/super intendents_memos/2020/index.shtml).

12. Author's telephone interview with Lilian Peake, September 10, 2020.

13. Virginia reported its first case on March 7, 2020, but its first death was not reported until March 13, one day after the legislature adjourned. By March 22 the state had 219 reported cases and three deaths. Virginia Department of Health, "COVID-19 in Virginia," http://www.vdh.virginia.gov/coronavirus/.

14. William Wan, "WHO Declares a Pandemic of Coronavirus Disease Covid-19," *Washington Post*, March 3, 2011. The CDC estimated that, between April 12, 2009, and April 10, 2010, the H1N1 influenza virus, the cause of the most recent worldwide pandemic, led to 274,304 hospitalizations and 12,469 deaths in the

United States alone. US Centers for Disease Control and Prevention, "2009 H1N1 Pandemic (H1N1pdm09 Virus)," https://www.cdc.gov/flu/pandemic-resources/2009-h1n1-pandemic.html.

15. "17 Coronavirus Cases in Virginia; Northam Declares State of Emergency," *Richmond Times-Dispatch*, March 12, 2020.

16. Katie Rogers, "Trump Now Claims He Always Knew the Coronavirus Would Be a Pandemic," *New York Times*, March 17, 2020. In September 2020 the public was made aware that Trump actually knew much earlier how serious the pandemic was likely to be. The details are recounted in Bob Woodward, *Rage* (New York: Simon & Schuster, 2020).

17. Blair Shiff, "Coronavirus Will Have 'Minimal Impact' on Us Economy, Larry Kudlow Says," *Fox Business*, January 29, 2020.

18. During a campaign rally in South Carolina on February 28, Mr. Trump accused Democrats and the news media of hysteria and of unfairly criticizing his administration by engaging in what he said was a political "hoax." Rogers, "Trump Now Claims He Always Knew the Coronavirus Would Be a Pandemic."

19. When Governor Inslee suggested that the president should follow the advice of the nation's scientists, Trump called him a "snake." Matthew Choi, "Trump Calls Inslee a 'Snake' over Criticism of Coronavirus Rhetoric," *Politico*, March 6, 2020.

20. Michael Ollove and Alex Brown, "States Have 'Immense' Powers to Fight Coronavirus," *Stateline* (blog), Pew Charitable Trusts, March 5, 2020, https://www.pewtrusts.org/en/research-and-analysis/blogs/stateline/2020/03/05/states-have-immense-powers-to-fight-coronavirus.

21. Kate Irby, "States Shouldn't Fight over Coronavirus Equipment, Gavin Newsom Says. Should Trump Take Charge?," *Sacramento Bee*, March 26, 2020.

22. Lenny Bernstein, "Did Ohio Get It Right? Early Intervention, Preparation for Pandemic May Pay Off," *Washington Post*, April 10, 2020.

23. Jesse McKinley and Edgar Sandoval, "Coronavirus in N.Y.: Cuomo Declares State of Emergency," *New York Times*, March 7, 2020.

24. Sarah Maslin Nir and Jesse McKinley, "'Containment Area' Is Ordered for New Rochelle Coronavirus Cluster," *New York Times*, March 10, 2020.

25. Alexa Lardieri, "New York Bans Large Gatherings, Closes Broadway as Coronavirus Spreads," *US News*, March 12, 2020.

26. Taylor Goldenstein, "Gov. Abbott Activates Texas National Guard for Coronavirus Response," *Houston Chronicle*, March 17, 2020.

27. "Map: Coronavirus and School Closures," *Education Week*, March 20, 2020.

28. Julie Carr Smyth and Terry Spencer, "Health Chief Halts Ohio Primary; 3 Other States Forge Ahead," *AP News*, March 17, 2020.

29. National Conference of State Legislatures, "2020 State Legislative Session Calendar," March 20, 2020, https://www.ncsl.org/research/about-state-legislatures/2020-state-legislative-session-calendar.aspx.

30. Some notable exceptions included Missouri governor Mike Parson, who said staying at home was a matter of "individual responsibilities," Arkansas governor Asa

Hutchinson, who asserted there was nothing "magical" about such directives, and Iowa governor Kim Reynolds, who proclaimed, "I can't lock everybody in their home." Quoted in Editorial Board, "Foot-Dragging GOP Governors Are Imperiling the Whole Country," *Washington Post,* April 4, 2020.

31. Bill Chappell, "8 in 10 Americans Support COVID-19 Shutdown, Kaiser Health Poll Finds," NPR, April 23, 2020, https://www.npr.org/sections/coronavirus -live-updates/2020/04/23/843175656/8-in-10-americans-support-covid-19 -shutdown-kaiser-health-poll-finds?utm_medium=RSS&utm_campaign=npr blogscoronavirusliveupdates.

32. Michelle L. Price and Scott Sonner, "Nevada Governor Shutters Gambling, Dining to Halt Virus," *AP News,* March 15, 2020.

33. Bernadette Hogan, Julia Marsh, and Nolan Hicks, "Coronavirus in NY: Cuomo Orders Lockdown, Shuts Down Non-Essential Businesses," *New York Post,* March 20, 2020.

34. Taryn Luna, "Gov. Newsom Orders All Californians to Stay Home as Coronavirus Cases Top 1,000," *Los Angeles Times,* March 20, 2020.

35. John Cassidy, "The Most Alarming Thing about the Worst Jobs Report in History," *New Yorker,* May 8, 2020.

36. Paul Roberts, "Washington's Unemployment System Flooded with Claims as Coronavirus Fallout Grows," *Seattle Times,* March 22, 2020.

37. Ned Oliver, "Unemployment Claims in Virginia Spiked 1,500% This Week," *Virginia Mercury,* March 20, 2020.

38. Michael Martz, "Virginia May Take $1 Billion Annual Revenue Hit in New Budget Because of Coronavirus," *Richmond Times-Dispatch,* Mar 24, 2020.

39. "U.S. Leading Indicator Points to Deep Economic Slump," Reuters, April 17, 2020, https://www.reuters.com/article/us-usa-economy-leadingindicator/u-s -leading-indicator-points-to-deep-economic-slump-idUSKBN21Z2EP.

40. Kelsey Piper and Christina Animashaun , "Why We're Not Overreacting to the Coronavirus, in One Chart," *Vox,* March 20, 2020.

41. Erik Gunn, "'We Put the Value of Human Life at a Higher Level,'" *Wisconsin Examiner,* March 25, 2020.

42. Bill Scher, "Coronavirus vs. Governors: Ranking the Best and Worst State Leaders," *Politico,* April 1, 2020.

43. *Seattle Times* Staff, "Coronavirus Daily News Updates, March 26: What to Know Today about Covid-19 in the Seattle Area, Washington State and the Nation," *Seattle Times,* March 26, 2020.

44. Quint Forgey, Gabby Orr, Nancy Cook, and Caitline Oprysko, "'I'd Love to Have It Open by Easter': Trump Says He Wants to Restart Economy by Mid-April," *Politico,* March 24, 2020. Trump further exclaimed, "You are going to lose a number of people to the flu, but you are going to lose more people by putting a country into a massive recession or depression."

45. James Urton, "US Approaching Peak of 'Active' Covid-19 Cases, Strain on Medical Resources, New Modeling Shows," *UW News,* April 10, 2020.

46. Dan Goldberg, "Governors' Coronavirus Pacts Could Thwart Trump Goal of Reopening Country," *Politico,* March 27, 2020.

47. A summary of the president's misstatements during the early days of the crisis are chronicled in Christian Paz, "All the President's Lies about the Coronavirus," *Atlantic,* March 24, 2020.

48. Matt Zapotosky, "Barr Calls Lockdown Measures 'Draconian,' and Suggests They Should Be Revisited Next Month," *Washington Post,* April 9, 2020.

49. White House Coronavirus Task Force Briefing, C-Span, April 13, 2020, at 1:09:31, https://www.c-span.org/video/?471160–1/white-house-coronavirus-task-force-briefing.

50. William A. Galston, "Trump or Governors: Who's the Boss?," *FixGov* (blog), Brookings Institution, March 25, 2020, https://www.brookings.edu/blog/fixgov/2020/03/25/trump-or-governors-whos-the-boss/; and Robert Chesney, "Can the Federal Government Override State Government Rules on Social Distancing to Promote the Economy?," *Lawfare* (blog), Lawfare Institute in cooperation with Brookings Institution, March 24, 2020, https://www.lawfareblog.com/can-federal-government-override-state-government-rules-social-distancing-promote-economy.

51. A Gallup poll reported 10 percent of respondents would wait indefinitely, another 20 percent said they would return to their normal activities immediately, and over 70 percent would wait and see what happened with the spread of the virus before they did anything. Lydia Saad, "Americans Remain Risk Averse about Getting Back to Normal," Gallup, April 14, 2020, https://news.gallup.com/poll/308264/americans-remain-risk-averse-getting-back-normal.aspx?utm_source=alert&utm_medium=email&utm_content=morelink&utm_campaign=syndication.

52. Dhrumil Mehta, "Most Americans Like How Their Governor Is Handling the Coronavirus Outbreak," FiveThirtyEight, April 10, 2020, https://fivethirtyeight.com/features/most-americans-like-how-their-governor-is-handling-the-coronavirus-outbreak/.

53. Justin Mattingly, "76% of Virginians Approve of Northam's Response to Pandemic, VCU Poll Says," *Roanoke Times,* April 15, 2020.

54. Laurie Sobel, Amrutha Ramaswamy, Brittni Frederiksen, and Alina Salganicoff, "State Action to Limit Abortion Access during the COVID-19 Pandemic," Kaiser Family Foundation, April 14, 2020, https://www.kff.org/womens-health-policy/issue-brief/state-action-to-limit-abortion-access-during-the-covid-19-pandemic/.

55. At its reconvened session in April 2020, the Virginia General Assembly accepted Northam's recommendation that delayed the increase in the minimum wage by eight months. Ned Oliver, Kate Masters, and Robert Zullo, "Lawmakers Delay Minimum Wage, Maintain Election Schedule in Extraordinary Session," *Virginia Mercury,* April 23, 2020.

56. Orders in Pennsylvania, Delaware, New Jersey, Michigan, Massachusetts, New Mexico, New York, and Washington initially required gun stores to close while

stay-at-home orders were in effect. Most other states allowed them to remain open. See Jacob Fischler, "COVID-19 Pandemic Fuels State Feuds over Gun Rights," *AZ Mirror*, April 23, 2020.

57. Todd Richmond, "Wisconsin High Court Tosses Out Governor's Stay-Home Order," *Star Tribune*, May 14, 2020. The Michigan Supreme Court took similar action that summer. By late November, legislation was introduced in at least twenty-six states to limit governors' powers or executive spending during the COVID-19 pandemic or other emergencies. Such bills or resolutions were adopted in at least eight states, including a proposed constitutional amendment limiting the governor's power in Pennsylvania.

58. Alex Samuels, "For Some, Forgoing Masks in Public during the Coronavirus Pandemic Has Become a Political Statement," *Texas Tribune*, May 22, 2020.

59. Shefali Luthra, "Donald Trump's Claim That US Tested More than All Countries Combined Is Pants on Fire Wrong," *Politifact*, April 30, 2020.

60. Johns Hopkins University, Coronavirus Resource Center, "All State Comparison of Testing Efforts," n.d., https://coronavirus.jhu.edu/testing/states-comparison.

61. Mark J. Rozell, "Northam Stumbles through a Crisis That Should Have Made Him a Rock Star," *Washington Post*, May 22, 2020.

62. Fenit Nirappil, Erin Cox, and Gregory S. Schneider, "With Focus on Testing, Maryland Buys 500,000 Coronavirus Test Kits from South Korea," *Washington Post*, April 20, 2020.

63. Alex Brown, "Washington State to Buy 1M Chinese Test Swabs in Bid to Reopen," *Stateline* (blog), Pew Charitable Trusts, April 23, 2020 https://www.pewtrusts.org/en/research-and-analysis/blogs/stateline/2020/04/23/washington-state-to-buy-1m-chinese-test-swabs-in-bid-to-reopen?utm_campaign=2020-4-23+SD&utm_medium=email&utm_source=Pew.

64. Hayley C. Cuccinello, "Michael Bloomberg Contributes $10.5 Million to Tri-State COVID-19 Tracing Program," *Forbes*, April 20, 2020.

65. "Five Questions for Northam," editorial, *Roanoke Times*, April 23, 2020.

66. Brian Resnick, "4 Reasons State Plans to Open up May Backfire—and Soon," *Vox*, May 9, 2020.

67. Donald G. McNeil Jr., "As States Rush to Reopen, Scientists Fear a Coronavirus Comeback," *New York Times*, May 11, 2020.

68. Bobby Harrison, "Legislature's Top Leaders Test Positive for Coronavirus," *Mississippi Today*, July 7, 2020.

69. Erin Cox, "There's No National Testing Strategy for Coronavirus. These States Banded Together to Make One," *Washington Post*, August 4, 2020.

70. Tucker Doherty, Victoria Guida, Bianca Quilantan, and Gabrielle Wanneh, "Which States Had the Best Pandemic Response?" *Politico*, October 15, 2020, https://www.politico.com/news/2020/10/14/best-state-responses-to-pandemic-429376?cid=apn.

71. A comparison of policies and requirements can be found in National Academy

for State Health Policy, "Chart: Each State's COVID-19 Reopening and Reclos-
ing Plans and Mask Requirements" (updated October 16, 2020), https://www
.nashp.org/governors-prioritize-health-for-all/, and Kaiser Family Foundation,
"State Data and Policy Actions to Address Coronavirus," Oct 23, 2020, https://
www.kff.org/coronavirus-covid-19/issue-brief/state-data-and-policy-actions
-to-address-coronavirus/.

72. Deborah Berkowitz, "Which States and Cities Have Adopted Comprehensive
COVID-19 Worker Protections?," NELP, October 23, 2020, https://www.nelp
.org/blog/which-states-cities-have-adopted-comprehensive-covid-19-worker
-protections/.

73. David R. Baker, Angelica LaVito, and Elise Young, "America Locks Down from
Atlantic to Pacific as Covid Rages," *Bloomberg News*, November 16, 2020.

74. "COVID-19 Restrictions: Map of COVID-19 Case Trends, Restrictions and
Mobility," *USA Today*, November 21, 2020.

75. Rebecca Cooper, Ariella Levisohn, Trish Riley, and Jill Rosenthal, "With Federal
Guidance Evolving and Vaccine Supplies Uncertain, States' COVID-19 Vaccine
Distribution Plans Remain Works in Progress," National Academy for State
Health Policy, December 8, 2020.

## 2. Laboratories of Democracy

1. "Just 37% of Americans Can Name Their Representative," Haven Insights, May
31, 2017, https://www.haveninsights.com/just-37-percent-name-representative/.
See also Elizabeth Mendes, "Americans Down on Congress, OK with Own Representative," Gallup poll, May 9, 2013, https://news.gallup.com/poll/162362
/americans-down-congress-own-representative.aspx.

2. Kendall Breitman, "Poll: Majority of Millennials Can't Name a Senator from
Their Home State," *Politico*, February 3, 2015.

3. "JHU Survey: Americans Don't Know Much about State Government," press
release, Johns Hopkins University, December 11, 2018, https://releases.jhu.edu
/2018/12/11/jhu-survey-americans-dont-know-much-about-state-government/.

4. Katerina Eva Matsa and Jan Lauren Boyles, "America's Shifting Statehouse
Press," Pew Research Center (Journalism and Media), July 10, 2014, http://www
.journalism.org/2014/07/10/americas-shifting-statehouse-press/.

5. Daniel J. Hopkins, *The Increasingly United States: How and Why American
Political Behavior Nationalized* (Chicago: University of Chicago Press, 2018).
Hopkins found, in looking at eight southern states, that congressional races
are becoming increasingly nationalized and that voters are looking less at their
personal relationship with their incumbent and more at the salient national
issues at the time.

6. Lilliana Mason, *Uncivil Agreement: How Politics Became Our Identity* (Chicago:
University of Chicago Press, 2018). Mason reviewed data from the American
National Election Studies (ANES) and found that the major political parties have
been growing more ideologically distinct from each other for the last several

decades, with the Republican ideological identity rising in greater strength than the Democratic ideological identity. In Mason's view, factors such as class, race, religion, gender, and sexuality used to cut across one another politically. More recently, she believes, there is a growing alignment of partisan and ideological views based on identity factors such as race, ethnicity, and religiosity.

7. Aaron Bycoffe and Dhrumil Mehta, "How Popular/Unpopular Is Trump?" (as of May 23, 2019), FiveThirtyEight, https://projects.fivethirtyeight.com/trump-approval-ratings/.

8. Megan Brenan, "Trump Approval Edges Down to 42%," Gallup poll, May 17, 2019, https://news.gallup.com/poll/257645/trump-approval-edges-down.aspx.

9. Alan I. Abramowitz, *The Great Alignment: Race, Party Transformation, and the Rise of Donald Trump* (New Haven, CT: Yale University Press, 2018). In Virginia, Rachel Bitecofer of Christopher Newport University's Wason Center recently gained national attention with her argument that there are few, if any, "swing voters." See Rachel Bitecofer," Hate Is on the Ballot," *New Republic*, February 26, 2020; and David Freedlander, "An Unsettling New Theory: There Is No Swing Voter," *Politico*, February 6, 2020.

10. Abby Vesoulis, "The 2018 Elections Saw Record Midterm Turnout," *Time*, November 13, 2018.

11. Virginia Department of Elections, "Summary of Virginia Registration and Turn-out Statistics," https://www.elections.virginia.gov/resultsreports/registration-statistics/registrationturnout-statistics/index.html. Graph created by the *Virginia Mercury*.

12. US Burden of Disease Collaborators, "The State of US Health, 1990–2016: Burden of Diseases, Injuries, and Risk Factors among US States," *Journal of the American Medical Association* 319, no. 14 (2018): 1444–72, tables 3 and 4.

13. Sentencing Project, "The Facts: State-by-State Data, State Rankings, State Imprisonment Rates," https://www.sentencingproject.org/the-facts/#rankings?dataset-option=SIR. For an earlier comparison, see Adam Liptak, "Inmate Count in U.S. Dwarfs Other Nations'," *New York Times*, April 23, 2008 ("Maine has the lowest incarceration rate in the United States, at 273 [people per 100,000]; and Louisiana the highest, at 1,138").

14. Data USA, "COVID-19 in Numbers: South Carolina, New York," https://datausa.io/profile/geo/south-carolina/?compare=new-york.

15. Madeline Will, "Which States Have the Highest and Lowest Teacher Salaries?," *Education Week*, April 30, 2019.

16. Chapter 14, section 72(a) of the North Carolina General Statutes, https://www.ncleg.gov/EnactedLegislation/Statutes/PDF/BySection/Chapter_14/GS_14-72.pdf, and chapter 15A, section 1340.23 N.C.G.S., https://www.ncleg.gov/EnactedLegislation/Statutes/PDF/BySection/Chapter_15A/GS_15A-1340.23.pdf.

17. See Law LIS (Legislative Information System), "Virginia Law," chapter 5, section 18, https://law.lis.virginia.gov/vacode/title18.2/chapter5/section18.2-95/. The felony threshold was raised in 2020 to $1,000.

18. Samuel Stebbins, "Dangerous States: Which States Have the Highest Rates of Violent Crime and Most Murders?," *USA Today,* January 13, 2020.

19. Elisabeth Garber-Paul and Tana Ganeva, "The State-by-State Guide to Weed in America," *Rolling Stone,* April 20, 2018.

20. Gregory S. Schneider, "Two Cities Share a Name, Water and a Library. But One Is in Big Trouble," *Washington Post,* July 9, 2018.

21. A national report ranking state funding for higher education showed that between 2013 and 2018, Wisconsin saw the fourth largest decline in per student spending of all the states. The only states with larger decreases in that time frame were Mississippi, West Virginia, and Oklahoma. See State Higher Education Executive Officers Association, *State Higher Education Finance: FY 2018* (Boulder, CO: State Higher Education Executive Officers Association, 2019), https://sheeo.org/wp-content/uploads/2019/04/SHEEO_SHEF_FY18_Report.pdf.

22. David Cooper, "As Wisconsin's and Minnesota's Lawmakers Took Divergent Paths, So Did Their Economies," Economic Policy Institute, May 8, 2018, https://www.epi.org/publication/as-wisconsins-and-minnesotas-lawmakers-took-divergent-paths-so-did-their-economies-since-2010-minnesotas-economy-has-performed-far-better-for-working-families-than-wisconsin/.

23. More recently, the two states have charted difference paths on energy policy. Minnesota has been more aggressive in promoting renewable energy than the Badger State. Chris Hubbuch, "Border Battles: When It Comes to Clean Energy, Minnesota Outshines Wisconsin," *Wisconsin State Journal,* January 5, 2020.

24. National Consumer Law Center, "Major Consumer Protections Announced in Response to COVID-19," June 17, 2020, https://library.nclc.org/major-consumer-protections-announced-response-covid-19#content-1.

25. Dan Keating and Lauren Tierney, "Which States Are Doing a Better Job Protecting Renters from Being Evicted during the Coronavirus Pandemic?," *Washington Post,* April 29, 2020.

26. Kelly Bauer, "New $900 Million Coronavirus Recovery Programs Will Focus on Businesses, Rent Relief and More," Block Club Chicago, June 17, 2020, https://blockclubchicago.org/2020/06/17/state-announces-new-900-million-coronavirus-recovery-fund-for-businesses-renters-and-more/. Decisions were being made state by state, with implications for millions.

27. Teresa Wiltz, "As COVID-19 Tanks the Economy, Eviction Moratoriums Expire," *Stateline* (blog), Pew Charitable Trusts, August 6, 2020, https://www.pewtrusts.org/en/research-and-analysis/blogs/stateline/2020/08/06/as-covid-19-tanks-the-economy-eviction-moratoriums-expire?utm_campaign=2020-08-06+SD&utm_medium=email&utm_source=Pew.

28. Sean Williams, "The Average Social Security Benefit Goes Farther in These 10 States," Motley Fool, March 15, 2019.

29. Wyoming has no income, estate, or inheritance taxes, and the average combined state and local sales tax rate is only 5.32 percent. See Rocky Mengle and

David Muhlbaum, "10 Most Tax-Friendly States for Retirees, 2019," *Kiplinger*, November 5, 2019.

30. Cheyenne Buckingham and Grant Suneson of 24/7wallst.com, "Where Is the Best Place to Live in America? All 50 States Ranked," *USA Today*, November 6, 2018. Original article published November 2, 2018, by 24/7 Wall Street and available at https://247wallst.com/special-report/2018/11/02/americas-best-states-to-live-in-3/.

31. "Best States Rankings," *U.S. News & World Report*, https://www.usnews.com/news/best-states/rankings (accessed June 19, 2019).

32. "America's Top States for Business 2018," CNBC, July 10, 2018, https://www.cnbc.com/2018/07/10/americas-top-states-for-business-2018.html; "Amazon Had It Right: Virginia Is America's Top State for Business in 2019," CNBC, July 10, 2019, https://www.cnbc.com/2019/07/09/virginia-is-americas-top-state-for-business-in-2019.html.

33. Adam McCann, "Happiest States in America," *WalletHub*, September 10, 2018, https://wallethub.com/edu/happiest-states/6959/.

34. *Smart Asset*, a financial advising periodical, consistently ranks the common-wealth as among the best states for higher education; in 2019, it was rated the "best state for higher education." Derek Miller, "Top States for Higher Education—2019 Edition," *Smart Asset*, March 5, 2019, https://smartasset.com/checking-account/top-states-for-higher-education-2019.

35. "How States Compare in the 2019 Best High Schools Rankings," *U.S. News & World Report*, April 29, 2019, https://www.usnews.com/education/best-high-schools/articles/how-states-compare.

36. Lauren Harmon, Charles Posner, Michele L. Jawando, and Matt Dhaiti, *The Health of State Democracies* (Washington, DC: Center for American Progress Action Fund, 2015).

37. Oxfam America, *The Best States to Work Index: A Guide to Labor Policy in US States* (Washington, DC: Oxfam America, 2018).

38. By Virginia FREE's tally, Virginia is the sixth best state for workers (based on the assemblage of rankings from other sources, catalogued at https://files.constant contact.com/005ceb5f201/f415139e-f39d-4946-a3c0-1b4773b3f3c0.pdf).

39. Among the groups taking this view is the Thomas Jefferson Institute for Public Policy (https://www.thomasjeffersoninst.org/).

40. United Health Foundation, *America's Health Rankings Annual Report*, 2019, www.AmericasHealthRankings.org. Vermont, Massachusetts, Hawaii, Connecticut, and Utah were ranked in top five; Oklahoma, Alabama, Arkansas, Louisiana, and Mississippi were ranked the lowest. Virginia ranked fifteenth best in the latest ranking.

41. Kim Keating, Sarah Daily, Patricia Cole, David Murphey, Gabriel Pina, Renee Ryberg, Leanna Moron, and Jessie Laurore, *State of Babies Yearbook: 2019* (Washington, DC: Zero to Three; Bethesda, MD: Child Trends, 2019).

42. Keating et al., *State of Babies Yearbook: 2019*, 26; data source, Appendix B, 261.

(Source from which *State of Babies Yearbook: 2019* got this information: Centers for Disease Control and Prevention, "Infant Mortality Rates by State, 2016," https://www.cdc.gov/nchs/pressroom/sosmap/infant_mortality_rates/infant_mortality.htm.)

43. Annie E. Casey Foundation, *2019 KIDS COUNT Data Book: State Trends in Child Well-Being* (Baltimore, MD: Annie E. Casey Foundation, 2019). The report measures child well-being in four general areas: (1) economic well-being, (2) education, (3) health, and (4) family and community.

44. "If You're an Average American, You'll Live to Be 78.6 Years Old," *National Geographic,* December 7, 2018. There are large regional differences as well. People residing in politically "red" states die, on average, five years earlier than those who live in "blue" states. Arlie Russell Hochschild, *Strangers in Their Own Land: Anger and Mourning on the American Right* (New York: New Press, 2018), 8.

45. In 2017, Gillespie lost a bid to become Virginia governor to Ralph Northam.

46. Vann R. Newkirk II, "How Redistricting Became a Technological Arms Race," *Atlantic,* October 28, 2017, referencing David Daley, *Ratf\*\*ked: Why Your Vote Doesn't Count* (New York: Liveright, 2016).

47. Dan Balz, "The Republican Takeover in the States," *Washington Post,* November 14, 2010.

48. At that time, there were two independents serving in the House, but both, Lacey Putney and Watkins Abbitt, caucused with the Republicans.

49. Ally Mutnick, "Democrats Stockpile Cash for State-by-State Redistricting Fight," *Politico,* December 19, 2019.

50. Scott Bland, "Scott Walker Joins GOP Redistricting Group as Finance Chair," *Politico,* March 21, 2019.

51. See Matt Vasilogambros, "The Tumultuous Life of an Independent Redistricting Commissioner," *Stateline* (blog), Pew Charitable Trusts, November 26, 2019, https://www.pewtrusts.org/en/research-and-analysis/blogs/stateline/2019/11/26/the-tumultuous-life-of-an-independent-redistricting-commissioner. They differ in structure and operation. See Brennan Center for Justice, "Redistricting Commissions: What Works" (New York University School of Law, n.d.), https://www.brennancenter.org/sites/default/files/analysis/Redistricting%20Commissions%20-%20What%20Works.pdf.

52. Vasilogambros, "The Tumultuous Life of an Independent Redistricting Commissioner." IRCs differ in structure and operation. See Brennan Center for Justice, "Redistricting Commissions."

53. For an amendment to be added to the Virginia Constitution, the legislature has to pass the measure in two successive sessions separated by an election. The proposed amendment then goes before the voters in the next election for approval or rejection.

54. Gregory S. Schneider, "Divided Democrats in Virginia House Pass Proposed Amendment for Redistricting Commission," *Washington Post,* March 6, 2020.

## 3. State Constitutions Matter

1. Robert F. Williams, *The Law of American State Constitutions* (New York: Oxford University Press, 2009). The more recent study found that 63 percent were not aware that their state had its own constitution. "JHU Survey: Americans Don't Know Much about State Government," press release, Johns Hopkins University, December 14, 2018, https://releases.jhu.edu/2018/12/11/jhu-survey -americans-dont-know-much-about-state-government/.

2. Jeffrey S. Sutton, *51 Imperfect Solutions: States and the Making of American Constitutional Law* (New York: Oxford University Press, 2018). Sutton is a judge of the US Court of Appeals for the Sixth Circuit.

3. John Dinan, *State Constitutional Politics: Governing by Amendment in the American States* (Chicago: University of Chicago Press, 2018).

4. Emily Parker, "50 State Review: Constitutional Obligations for Public Education," Education Commission of the States, March 2016, https://www.ecs.org/ wp-content/uploads/2016-Constitutional-obligations-for-public-education-1.pdf.

5. Constitution of Alabama, 1901, Section 256.

6. Julia Zebley, "Alabama Voters Decline to Remove Racist Language from Constitution over Right to Education Concerns," *Jurist*, November 7, 2012, https:// www.jurist.org/news/2012/11/alabama-voters-decline-to-remove-racist-language -from-constitution-over-right-to-education-conerns/.

7. California Constitution, Article I, Section 1.

8. Constitution of Virginia, Article V, Section 1.

9. National Conference on State Legislatures, "State Balanced Budget Provisions," October 2010, https://www.ncsl.org/documents/fiscal/StateBalanced BudgetProvisions2010.pdf. Four other states include such a provision in their state statutes, not their constitutions. Vermont does not include a requirement in its state constitution or its state law. In 2018, Indiana voters added a provision to its constitution requiring a balanced budget. See Domenica Bongiovanni, "Indiana's Balanced Budget Amendment, Championed by Mike Pence, Easily Passes," *Indianapolis Star*, November 6, 2018.

10. National Conference on State Legislatures, Center for Legislative Strengthening, "State Legislative Policymaking in an Age of Political Polarization," February 2018, 11, https://www.ncsl.org/Portals/1/Documents/About_State _Legislatures/Partisanship_030818.pdf.

11. Journals of the Continental Congress—Letter from the Provincial Convention of Massachusetts; June 2, 1775, Yale Law School Avalon Project, https://avalon .law.yale.edu/18th_century/contcong_06-02-75.asp.

12. Quoted in Jerrilyn Greene Marston, *King and Congress: The Transfer of Political Legitimacy, 1774–1776* (Princeton, NJ: Princeton University Press, 1987), 263.

13. G. Alan Tarr, "State Constitutional Design and Interpretation," *Montana Law Review* 72, no. 1 (Winter 2011): 8–26.

14. Tarr, "State Constitutional Design and Interpretation," 13.

15. Scott L. Kafker, "America's Other Constitutions: Book Review of *The Law of American State Constitutions*" (quoting *Federalist* No. 45), *New England Law Review* 45, no. 4 (2011): 835, 839.

16. Detailed expositions of the nature of state constitutions can be found in Robert F. Williams, *The Law of American State Constitutions* (New York: Oxford University Press, 2009); G. Alan Tarr, *Understanding State Constitutions* (Princeton, NJ: Princeton University Press, 1998); John Dinan, "State Constitutional Developments," in *The Book of the States* (2009); and *The Oxford Commentaries on the State Constitutions of the United States*, 45 vols., edited by G. Alan Tarr (New York: Oxford University Press, 2011).

17. *Goodridge v. Dept. of Public Health*, 798 N.E.2d 941 (Mass. 2003). This is the argument made in Jeffrey S. Sutton, Randy J. Holland, Stephen R. McAllister, and Jeffrey M. Shaman, *State Constitutional Law: The Modern Experience*, 3rd ed., American Casebook Series (Eagan, MN: West, 2019).

18. Elizabeth Weeks Leonard, "State Constitutionalism and the Right to Health Care," *Journal of Constitutional Law* 12, no. 5 (2010).

19. David M. Primo, "State Constitutions and Fiscal Policy" (Arlington, VA: George Mason University, Mercatus Center, August 2016), http://www.sas.rochester .edu/psc/primo/PrimoStateConstMercatus2016.pdf.

20. Mike Baker, "Oregon Republicans Disappear for Another Climate Vote," *New York Times*, February 24, 2020.

21. Emily Parker, "50 State Review: Constitutional Obligations for Public Education," Education Commission of the States, March 2016, https://www.ecs.org /wp-content/uploads/2016-Constitutional-obligations-for-public-education -1.pdf.

22. Minnesota Constitution, Article XIII, Section 1; Pennsylvania Constitution, Article III, part B, Section 14; Colorado Constitution, Article IX, Section 2.

23. At the Constitutional Commission that drafted the current Virginia constitution in 1971, there was considerable discussion about including language that would require "an educational program of high quality" rather than the current wording that the state "shall seek to ensure" it. Ultimately, any duty to provide a certain level of quality was rejected in favor of aspirational language. See A. E. Dick Howard, *Commentaries on the Constitution of Virginia*, vol. 2 (Charlottesville: University of Virginia Press, 1974), 895–97.

24. *Reid Scott, et al. v. Commonwealth of Virginia*, 247 Va. 379, 443 S.E.2d 138 (1994).

25. The case was styled *Luke Gannon, by his next friends and guardians, et al. v. State of Kansas, et al.*, and has come to be known as "Gannon."

26. Erik Eckholm, "Outraged by Kansas Justices' Rulings, Republicans Seek to Reshape Court," *New York Times*, April 1, 2016.

27. Associated Press, "Frustrated Kansas GOP Lawmakers Weigh Move to Impeach Top Judges," *Kansas City Star*, March 7, 2016.

28. Dion Lefler, Hunter Woodall, Katy Bergen, and Suzanne Tobias, "Kansas School Funding Still Inadequate, Supreme Court Says," *Kansas City Star*, June 25, 2018.

29. Jonathan Shorman, "'I've Been There, Done That': Laura Kelly Navigates GOP Skepticism to Score Early Wins," *Wichita Eagle*, April 23, 2019.

30. Jonathan Shorman and Dion Lefler, "Kansas School Funding Is Adequate, High Court Says. But Justices Still Will Oversee Case," *Wichita Eagle*, June 14, 2019.

31. Erica Bryant, "Do Lawsuits Have a Good Track Record in Forcing Education Reforms?." *Rochester Democrat and Chronicle*, April 11, 2019. In New Mexico, for example, a state court ruled in 2018 that the level of school funding was violating provisions of the state's constitution by providing insufficient funding for at-risk students. Dan McKay and Shelby Perea, "New Mexico Loses Education Lawsuit," *Albuquerque Journal*, July 20, 2018.

32. Jack R. Tuholske, "U.S. State Constitutions and Environmental Protection: Diamonds in the Rough," *Widener Law Review* 21 (2015): 239–55.

33. Oliver A. Pollard, "A Promise Unfulfilled: Environmental Provisions in State Constitutions and the Self-Execution Question," *Virginia Journal of Natural Resources Law* 5, no. 2 (1986): 351–81. See *Rudder v. Wise County Redevelopment & Hous. Auth.*, 219 Va. 592, 249 S.E.2d 177 (1978) and *Robb v. Shockoe Slip Found.*, 228 Va 678, 324 S.E.2d 674 (1985), for further discussion of what it means to be a "self executing" clause of the Virginia Constitution.

34. Tuholske, "U.S. State Constitutions and Environmental Protection," 241.

35. *Montana Environmental Information Center ("MEIC") v. Department of Environmental Quality*, 988 P.2d 1236 (Mont. 1999).

36. *Robinson Twp. v. Commonwealth*, 623 Pa. 564, 83 A.3d 901 (Pa. 2013).

37. See *Mauna Kea Anaina Hou v. Bd. of Land & Nat. Res.*, 136 Haw. 376 (2015); *County of Hawaii v. Ala Loop Homeowners*, 123 Haw. 391 (2010).

38. In 2018 alone, Alabama voters approved four constitutional amendments.

39. For an overview and state-by-state explanation, see "Amending State Constitutions," *Ballotpedia*, https://ballotpedia.org/Amending_state_constitutions (accessed June 27, 2019).

40. Following passage of the amendment, the state legislature passed a law requiring former felons to pay the fines and fee payments associated with their convictions prior to formal restoration, sparking major controversy and lawsuits. Nina Totenburg, "Supreme Court Deals Major Blow to Felons' Right to Vote in Florida," NPR, July 17, 2020.

41. J. Brian Charles, "Ten Commandments Amendment Cruises to Victory in Alabama," *Governing*, November 7, 2018.

42. Candice Norwood, "'People Want Their Power Back:' Voters Approve Redistricting Reforms," *Governing*, November 7, 2018.

43. For more on citizen initiatives, see the USC Gould School of Law's Initiative & Referendum Institute website at http://www.iandrinstitute.org/. According to IRI's research, a total of 2,609 state-level initiatives have been on the ballot since the first ones went before the voters in Oregon in 1904, and 1,079 (41 percent) have been approved. "Overview of Initiative Use, 1900–2018," IRI,

January 2019, http://www.iandrinstitute.org/docs/IRI%20Initiative%20Use%20(1904–2018).pdf.

44. Vann R. Newkirk II, "American Voters Are Turning to Direct Democracy," *Atlantic*, April 18, 2018.

45. News Staff, "The Most Important Ballot Measure Results," *Governing*, October 3, 2018 (last updated November 7, 2018).

46. IRI, "Overview of Initiative Use, 1900–2019," December 2019, http://www.iandrinstitute.org/docs/IRI%20Initiative%20Use%20(1904-2018).pdf.

47. On Florida increasing the minimum wage, see Lawrence Mower, Sara DiNatale and Carlos Frias, "Florida Voters Passed a Minimum Wage Increase. What Does That Mean?," *Tampa Bay Times*, November 4, 2020. On Nevada's amendment to obtain electricity from renewable sources, see David Roberts, "Nevada Voters Seal Renewable Energy Goals in Their State Constitution," *Vox*, November 4, 2020, https://www.vox.com/2020/11/4/21536321/nevada-question-6-renewable-energy-results.

48. IRI, "Overview of Initiative Use, 1900–2019."

49. Virginia Department of Elections, "2016 November General Election Official Results" for proposed constitutional amendment Question 1, last modified December 1, 2016, https://results.elections.virginia.gov/vaelections/2016%20November%20General/Site/Referendums.html. Noam Scheider, "Missouri Voters Reject Anti-Union Law in a Victory for Labor," *New York Times*, August 7, 2018.

50. Virginia Department of Elections, Elections Database, Ballot Questions, 2006, https://historical.elections.virginia.gov/ballot_questions/search/year_from:2006/year_to:2006/type:is_amendment (accessed June 25, 2019).

51. Virginia Department of Elections, Elections Database, Ballot Questions, 2006, https://historical.elections.virginia.gov/ballot_questions/search/year_from:2006/year_to:2006/type:is_amendment (accessed June 25, 2019).

52. *Bostic v. Schaefer*, 760 F.3d 352 (4th Cir. 2014).

53. *Obergefell v. Hodges*, 135 S.Ct. 2584 (2015).

54. The costs of the 2006 marriage amendments, state by state, are detailed in Megan Moore, "The Money Behind the 2006 Marriage Amendments," National Institute on Money in Politics (FollowTheMoney.org), July 23, 2007, https://www.followthemoney.org/research/institute-reports/the-money-behind-the-2006-marriage-amendments. In Virginia, almost $2 million was spent, two-thirds of which was in opposition to the amendment.

55. Jack Healy, "Voters Ease Marijuana Laws in 2 States, but Legal Questions Remain," *New York Times*, November 7, 2012.

56. Sarah Rense, "Here Are All the States That Have Legalized Weed in the U.S.," *Esquire*, June 27, 2019.

57. Sophie Quinton, "Voters Approve Marijuana Measures in Five States," *Stateline* (blog), Pew Charitable Trusts, November 4, 2020, https://www.pewtrusts.org/en/research-and-analysis/blogs/stateline/2020/11/04/voters-approve

-marijuana-measures-in-five-states?utm_campaign=2020-11-04+SD&utm
_medium=email&utm_source=Pew.

58. Tom Angell, "These States Are Most Likely to Legalize Marijuana in 2019," *Forbes,* December 26, 2018.

59. Pat Evans, "8 Incredible Facts about the Booming US Marijuana Industry," *Markets Insider,* May 7, 2019; Bruce Barcott and Beau Whitney, "Special Report: Cannabis Jobs Count," Leafly, March 2019, https://d3atagtornqk7k.cloudfront .net/wp-content/uploads/2019/03/01141121/CANNABIS-JOBS-REPORT-FINAL -2.27.191.pdf.

60. Rense, "Here Are All the States That Have Legalized Weed in the U.S."

61. Emma Green, "What Tennessee's New Abortion Amendment Means for America," *Atlantic,* November 5, 2014. Under the Tennessee Constitution, an amendment will be added to the constitution if the number of yes votes exceeds 50 percent of all votes cast in the election. The vote was unsuccessfully challenged in federal court.

62. Emma Sarappo, "The Legal Strategy behind Alabama and West Virginia's New Anti-Abortion Amendments," *Pacific Standard,* November 7, 2018.

## 4. The Cards You Are Dealt

1. In Virginia, the state has historically provided massive tax subsidies to the coal industry to increase employment and production; ironically, the subsidies have done neither, but the coal companies and the utilities have nonetheless benefited from the state's largesse. David J. Toscano, "Toscano: Tough Choices about Coal Tax Credits," *Richmond Times Dispatch,* December 12, 2012.

2. Dylan Matthews, "The Sequester: Absolutely Everything You Could Possibly Need to Know, in One FAQ," *Washington Post,* March 3, 2013.

3. Jenna Portnoy, "McAuliffe Announces $2.4 billion Projected Budget Gap in Va.; Blames Defense Cuts," *Washington Post,* August 14, 2014.

4. "QuickFacts: California," population estimate July 1, 2019, US Census Bureau, www.census.gov/quickfacts/ca.

5. For data on the number of students enrolled in California's public schools, see "Fingertip Facts on Education in California—CalEdFacts," California Department of Education, 2018–19, www.cde.ca.gov/ds/sd/cb/ceffingertipfacts.asp. On Maryland's population, see "QuickFacts: Maryland," population estimate July 1, 2019, US Census Bureau QuickFacts, www.census.gov/quickfacts/md. On Wisconsin's population, see "QuickFacts: Wisconsin," population estimate July 1, 2019, US Census Bureau QuickFacts, www.census.gov/quickfacts/wi. On Colorado's population, see "QuickFacts: Colorado," population estimate July 1, 2019, US Census Bureau QuickFacts, www.census.gov/quickfacts/co.

6. For information on Florida, see "QuickFacts: Florida," age estimate July 1, 2019, US Census Bureau Quick Facts, www.census.gov/quickfacts/fact/table /fl/AGE775217#AGE775217. For information on Utah, see "QuickFacts: Utah,"

age estimate July 1, 2019, US Census Bureau QuickFacts, www.census.gov /quickfacts/ut.

7.  Florida Division of Elections, "Voter Turnout," https://dos.myflorida.com /elections/data-statistics/elections-data/voter-turnout/.

8.  For West Virginia's population ages, see QuickFacts: West Virginia," age estimate July 1, 2019, US Census Bureau QuickFacts, www.census.gov/quickfacts /wv. For Pennsylvania's population ages, see "QuickFacts: Pennsylvania," age estimate July 1, 2019, US Census Bureau QuickFacts, www.census.gov /quickfacts/pa. For Maine's, see "QuickFacts: Maine," age estimate July 1, 2019, US Census Bureau QuickFacts, www.census.gov/quickfacts/me.

9.  Jynnah Radford, "Key Findings about U.S. Immigrants," Pew Research Center, June 17, 2019, https://www.pewresearch.org/fact-tank/2019/06/17/key-findings -about-u-s-immigrants/.

10. Radford, "Key Findings about U.S. Immigrants."

11. Steven A. Camarota and Bryan Griffith, "Immigration Brief: The Numbers Matter" (Washington, DC: Center for Immigration Studies, January 13, 2020).

12. By 2019, Asian groups constituted approximately 6.9 percent of the Virginia population. See "QuickFacts: Virginia," Asian population estimate July 1, 2019, US Census Bureau QuickFacts, www.census.gov/quickfacts/va.

13. "QuickFacts: Fairfax County, Virginia," Asian population estimate July 1, 2019, US Census Bureau QuickFacts, www.census.gov/quickfacts/fairfax countyvirginia.

14. "QuickFacts: Prince William County, Virginia," Asian population estimate July 1, 2019, US Census Bureau QuickFacts, www.census.gov/quickfacts/prince williamcountyvirginia.

15. Kendra Sena, "Driver's Licenses and Undocumented Immigrants," Albany Law School Government Law Explainer, July 15, 2019 https://www.albanylaw .edu/centers/government-law-center/Immigration/explainers/Documents /DriversLicensesExplainer.pdf. Virginia was among the most recent states to enact this provision, the law taking effect on July 1, 2020.

16. Emma North, "Population Expected to Shrink in Rural Virginia," *Virginia Mercury*, September 19, 2019.

17. "New Census Bureau Report Analyzes U.S. Population Projections," US Census Bureau, January 7, 2017, www.census.gov/newsroom/press-releases/2015 /cb15-tps16.html.

18. Li Zhou, "Exclusive: New Poll Shows Asian American Voters Could Give Democrats a Big Boost in 2020 Battleground Districts," *Vox*, March 19, 2020; Jens Manuel Krogstad, Ana Gonzalez-Barrera, and Christine Tamir, "Latino Democratic Voters Place High Importance on 2020 Presidential Election," Pew Research Center, January 17, 2020, https://www.pewresearch.org /fact-tank/2020/01/17/latino-democratic-voters-place-high-importance-on -2020-presidential-election/.

19. Data sources: Connecticut, "QuickFacts: Connecticut," Latino population estimates July 1, 2019, US Census Bureau QuickFacts, www.census.gov/quickfacts /ct; New Jersey, "QuickFacts: New Jersey," Latino population estimates July 1, 2019, US Census Bureau QuickFacts, www.census.gov/quickfacts/nj; "QuickFacts: Rhode Island," Latino population estimates July 1, 2019, US Census Bureau QuickFacts, www.census.gov/quickfacts/ri.

20. Data sources: New Mexico: QuickFacts: New Mexico," Native American population estimate July 1, 2019, US Census Bureau QuickFacts, www.census.gov /quickfacts/nm; South Dakota: "QuickFacts: South Dakota," Native American population estimate July 1, 2019, US Census Bureau QuickFacts, www.census .gov/quickfacts/sd; Oklahoma: "QuickFacts: Oklahoma," Native American population estimate July 1, 2019, US Census Bureau QuickFacts, www.census .gov/quickfacts/ok; "QuickFacts: Alaska," Native American population estimate July 1, 2019, US Census Bureau QuickFacts, www.census.gov/quickfacts/ak.

21. "What Unites and Divides Urban, Suburban and Rural Communities," Pew Research Center, May 22, 2018, https://www.pewsocialtrends.org/2018/05/22 /what-unites-and-divides-urban-suburban-and-rural-communities/.

22. "The Partisan Divide on Political Values Grows Even Wider," Pew Research Center, October 5, 2017, https://www.pewsocialtrends.org/2018/05/22/what -unites-and-divides-urban-suburban-and-rural-communities/.

23. "Advanced Member Search," House of Delegates demographics, Virginia House of Delegates Clerks Office, 2010, History.house.virginia.gov.

24. "General Assembly: Legislators," VPAP.org, 2019, www.vpap.org/general -assembly/legislators/?display=gender.

25. "General Assembly: Legislators," VPAP.org, 2019, https://www.vpap.org /general-assembly/legislators/?display=race.

26. National Conference of State Legislatures, "Women in State Legislatures for 2019," July 25, 2019, http://www.ncsl.org/legislators-staff/legislators/womens -legislative-network/women-in-state-legislatures-for-2019.aspx. Nevada had the highest percentage at 52.4 percent; Mississippi the lowest at 13.8 percent.

27. "Women of Color in Elective Office 2019" (New Brunswick, NJ: Rutgers University, Eagleton Institute of Politics, Center for American Women and Politics, n.d.), https://cawp.rutgers.edu/women-color-elective-office-2019 (accessed June 21, 2019).

28. Richard H. Frey, "The Millennial Generation: A Demographic Bridge to America's Diverse Future," Brookings Institution, January 2018, https://www .brookings.edu/research/millennials/.

29. Richard L. Florida, *The Rise of the Creative Class: And How It's Transforming Work, Leisure, Community and Everyday Life* (New York: Basic Books, 2002).

30. Mike Maciag, "Millennials Remade Cities, but Will They Keep Living in Them?," *Governing*, July 2015.

31. "The Generation Gap in American Politics," Pew Research Center, March 1, 2018,

https://www.people-press.org/2018/03/01/the-generation-gap-in-american
-politics/.

32. Julie Beck and Caroline Kitchener, "Early Signs of a Youth Wave," *Atlantic*,
November 6, 2018.

33. Hannah Hartig, "In Year of Record Midterm Turnout, Women Continued to
Vote at Higher Rates Than Men," Pew Research Center, May 3, 2019, https://
www.pewresearch.org/fact-tank/2019/05/03/in-year-of-record-midterm
-turnout-women-continued-to-vote-at-higher-rates-than-men/.

34. "Election Week 2020: Youth Key to Biden Wins in Midwest" (Medford, MA: Tufts
University, Center for Information and Research on Civic Learning and Engagement, November 24, 2020), https://circle.tufts.edu/latest-research/election
-week-2020.

35. Daniel J. Elazar, *American Federalism: A View from the States* (New York: Crowell,
1966).

36. V. O. Key Jr., *Southern Politics in State and Nation* (New York: Knopf, 1949).

37. Joel Lieske. "American State Cultures: Testing a New Measure and Theory,"
*Publius* 42, no. 1 (2012): 108–33.

38. See, for example, Colin Woodard, *American Nations: A History of Eleven Rival
Regional Cultures in North America* (New York: Penguin, 2012). Woodard defined
eleven distinct cultural areas of the United States. Delaware, North Carolina,
and the portion of Virginia east of the Blue Ridge Mountains were labeled
"Tidewater" and characterized primarily by their respect for authority and
tradition. Part of Virginia is included in Woodard's region labeled "Greater
Appalachia."

39. Associated Press, "California Is Now the World's Fifth-largest Economy, Sur-
passing United Kingdom," *Los Angeles Times*," May 4, 2018.

40. Noah Robertson, "Why Secession Is the Talk of This Pro-Gun County in Virginia," *Christian Science Monitor*, February 7, 2020.

41. See Arlie Russell Hochschild, *Strangers in Their Own Land: Anger and Mourning
on the American Right* (New York: New Press, 2016), and J. D. Vance, *Hillbilly
Elegy: A Memoir of a Family and Culture in Crisis* (New York: HarperCollins,
2016).

42. C. Wright Mills, *The Sociological Imagination* (New York: Oxford University
Press, 1959).

43. Edwin Witte, *The Development of the Social Security Act* (Madison: University of
Wisconsin Press, 1963); Arthur Altmeyer, *The Formative Years of Social Security*
(Madison: University of Wisconsin Press, 1968).

44. US Centers for Disease Control, "Overdose Death Maps," August 13, 2019,
https://www.cdc.gov/drugoverdose/data/prescribing/overdose-death-maps
.html.

45. National Conference of State Legislatures, "Prescribing Policies: States Confront Opioid Overdose Epidemic," October 31, 2018, http://www.ncsl.org

/research/health/prescribing-policies-states-confront-opioid-overdose-epidemic
.aspx.

46. National Conference of State Legislatures, "Autism and Insurance Coverage, State Laws," August 8, 2018, http://www.ncsl.org/research/health/autism-and -insurance-coverage-state-laws.aspx.

## 5. Players on the Stage

1. Elaine S. Povich, "Governors Leapfrog Feds on Coronavirus Response," *State-line* (blog), Pew Charitable Trusts, March 20, 2020, https://www.pewtrusts.org /en/research-and-analysis/blogs/stateline/2020/03/20/governors-leapfrog -feds-on-coronavirus-response?utm_campaign=2020-03-20+SD&utm _medium=email&utm_source=Pew. In strict contrast, Trump exclaimed at a news conference on March 13 when asked whether he should take responsibility for the inability of the federal government to distribute more coronavirus tests earlier, "I don't take responsibility at all."

2. Council of State Governments, *The Book of the States* (Lexington, KY: Council of State Governments, 2008), 40:195–96, table 4.9.

3. "Term Limits on Governor," TermLimits.com, 2020, https://www.termlimits .com/governor_termlimits/. Former Iowa governor Terry Branstad holds the record for the longest-serving governor in US history. He was elected to six four-year terms and served a combined twenty-four years.

4. Allen's mistake occurred when he was campaigning from the back of his pickup truck and made a disparaging comment to a college-aged student of Indian descent, who was working as what people call a "tracker," someone who follows and records information on an opponent's campaign. "Macaca" is a slur to Indians. Allen's comment went viral and opened up the larger issue of the former governor's alleged racial insensitivity. He never recovered, and lost his Senate race to little-known Jim Webb. Warren Fiske, "George Allen's 'Macaca' Moment Enshrined in a Political Manual," *Virginian-Pilot*, June 16, 2007; David Stout, "Senator Says He Meant No Insult by Remark, *New York Times*, August 16, 2006.

5. Allen Cooper, "Jim Gilmore Formally Joins GOP Presidential Race," *USA Today*, July 30, 2015.

6. Warner's stature was enhanced when, in 2004, he was able to convince the Republican-controlled state legislature to support a major tax increase to fund schools and other critical services after a substantial tax cut enacted by the previous Republican governor had unbalanced the state's finances and posed risks to the state's triple-A bond rating.

7. Benjamin Wermund, "The Red State That Loves Free College," *Politico*, January 16, 2019.

8. Jen Mishory, "The Future of Statewide College Promise Programs" (New York: Century Foundation, March 6, 2018), https://tcf.org/content/report/future -statewide-college-promise-programs/?agreed=1. The New York Excelsior

Scholarship includes a guarantee of free tuition at four-year institutions, and programs similar to Tennessee's exist in Georgia, Florida, Oregon, and West Virginia. See, for example, Adam Tamburin, "Free Community College Spreads from Tennessee to Oregon," *Statesman Journal*, February 12, 2017.

9. By comparison, the president of the United States does not have line-item veto power. In fact, the Supreme Court ruled in 1998 that Congress's attempt to grant this power to the president was unconstitutional as violating the present-ment clause of the US Constitution. *Clinton v. City of New York*, 524 U.S. 417 (1998).

10. National Association of State Budget Officers, "Budget Processes in the States," summer 2008.

11. Michael Callaghan, "Holding Court with John," *Garden and Gun*, October/November 2016.

12. For a summary of numbers, see National Conference of State Legislatures, "2010 Constituents per State Legislative District" (table), http://www.ncsl.org/research/about-state-legislatures/2010-constituents-per-state-legislative-district.aspx.

13. Spitzer became known as the "sheriff of Wall Street" for his efforts to crack down on white-collar crime and financial abuse. Charles Gasparino, "Wall Street Has Unlikely New Cop In New York State's Eliot Spitzer," *Wall Street Journal*, April 25, 2002.

14. Paul Nolette, *Federalism on Trial: State Attorneys General and National Policymaking in Contemporary America* (Lawrence: University Press of Kansas, 2015), 1.

15. Michael Janofsky, "Mississippi Seeks Damages from Tobacco Companies," *New York Times*, May 24, 1994, and Allan M. Brandt, *The Cigarette Century: The Rise, Fall, and Deadly Persistence of the Product That Defined America* (New York: Basic Books, 2007).

16. Christina Nuckols, "McDonnell Rules Kaine Out of Order on Gay-Discrimination Ban," *Virginian-Pilot*, February 25, 2006. Although their legal reasoning is often cited in court opinions, Attorney General Opinions under Virginia law do not carry the force of law, and only reflect the legal views of office at the time of their issuance.

17. Dan Levine, "Exclusive: As Democratic Attorneys General Target Trump, Republican AGs Target Them," Reuters, March 28, 2017.

18. Paul Nolette, "State Litigation during the Obama Administration: Diverging Agendas in an Era of Polarized Politics," *Publius: The Journal of Federalism* 44, no. 3 (Summer 2014): 451–74.

19. Sheila Kaplan and Jan Hoffman, "Mallinckrodt Reaches $1.6 Billion Deal to Settle Opioid Lawsuits," *New York Times*, February 25, 2020.

20. While at the EPA, Pruitt was immediately embroiled in a series of ethical alle-gations, including spending abuses for furniture, first class travel, and cozy relationships with lobbyists. Under pressure, he resigned his position in July 2018. See Coral Davenport, Lisa Friedman, and Maggie Haberman, "EPA's

Chief Scott Pruitt Resigns Under a Cloud of Ethics Scandals," *New York Times,* July 5, 2018.

21. Elaine S. Povich, "When a State Attorney General Takes On a National Fight, What's He Gunning For?," *Stateline* (blog), Pew Charitable Trusts, November 11, 2019, https://www.pewtrusts.org/en/research-and-analysis/blogs/stateline /2019/11/11/when-a-state-attorney-general-takes-on-a-national-fight-whats-he -gunning-for.

22. Elizabeth Daigneau, "Hoping for Success They Had against Tobacco, State AGs Unite to Fight Climate Change," *Governing,* October 2016.

23. Rick Pluta, "Nessel Says She Will Use AG Powers to Protect against Voter Intimidation," Michigan Public Radio, September 2, 2020.

24. Erik Larson, "Republican State AGs Challenge Arizona Ruling on Ballot Signatures, *Bloomberg News,* September 25, 2020.

25. Allen Greenblatt, "The Story behind the Prominent Rise of State AGs," *Governing,* June 2015.

26. Nolette, *Federalism on Trial.*

27. Margaret H. Lemos and Ernest A. Young, "State Public-Law Litigation in an Age of Polarization," *Texas Law Review* 97, no. 1 (2020), https://texaslawreview.org /state-public-law-litigation-in-an-age-of-polarization/.

28. Joshua Hersh, "Cuccinelli's War," *New Republic,* March 17, 2011. The case was subsequently dismissed in 2011. See Anita Kumar and N.C. Aizenman, "Appeals Court Dismisses Virginia's Health Law Challenge," *Washington Post,* September 8, 2011.

29. Brittany Daniels, "Cuccinelli Says Colleges Can't Protect Gays," *Loudoun Times Mirror,* March 8, 2010.

30. Anita Kumar and Rosalind Helderman, "VA. Permits Wider Police Immigration Status Check," *Washington Post,* August 3, 2010.

31. "Attorney General Herring Sues EPA over Attacks on Clean Air and Climate Change Efforts," press release, Office of Virginia Attorney General, November 15, 2019, https://www.oag.state.va.us/media-center/news-releases/1577 -november-15–2019-herring-sues-epa-over-attacks-on-clean-air-and-climate -change-efforts.

32. This case will undoubtedly end up before the US Supreme Court, and there are many thorny legal questions to be resolved. As an example, five states—Idaho, Kentucky, Nebraska, Tennessee, and South Dakota—have rescinded their ratifications. In addition, Congress had previously set a deadline for ratification. Patricia Sullivan, "Herring, Other State AGs File Lawsuit Demanding Addition of ERA to Constitution," *Washington Post,* January 30, 2020.

33. Associated Press, "GOP Attorneys General Seek to Block Equal Rights Amendment," *New York Times,* February 21, 2020.

34. The 2020 election also provided some understanding of yet another official frequently elected statewide and who can have an impact on public policy, state secretaries of state. Forty-seven of the fifty states have such officials and in

thirty-five of them they are elected, usually as members of parties. They control the operation of elections. In most cases, they are not viewed as partisan, even though Katherine Harris, the Florida secretary of state, gained notoriety during the 2000 election when she decided that the state would stop counting votes. A history of this group is found in Jocelyn F. Benson, *State Secretaries of State: Guardians of the Democratic Process* (Farnham, UK: Ashgate, 2010). Georgia Republican secretary of state Brad Raffensperger gained public attention in 2020 when he claimed that the Republicans were pressuring him not to count legitimate ballots, resisted the Trump narrative that the state's election was tainted, and insisted that the election was conducted without fraud and in keeping with the laws of the state. Amy Gardner, "Ga. Secretary of state Says Fellow Republicans Are Pressuring Him to Find Ways to Exclude Ballots," *Washington Post*, November 16, 2020.

35. Rob O'Dell and Nick Penzenstadler, "You Elected Them to Write New Laws. They're Letting Corporations Do It Instead," *USA Today*, April 4, 2019.

36. Although the Democrats have not been as effective in creating national groups having influence similar to ALEC, they continue to make efforts. See Alan Greenblatt, "Have Democrats Found Their ALEC?," *New Republic*, January 3, 2020.

37. Jessie Van Berkel and Torey Van Oot, "Some Minnesota Bills Copied from Other States, Even Written by Special Interests," *Star Tribune*, July 22, 2019.

38. Nancy Scola, "Exposing ALEC: How Conservative-Backed State Laws Are All Connected," *Atlantic*, April 14, 2012.

39. Alexander Hertel-Fernandez, *State Capture: How Conservative Activists, Big Businesses, and Wealthy Donors Reshaped the American States—and the Nation* (New York: Oxford University Press, 2019).

40. Trevor Bragdon, State Workplace Freedom Toolkit, Arlington, VA: State Policy Network, n.d.; quoted in Hertel-Fernandez, *State Capture*, 11.

41. Ethan Magoc, "Flurry of Photo ID Laws Tied to Conservative ALEC Group," *News21*, August 20, 2012, https://www.minnpost.com/politics-policy/2012/08/flurry-photo-id-laws-tied-conservative-alec-group/.

42. Michael Waldman, *The Fight to Vote* (New York: Simon & Schuster, 2016), 200–201.

43. Brendan Greeley and Alison Fitzgerald, "Pssst . . . Wanna Buy a Law?," *Bloomberg Businessweek*, December 1, 2011.

44. Hertel-Fernandez, *State Capture*, 5.

## 6. Controlling the Nation One State at a Time

1. David Margolick, Evgenia Peretz, and Michael Shnayerson, "The Path to Florida," *Vanity Fair*, October 2004.

2. *Bush v. Gore*, 531 U.S. 98 (2000).

3. When ballots mailed to the local registrar had not been placed inside this second envelope, they were called "naked ballots" and the courts ruled they could not be counted under state law.

4. Christa Case Bryant, "Why Pennsylvania Is Ground Zero for Mail-in Voting Debate," *Christian Science Monitor*, September 4, 2020.

5. National Conference of State Legislatures, "VOPP Table 16: When Absentee/Mail Ballot Processing and Counting Can Begin," October 2, 2020, https://www.ncsl.org/research/elections-and-campaigns/vopp-table-16-when-absentee-mail-ballot-processing-and-counting-can-begin.aspx.

6. Anita Kumar, "Trump Readies Thousands of Attorneys for Election Fight," *Politico*, September 27, 2020.

7. Steve Peoples and Thomas Beaumont, "Trump Triggers Massive Midterm Turnout," Associated Press, November 9, 2018.

8. Nonprofit VOTE and U.S. Elections Project, *America Goes to the Polls, 2018* (Cambridge, MA: Nonprofit VOTE, 2019), https://www.nonprofitvote.org/documents/2019/03/america-goes-polls-2018.pdf/. This number surpasses the 48.7 percent turnout in 1966. For midterm participation rates above that, you'd have to look as far back as 1914 (http://www.electproject.org/2018g).

9. Virginia Department of Elections, "Summary of Virginia Registration & Turnout Statistics, 2017."

10. National Conference of State Legislatures, "Same Day Voter Registration," October 6, 2020; Nonprofit VOTE and U.S. Elections Project, *America Goes to the Polls 2016* (Cambridge, MA: Nonprofit VOTE, 2017), 9–10, http://npvote.wpengine.com/documents/2017/03/america-goes-polls-2016.pdf/.

11. NIU Newroom, "How Hard Is It to Vote in Your State?," Northern Illinois University, October 13, 2020, https://newsroom.niu.edu/2020/10/13/how-hard-is-it-to-vote-in-your-state/.

12. NIU Newroom, "How Hard Is It to Vote in Your State?"

13. Nonprofit VOTE and U.S. Elections Project, *America Goes to the Polls 2018*, 6.

14. Nonprofit VOTE and U.S. Elections Project, *America Goes to the Polls 2018*, 6.

15. Quan Li, Michael J. Pomante II, and Scot Schraufnagel, "Cost of Voting in the American States," *Election Law Journal: Rules, Politics, and Policy* 17, no. 3 (2018).

16. Virginia made major changes in its voting practices in 2020, providing for automatic registration, the end of photo ID, and no-excuse absentee voting.

17. Nonprofit VOTE and U.S. Elections Project, *America Goes to the Polls, 2016*.

18. "Voter Turnout Rate in the Presidential Election in the United States as of November 16, 2020, by State" (graphic), Statista, https://www.statista.com/statistics/1184621/presidential-election-voter-turnout-rate-state/.

19. Virginia Department of Elections, "Summary of Virginia Registration & Turnout Statistics," https://www.elections.virginia.gov/resultsreports/registration-statistics/registrationturnout-statistics/index.html.

20. Virginia Department of Elections, "Summary of Virginia Registration & Turnout Statistics."

21. Alexander Keyssar, *The Right to Vote* (New York: Basic Books, 2009).

22. Carol Anderson, *One Person, No Vote: How Voter Suppression Is Destroying Our Democracy* (New York: Bloomsbury, 2018).

23. Carol Anderson, "The Republican Approach to Voter Fraud: Lie," *New York Times*, September 9, 2018.

24. Justin Levitt, "A Comprehensive Investigation of Voter Impersonation Finds 31 Credible Incidents out of One Billion Ballots Cast," *Washington Post*, August 6, 2014.

25. Matthew Vadum, "Registering the Poor to Vote Is Un-American," *American Thinker*, September 1, 2011, quoted in Michael Waldman, *The Fight to Vote* (New York: Simon & Schuster, 2016), 196.

26. Waldman, *The Fight to Vote*, 197.

27. Quoted in Anderson, *One Person, No Vote*, 48.

28. Waldman, *The Fight to Vote*, 201.

29. Reid Wilson, "Voter Turnout Dipped in 2016, Led by Decline among Blacks," *The Hill*, May 11, 2017.

30. Ari Berman, "The GOPs Attack on Voting Rights Was Most Undercovered Story of 2016," *The Nation*, November 9, 2016.

31. Anderson, *One Person, No Vote*.

32. Mark Joseph Stern, "New Hampshire Republicans Passed a Bill to Suppress the Student Vote. Democrats Have One Last Chance to Defeat It," *Slate*, July 16, 2018.

33. Georgia is one of nine states with a "use it or lose it" law: if a voter fails to exercise the franchise for a certain number of elections, he or she can be purged from the voting rolls. Some argue that this is unconstitutional. See Mark Niesse, "Judge Allows Georgia to Purge 309K Voter Registrations Overnight," *Atlanta Journal-Constitution*, December 16, 2019.

34. Greg Bluestein, "Georgia 2018: Stacey Abrams Resigns from House to Focus on Gov Run," *Atlanta Journal-Constitution*, August 25, 2017.

35. Nate Cohn, Matthew Conlen, and Charlie Smart, "Detailed Turnout Data Shows How Georgia Turned Blue," *New York Times*, November 17, 2020.

36. Jamie Azure, "North Dakota's Voter-ID Law Aimed to Silence Native American Voters: Instead, It Rallied My Tribe," *Washington Post*, November 1, 2018.

37. Jonathan Brater, Kevin Morris, Myrna Pérez, and Christopher Deluzio, *Purges: A Growing Threat to the Right to Vote*, Brennan Center for Justice, New York University School of Law, 2018, 3, https://www.brennancenter.org/sites/default/files/publications/Purges_Growing_Threat_2018.pdf.

38. Brater et al., *Purge*, 4. A federal court struck down another Texas effort to purge over 100,000 voters in 2019. Niraj Chokshi, "Federal Judge Halts 'Ham Handed' Texas Voter Purge," *New York Times*, February 28, 2019.

39. Ben Nadler, "Voting rights become a Flashpoint in Georgia Governor's race," *US News & World Report*, October 9, 2018.

40. "Inaccurate, Costly, and Inefficient: Evidence That America's Voter Registration

System Needs an Upgrade," Pew Center on the States, February 2012, https://www.pewtrusts.org/~/media/legacy/uploadedfiles/pcs_assets/2012/pewupgradingvoterregistrationpdf.pdf.

41. Jonathan Brater, "Virginia Offers Lessons for Voter List Maintenance," Brennan Center for Justice, New York University School of Law, November 25, 2013, https://www.brennancenter.org/analysis/virginia-offers-lessons-voter-list-maintenance.

42. Scott Simpson et al., *The Great Poll Closure* (Washington, DC: Leadership Conference Education Fund, November 2016), http://civilrightsdocs.info/pdf/reports/2016/poll-closure-report-web.pdf.

43. Mark Niesse, Maya T. Prabhu, and Jacquelyn Elias, "Voting Precincts Closed across Georgia since Election Oversight Lifted," *Atlanta Journal-Constitution*, August 31, 2018.

44. Office of Civil Rights Evaluation, US Commission on Civil Rights, *An Assessment of Minority Voting Rights Access in the United States* (Washington, DC: US Commission on Civil Rights, 2018), https://www.usccr.gov/pubs/2018/Minority_Voting_Access_2018.pdf.

45. Daniel Moritz-Rabson, "Almost Half of North Carolina Counties Shut Down Polling Places Used for Early Voting," *Newsweek*, September 25, 2018.

46. Steve Bousquet, "Judge: Florida's Early Voting-on-Campus Ban Shows 'Stark Pattern of Discrimination,'" *Tampa Bay Times*, July 24, 2018.

47. Frances Robles, "1.4 Million Floridians with Felonies Win Long-Denied Right to Vote," *New York Times*, November 7, 2018.

48. Editorial Board, "The Return of the Poll Tax in Florida," *New York Times*, March 22, 2019.

49. Brennan Center for Justice, "Automatic Voter Registration," New York University School of Law, July 10, 2019, https://www.brennancenter.org/analysis/automatic-voter-registration.

50. National Conference of State Legislatures, "Automatic Voter Registration," April 22, 2019, http://www.ncsl.org/research/elections-and-campaigns/automatic-voter-registration.aspx. Virginia was added to the list in 2020.

51. Brennan Center for Justice, "Policy Differences of Automatic Voter Registration," New York University School of Law, June 19, 2019, https://www.brennancenter.org/analysis/policy-differences-automatic-voter-registration.

52. National Conference of State Legislatures, "Same Day Voter Registration," June 28, 2019, http://www.ncsl.org/research/elections-and-campaigns/same-day-registration.aspx. New Mexico adopted legislation in 2019 but will be phasing in same-day registration over the next several years.

53. Nonprofit VOTE and U.S. Elections Project, *America Goes to the Polls 2018* (Cambridge, MA: Nonprofit VOTE, 2019), 6, https://www.nonprofitvote.org/america-goes-to-the-polls-2018/.

54. Nonprofit VOTE and U.S. Elections Project, *America Goes to the Polls 2018*, 6.

55. Joey Garrison, "Voter Turnout 2020: Early Voting Tops 100 Million Ballots Cast," *USA Today*, November 3, 2020.

56. Dennis Romboy, "It's Official: Utah voters Went 'Bonkers,' Turned Out in Record Numbers," *Deseret News*, November 23, 2020.

57. Natalie Colarossi, "The Highest Voter Turnouts in History of U.S. Elections," *Newsweek*, November 5, 2020.

58. Matt Vasilogambros, "How to Bring the Ballot to Aging Americans," *Stateline* (blog), Pew Charitable Trusts, July 23, 2018, https://www.pewtrusts.org/en/research-and-analysis/blogs/stateline/2018/07/23/how-to-bring-the-ballot-to-aging-americans.

59. In Texas, the state supreme court held in May 2020 that the risk of contracting the virus alone does not meet the state's qualifications as a "disability" that would qualify a voter to vote by mail. See Alexa Ura, "Texas Supreme Court: Lack of Immunity to Coronavirus Alone Isn't Enough for Mail-in Ballot," *Texas Tribune*, May 27, 2020.

60. Deb Riechmann and Anthony Izaguirre, "Trump Admits He's Blocking Postal Cash to Stop Mail-in Votes," *AP News*, August 14, 2020.

61. US Constitution, Article I, Section 2.

62. Erick Trickey, "Where Did the Term 'Gerrymander' Come From?," *Smithsonian Magazine*, July 20, 2017.

63. Jenna Portnoy, "Hogan on High Court ruling: 'Gerrymandering Is Wrong, and Both Parties Are Guilty,'" *Washington Post*, June 27, 2019.

64. For updates, see Brennan Center for Justice, New York University School of Law (https://www.brennancenter.org/blog/state-redistricting-litigation).

65. David A. Lieb, "Pennsylvania, North Carolina Election Results Illustrate Power of Gerrymandering," *Washington Times*, November 18, 2018.

66. Josh Gerstein, "Court Won't Force North Carolina Redistricting This Year," *Politico*, August 4, 2018.

67. Jonathan Oosting, "Federal Court: Michigan Political Maps Illegally Rigged to 'Historical Proportions,'" *Detroit News*, April 25, 2019. Given the decision in *Rucho* discussed below, most observers believe the Michigan case will also be dismissed.

68. The Maryland case, *Lamone v. Benisek*, was consolidated with *Rucho v. Common Cause* by the US Supreme Court and remanded to the Maryland district court with instructions to dismiss both cases for lack of jurisdiction. *Rucho v. Common Cause*, 588 U.S. ___ (2019), slip opinion at 34. The plaintiffs in Wisconsin (*Gill v. Whitford*) won some rulings in lower courts, but following the decision in *Rucho v. Common Cause* that such partisan gerrymandering claims are non-justiciable, the parties requested and the court granted dismissal (https://www.brennancenter.org/legal-work/whitford-v-gill).

69. *Rucho v. Common Cause*, 588 U.S. ___ (2019), slip opinion, dissent at p. 33.

70. Michael Wines and Richard Fausset, "North Carolina's Legislative Maps Are

Thrown Out by State Court Panel," *New York Times*, September 3, 2019. The defendants were further hindered by the fact that while they claimed race played no role in their redistricting, a memo from a Republican operative advising the legislators suggested just the opposite.

71. *Page v. Virginia State Bd. of Elections*, 2015 WL 3604029 (June 5, 2015), appeal dismissed *sub nom. Wittman v. Personhuballah*, 578 U.S. ___ (2016).

72. *Bethune-Hill v. Virginia State Bd. of Elections*, 326 F. Supp. 3d 128 (E.D.Va. 2018).

73. Associated Press, "Number of States Using Redistricting Commissions Growing," *AP News*, March 21, 2019, https://www.apnews.com/4d2e2aea7e224549af 61699e51c955dd. For information on OneVirginia2021, see the website at https://www.onevirginia2021.org.

74. Emily Moon, "How Did Citizen-Led Redistricting Initiatives Fare in the Midterms? The Answer: Very Well," *Pacific Standard*, November 7, 2018.

75. Brennan Center for Justice, "Who Draws the Maps? Legislative and Congressional Redistricting," New York University School of Law, January 30, 2019, https://www.brennancenter.org/analysis/who-draws-maps-states-redrawing -congressional-and-state-district-lines.

76. Brennan Center for Justice, "Who Draws the Maps?"

77. Brennan Center for Justice, "Who Draws the Maps?"

78. Senate Joint Resolution 306 (2019), https://lis.virginia.gov/cgi-bin/legp604.exe ?191+sum+SJ306.

## 7. States of Knowledge

1. Jim Nolan "After Passionate Debate, Va. Senate Passes Bill That Lets Parents Object to Books," *Roanoke Times*, March 1, 2016.

2. Stephen Q. Cornman, Lei Zhou, Malia R. Howell, and Jumaane Young, *Revenues and Expenditures for Public Elementary and Secondary Education: School Year 2014–15 (Fiscal Year 2015); First Look*, NCES 2018–301 (Washington, DC: US Department of Education, National Center for Education Statistics, 2017), 2, https://nces.ed.gov/pubs2018/2018301.pdf.

3. Mike Maciag, "States That Spend the Most (and the Least) on Education," *Governing*, June 4, 2019.

4. Urban Institute, "How Do School Funding Formulas Work?" (Washington, DC: Urban Institute, November 29, 2017), https://apps.urban.org/features/funding -formulas/.

5. Ellen Dewitt, "States Spending the Most and Least per Student on Education," *Stacker*, November 16, 2020.

6. Another source is found in US Census data. US Census Bureau, Annual Survey of School System Finances, 2017 Public Elementary-Secondary Education Finance Data (Washington, DC: US Department of Commerce, Census Bureau, last revised April 19, 2019), Summary Tables at table 8, https://www.census .gov/data/tables/2017/econ/school-finances/secondary-education-finance .html.

7. Bruce D. Baker, Matthew Di Carlo, and Mark Weber, "The Adequacy and Fairness of State School Finance Systems," Rutgers Graduate School of Education and Albert Shanker Foundation, April 2019, http://schoolfinancedata.org/wp -content/uploads/2019/03/SFID_AnnualReport_2019.pdf.

8. Mike Maciag, "The States That Spend the Most (and the Least) on Education," *Governing*, August 2016.

9. A good example of how this works is found in Cary Lou and Kristin Blagg, *School District Funding in Virginia: Computing the Effects of Changes to the Standards of Quality Funding Formula* (Washington, DC: Urban Institute Center on Education Data and Policy, December 2018), https://www.urban.org/sites /default/files/publication/99540/school_district_funding_in_virginia_2.pdf.

10. Education Commission of the States, "50-State Comparison: K–12 Funding," August 5, 2019, https://www.ecs.org/50-state-comparison-k-12-funding/.

11. "Editorial: Letter to the General Assembly's New Democratic Leaders," *Roanoke Times*, November 17, 2019.

12. These funding formulas also create complexities for state lawmakers who are trying to determine comparative teacher salaries—and raise them. Because larger and wealthier jurisdictions can invest more, their teacher salaries can be much higher than in poorer communities. And this creates challenges in assessing how states rank in terms of their salaries. The figures from 2019 showed Arlington County's average salary at $78,617, much higher than either the state average ($49,457) or that in some Southwest Virginia jurisdictions, where teachers can earn as little as $33,000 per year. And simply putting more state money into teacher salaries typically requires a local match, again placing greater burdens on poorer communities. Mechelle Hankerson, "What's the Average Teacher Salary in Virginia? Depends Who Does the Math, Lawmakers Find," *Virginia Mercury*, November 20, 2019.

13. Kevin Richert, "Education Week: Idaho Lags in K–12 Spending, and Struggles with Funding Equity," *Idaho Education News*, June 5, 2019.

14. Anna Gronewold and Nick Niedzwiadek, "An Albany Tradition Andrew Cuomo Can't Change," *Politico*, February 27, 2020.

15. "Virginia Board of Education Considers Updated Proposed Standards of Quality Revisions with Potential $1.2 Billion Fiscal Impact," Virginia Association of Counties blog, July 30, 2019, https://www.vaco.org/virginia-board-of-education -considers-updated-proposed-standards-of-quality-revisions-with-potential -1-2-billion-fiscal-impact/.

16. State Science and Technology Institute, "Per capita GDP by state (2008– 2017)," *Useful Stats* (blog), SSTI, May 10, 2018, https://ssti.org/blog/useful -stats-capita-gdp-state-2008-2017. 2017 version of "Best States Rankings," *U.S. News & World Report*, n.d., https://www.usnews.com/media/best-states/overall -rankings-2017.pdf.

17. Education Week Research Center, *Quality Counts 2020: Grading the States, Education Week*, September 1, 2020.

18. Samuel Stebbins and Thomas C. Frohlich, "Geographic Disparity: States with the Best (and Worst) Schools," *USA Today*, February 12, 2018.

19. Education Week Research Center, "State Grades on K-12 Education: Map and Rankings," in *Quality Counts 2018: Grading the States* (special report), *Education Week*, January 17, 2018 (updated online October 10, 2018), https://www.edweek.org/ew /collections/quality-counts-2018-state-grades/report-card-map-rankings.html.

20. Stebbins and Frohlich, "Geographic Disparity."

21. Rex Springston, "Happy Slaves? The Peculiar Story of Three Virginia School Textbooks," *Richmond Times Dispatch*, April 14, 2018; Donald Yacovone, "Textbook Racism: How Scholars Sustained White Supremacy," *Chronicle of Higher Education*, April 8, 2018.

22. Mechelle Hankerson, "A Governor-Appointed Commission Begins Work on Improving Black History Education in Virginia," *Virginia Mercury*, October 29, 2019.

23. Lauren McGaughy, "Texas History Curriculum: Hillary Clinton and Alamo 'Heroes' Are In. Oprah's Out," *Dallas Morning News*, November 13, 2018 (updated online November 16, 2018).

24. Emily Weyrauch, "Florida's Textbooks Are a New Battleground in America's Fight over Facts," *Time*, August 30, 2017.

25. Dana Goldstein, "Two States. Eight Textbooks. Two American Stories," *New York Times*, January 12, 2020.

26. Leslie Postal, "DeSantis Signs Bill Creating Florida's Fifth School Voucher Program," *Orlando Sentinel*, May 9, 2019.

27. Examples include *McCall v. Scott*, 199 So. 3d 359 (Fla. 1st DCA 2016) (no taxpayer standing to sue when there is no disbursement from the public treasury), and *Citizens for Strong Schools, Inc. v. Florida State Board of Education*, No. 1D16–2862, 232 So. 3d 1163 (Fla. Dist. Ct. App. 2017), affirmed, *Citizens for Strong Schools, Inc. v. Florida State Board of Education*, case No. SC18–67 (Fla. Jan 4, 2019) (available at https://law.justia.com/cases/florida/supreme-court/2019 /sc18-67.html), which upheld the constitutionality of the state's "scholarship" funding program for students with disabilities under the Florida Constitution. The Florida Supreme Court, however, has ruled that a direct-public-funds voucher program, as opposed to tax credit initiatives like the one at issue in *McCall*, violates the state's constitutional duty to provide a "uniform system of free public schools." *Bush v. Holmes*, 919 So. 2d 392 (Fla. 2006).

28. American Federation for Children, "The School Choice Fact Sheet 2019," https://www.federationforchildren.org/wp-content/uploads/2016/09/AFC -School-Choice-FactSheet-6–2019.pdf. We looked briefly at Virginia's program in chapter 6.

29. Jackson, C. Kirabo Jackson, Cora Wigger, and Heyu Xiong, "Do School Spending Cuts Matter? Evidence from the Great Recession," NBER Working Paper 24203 (Cambridge, MA: National Bureau of Economic Research, January 2018), https://www.nber.org/papers/w24204.

30. Brooke Auxier and Monica Anderson, "As Schools Close due to the Coronavirus, Some U.S. Students Face a Digital 'Homework Gap,'" Pew Research Center, March 16, 2020; D. Antonio Cantù, "Initiatives to Close the Digital Divide Must Last beyond the COVID-19 Pandemic to Work," *The Conversation*, October 27, 2020, https://theconversation.com/initiatives-to-close-the-digital-divide-must-last-beyond-the-covid-19-pandemic-to-work-146663.

31. Andrew Bacher-Hicks, Joshua Goodman, and Christine Mulhern, "Inequality in Household Adaptation to Schooling Shocks: Covid-Induced Online Learning Engagement in Real Time," NBER Working Paper w27555 (Cambridge, MA: National Bureau of Economic Research, July 2020).

32. Rachel Fishman, Sophie Nguyen, Alejandra Acosta, and Ashley Clark, *Varying Degrees 2019: New America's Third Annual Survey on Higher Education* (Washington, DC: New America, September 2019), https://d1y8sb8igg2f8e.cloudfront.net/documents/Varying_Degrees_2019_2019-09-11_202908.pdf.

33. Anna Brown, "Most Americans Say Higher Ed Is Heading in Wrong Direction, but Partisans Disagree on Why," Pew Research Center, July 26, 2018, https://www.pewresearch.org/fact-tank/2018/07/26/most-americans-say-higher-ed-is-heading-in-wrong-direction-but-partisans-disagree-on-why/.

34. Jeffrey M. Jones, "Confidence in Higher Education Down since 2015," *Gallup Blog*, October 9, 2018, https://news.gallup.com/opinion/gallup/242441/confidence-higher-education-down-2015.aspx.

35 Justin Ware, "Tennessee State GOP Lawmaker Says Getting Rid of Higher Education Would 'Save America,'" *The Hill*, September 9, 2019.

36. Paul Tough, *The Years That Matter Most: How College Makes or Breaks Us* (Boston: Houghton Mifflin Harcourt, 2019).

37. Tara Westover, "Is College Merely Helping Those Who Need Help Least?," *New York Times*, September 11, 2019.

38. Adam Looney and Constantine Yannelis, "Borrowers with Large Balances: Rising Student Debt and Falling Repayment Rates," Brookings Institution, February 2018, https://www.brookings.edu/wp-content/uploads/2018/02/es_20180216_looneylargebalances.pdf.

39. Susan Svrluga, "Alumnae Vowed to Save Sweet Briar from Closing Last Year. And They Did," *Washington Post*, March 3, 2016.

40. Eliza Gray, "Are Liberal Arts Colleges Doomed?," *Washington Post Magazine*, October 21, 2019.

41. Education Dive Staff, "A Look at Trends in College and University Consolidation since 2016," *Education Dive*, October 2, 2019.

42. Sophie Quinton, "Merging Colleges to Cut Costs and Still Boost Graduation Rates," *Stateline* (blog), Pew Charitable Trusts, March 29, 2017, https://www.pewtrusts.org/en/research-and-analysis/blogs/stateline/2017/03/29/merging-colleges-to-cut-costs-and-still-boost-graduation-rates.

43. "Two Decades of Change in Federal and State Higher Education Funding," Pew Issue Brief, Pew Charitable Trusts, October 15, 2019, https://www.pewtrusts

.org/en/research-and-analysis/issue-briefs/2019/10/two-decades-of-change
-in-federal-and-state-higher-education-funding.

44. F. King Alexander, "The Reality of State Disinvestment in Public Higher Education," *Inside Higher Ed,* November 26, 2019.

45. Richard Vedder, "There Is NO Public 'Disinvestment' in College," *Forbes,* October 1, 2020.

46. Michael Mitchell, Michael Leachman, and Kathleen Masterson, "A Lost Decade in Higher Education Funding" (Washington, DC: Center on Budget and Policy Priorities, August 23, 2017), https://www.cbpp.org/research/state-budget-and-tax/a-lost-decade-in-higher-education-funding.

47. Dina El Boghdady, "How Student Debt Crushes Your Chances of Buying a Home," *Washington Post,* August 22, 2014.

48. Madeline St. Amour, "Report: Enrollment Continues to Trend Downward," *Inside Higher Ed,* October 15, 2020.

49. Grace Turner, "Report: Apprenticeships for Community College Students Can Lessen Tech Talent Shortage," *dBusiness,* November 11, 2019.

50. State Higher Education Executive Officers Association, "SHEF: FY 2018—State Higher Education Finance" (2018), quoted in "'Lost Decade' Casts a Post-Recession Shadow on State Finances," Pew Charitable Trusts, June 4, 2019, https://www.pewtrusts.org/en/research-and-analysis/issue-briefs/2019/06/lost-decade-casts-a-post-recession-shadow-on-state-finances.

51. "'Lost Decade' Casts a Post-Recession Shadow on State Finances."

52. Jennifer Ma, Sandy Baum, Matea Prender, and C. J. Libassi, *Trends in College Pricing* (New York: College Board, 2018), 15, https://trends.collegeboard.org/sites/default/files/2018-trends-in-college-pricing.pdf.

53. State Higher Education Executive Officers Association, *State Higher Education Finance: FY 2018* (Boulder, CO: State Higher Education Executive Officers Association, 2019). https://sheeo.org/wp-content/uploads/2019/04/SHEEO_SHEF_FY18_Report.pdf.

54. "Virginia College Affordability Profile 2018" (Atlanta: Southern Regional Education Board, November 2018), 6, https://www.sreb.org/publication/virginia.

55. Susan Svrluga, "Virginia Public Colleges Freeze Tuition for Coming School Year," *Washington Post,* May 29, 2019

56. "Virginia College Affordability Profile 2018," 3.

57. G. Gilmer Minor III and Dennis H. Treacy, "A Year of Great Progress, and More Work to Do," *Richmond Times Dispatch,* June 8, 2019.

58. "Tuition-Free College Is Now a Reality in Nearly 20 States," CNBC, March 12, 2019.

59. Alain Poutre and Mamie Voight, "The State of Free College: Tennessee Promise and New York's Excelsior Scholarship," Institute for Higher Education Policy, September 2018, http://www.ihep.org/research/publications/state-free-college-tennessee-promise-and-new-yorks-excelsior-scholarship.

60. Emily S. Rueb, "Washington State Moves Toward Free and Reduced College Tuition, With Businesses Footing the Bill," *New York Times,* May 8, 2019.

61. Hannah Natanson, "Gov. Northam Proposes Making Community College Free for Some Job-seekers in Virginia," *Washington Post,* December 19, 2019.

62. Madeline St. Amour, "Free College for All in New Mexico," *Inside Higher Education,* September 19, 2019.

63. Wesley Whistle and Tamara Hiler, "Why Free College Could Increase Inequality," Third Way, March 19, 2019, https://www.thirdway.org/memo/why-free-college-could-increase-inequality. The proposed Virginia program is attempting to address this by targeting grants to low- and moderate-income students.

64. Many studies have found that full-time online learning does not deliver the academic results of in-class instruction. Emma Dorn, Bryan Hancock, Jimmy Sarakatsannis, and Ellen Viruleg, "COVID-19 and Student Learning in the United States: The Hurt Could Last a Lifetime," McKinsey, June 1, 2020, https://www.mckinsey.com/industries/public-and-social-sector/our-insights/covid-19-and-student-learning-in-the-united-states-the-hurt-could-last-a-lifetime.

65. Sumit Chandra, Amy Chang, Lauren Day, et al., *Closing the K–12 Digital Divide in the Age of Distance Learning* (Boston: Boston Consulting Group and Common Sense Media, 2020), https://www.commonsensemedia.org/sites/default/files/uploads/pdfs/common_sense_media_report_final_7_1_3pm_web.pdf.

66. "States Tap Federal CARES Act to Expand Broadband," Pew Issue Brief, Pew Charitable Trusts, November 16, 2020.

## 8. Crime, Punishment, and Justice

1. Jennifer Bronson and E. Ann Carson, *Prisoners in 2017,* NCJ 252156 (Washington, DC: US Department of Justice, Office of Justice Programs, Bureau of Justice Statistics, April 2019), https://www.bjs.gov/content/pub/pdf/p17.pdf.

2. Zhen Zeng, *Jail Inmates in 2017,* NCJ 251774 (Washington, DC: US Department of Justice, Office of Justice Programs, Bureau of Justice Statistics, April 2019), https://www.bjs.gov/content/pub/pdf/ji17.pdf.

3. Campbell Robertson, "Crime Is Down, Yet U.S. Incarceration Rates Are Still among the Highest in the World," *New York Times,* April 25, 2019.

4. "Correctional Populations in the United States, 2016," NCJ 251211 (Washington, DC: US Department of Justice, Office of Justice Programs, Bureau of Justice Statistics, April 2018), https://www.bjs.gov/content/pub/pdf/cpus16.pdf.

5. Sentencing Project, "U.S. Prison Decline: Insufficient to Undo Mass Incarceration," https://www.sentencingproject.org/.

6. "Virginia's Offender Population Forecasts," presentation to Virginia House Appropriations Committee, January 14, 2015, http://hac.virginia.gov/subcommittee/2015_Subcommittee/public_safety/files/01-15-15/Offender%20Forecasts.pdf.

7. Sentencing Project, "State-by-State Data," 2019, https://www.sentencingproject.org/the-facts/#detail?state1Option=Virginia&state2Option=Virginia.

8. Peter Wagner and Wendy Sawyer, "States of Incarceration: The Global Context 2018" (Easthampton, MA: Prison Policy Institute, June 2018), https://www.prisonpolicy.org/global/2018.html.

9. Wagner and Sawyer, "States of Incarceration."

10. "State and Federal Prisoners, 1925–85," *Bureau of Justice Statistics Bulletin*, October 1986, 1–8, https://www.bjs.gov/content/pub/pdf/sfp2585.pdf.

11. Sentencing Project, "People Serving Life Exceeds Entire Prison Population of 1970," January 2020, https://www.sentencingproject.org/wp-content/uploads/2020/02/People-Serving-Life-Exceeds-Entire-Prison-Population-of-1970.pdf?eType=EmailBlastContent&eId=69d58b43-5227-4d54-8177-d2fdf5ab520f.

12. Jeremy Travis, Bruce Western, and F. Stevens Redburn, eds., *The Growth of Incarceration in the United States: Exploring Causes and Consequences of High Rates of Incarceration* (Washington, DC: National Academies Press, 2014), chap. 1.

13. Darryl K. Brown, "Why Do We Sentence People to Hundreds of Years in Prison?," *Virginia Mercury*, July 28, 2019.

14. Jennifer Bronson and E. Ann Carson, *Prisoners in 2017*, NCJ 252156 (Washington, DC: US Department of Justice, Office of Justice Programs, Bureau of Justice Statistics, April 2019), https://www.bjs.gov/content/pub/pdf/p17.pdf.

15. E. A. Carson, *Prisoners in 2014* (Washington, DC: US Department of Justice, Bureau of Justice Statistics, 2015), quoted in Ashley Nellis, *The Color of Justice: Racial and Ethnic Disparity in State Prisons* (Washington, DC: Sentencing Project, June 14, 2016), https://www.sentencingproject.org/publications/color-of-justice-racial-and-ethnic-disparity-in-state-prisons/, 4.

16. The National Conference of State Legislatures has put together misdemeanor offenses and penalties by state. See NCSL, "Misdemeanor Sentencing Trends," January 29, 2019, http://www.ncsl.org/research/civil-and-criminal-justice/misdemeanor-sentencing-trends.aspx.

17. Jury discretion to select sentences in felony cases was first adopted in the United States as part of Virginia's 1796 penal code. Nancy J. King, "The Origins of Felony Jury Sentencing in the United States," *Chicago-Kent Law Review* 78 (2003): 937. Virginia modified its law in 2020. Defendants can now request that they be sentenced by a judge.

18. Richard S. Frase, "Sentencing Guidelines in American Courts: A Forty-Year Retrospective," *Federal Sentencing Reporter* 32, no. 2 (2019): 109–23.

19. *Trends in State Parole, 1990–2000* (Washington, DC: US Department of Justice, Office of Justice Programs, Bureau of Justice Statistics, October 2001), https://www.prisonpolicy.org/scans/bjs/tsp00.pdf.

20. Peter Enns, *Incarceration Nation: How the United States Became the Most Punitive Democracy in the World* (New York: Cambridge University Press, 2016).

21. Terry McAuliffe, "Reconsidering Parole in Virginia," *Washington Post*, August 28, 2015.

22. Dan Nagin, Frank Cullen, and Cheryl Lero-Jonson, "Imprisonment and

Reoffending," in *Crime and Justice: An Annual Review of Research*, vol. 38, ed. Michael Tonry (Chicago: University of Chicago Press, 2009).

23. Pew Charitable Trusts, "The Effects of Changing Felony Theft Thresholds," April 12, 2017, https://www.pewtrusts.org/en/research-and-analysis/issue-briefs/2017/04/the-effects-of-changing-felony-theft-thresholds.

24. Pew Center on the States, *Time Served: The High Cost, Low Return of Longer Prison Terms*, June 2012, https://www.pewtrusts.org/~/media/legacy/uploadedfiles/wwwpewtrustsorg/reports/sentencing_and_corrections/prisontimeservedpdf.pdf.

25. Jonathan Rothwell, *Drug Offenders in American Prisons: The Critical Difference between Stock and Flow* (Washington, DC: Brookings Institution Press, 2015), quoted in Cassia Spohn, Miriam DeLone, and Samuel Walker, *The Color of Justice: Race, Ethnicity, and Crime in America*, 6th ed. (Boston: Cengage Learning), 10.

26. Michelle Alexander, *The New Jim Crow: Mass Incarceration in the Age of Colorblindness* (New York: New Press, 2012).

27. Peter Wagner and Bernadette Rabuy, "Following the Money of Mass Incarceration" (Eastham, MA: Prison Policy Institute, January 25, 2017), https://www.prisonpolicy.org/reports/money.html.

28. Justin McCarthy, "Americans' Views Shift on Toughness of Justice System," Gallup poll, October 20, 2016, https://news.gallup.com/poll/196568/americans-views-shift-toughness-justice-system.aspx.

29. Public Opinion Strategies Memo, National Poll Results, January 25, 2018, https://www.politico.com/f/?id=00000161-2ccc-da2c-a963-efff82be0001. This poll is being cited on liberal and conservative websites, including that of conservative Kansas senator Charles Grassley, who is a cosponsor of a major criminal justice reform bill in the US Senate.

30. John Gramlich, "From Police to Parole, Black and White Americans Differ Widely in Their Views of Criminal Justice System," Pew Research, May 21, 2019, https://www.pewresearch.org/fact-tank/2019/05/21/from-police-to-parole-black-and-white-americans-differ-widely-in-their-views-of-criminal-justice-system/.

31. Jennifer Agiesta, "CNN Poll: Trump Losing Ground to Biden amid Chaotic Week," *CNN Politics*, June 8, 2020, https://www.cnn.com/2020/06/08/politics/cnn-poll-trump-biden-chaotic-week/index.html.

32. Russell Berman, "The State Where Protests Have Already Forced Major Police Reform," *Atlantic*, July 17, 2020.

33. Orion Rummier, "The Major Police Reforms Enacted since George Floyd's Death," *Axios*, July 27, 2020.

34. Maggie Astor, "Left and Right Agree on Criminal Justice: They Were Both Wrong Before," *New York Times*, May 16, 2019.

35. Ronald J. Lampard and Rep. Alan Clemmons, "States Have Been the Cultivators of Sound Criminal Justice Policies," ALEC, October 25, 2019, https://www.alec.org/article/states-have-been-the-cultivators-of-sound-criminal-justice-policies/.

36. Jared Meyer, "Van Jones: Conservatives 'Now the Leader' on Criminal Justice Reform," *Forbes*, April 1, 2019.

37. German Lopez, "Marijuana Legalization Is Very Popular," *Vox*, April 15, 2019.

38. Niall McCarthy, "Marijuana in 2018?" (infographic), *Forbes*, March 26, 2019.

39. Brian J. Ostrom and Neal B. Kauder, eds., *Examining the Work of State Courts, 1996: A National Perspective from the Court Statistics Project* (Williamsburg, VA: National Center for State Courts, 1997), 66–67. (An NCSC report states "drug offenses"; the parenthetical addition of "possession or trafficking" comes from Office of the Executive Secretary, Virginia Supreme Court, "About Drug Treatment Courts," November 24, 2014, http://www.courts.state.va.us/courtadmin/aoc /djs/programs/dtc/general_info/about.html.)

40. Bob Egeklo, "How California Reduced Its Inmate Population to a 30-Year Low," *San Francisco Chronicle*, August 3, 2020, 1.

41. Mia Bird, Magnus Lofstrom, Brandon Martin, Steven Raphael, and Viet Nguyen, *The Impact of Proposition 47 on Crime and Recidivism* (Sacramento: Public Policy Institute of California, June 2018), https://www.ppic.org/wp-content /uploads/r_0618mbr.pdf.

42. Dana Shoenberg, Casey Pheiffer, and Ruth Rosenthal, "Kansas Sees 63% Decline in Youth Confinement," Pew Charitable Trusts, April 24, 2019, https:// www.pewtrusts.org/en/research-and-analysis/articles/2019/04/24/kansas-sees -63-percent-decline-in-youth-confinement.

43. "Nation's 'Most Incarcerated State' Chooses a New Path," Pew Charitable Trusts, July 31, 2017, https://www.pewtrusts.org/en/research-and-analysis/fact -sheets/2017/07/nations-most-incarcerated-state-chooses-a-new-path.

44. William R. Horton was convicted and serving a life sentence for murder in Massachusetts without the possibility of parole when he was released under a weekend furlough program offered by the state. He did not return at the end of the weekend and went on a crime spree that included assault, armed robbery, and rape before he was captured. Republican candidate George H. W. Bush seized on the Horton case in his 1988 presidential contest against Michael Dukakis, who was Massachusetts governor at that time and who not only had supported the furlough program but had vetoed a bill that would have ended it. Bush campaign manager Lee Atwater remarked during the campaign that "by the time we're finished, they're going to wonder whether Willie Horton is Dukakis' running mate." Some believe that this attack cost Dukakis the election. See Roger Simon, "How a Murderer and Rapist Became the Bush Campaign's Most Valuable Player," *Baltimore Sun*, November 11, 1990.

45. Robert LaFountain et al., National Center for State Courts, *Examining the Work of State Courts: An Analysis of 2009 State Court Caseloads*, 2011, http://www .courtstatistics.org/FlashMicrosites/CSP/images/CSP2009.pdf.

46. Alicia Bannon, "Choosing State Judges: A Plan for Reform," Brennan Center for Justice, New York University School of Law, 2018, https://www.brennancenter .org/sites/default/files/publications/2018_09_JudicialSelection.pdf.

47. In nineteen states, justices who have been appointed must, at the end of their terms, go before state voters in uncontested up-or-down votes to retain their seats. Bannon, "Choosing State Judges."

48. Salmon Shomade, *Decision Making and Controversies in State Supreme Courts* (Lanham, MD: Rowman & Littlefield, 2019).

49. Melinda Gann Hall, "Electoral Politics and Strategic Voting in State Supreme Courts," *Journal of Politics* 54, no. 2 (May 1992): 427–46.

50. *Varnum v. Brien*, 763 N.W.2d 862 (Iowa 2009).

51. This process was originally known as the "Missouri system," named for the state that adopted it in 1940.

52. A summary of each state's process is described on the website of the National Center for State Courts (http://judicialselection.us/judicial_selection/reform _efforts/altering_selection_methods.cfm?state=).

53. Scott Greytak, Alicia Bannon, Allyse Falce, and Linda Casey, "Bankrolling the Bench," Brennan Center for Justice, New York University School of Law, October 2015, https://www.brennancenter.org/sites/default/files/publications/The _New_Politics_of_Judicial_Election_2013_2014.pdf.

54. Tyler Bishop, "The Most Expensive Judicial Election in U.S. History," *Atlantic*, November 10, 2015.

55. Alicia Bannon, Cathleen Lisk, and Peter Hardin, "Who Pays for Judicial Races?," Brennan Center for Justice, New York University School of Law, 2017, https:// www.brennancenter.org/sites/default/files/publications/Politics of Judicial _Elections_Final.pdf.

56. Wisconsin Democracy Campaign, "2019 Supreme Court Race Cost Record $8.2 Million+," press release, July 17, 2019, https://www.wisdc.org/news/press -releases/126-press-release-2019/6380-2019-supreme-court-race-cost-record -8-2-million.

57. Wisconsin Elections Commission, "2019 Spring Election Results," https:// elections.wi.gov/elections-voting/results/2019/spring-election, and Wisconsin Elections Commission, "Canvass Results for 2019 Spring Election," https:// elections.wi.gov/sites/electionsuat.wi.gov/files/Canvass%20Results-Spring %20Election%20and%20Assm%2064%20Primary.pdf. Just one year later, Jill Karofsky shocked the Wisconsin political world by ousting the conservative incumbent, Daniel Kelly, by 120,000 votes in the middle of the pandemic.

58. Jonathan Oosting, Riley Beggin, and Kelly House, "Michigan Supreme Court Rules Whitmer Lacks COVID-19 Emergency Powers," *Bridge Michigan*, October 2, 2020.

59. A study of the Nevada Supreme Court found that in 60 percent of civil cases in 2008–9, at least one of the litigants or attorneys involved in the case had contributed to the campaign of at least one justice. "Campaign Contributors and the Nevada Supreme Court, American Judicature Society," 2010, 2, http://www.judicialselection.us/uploads/documents/AJS_NV_study_FINAL _A3A7D42494729.pdf; quoted in Bannon, "Choosing State Judges." See also

Joanna M. Shepherd, "Money, Politics, and Impartial Justice," *Duke Law Journal* 623 (2009): 665–66, and Michael S. Kang and Joanna M. Shepherd, "The Partisan Price of Justice: An Empirical Analysis of Campaign Contributions and Judicial Decisions," *New York University Law Review* 86 (2011): 104.

60. Scott Greytak, Alicia Bannon, and Allyse Falce, *Bankrolling the Bench: The New Politics of Judicial Elections 2013–2014*, Brennan Center for Justice, New York University School of Law; Justice at Stake; and the National Institute on Money in State Politics, 2015, 1–4.

61. Dan Levine and Kristina Cooke, "In States with Elected High Court Judges, a Harder Line on Capital Punishment," Reuters, September 22, 2015, https://www.reuters.com/investigates/special-report/usa-deathpenalty-judges/#graphic-deathpenalty.

62. Patrick Berry and Douglas Keith, "In 2018, A Spate of Partisan Attacks on State Courts," Brennan Center for Justice, New York University School of Law, December 18, 2018, https://www.brennancenter.org/blog/2018-spate-partisan-attacks-state-courts.

63. Billy Corriher, "Court Packing? It's Already Happening at the State Level," *Governing*, September 30, 2020.

64. The Brennan Center for Justice conducted a study of Virginia, South Carolina, and Rhode Island appointment processes (Rhode Island used a legislative appointment process until 1994) that reveals a number of the problems discussed in this section. Douglas Keith and Laila Robbins, "Legislative Appointments for Judges: Lessons from South Carolina, Virginia, and Rhode Island," Brennan Center for Justice, New York University School of Law, September 29, 2017, https://www.brennancenter.org/our-work/research-reports/legislative-appointments-judges-lessons-south-carolina-virginia-and-rhode.

65. Levine and Cooke, "In States with Elected High Court Judges."

66. Under the Virginia Constitution, the governor has the power to make judicial appointments to seats that become vacant when the General Assembly is not in session. Constitution of Virginia, Article V, Section 7, and Article VI, Section 7. To get around this provision, the Republican-controlled General Assembly has frequently chosen to remain in session, even though there is no business to transact, in order to deny the governor the ability to make a "recess appointment."

67. A University of Georgia study estimated that, as of 2010, 3 percent of the total US population and 15 percent of the African American male population had served time in prison; that amounts to over eight million Americans. Alan Flurry, "Study Estimates U.S. Population with Felony Convictions," *UGA Today*, October 1, 2017. A Pew study reported that, in 2015, there were 1.9 million people on felony probation in the United States. Tim Henderson, "Felony Conviction Rates Have Risen Sharply, but Unevenly," *Stateline* (blog), Pew Charitable Trusts, January 2, 2018, https://www.pewtrusts.org/en/research

-and-analysis/blogs/stateline/2018/01/02/felony-conviction-rates-have-risen
-sharply-but-unevenly.

## 9. Building State Economies

1. Enrico Moretti, *The New Geography of Jobs* (New York: Houghton Mifflin, 2012).
2. Luke Mullins, "The Real Story of How Virginia Won Amazon's HQ2," *Washingtonian,* June 2019.
3. "The Big Reveal," *Virginia Economic Review,* First Quarter 2019, 16.
4. Susan Adams, "Virginia Tech's Promise to Build a New Campus Helped Seal Amazon's Virginia Headquarters Deal," *Forbes,* November 13, 2018.
5. Laura Stevens, Jimmy Vielkind, and Katie Honan, "Amazon Cancels HQ2 Plans in New York City," *Wall Street Journal,* February 14, 2019.
6. Ed Shanahan, "Amazon Grows in New York, Reviving Debate over Abandoned Queens Project," *New York Times,* December 9, 2019.
7. Scott Cohn, "Texas Is CNBC's Top State for Business in America This Year," CNBC, July 10, 2018, https://www.cnbc.com/2018/06/29/texas-rebounds -to-become-americas-top-state-for-business-in-2018.html; Scott Cohn, "Amazon Had It Right: Virginia Is America's Top State for Business in 2019," CNBC, July 10, 2019, https://www.cnbc.com/2019/07/09/virginia-is-americas-top -state-for-business-in-2019.html.
8. Nelson D. Schwartz, Patricia Cohen, and Julie Hirschfeld Davis, "Wisconsin's Lavish Lure for Foxconn: $3 Billion in Tax Subsidies," *New York Times,* July 27, 2017.
9. Scott Bauer, "Wisconsin tells Foxconn No Tax Credits without New Deal," *AP News,* October 12, 2020.
10. Peter T. Calcagno and Frank Hefner, "Economic Development Tax Incentives: A Review of the Perverse, Ineffective, and Unintended Consequences," in *For Your Own Good: Taxes, Paternalism, and Fiscal Discrimination in the Twenty-First Century,* ed. Adam J. Hoffer and Todd Nesbit (Arlington, VA: George Mason University, Mercatus Center, 2018).
11. Timothy J. Bartik, "Who Benefits from Economic Development Incentives? How Incentive Effects on Local Incomes and the Income Distribution Vary with Different Assumptions about Incentive Policy and the Local Economy," Upjohn Institute Technical Report 18-034 (Kalamazoo, MI: W. E. Upjohn Institute for Employment Research, 2018).
12. Timothy J. Bartik, "'But For' Percentages for Economic Development Incentives: What Percentage Estimates Are Plausible Based on the Research Literature?," Upjohn Institute Working Paper 18-289 (Kalamazoo, MI: W. E. Upjohn Institute for Employment Research, 2018).'
13. Bruce McDonald, John Decker, Brad Johnson, and Michelle Allen, "You Don't Always Get What You Want: The Effect of Financial Incentives on State Fiscal Health," *Public Administration Review,* May 23, 2019 (last revised May 8, 2020).

Another study, which places total state incentives in the range of $96 billion over a fifteen-year period, questions whether the high costs of these incentives are justified in terms of the jobs produced or revenue raised. Cailin R. Slattery and Owen M. Zidar, "Evaluating State and Local Business Tax Incentives," NBER Working Paper 26603 (Cambridge, MA: National Bureau of Economic Research, January 2020).

14. Terry McAuliffe, *Four Years: Celebrating the New Virginia Economy,* Commonwealth of Virginia, 2018, https://www.terrymcauliffe.com/wp-content/uploads/2020/08/Four-YearReport-3.pdf.

15. Jeff Sturgeon, "Money for Nothing: Sweet Appomattox Deal Turned Sour for Virginia, Mcauliffe," *Roanoke Times,* January 16, 2016.

16. R. L. Nave, "With Safety History, Is Yokohama a Good Deal?," *Jackson Free Press,* May 1, 2013.

17. Josh Goodman, "New Jersey Tax Incentives Need a Periodic Checkup," Pew Charitable Trusts, June 9, 2019, https://www.pewtrusts.org/en/about/news-room/opinion/2019/06/09/new-jersey-tax-incentives-need-a-periodic-checkup.

18. Virginia Joint Legislative Audit and Review Commission, "Management and Accountability of the Virginia Economic Development Partnership," November 2016, http://jlarc.virginia.gov/pdfs/reports/Rpt488.pdf.

19. Josh Goodman, Alison Wakefield and Shane Benz, "Pennsylvania Revises Tax Credits after First State Evaluations," Pew Charitable Trusts, July 29, 2019, https://www.pewtrusts.org/en/research-and-analysis/articles/2019/07/29/pennsylvania-revises-tax-credits-after-first-state-evaluations.

20. Virginia Division of Legislative Services, "Joint Subcommittee to Evaluate Tax Preferences: Preference Reports," http://dls.virginia.gov/commissions/tax.htm?x=rep (accessed February 1, 2017).

21. David J. Toscano, "Toscano: Tough Choices about Coal Tax Credits," *Richmond Times Dispatch,* December 17, 2012.

22. Aaron Williams and Michael J. Cassidy, "Coal Tax Credits Aren't Working," Commonwealth Institute, March 2, 2016, https://www.thecommonwealthinstitute.org/2016/03/02/coal-tax-credits-arent-working/.

23. "How States Are Improving Tax Incentives for Jobs and Growth," Pew Charitable Trusts, May 3, 2017, https://www.pewtrusts.org/en/research-and-analysis/reports/2017/05/how-states-are-improving-tax-incentives-for-jobs-and-growth.

24. National Conference of State Legislatures, State Tax Incentives Evaluations Database, October 10, 2018, http://www.ncsl.org/research/fiscal-policy/state-tax-incentive-evaluations-database.aspx.

25. Michael Thom, "Lights, Camera, but No Action? Tax and Economic Development Lessons from State Motion Picture Incentive Programs," *American Review of Public Administration* 48, no. 1 (January 2018), 33–51. A similar critique is found in Mark F. Owens and Adam D. Rennhoff, "Motion Picture Production

Incentives and Filming Location Decisions: A Discrete Choice Approach," *Journal of Economic Geography*, November 23, 2018.

26. National Conference of State Legislatures, "State Film Production Incentives and Programs," February 5, 2018, http://www.ncsl.org/research/fiscal-policy/state-film-production-incentives-and-programs.aspx.

27. James Salzer, "Auditors Say Impact of Georgia's Film Tax Credits Has Been Exaggerated," *Atlanta Journal-Constitution*, January 9, 2020.

28. The Georgia film credit is among the most lucrative of all the states. The yearly cost to fund the film tax credits grew from $141 million in 2010 to an estimated $870 million in 2019. Since its inception, about $4 billion in tax credits have been issued by the state. New York distributed $621 million in 2017 to support the film industry. See Ben Paviour, "Lights, Camera, Subsidies: Legislature Debates Increasing Film Incentives," *VPM News*, February 13, 2020.

29. Joint Legislative Audit and Review Commission, *Evaluation: Film Incentives Economic Development Incentives Evaluation Series*, JLARC Report 501, 2017, http://jlarc.virginia.gov/pdfs/reports/Rpt501.pdf.

30. Baker Tilly, "Virginia's Historic Rehabilitation Tax Credits," Preservation Virginia, December 2017, http://preservationva.wpengine.com/wp-content/uploads/2018/08/VA_HTC_Full_Report_.pdf, and Sarin Adhlkri, Jeffrey Crawford, Fabrizio Fasulo, and Michael Mackenzie, *Preserving The Past, Building the Future: HRTC at Work in Virginia* (Richmond: Virginia Commonwealth University, Virginia: L. Douglas Wilder School of Government and Public Affairs, January 2018).

31. Renee Kuhlman, "Historic Tax Credits: A Good Return for the Money," *Main Street America*, June 17, 2015, https://www.mainstreet.org/blogs/hl-admin/2017/05/11/historic-tax-credits-a-good-return-for-the-money.

32. It is for this reason that Virginia has been seeking to increase monies reserved in the state budget for site readiness. See Michael Martz, "New State Study Shows Few Large Sites in Virginia Are Ready to Market for Economic Development Projects," *Richmond Times-Dispatch*, December 10, 2019.

33. National Conference of State Legislatures, "State Minimum Wages: 2020 Minimum Wage by State," January 6, 2020, https://www.ncsl.org/research/labor-and-employment/state-minimum-wage-chart.aspx. California has differential minimum wages based on company size, and New York's minimum differs by region.

34. Elise Gould and Will Kimball, "'Right-to-Work' States Still Have Lower Wages," Economic Policy Institute, April 22, 2015, https://www.epi.org/publication/right-to-work-states-have-lower-wages/.

35. National Conference of State Legislatures, "Right-To-Work Resources," http://www.ncsl.org/research/labor-and-employment/right-to-work-laws-and-bills.aspx. Michigan, West Virginia, Indiana, and Wisconsin added right-to-work clauses to their state codes in the last five years, though the action of the Mountain

State is being challenged in the courts. Eight states—Arizona, Oklahoma, Nebraska, South Dakota, Arkansas, Mississippi, Alabama, and Florida—even include it in their constitutions. The National Right to Work Committee is the national group advocating for these laws (see the website at https://nrtwc.org/).

36. Annie Gowen, "How the Democrats Finally Defeated Wisconsin Gov. Scott Walker," *Washington Post*, November 7, 2018.

37. Jeffrey A. Eisenach, "Right-to-Work Laws: The Economic Evidence," NERA Economic Consulting, May 2018, https://www.nera.com/content/dam/nera/publications/2018/PUB_Right_to_Work_Laws_0518_web.pdf.

38. Thomas J. Holmes, "The Effect of State Policies on the Location of Manufacturing: Evidence from State Borders," *Journal of Political Economy* 106, no. 4 (August 1998): 667–705.

39. Ozkan Eren and Serkan Ozbeklik, "What Do Right-to-Work Laws Do? Evidence from a Synthetic Control Method Analysis," *Journal of Policy Analysis and Management* 35, no. 1 (July 2015): 173–94.

40. Frank Manzo IV and Robert Bruno, "The Impact of 'Right-to-Work' Laws on Labor Market Outcomes in Three Midwest States: Evidence from Indiana, Michigan, and Wisconsin (2010–2016)" (Urbana-Champaign: University of Illinois, School of Labor & Employment Relations, April 2017), https://ler.illinois.edu/wp-content/uploads/2017/03/RTW-in-the-Midwest-2010–2016.pdf.

41. James Feigenbaum, Alexander Hertel-Fernandez, and Vanessa Williamson, "From the Bargaining Table to the Ballot Box: Political Effects of Right to Work Laws," NBER Working Paper w24259 (Cambridge, MA: National Bureau of Economic Research, January 2018).

42. Benjamin Collins, "Right to Work Laws: Legislative Background and Empirical Research" (Washington, DC: Congressional Research Service, January 6, 2014).

43. Andriy Blokhin, "5 States with the Highest Real GDP Per Capita," *Investopedia*, October 24, 2018, https://www.investopedia.com/contributors/53892/.

44. "Per Capita Real Gross Domestic Product (GDP) of the United States in 2018, by State (in Chained 2012 U.S. Dollars)," Statista, https://www.statista.com/statistics/248063/per-capita-us-real-gross-domestic-product-gdp-by-state/.

45. Brad Plumer, "What Do 'Right-to-Work' Laws Do to a State's Economy?" *Washington Post*, December 10, 2012.

46. According to the US Labor Department, only 4.6 percent of Virginia's workers are unionized, well below the national rate of 10.5 percent. Sean Higgins, "After Years of Pursuit, Virginia Democrats Slow-Walk Right-to-Work Repeal," *Washington Examiner*, November 13, 2019.

47. *Janus v. AFSCME, Council 31, et al.*, 138 U.S. (2018).

48. *Abood v. Detroit Board of Education*, 431 U.S. 209 (1977).

49. Trey Kovacs, "Post-'Janus', Unions Continue Undermining Public Workers' First Amendment Rights," Competitive Enterprise Institute, June 24, 2019, https://cei.org/blog/post-janus-unions-continue-undermining-public-workers-first-amendment-rights.

50.  Katherine Barnett and Richard Greene, "How States Are Making It Harder to Leave Unions," *Governing*, July 16, 2018.

51.  Michael J. Reitz, "Public Employees Should Be Allowed to Exercise Their Rights," *The Hill*, August 21, 2019. A legal approach to this issue is outlined in Aaron Tang, "Life after Janus," *Columbia Law Review* 119, no. 3 (2019): 677–762.

52.  His actual quotation, taken from a dissent he wrote in *Compania General de Tabacos v. Collector*, 275 U.S. 87, 100 (1927), was "every exaction of money for an act is a discouragement to the extent of the payment required, but that which in its immediacy is a discouragement may be part of an encouragement when seen in its organic connection with the whole. Taxes are what we pay for civilized society. . . ."

53.  David Brunori, *State Tax Policy: A Primer* (Lanham, MD: Rowman & Littlefield, 2016).

54.  Janelle Cammenga, "State and Local Sales Tax Rates, 2019" (Washington, DC: Tax Foundation, January 30, 2019), https://taxfoundation.org/sales-tax-rates-2019/.

55.  Jared Walczak, Scott Drenkard, and Joseph Bishop-Henchman, "2019 State Business Tax Climate Index" (Washington, DC: Tax Foundation, n.d.), https://files.taxfoundation.org/20180925174436/2019-State-Business-Tax-Climate-Index.pdf.

56.  Meg Wehe, Aidan Davis, Carl Davis, Matt Gardner, Lisa Christensengee, and Dillon Grundman, *Who Pays? A Distributional Analysis of the Tax Systems in All Fifty States*, 6th ed. (Washington, DC: Institute on Taxation and Economic Policy, October 2018).

57.  Institute on Taxation and Economic Policy, "Low Tax States Are Often High-Tax for the Poor," October 17, 2018, https://itep.org/low-tax-states-are-often-high-tax-for-the-poor/.

58.  Eileen Norcross and Olivia Gonzalez. "Ranking the States by Fiscal Condition, 2018 Edition" (Arlington, VA: George Mason University, Mercatus Center, October 2018), https://www.mercatus.org/system/files/norcross-fiscal-rankings-2018-mercatus-research-v1.pdf.

59.  Heather Boushey, "Failed Tax-Cut Experiment in Kansas Should Guide National Leaders," *The Hill*, November 29, 2018.

## 10. Don't Forget Health Care!

1.  Carmen Forman, "Remote Area Medical Founder: Donald Trump Should Be Here," *Roanoke Times*, July 23, 2017

2.  Tim Dodson, "Remote Area Medical to Discontinue Wise County Clinic Next Year," *Bristol Herald Courier*, July 12, 2019.

3.  The COVID-19 pandemic forced a cancellation of the clinic in 2020, yet another manifestation of the effect of the virus.

4.  Edward R. Berchick, Jessica C. Barnett, and Rachel D. Upton, "Health Insurance Coverage in the United States: 2018" (Washington, DC: US Census Bureau,

November 2019), https://www.census.gov/content/dam/Census/library/publications/2019/demo/p60-267.pdf.

5. Hristina Byrnes and Thomas C. Frohlich, "Life Expectancy in the US: You're Most Likely to Live a Long Life in Hawaii and California," *USA Today*, February 21, 2019.

6. US Public Health Service, Department of Health, Education, and Welfare, "Infant Mortality Rates by Color: United States, Each Division and State," in *Vital Statistics of the United States, 1967: Volume II-Mortality, Part A* (Washington, DC: US Government Printing Office, 1969), table 2-6.

7. Danielle M. Ely and Anne K. Driscoll, "Infant Mortality in the United States, 2017: Data from the Period Linked Birth/Infant Death File," *National Vital Statistics Report* 68, no. 10 (August 1, 2019): 14, table 3.

8. Massachusetts Department of Public Health, "Life Expectancy Rises in Massachusetts, Breaking with National Trend," press release, December 26, 2018, https://www.mass.gov/news/life-expectancy-rises-in-massachusetts-breaking-with-national-trend.

9. Laura Snyder and Robin Rudowitz, "Medicaid Financing: How Does It Work and What Are the Implications?," issue brief, Kaiser Family Foundation, May 20, 2015, https://www.kff.org/report-section/medicaid-financing-how-does-it-work-and-what-are-the-implications-issue-brief/.

10. *NFIB v. Sebelius*, 567 U.S. 519 (2012).

11. Kaiser Family Foundation, "Status of State Medicaid Expansion Decisions: Interactive Map," August 5, 2020, https://www.kff.org/medicaid/issue-brief/status-of-state-medicaid-expansion-decisions-interactive-map/. In 2020, the Kansas legislature indicated its intention to expand Medicaid as well.

12. Families USA, "A 50-State Look at Medicaid Expansion," November 2018, https://familiesusa.org/product/50-state-look-medicaid-expansion. Oklahoma's ballot initiative was notable because it added the Medicaid expansion to the state's constitution. Carmen Foreman, "Oklahoma Voters Approve Medicaid Expansion at the Ballot Box," *The Oklahoman*, July 1, 2020.

13. Greg Sargent, "Have Republicans Lost the Argument over the Medicaid Expansion?," *Washington Post*, January 9, 2020.

14. Robin Rudowitz, Elizabeth Hinton, Maria Diaz, Madeline Guth, and Marina Tian, "Medicaid Enrollment & Spending Growth: FY 2019 & 2020," Kaiser Family Foundation, October 18, 2019, https://www.kff.org/medicaid/issue-brief/medicaid-enrollment-spending-growth-fy-2019-2020/.

15. Andrew Soergel, "New York, Rhode Island Spend Highest Percentages of Budgets on Medicaid," *US News*, January 14, 2020.

16. Laura Snyder and Robin Rudowitz, "Trends in State Medicaid Programs: Looking Back and Looking Ahead," Kaiser Family Foundation, June 21, 2016, https://www.kff.org/medicaid/issue-brief/trends-in-state-medicaid-programs-looking-back-and-looking-ahead/view/print/.

17. Robin Rudowitz, Elizabeth Hinton, and Larisa Antonisse, "Medicaid Enrollment

& Spending Growth: FY 2018 & 2019," Kaiser Family Foundation, October 25, 2018, https://www.kff.org/medicaid/issue-brief/medicaid-enrollment-spending-growth-fy-2018-2019/.

18. Larisa Antonisse, Rachel Garfield, Robin Rudowitz, and Madeline Guth, "The Effects of Medicaid Expansion under the ACA: Updated Findings from a Literature Review," Kaiser Family Foundation, August 15, 2019, https://www.kff.org/medicaid/issue-brief/the-effects-of-medicaid-expansion-under-the-aca-updated-findings-from-a-literature-review-august-2019/. A 2019 study argues that Medicaid expansion saves lives. See Sarah Miller, Sean Altekruse, Norman Johnson, and Laura R. Wherry, "Medicaid and Mortality: New Evidence from Linked Survey and Administrative Data," NBER Working Paper w26081 (Cambridge, MA: National Bureau of Economic Research, July 2019, rev. August 2019), https://www.nber.org/papers/w26081.

19. Colby Itkowitz, "Where Are the Most Expensive ACA Plans in America? Charlottesville," *Washington Post,* November 16, 2017.

20. Rachel Fehr, Rabah Kamal, and Cynthia Cox, "Insurer Participation on ACA Marketplaces, 2014–2020," Kaiser Family Foundation, November 21, 2019, https://www.kff.org/private-insurance/issue-brief/insurer-participation-on-aca-marketplaces-2014-2020/.

21. Linda J. Blumberg, Matthew Buettgens, and Robin Wang, "The Potential Impact of Short-Term Limited Duration Policies on Insurance Coverage, Premiums, and Federal Spending" (Washington, DC: Urban Institute, February 2018), https://www.urban.org/sites/default/files/publication/96781/2001727_0.pdf.

22. Rabah Kamal, Cynthia Cox, Rachel Fehr, Marco Ramirez, Katherine Horstman, and Larry Levitt, "How Repeal of the Individual Mandate and Expansion of Loosely Regulated Plans Are Affecting 2019 Premiums," Kaiser Family Foundation, October 26, 2018, https://www.kff.org/health-costs/issue-brief/how-repeal-of-the-individual-mandate-and-expansion-of-loosely-regulated-plans-are-affecting-2019-premiums/.

23. Steven Findlay, "As States Strive To Stabilize Insurance Marketplaces, Insurers Return," *Kaiser Health News,* August 14, 2019, https://khn.org/news/as-states-strive-to-stabilize-insurance-marketplaces-insurers-return.

24. Colleen Becker, "Insuring the Health Insurers—Reinsurance Explained," *The NCSL Blog,* May 7, 2018, http://www.ncsl.org/blog/2018/05/07/insuring-the-health-insurers-reinsurance-explained.aspx.

25. Elizabeth Hayes, "Oregon Health Insurance Rates Could Rise Less Than Anticipated Next Year," *Portland Business Journal,* June 30, 2017.

26. John Holahan, Linda J. Blumberg, and Erik Wengle, *Changes in Marketplace Premiums, 2017 to 2018* (Washington, DC: Urban Institute, March 2018), https://www.urban.org/sites/default/files/publication/97371/changes_in_marketplace_premiums_2017_to_2018_0.pdf.

27. Katie Keith, "CMS Approves Reinsurance Waivers in DE, RI," *Health Affairs,* August 27, 2019.

28. Coleman Drake, Brett Fried, and Lynn A. Blewett, "Estimated Costs of a Rein-surance Program to Stabilize the Individual Health Insurance Market: National- and State-Level Estimates," *Inquiry* 56 (March 21, 2019), https://www.ncbi.nlm .nih.gov/pmc/articles/PMC6429648/.

29. Michael Ollove, "To Curb Rising Health Insurance Costs, Some States Try 'Reinsurance Pools,'" *Stateline* (blog), Pew Charitable Trusts, April 9, 2018, https://www.pewtrusts.org/en/research-and-analysis/blogs/stateline/2018/04 /09/to-curb-rising-health-insurance-costs-some-states-try-reinsurance-pools.

30. John Ingold, "Hospitals Are Backing Off a Budget Fight over Colorado's Rein-surance Program. Is a Deal Possible?," *Colorado Sun*, January 30, 2020.

31. Joseph O'Sullivan, "Washingtonians to Get Public Option on State's Health-Insurance Exchange," *Seattle Times*, May 14, 2019.

32. Michael Ollove, "Medicaid 'Buy-In' Could Be a New Health Care Option for the Uninsured," *Stateline* (blog), Pew Charitable Trusts, January 10, 2019, https:// www.pewtrusts.org/en/research-and-analysis/blogs/stateline/2019/01/10 /medicaid-buy-in-could-be-a-new-health-care-option-for-the-uninsured.

33. Harris Meyer, "States Giving Public Option Health Plans a Hard Look," *Modern Health Care*, June 1, 2019.

34. Sarah Gantz, "Pennsylvania to Shift from Healthcare.gov to State-Based Insur-ance Exchange," *Philadelphia Inquirer*, July 2, 2019.

35. Ned Oliver, "Va. Democrats Weigh Medicaid Dental Coverage, a Cheaper Mar-ketplace and, Maybe, a Public Option," *Virginia Mercury*, January 7, 2020.

36. Harris Meyer, "Cigna Helps Shoot Down Connecticut Public-Option Bill," *Modern Healthcare*, May 30, 2019.

37. Rachel Schwab and JoAnn Volk, "States Looking to Run Their Own Health Insurance Marketplace See Opportunity for Funding, Flexibility," *To the Point* (blog), Commonwealth Fund, June 28, 2019, https://www.commonwealthfund .org/blog/2019/states-looking-to-run-their-own-health-insurance-marketplace -see-opportunity.

38. Harris Meyer, "Maine Will Shift to State-Based ACA Exchange," *Modern Health-care*, August 29, 2019, https://www.modernhealthcare.com/insurance/maine -will-shift-state-based-aca-exchange.

39. Lauren Weber, Laura Ungar, Michelle R. Smith, Hannah Recht, and Anna Maria Barry-Jester, "Hollowed-Out Public Health System Faces More Cuts Amid Virus," Kaiser Family Foundation, July 1, 2020,

40. Margot Sanger-Katz, Sarah Kliff and Alicia Parlapiano, "These Places Could Run Out of Hospital Beds as Coronavirus Spreads," *New York Times*, March 17, 2020; Jesse C. Baumgartner, David C. Radley, Sara R. Collins, Melinda K. Abrams, and Eric C. Schneider "Assessing Underlying State Conditions and Ramp-Up Challenges for the COVID-19 Response," Commonwealth Fund, March 25, 2020, https://www.commonwealthfund.org/publications/issue-briefs/2020 /mar/assessing-underlying-state-conditions-and-ramp-challenges-covid.

41. Dan Goldberg, "Pandemic Upends State Plans to Expand Health Insurance," *Politico*, May 28, 2020.

42. Josh Bivens and Ben Zipperer, "Health Insurance and the Covid-19 Shock," Economic Policy Institute, August 26, 2020, https://www.epi.org/publication /health-insurance-and-the-covid-19-shock/.

43. Progressive Policy Institute, "Medicaid Will Be Crucial Safety Net in COVID-19 Crisis," June 3, 2020, https://www.progressivepolicy.org/publication/medicaid -will-be-crucial-safety-net-in-covid-19-crisis/.

44. Heather Howard and Sonia Pandit, "States Lead the Way in Responding to COVID-19 and Advancing Innovative Health Policy Solutions on Many Fronts," *Health Affairs* (blog), HealthAffairs.org, May 18, 2020 https://www.healthaffairs .org/do/10.1377/hblog20200513.980735/full/.

45. Kate Masters, "Nurse Practitioners Say Supervision Requirements are a Hindrance amid COVID-19 Pandemic," *Virginia Mercury*, April 13, 2020.

46. Geoffrey A. Fowler, "I Downloaded America's First Coronavirus Exposure App. You Should Too," *Washington Post*, August 18, 2020.

## 11. Flashpoints in the Culture Wars of States

1. *Roe v. Wade*, 410 U.S. 113 (1973).

2. *Planned Parenthood v. Casey*, 505 U.S. 833 (1992).

3. "The New Push to Overturn Roe v Wade," *Economist*, April 13, 2019.

4. Emily Wax-Thibodeaux, "Restrictive Abortion Bill Weighs on Alabama Republicans, Who Struggle with Lack of Exceptions for Rape, Incest," *Washington Post*, May 13, 2019.

5. Guttmacher Institute, "Abortion Policy in the Absence of Roe," July 1, 2019, https://www.guttmacher.org/state-policy/explore/abortion-policy-absence-roe.

6. The US Centers for Disease Control and Prevention found that from 2006 to 2015, "the number, rate, and ratio of reported abortions decreased 24 percent, 26 percent, and 19 percent, respectively. In 2015, all three measures reached their lowest level for the entire period of analysis (2006–2015)." CDC's Abortion Surveillance System FAQs, November 19, 2018, https://www.cdc.gov /reproductivehealth/data_stats/abortion.htm. The Guttmacher Institute estimates the number of abortions in the United States in 2014 was about 926,000, down from a high of about 1.5 million annually in the early 1990s. Guttmacher Institute, "Induced Abortion in the United States" (fact sheet), January 2018, https://www.guttmacher.org/fact-sheet/induced-abortion-united -states. See also National Academies of Sciences, Engineering, and Medicine, *The Safety and Quality of Abortion Care in the United States* (Washington, DC: National Academies Press, 2018).

7. Tara C. Jatlaoui, Maegan E. Boutot, Michelle G. Mandel, et al., "Abortion Surveillance—United States, 2015," *MMWR Surveillance Summaries* 67, no. 13 (2018):1–45.

8. National Right to Life Committee, *The State of Abortion in the United States* (Washington, DC: NRLC, January 2019), 5–6.

9. Michael Scherer and Felicia Sonmez, "Abortion Ban Reaction: Democrats Erupt, Republicans Stay Quiet as Both Sides See an Impact in the 2020 Election," *Washington Post*, May 15, 2019.

10. Tara Law, "Here Are the Details of the Abortion Legislation in Alabama, Georgia, Louisiana and Elsewhere," *Time*, May 18, 2019 (updated online July 2, 2019).

11. David Pitt and Paul J. Weber, "Judges Slow Abortion Bans in Texas, Ohio, Alabama amid Virus," *AP News*, March 31, 2020.

12. The Tennessee situation is especially significant since a state supreme court decision issued a decade earlier, *Planned Parenthood of Middle Tennessee v. Sundquist*, 38 S.W.3d 1 (Tenn. 2000), found that the state's constitution provided stronger abortion protections than the federal constitution, concluding that "a woman's right to terminate her pregnancy is a vital part of the right to privacy guaranteed by the Tennessee Constitution." *Sundquist*, 38 S.W. 3d at 19. This is one reason why anti-abortion activists targeted Tennessee for the anti-abortion constitutional amendment. Since the passage of the amendment, Tennessee has once again implemented a forty-eight-hour waiting period, a ban on public funding, and a ban on abortion after viability.

13. Emma Sarappo, "The Legal Strategy behind Alabama and West Virginia's New Anti-Abortion Amendments," *Pacific Standard*, November 7, 2018.

14. Lolly Bowean, "Gov. J.B. Pritzker Signs Abortion Rights Law Making Procedure a 'Fundamental Right' for Women in Illinois," *Chicago Tribune*, June 12, 2019.

15. Aris Folley, "GOP Vermont Governor Signs Sweeping Abortion Rights Bill into Law," *The Hill*, June 11, 2019.

16. Gallup, "Abortion," *In Depth: Topics A–Z*, https://news.gallup.com/poll/1576 /abortion.aspx; Emily Guskin and Scott Clement, "Abortion Support Is the Highest It's Been in Two Decades as Challenges Mount," *Washington Post*, July 10, 2019.

17. Anna North, "How the Abortion Debate Moved Away from 'Safe, Legal, and Rare,'" *Vox*, October 18, 2019.

18. Ryan W. Miller, "Virginia Gov. Northam Signs Host of Gun Control Bills into Law Months after Richmond Rally," *USA Today*, April 10, 2020.

19. US Bureau of Alcohol, Tobacco, Firearms and Explosives, "Firearms Commerce in the United States, Annual Statistical Update, 2015," updated March 15, 2016, https://www.atf.gov/file/89561/download.

20. Megan Brenan, "Nearly Half in U.S. Fear Being the Victim of a Mass Shooting," Gallup poll, September 10, 2019, https://news.gallup.com/poll/266681/nearly -half-fear-victim-mass-shooting.aspx?.

21. Christopher Ingraham, "There Are Now More Guns Than People in the United States," *Washington Post*, October 5, 2015. The *Post* also presents some evidence

that this number may actually be a little lower; nonetheless, there is broad consensus that the numbers far exceed 200 million.

22. Jeff Edwards, "Gun Ownership Mapped: How Many Guns Each State Had in 2017?," *Hunting Mark,* February 18, 2018.

23. Centers for Disease Control and Prevention, Web-Based Injury Statistics Query and Reporting System (WISQARS) (Atlanta, GA: National Center for Injury Prevention and Control, 2017), quoted in Jane McClenathan, Molly Pahn, and Michael Siegel, "The Changing Landscape of U.S. Gun Policy: State Firearm Laws, 1991–2016," Robert Wood Foundation and Boston University School of Public Health, 2017, http://www.statefirearmlaws.org/sites/default/files/2017–12/report_0.pdf.

24. Joseph Tartakovsky, "Firearm Preemption Laws and What They Mean for Cities," *Municipal Lawyer* 54, no. 5 (September/October 2013).

25. Ashley Murray, "City Agrees to Stay on Three Gun-Control Bills while Lawsuits Play Out in Court," *Pittsburgh Post-Gazette,* July 19, 2019.

26. US Secret Service National Threat Assessment Center, *Mass Attacks in Public Spaces-2018* (Washington, DC: US Department of Homeland Security, July, 2019), https://www.secretservice.gov/data/press/reports/USSS_FY2019_MAPS.pdf.

27. Maurizio Pompili, Roberto Tatarelli, et al., "Suicide Risk among Epileptic Patients," in *New Research on Epilepsy and Behavior,* ed. K. J. Hollaway (New York: Nova Science, 2007), 144, table 1. Hollaway's book is referenced on the web page "Suicide," Mental Health America, http://www.mentalhealthamerica.net/suicide.

28. Aaron J. Kivisto and Peter Lee Phalen, "Effects of Risk-Based Firearm Seizure Laws in Connecticut and Indiana on Suicide Rates, 1981–2015," *Psychiatry Online,* June 1, 2018, https://doi.org/10.1176/appi.ps.201700250.

29. On Florida's laws, see Patricia Mazzei, "Florida Governor Signs Gun Limits into Law, Breaking with the N.R.A.," *New York Times,* March 9, 2018. On New Mexico's laws, see Jens Gould, "Governor Signs Controversial 'Red-Flag' Bill into Law," *Santa Fe New Mexican,* February 25, 2020. On Virginia's laws, see Miller, "Virginia Gov. Northam Signs Host of Gun Control Bills into Law Months after Richmond Rally."

30. *The Science of Gun Policy: A Critical Synthesis of Research Evidence on the Effects of Gun Policies in the United States* (Santa Monica, CA: Rand Corp., 2018).

31. Michael Siegel and Claire Boine, "What Are the Most Effective Policies in Reducing Gun Homicides?," Regional Gun Violence Research Consortium Policy Brief (Albany, NY: SUNY Rockefeller Institute of Government, 2019), https://rockinst.org/wp-content/uploads/2019/08/8-13-19-Firearm-Laws-Homicide-Brief.pdf.

32. Peter Jamison, "Red Flag Laws May Play Role in Preventing Mass Shootings, Study Finds," *Washington Post,* August 19, 2019.

33. Jane McClenathan, Molly Pahn, and Michael Siegel, *The Changing Landscape of U.S. Gun Policy: State Firearm Laws, 1991–2016*, Robert Wood Foundation and Boston University School of Public Health, 2017, http://www.statefirearmlaws .org/sites/default/files/2017-12/report_0.pdf; Michael Siegel, Benjamin Solomon, Anita Knopov, Emily F. Rothman, Shea W. Cronin, Ziming Xuan, and David Hemenway, "The Impact of State Firearm Laws on Homicide Rates in Suburban and Rural Areas Compared to Large Cities in the United States, 1991–2016," *Journal of Rural Health*, July 30, 2019.

34. Daniel Trotta, "Defiant U.S. Sheriffs Push Gun Sanctuaries, Imitating Liberals on Immigration," Reuters, March 4, 2019.

35. Katherine Rosenberg-Douglas, "Second Amendment 'Sanctuary County' Movement Expands as Organizers Take Aim at New Gun Laws," *Chicago Tribune*, April 17, 2019.

36. David "Adam" McKelvey, "McKelvey: A Framework for True 2nd Amendment Sanctuary," *Roanoke Times*, November 27, 2019.

37. Gould, "Governor Signs Controversial 'Red-Flag' Bill into Law."

38. Alienation in rural life has been most recently chronicled in J. D. Vance, *Hillbilly Elegy: A Memoir of a Family and Culture in Crisis* (New York: Harper Press, 2016), Timothy P. Carney, *Alienated America* (New York: HarperCollins, 2019), and Arlie Russell Hochschild, *Strangers in Their Own Land: Anger and Mourning on the American Right* (New York: New Press, 2016).

39. Bradley Jones, "Majority of Americans Continue to Say Immigrants Strengthen the U.S.," Pew Research Center, January 31, 2019, https://www.pewresearch .org/fact-tank/2019/01/31/majority-of-americans-continue-to-say-immigrants -strengthen-the-u-s/.

40. For years, Republicans in Virginia distributed countless pieces of campaign literature linking their Democratic opponents to illegal immigrants and gangs such as MS-13. If recent election results in the commonwealth are any guide, these attacks appear to have lost some of their effectiveness.

41. Peter Wehner, *The Death of Politics: How to Heal Our Frayed Republic after Trump* (New York: Harper One, 2019), 16.

42. Alexia Fernandez Campbell, "Trump Says Undocumented Immigrants Are an Economic Burden. They Pay Billions in Taxes," *Vox*, October 25, 2018.

43. Campbell, "Trump Says Undocumented Immigrants Are an Economic Burden."

44. National Conference of State Legislatures, "State Laws Related to Immigration and Immigrants," January 16, 2019, https://www.ncsl.org/research /immigration/state-laws-related-to-immigration-and-immigrants.aspx.

45. Mel Leonor, "Northam Vetoes 'Sanctuary Cities' Bill," *Richmond Times-Dispatch*, March 19, 2019.

46. National Conference of State Legislatures, "Sanctuary Policy FAQ," April 16, 2019, http://www.ncsl.org/research/immigration/sanctuary-policy-faq635 991795.aspx.

47. *Plyler v. Doe*, 457 U.S. 202 (1982).

48. National Conference of State Legislatures, "Undocumented Student Tuition: Overview," March 14, 2019, http://www.ncsl.org/research/education/undocumented-student-tuition-overview.aspx.

49. Logan Albright, Ike Brannon, and M. Kevin McGee, "A New Estimate of the Cost of Reversing DACA," Cato Working Paper 49 (Washington, DC: Cato Institute, February 15, 2018).

50. "New Business Coalition, Texans for Economic Growth, and Texas Business Immigration Coalition Launch Texas Compact on Immigration," press release, New American Economy, February 26, 2019, https://www.newamerican economy.org/press-release/new-business-coalition-texans-for-economic-growth-and-texas-business-immigration-coalition-launch-texas-compact-on-immigration/.

51. National Conference of State Legislatures, "States Offering Driver's Licenses to Immigrants," February 6, 2020, https://www.ncsl.org/research/immigration/states-offering-driver-s-licenses-to-immigrants.aspx. For more information, see National Immigration Law Center, "State Laws Providing Access to Driver's Licenses or Cards, Regardless of Immigration Status" (last updated August 2019), https://www.nilc.org/wp-content/uploads/2015/11/drivers-license-access-table.pdf.

52. Kate Masters and Ned Oliver, "House, Senate Pass Long-Anticipated Immigrants' Rights Bills," *Virginia Mercury*, February 12, 2020.

53. Mary Duan, "Should States Driver's License to Unauthorized Residents?," *Insights by Stanford Business*, April 3, 2017, https://www.gsb.stanford.edu/insights/should-states-give-drivers-licenses-unauthorized-residents; Chris Burrell, "Licenses for Undocumented Immigrants Seem to Be Showing Benefits in Connecticut," *WGBH News*, April 16, 2019. Other studies in New Mexico and Utah cite reductions in the number of uninsured vehicles after changes in the law. See Bob Lewis, "License Undocumented Immigrants? It's Safer Than Having Unvetted, Unlicensed Drivers," *Virginia Mercury*, February 3, 2020.

54. Jimmy Vielkind, "New Yorkers Oppose Driver's Licenses for Illegal Immigrants, Poll Shows," *Wall Street Journal*, June 10, 2019.

55. After New York passed a law permitting greater access to licenses, the Trump administration became more actively involved, with the Department of Homeland Security arguing that the state's action "will protect criminals at the expense of the safety and security of law-abiding New York residents." Zachary Evans, "DHS Slams New York Law Allowing Illegal Immigrants to Obtain Driver's Licenses," *National Review*, December 17, 2019.

## 12. Tip O'Neill Is Still Dead

1. Thomas P. O'Neill with Gary Hymel, *All Politics Is Local: And Other Rules of the Game* (New York: Random House, 1994).

2. Steven Rogers, "National Forces in State Legislative Elections," *Annals of the*

*American Academy of Political and Social Science* 667 (2016): 207–25. Rogers argues there is an increasing nationalization of state elections and that "state legislators have relatively little control over their own elections."

3. The Tenth Amendment to the US Constitution states that "The powers not delegated to the United States by the Constitution, nor prohibited by it to the States, are reserved to the States respectively, or to the people."

4. Richard Florida, "America's 'Big Sort' Is Only Getting Bigger," *CityLab*, Bloomberg, October 25, 2016, https://www.citylab.com/equity/2016/10/the-big -sort-revisited/504830/.

5. Emily Badger, "Blue Cities Want to Make Their Own Rules. Red States Won't Let Them," *New York Times*, July 6, 2017.

6. Alan Greenblatt, "America's Governments Are at War with Each Other," *Governing*, July 24, 2020.

7. Steve Harrison, "Charlotte City Council Approves LGBT protections in 7–4 Vote," *Charlotte Observer*, February 23, 2016.

8. Michael Gordon, Mark S. Price, and Katie Peralta, "Understanding HB2: North Carolina's Newest Law Solidifies State's Role in Defining Discrimination," *Charlotte Observer*, March 26, 2016.

9. Emma G. Ellis, "Guess How Much that Anti-LGBTQ Law is Costing North Carolina," *Wired*, September 18, 2016.

10. Dan Levin, "North Carolina Reaches Settlement on 'Bathroom Bill,'" *New York Times*, July 23, 2019.

11. National League of Cities, "City Rights in an Era of Preemption: A State-by-State Analysis, 2018 Update," 2018, http://nlc.org/sites/default/files/2017–03 /NLC-SML%20Preemption%20Report%202017-pages.pdf.

12. Diana Ali, "The Rise and Fall of the Bathroom Bill: State Legislation Affecting Trans & Gender Non-Binary People," NAPSA Student Affairs Administrators in Higher Education, April 2, 2019, https://www.naspa.org/blog/the-rise-and-fall -of-the-bathroom-bill-state-legislation-affecting-trans-and-gender-non-binary -people.

13. Casey Leins, "Illinois Passes Gender-Neutral Bathroom Bill," *U.S. News and World Report*, July 29, 2019.

14. Human Rights Campaign, "Cities and Counties with Non-Discrimination Ordinances That Include Gender Identity," https://www.hrc.org/resources/cities -and-counties-with-non-discrimination-ordinances-that-include-gender.

15. A. E. S., "Dillon's Rule: The Case for Reform," *Virginia Law Review* 68, no. 3 (1982): 693–712.

16. John Forrest Dillon, *Commentaries on the Law of Municipal Corporations*, 2 vols. (Boston: Wentworth Press, 2016).

17. *City of Clinton v. Cedar Rapids and Missouri River Railroad Company*, 24 Iowa 455, 475 (1868).

18. *Hunter v. Pittsburgh*, 207 U.S. 161 (1907).

19. *Hunter v. Pittsburgh*, 207 U.S. 161 (1907), at 177.

20. *City of Winchester v. Redmond*, 93 Va. 711, 25 S.E. 1001 (1896).

21. Code of Virginia sections 15.2–901 and 15.2–1215, as amended by House Bill 177 in 2014 (Acts of Assembly 2014, chapter 385).

22. National League of Cities, "Local Government Authority," https://web.archive .org/web/20160804131854/http://www.nlc.org/build-skills-and-networks /resources/cities-101/city-powers/local-government-authority.

23. Jesse J. Richardson Jr., Meghan Zimmerman Gough, and Robert Puentes, "Is Home Rule the Answer? Clarifying the Influence of Dillon's Rule on Growth Management" (Washington, DC: Brookings Institute, January 1, 2003), https:// www.brookings.edu/research/is-home-rule-the-answer-clarifying-the-influence -of-dillons-rule-on-growth-management/.

24. *The Constitution of Virginia: Report of the Commission on Constitutional Revision to His Excellency, Mills E. Godwin, Jr., Governor of Virginia, the General Assembly of Virginia, and the People of Virginia, January 1, 1969* (Charlottesville, VA: Michie Co., 1969), 228–30; Richard Schragger and C. Alex Retzloff, "The Failure of Home Rule Reform in Virginia: Race, Localism, and the Constitution of 1971" (April 13, 2020), in *Essays on the Constitution of Virginia* (Charlottesville: University of Virginia Press, 2021).

25. A. E. Dick Howard, *Commentaries on the Constitution of Virginia* (Charlottesville: University Press of Virginia, 1974), 2:811–12. See also Jack Spain Jr., "The General Assembly and Local Government: Legislating A Constitution 1969–1970," *University of Richmond Law Review* 8 (1974): 387.

26. Richard Briffault, Nestor M. Davidson, Paul A. Diller, Sarah Fox, Laurie Reynolds, Erin A. Scharff, Richard Schragger, and Rick Su, "Principles of Home Rule for the Twenty-First Century," Fordham Law Legal Studies Research Paper 3539617 (National League of Cities, February 12, 2020).

27. "State Preemption of Local Laws: Preliminary Review of Substantive Areas," snapshot as of March 2017, http://docs.wixstatic.com/ugd/d91411_498e690 d818747359db094948ba1056d.pdf.

28. "State Plastic and Paper Bag Legislation," National Conference of State Legislatures, November 11, 2016, http://www.ncsl.org/research/environment-and -natural-resources/plastic-bag-legislation.aspx.

29. National League of Cities, "Restoring City Rights in an Era of Preemption," National League of Cities, 2019, https://www.nlc.org/sites/default/files/2019-11 /Preemption-3.pdf.

30. National Conference of State Legislatures, "What's a Sanctuary Policy? FAQ on Federal, State and Local Action on Immigration Enforcement," April 16, 2019, http://www.ncsl.org/research/immigration/sanctuary-policy-faq635991795 .aspx.

31. Mel Leonor, "Northam Vetoes 'Sanctuary Cities' Bill," *Richmond Times-Dispatch*, March 19, 2019. Ironically, no city in Virginia had passed an ordinance declaring itself a sanctuary city.

32. *City of Cleveland v. State*, 128 Ohio St. 3d 135 (2010).

33. National League of Cities, "State Plastic and Paper Bag Legislation," National League of Cities, August 15, 2019, http://www.ncsl.org/research/environment -and-natural-resources/plastic-bag-legislation.aspx. Many of these initiatives originated in model bills proposed by ALEC.

34. Henry Grabar, "Phoenix Has Beef with Arizona," *Slate,* September 19, 2016.

35. Jennifer L. Pomeranz et al., "State Preemption of Food and Nutrition Policies and Litigation: Undermining Government's Role in Public Health," *American Journal of Preventive Medicine* 56, no. 1 (2019): 47–57.

36. Christiana K. McFarland, Kyle Funk, Rose Kim, Domenick Lasorsa, and Brenna Rivett, "Local Tools to Address Housing Affordability: A State-by-State Analysis," National League of Cities, 2019. At least eleven states have preempted localities from enacting mandatory inclusionary zoning, or which limit their ability to develop voluntary inclusionary zoning policies. As of July 2019, cities in twenty states and the District of Columbia are expressly permitted or face no legal barriers to inclusionary housing.

37. Sophie Kasakove, "Red State Governments Ban Blue Cities from Passing Bills to Make Housing Affordable," *Pacific Standard,* July 23, 2019.

38. Richard Briffault, "The Challenge of the New Preemption," *Stanford Law Review* 70 (2018): 1995; Columbia Public Law Research Paper 14–580 (2018), https:// scholarship.law.columbia.edu/faculty_scholarship/2090.

39. *State v. City and County of Denver,* 139 P.3d 635 (Colo. 2006).

40. Luke Fowler and Stephanie L. Witt, "State Preemption of Local Authority: Explaining Patterns of State Adoption of Preemption Measures," *Publius: The Journal of Federalism* 49, no. 3 (Summer 2019): 540–59.

41. See Franklin R. Guenthner, "Note: Reconsidering Home Rule and City-State Preemption in Abandoned Fields of Law," *Minnesota Law Review,* 102 (2017): 427, at 428, A useful summary of preemption laws by state is found in Brooks Rainwater, "From the Director," in Nicole DuPuis, Trevor Langan, Christiana McFarland, Angelina Panettieri, and Brooks Rainwater, *City Rights in an Era of Preemption: A State-by-State Analysis* (Washington, DC: National League of Cities, 2018), https://www.nlc.org/wp-content/uploads/2017/02/NLC-SML -Preemption-Report-2017-pages.pdf.

42. Patrick Svitek, "Abbott Wants "Broad-Based Law" That Preempts Local Regulations," *Texas Tribune,* March 21, 2017.

43. A Florida court ruled, however, that while the state could preempt the local initiatives in the gun control area, it could not subject local officials to fines or removal by taking the action. Doug Hanks, "Judge Strikes Down Penalties for Local Governments That Pass Gun-Control Laws," *Tampa Bay Times,* July 28, 2019.

44. Ariz. Rev. Stat. Ann. § 41–194.01 (2016). Lauren E. Phillips, "Impeding Innovation: State Preemption of Progressive Local Regulations," *Columbia Law Review* 117, no. 8 (2017): 2225–63. Kentucky's law permits holding local officials civilly and, in some cases, criminally liable for violating certain preemption statutes.

45. Phillips, "Impeding Innovation," 2256.

46. Ballotpedia, "List of Current Mayors of the Top 100 Cities in the United States," https://ballotpedia.org/List_of_current_mayors_of_the_top_100_cities_in_the _United_States (accessed October 10, 2019).

47. Jared Bernstein, "Cities Would Like to Raise Their Minimum Wages, Too, but States Keep Blocking Them," *Washington Post*, July 19, 2019.

48. National Conference of State Legislatures, "State Minimum Wages: 2020 Minimum Wage by State," January 6, 2020, https://www.ncsl.org/research/labor -and-employment/state-minimum-wage-chart.aspx.

49. National Conference of State Legislatures, "State Minimum Wages."

50. Laura Huizar and Yannet Lathrop, "Fighting Wage Preemption: How Workers Have Lost Billions in Wages and How We Can Restore Local Democracy," National Employment Law Project, July 2019, https://s27147.pcdn.co/wp -content/uploads/Fighting-Wage-Preemption-Report-7-19.pdf.

51. Elizabeth Patton, "Alabama Senate Votes for Minimum Wage Uniformity, Blocks Birmingham Minimum Wage Increase," *Alabama Today*, February 25, 2016.

52. The case is still active. In 2018, the 11th US Circuit Court of Appeals reversed a lower court's decision to dismiss the suit. Yuki Noguchi, "In Battle Pitting Cities vs. States over Minimum Wage, Birmingham Scores a Win," NPR, July 27, 2018, https://www.npr.org/2018/07/27/632723920/in-battle-pitting-cities-vs -states-over-minimum-wage-birmingham-scores-a-win.

53. A partial victory for Kansas City was achieved, however, when the state supreme court held that approval of the hike by voter referendum would be sufficient to usher in the change. To date, the city has chosen not to pursue this option. Associated Press, "Missouri Supreme Court orders Kansas City Vote on Wage Hike," *Washington Times*, January 17, 2017.

54. Matthew Bultman, "Ky. High Court Strikes Louisville Minimum Wage Ordinance," *Law360*, October 21, 2016, https://www.law360.com/articles/854013 /ky-high-court-strikes-louisville-minimum-wage-ordinance.

55. DuPuis et al., *City Rights in an Era of Preemption*.

56. Leila Atassi, "Special Election for Phased-in $15 Minimum Wage Proposal Set for May 2 in Cleveland," Cleveland.com, September 12, 2016, http://perma.cc /X8H3-MHSJ.

57. Nick Beleiciks, "Oregon's Minimum Wage Increases on July 1, 2019," Oregon Employment Department, June 6, 2019, https://www.qualityinfo.org/-/oregon -s-minimum-wage-increases-on-july-1-2019; Chad Arnold, "Minimum Wage Increases Are Coming: What It Means for New Yorkers," *Democrat & Chronicle*, December 19, 2018.

58. Andrew Sheeler, "California's $15 an Hour Minimum Wage Is Coming, but When?," *Sacramento Bee*, July 12, 2019.

59. Anna Staver, "Colorado Cities Can Raise Minimum Wages Starting in January 2020," *Denver Post*, May 28, 2019.

60. LIS (Legislative Information System), "2019 Session: HB 2631 Minimum Wage; Local Alternative," https://lis.virginia.gov/cgi-bin/legp604.exe?ses=191&typ=bil&val=hb2631. The bill was introduced by Delegate Mark Levine. Several of these measures were proposed during my time in the legislature.

61. Huizar and Lathrop, "Fighting Wage Preemption," 20.

62. Alan Greenblatt, "Will State Preemption Leave Cities More Vulnerable?," *Governing*, April 3, 2020.

63. Christine Clarridge, "Snohomish County Sheriff Says He Won't Enforce Washington State's Stay-Home Order," *Seattle Times*, April 22, 2020. Fortney had also been active in the Second Amendment sanctuary movement.

64. Massachusetts might be called a limited home rule state. Certain powers are granted to localities, but most are still derived from the state.

65. New York's order was issued pursuant to "Section 29-a of Article 2-B of the Executive Law to temporarily suspend or modify any statute, local law, ordinance, order, rule, or regulation, or parts thereof, of any agency during a State disaster emergency, if compliance with such statute, local law, ordinance, order, rule, or regulation would prevent, hinder, or delay action necessary to cope with the disaster emergency or if necessary to assist or aid in coping with such disaster." See the website at https://www.governor.ny.gov/news/no-2028-continuing-temporary-suspension-and-modification-laws-relating-disaster-emergency.

66. Ben Kesslen and Phil McCausland, "A Southern Mayor Had Careful Plans to Reopen the City. His Governor Had Other Ideas," *NBC News*, May 1, 2020.

67. Bob Moser, "How Mississippi's Governor Undermined Efforts to Contain the Coronavirus," *New Yorker*, April 7, 2020.

68. Nestor Davidson and Kim Haddow, "State Preemption and Local Responses in the Pandemic," ACS Expert Forum, June 22, 2020, https://www.acslaw.org/expertforum/state-preemption-and-local-responses-in-the-pandemic/.

69. Emma Platoff, "Texas Attorney General Ken Paxton warns Austin, San Antonio, Dallas to Loosen Coronavirus Restrictions," *Texas Tribune*, May 12, 2020.

70. LSSC, "At a Glance: Preemption and Covid-19 April 30, 2020," https://static1.squarespace.com/static/5ce4377caeb1ce00013a02fd/t/5eb040daf1865620afc9fied/1588609242635/LSSC-COVID19-April30.pdf.

71. Greg Bluestein and Stephanie Toone, "'Too Soon,' Trump Says of Ga. Plan to Reopen Economy; Kemp Disagrees," *Atlanta Journal Constitution*, April 22, 2020, https://www.ajc.com/blog/politics/too-soon-trump-urges-kemp-reverse-coronavirus-rollback/bUQsnksgvm8vmrTQonrNtK/.

72. Joseph Bustos, "SC Hasn't Met Key White House Guideline to Reopen. McMaster Opened Some Businesses Anyway," *The State*, April 23, 2020.

73. Greg Hadley, "Benjamin Says Columbia Plans to Move Ahead with Coronavirus 'Stay at Home' Order," *The State*, March 28, 2020.

74. In contrast, when Alaska governor Mike Dunleavy announced his intention to supersede the emergency provisions of the Anchorage city order, he had to back off because Alaska is a home rule state and cities enjoy greater powers. A

compromise was struck, and the state and city reached agreement on opening some businesses. See Daniella Rivera, "Authority of Local Governments Questioned as State Prepares to Lift COVID-19 Restrictions," KTVA, April 23, 2020.

75. Kate Elizabeth Queram,"Florida Lifts Covid Restrictions on Bars and Restaurants, While Prohibiting Local Mask Penalties," Route Fifty, September 27, 2020, https://www.route-fifty.com/health-human-services/2020/09/florida-lifts-covid-restrictions-bars-and-restaurants-mask-penalties/168800/.

76. Claire Hansen, "Texas AG Threatens Austin, Dallas and San Antonio over Coronavirus Restrictions," *USA Today,* May 13, 2020, https://www.usnews.com/news/national-news/articles/2020-05-13/texas-ag-threatens-austin-dallas-and-san-antonio-over-coronavirus-restrictions.

## 13. Saving the Planet

1. The grid is actually made up of four major networks of interconnected power systems. Good descriptions may be found in Julie A. Cohn, *The Grid: Biography of an American Technology* (Cambridge, MA: MIT Press, 2017); Philip F. Schewe, *The Grid: A Journey Through the Heart of Our Electrified World* (Washington, DC: Joseph Henry Press, 2007); Gretchen Bakke, *The Grid: The Fraying Wires between Americans and Our Energy Future* (New York: Bloomsbury, 2016); and Mason Willrich, *Modernizing America's Electricity Infrastructure* (Cambridge, MA: MIT Press, 2017).

2. *Clean Energy Policy Guide for State Legislatures* (Fort Collins: Colorado State University, Center for the New Energy Economy, 2019).

3. Austa Somvichian-Clausen, "Several Renewable Energy Initiatives Passed in the 2020 Election. Here's What You Need to Know," *The Hill,* November 6, 2020.

4. Jeff St. John, "The 5 Biggest US Utilities Committing to Zero Carbon Emissions by 2050," *Grid Edge,* September 16, 2020.

5. Galen Barbose, "U.S. Renewables Portfolio Standards 2017 Annual Status Report," Lawrence Berkeley National Laboratory, July 2017, https://emp.lbl.gov/sites/default/files/2017-annual-rps-summary-report.pdf.

6. Coley Girouard,"Top 10 Utility Regulation Trends of 2019," *Advanced Energy Economy Perspectives* (blog), Advanced Energy Economy, December 9, 2019, https://blog.aee.net/top-10-utility-regulation-trends-of-2019?utm_source=hs_email&utm_medium=email&utm_content=80556881&_hsenc=p2ANqtz-_io4H76xHf_WyNnCyJW6T59NeCoDXB1It38wxw7ZPYbSQUlqs7NAU3DnZvOil2mVH9oCGM8_hIU5L8aIg-enQuiZbkSA&_hsmi=80556881.

7. Don Jenkins, "Inslee Signs Five Climate-Change Bills," *Capital Press,* May 8, 2019.

8. Liam Dillon, "California to Rely on 100% Clean Electricity by 2045 under Bill Signed by Gov. Jerry Brown," *Los Angeles Times,* September 18, 2018.

9. Mel Leonor, "Dominion Plans to Build Nation's Largest Offshore Wind Farm off Coast of Virginia," *Richmond Times-Dispatch,* September 19, 2019.

10. See the website at https://www.rggi.org/. See also Acadia Center, "The Regional Greenhouse Gas Initiative: Ten Years in Review," September 19, 2019, https://acadiacenter.org/wp-content/uploads/2019/09/Acadia-Center_RGGI_10-Years-in-Review_2019-09-17.pdf.

11. Jeff St. John, "Virginia Mandates 100% Clean Power by 2045," *Grid Edge,* March 06, 2020.

12. Matthew L. Wald, "State Energy Plan Would Alter New York Utilities," *New York Times,* April 5, 2014.

13. Davide Savenije, "Inside the REV: Audrey Zibelman's Bold Plan to Transform New York's Electricity Market," *Utility Dive,* November 3, 2014.

14. "Governor Baker Signs Legislation Directing $2.4 Billion to Climate Change Adaptation, Environmental Protection, and Community Investments," press release, Office of the Governor of Massachusetts, August 21, 2018, https://www.mass.gov/news/governor-baker-signs-legislation-directing-24-billion-to-climate-change-adaptation.

15. The US Energy Information Administration reported that in April 2019, renewable energy production surpassed coal-fired generation for the first time in history. US EIA, "Electric Power Monthly Data for April 2019," June 25, 2019, https://www.eia.gov/electricity/monthly/.

16. John Parnell, "Forget King Coal. Solar Is 'New King' of Global Power Markets, Says IEA," Greentech Media, October 13, 2020, https://www.greentechmedia.com/articles/read/forget-king-coal-solar-is-the-new-king-of-global-electricity-markets-says-iea.

17. The last decade has seen the following changes: (1) The use of coal to provide electricity dropped precipitously, from 45 percent in 2010 to 23 percent in 2019. (2) Natural gas–fired power, now the top producer of electricity, grew from 24 percent of US power needs in 2010 to 38 percent in 2019. (3) Renewables grew from providing 10 percent of the nation's electricity demand in 2010 to 18 percent in 2019. See Monique Hanis, "2020 'Factbook' Reveals a Decade's Shift to Advanced Energy," Advanced Energy Perspectives (blog), Advanced Energy Economy, February 19, 2020, https://blog.aee.net/2020-factbook-reveals-a-decades-shift-to-advanced-energy?utm_source=hs_email&utm_medium=email&utm_content=83641510&_hsenc=p2ANqtz-90qA1qWrqNPQcHoJu4Rju3-IPBYk8Gwu_xXCWfS9FZ5PFYmr5i2-aXA1W96koOePqJYmG7GxeGPnx-KENSoUoKzFhgnw&_hsmi=83641510.

18. C2 Energy Capital, "Walmart Executes Agreements for 46 Solar Projects across the US with C2 Energy Capital," press release, PR Newswire, May 8, 2019, https://www.prnewswire.com/news-releases/walmart-executes-agreements-for-46-solar-projects-across-the-us-with-c2-energy-capital-300845972.html.

19. Cassandra Sweet, "Salesforce, Microsoft, Apple Push Virginia Utility to Use More Renewables, Less Gas," *Greenbiz,* July 9, 2019.

20. Mark Wilson, "Denied: Indiana Utility Regulatory Commission Rejects Vectren's Power Plant Proposal," *Evansville Courier & Press,* April 25, 2019.

21. David Wichner, "Regulators Extend Ban on New Gas Power Plants in Arizona," *Arizona Daily Star*, February 8, 2019.

22. Jeff St. John, "Virginia Regulators Reject Key Parts of Dominion's Smart Meter, Grid Upgrade Plan," *Grid Edge*, March 27, 2020.

23. North Carolina Clean Energy Technology Center, *The 50 States of Grid Modernization: 2019 Review and Q4 2019 Quarterly Report*, February 2020, https://nccleantech.ncsu.edu/wp-content/uploads/2020/02/Q42019-GridMod-Exec-Final2.pdf.

24. Alec Tyson and Brian Kennedy, "Two-Thirds of Americans Think Government Should Do More on Climate," Pew Research Center, June 23, 2020, https://www.pewresearch.org/science/2020/06/23/two-thirds-of-americans-think-government-should-do-more-on-climate/.

25. The model was based on earlier state efforts to rein in the power of the railroads and other monopoly industries. The utilities were also granted certain legal powers, such as the power of eminent domain, so they could build and maintain the infrastructure necessary to produce energy and deliver it to the customer. See, for example, the history of Virginia regulation written by the Virginia State Corporation Commission, available at https://www.scc.virginia.gov/comm/reports/restrct3.pdf.

26. Advanced Energy Economy, "Public Utility Commission Engagement," https://www.aee.net/initiatives/puc-engagement.

27. "US Utility Commissioners: A Key Factor in Assessing Regulatory Risk," *S&P Global Market Intelligence*, May 23, 2019, https://www.spglobal.com/market intelligence/en/news-insights/blog/us-utility-commissioners-a-key-factor-in-assessing-regulatory-risk.

28. In Virginia, this is an extremely complicated phenomenon. For years, proponents of renewable energy have criticized the SCC because of its unwillingness to approve projects by the utilities in this area. The commission has argued that the costs of these projects will show up in the bills of the ratepayers, and opposes the new initiatives as a result. The utilities have often come to the legislature to pass legislation to compel the SCC to act.

29. Pew Research Center, "Public Opinion on Renewables and Other Energy Sources," October 4, 2016, https://www.pewresearch.org/science/2016/10/04/public-opinion-on-renewables-and-other-energy-sources/. A recent Public Opinion Strategies poll of Virginians found that 86 percent want to accelerate the growth of clean energy (http://www.cleanenergyconservatives.com).

30. Comparing electric rates and bills is a complicated endeavor, but according to 2016 data analyzed by the US Energy Information Agency, the costliest electricity rates are found in Hawaii and the cheapest are in Louisiana; Virginia was ranked twenty-fifth. US Energy Information Administration, "Today in Energy," February 13, 2018, https://www.eia.gov/todayinenergy/detail.php?id=34932.

31. Solar Energy Industries Association, "U.S. Solar Market Insight," September 17, 2019, https://www.seia.org/us-solar-market-insight.

32. Anmar Frangoul, "From California to Texas, These Are the US States Leading the Way in Solar," CNBC, September 19, 2018.

33. Andrea Thompson, "Utility-Scale Energy Storage Will Enable a Renewable Grid," *Scientific American*, July 1, 2019. A 2019 government-funded report published by the National Renewable Energy Laboratory concluded that battery technology is now at a stage where short-duration, four-hour battery storage systems can actually provide alternatives to fossil fuel generation for peak demand. Paul Denholm, Jacob Nunemaker, Pieter Gagnon, and Wesley Cole, *The Potential for Battery Energy Storage to Provide Peaking Capacity in the United States*, Technical Report NREL/TP-6A20–74184 (Golden, CO: National Renewable Energy Laboratory, 2019).The Energy Storage Association (http:// energystorage.org/) provides periodic updates on developments in this field.

34. Tsvetana Paraskova, "Replacing the US Electric Grid Could Cost $5 trillion," *Business Insider*, March 25, 2017. The American Society of Civil Engineers (ASCE) gave energy infrastructure a grade of D+ in its 2017 Infrastructure Report Card (https://www.infrastructurereportcard.org/wp-content/uploads /2017/01/Energy-Final.pdf). A caveat is in order here: almost every US infrastructure rating in the report was a D.

35. Michelle Lewis, "EGEB: Wind Is Now the Largest Source of Electricity in Iowa and Kansas," Electrek, April 20, 2020, https://electrek.co/2020/04/20/egeb -wind-electricity-iowa-kansas-austria-coal/.

36. American Council for an Energy-Efficient Economy, "State Energy Efficiency Resource Standards (EERS), May 2019," EERS Policy Brief, ACEEE, May 2019, state-eers-0519.pdf (aceee.org).

37. Hannah Natanson, "Electric School Buses Are Coming to Virginia," *Washington Post*, September 7, 2019.

38. "Aligning Utility Business Models with Energy Efficiency," ACEEE, February 5, 2020, https://www.aceee.org/toolkit/2020/02/aligning-utility-business -models-energy-efficiency.

39. One group attempting to build this capacity is the Center for the New Energy Economy at Colorado State University. Led by former governor Bill Ritter, the center works with policymakers and stakeholders across the country to develop a deeper understanding of the energy challenges before us (https:// cnee.colostate.edu/). The center publishes briefs describing energy policies in the various states (https://www.aeltracker.org/).

## Conclusion

1. Over the years, some controversy has emerged about whether he actually uttered these precise words. Nonetheless, the fact that so many reference the anecdote shows the insight of the statement. See Gilliam Brockell, "'A Republic, If You Can Keep It': Did Ben Franklin Really Say Impeachment Day's Favorite Quote?," *Washington Post*, December 18, 2019.

2. A recent national survey conducted by the Pew Research Center found that

more than eight in ten Americans say they are worried about the way the government in Washington works, including 49 percent who are "very worried." Kim Parker, Rich Morin, and Juliana Menasce Horowitz, "Looking to the Future, Public Sees an America in Decline on Many Fronts," Pew Research Center, March 21, 2019, https://www.pewsocialtrends.org/2019/03/21/public -sees-an-america-in-decline-on-many-fronts/. Pew further reports that public trust in the government remains near historic lows. Pew Research Center, "Public Trust in Government: 1958–2019," April 11, 2019, https://www.people -press.org/2019/04/11/public-trust-in-government-1958-2019/.

3. Steven Levitsky and Daniel Ziblatt in *How Democracies Die* (New York: Broadway Books, 2019) describe the breakdown of democracies in Europe and Latin America, arguing that they usually end not with the bang of revolution or coup but instead with the slow erosion of critical institutions and the decline of long-standing norms.

4. Aaron Rupar, "New Congress Member Creates Stir by Saying of Trump: 'We're Going to Impeach This Motherfucker!,'" *Vox*, January 4, 2019.

5. Gerald J. Postema, "Is Being Incivil a Morally Justifiable Choice?," *Charlotte Observer*, July 16, 2018.

6. David Jackson, "'You Can't Send Us Back!' Virginia House Delegate Ibraheem Samirah Interrupts Trump's Jamestown Speech," *USA Today*, July 31, 2019.

7. Tom Lindsay, "Outlawing the 'Heckler's Veto': Drive to Restore Free Speech on Campus Gathers Steam in the States," *Forbes*, January 26, 2018.

8. "'Hear Me by Any Means Necessary': Charlottesville Is Forced to Redefine Civility," *Morning Edition*, NPR, March 20, 2019.

9. Katy Steinmetz, "Fighting Words: A Battle in Berkeley over Free Speech," *Time*, June 1, 2017.

10. Marissa J. Lang, "'We Will Not Obey': 575 Arrested as Hundreds of Women Rally in D.C. to Protest Trump's Immigration Policy," *Washington Post*, June 28, 2018.

11. David J. Toscano, "The Gun Sanctuary Movement Is Exploding," *Slate*, December 11, 2019.

12. David Blankenhorn, "The Top 14 Causes of Political Polarization," *American Interest*, May 16, 2018.

13. Weber Shandwick, "Civility in America 2019: Solutions for Tomorrow," WebersHandwick.com, 2019, 9, https://www.webershandwick.com/wp -content/uploads/2019/06/CivilityInAmerica2019SolutionsforTomorrow.pdf. The increase in blaming the internet and social media for civility's demise has more than doubled since this group began investigating its role (from 24 percent in 2012 to 57 percent in 2019).

14. Keith J. Bybee, *How Civility Works* (Stanford, CA: Stanford University Press, 2018).

15. John Rawls, *Political Liberalism* (New York: Columbia University Press, 2005), 217.

16. See Teresa Bejan, *Mere Civility: Disagreement and the Limits of Toleration* (Cambridge, MA: Harvard University Press, 2017), for the origins of the concept.

17. A 2018 NPR/PBS *NewsHour*/Marist poll found that the country's civility crisis is deepening and that a majority of Americans fear it will lead to violence. Seven in ten (70 percent) Americans believe the tone of the discourse between Republicans and Democrats has gotten worse since President Donald Trump was elected (NPR/PBS NewsHour/Marist Poll Results November 1, 2018, http://maristpoll.marist.edu/?page_id=43329%23sthash.LoxbWsk5.dpbs%20#sthash.ZosONIWZ.gMcJF83i.dpbs).

18. Candice Delmas, "Civil Disobedience," *Philosophy Compass* 11, no. 1 (2016): 681–91.

19. Michelangelo Signorile, "Fuck Civility," *Huffington Post*, June 27, 2018.

20. Weber Shandwick, "Civility in America, 2019: Solutions for Tomorrow," 14.

21. Defining polarization as "the average ideological distance between the median Democrat and median Republican," political scientists Boris Shor and Nolan McCarty claim that chambers in roughly half the states are even more polarized than our national legislature, and that the level of polarization in states is steadily increasing. They argue that California is the most polarized and Rhode Island, New Jersey, and Louisiana are the least; Virginia was ranked twenty-third most polarized. See Boris Shor and Nolan McCarty, "May 2018 Update to Shor-McCarty State Legislatures Data," *Measuring American Legislatures* (blog), AmericanLegislatures.com, May 14, 2018. https://americanlegislatures.com/blog/.

22. P. M. Forni's classic, *Choosing Civility* (New York: St. Martin's Press, 2002), listed twenty-five rules. George Washington listed 110. George Washington, *George Washington's Rules of Civility & Decent Behavior in Company and Conversation* (Williamsburg, VA: Beaver Press, 1971).

23. Martin Luther King Jr., "Letter from a Birmingham Jail," in *Why We Can't Wait* (New York: Signet, 1960).

24. The *New York Times* columnist and American Enterprise Institute scholar Arthur C. Brooks discusses the tendency to treat our adversaries with contempt in "Our Culture of Contempt," *New York Times*, March 2, 2019.

25. William Branigin, "Warner Apologizes to Victims of Eugenics," *Washington Post*, May 3, 2002.

26. Alicia Petska, "Victims of Forced Sterilization to Receive Compensation from State," *News and Advance*, February 27, 2015.

27. Bob Gibson, "Slavery Apology Measure Ignites Legislative Debate," *Daily Progress*, January 16, 2007.

28. Sydney Trent, "Alabama's Governor Apologizes to Survivor of 1963 Klan Bombing of Birmingham Church," *Washington Post*, September 30, 2020.

29. "States Race to Pass Policing Reforms after Floyd's Death," CNBC, August 8, 2020.

30.  Noah Robertson, "After Blackface Scandal, Va. Governor Has Hung on—and Is Making Amends," *Christian Science Monitor,* October 9, 2019.

31.  Gregory S. Schneider, "Northam Names First Diversity Chief for Virginia State Government, *Washington Post,* September 9, 2019.

32.  Office of the Governor, Commonwealth of Virginia, Executive Order Number Thirty-Nine (2019) Establishment of the Commission on African American History Education in the Commonwealth. https://www.governor.virginia.gov /media/governorvirginiagov/executive-actions/EO-39-Establishment-of-the -Commission-on-African-American-History-Education-in-the-Commonwealth .pdf. See also Mechelle Hankerson, "A Governor-Appointed Commission Begins Work on Improving Black History Education in Virginia," *Washington Post,* October 29, 2019.

33.  Roger Chesley, "Governor's Support of HBCUs Laudable, Though Financial, Other Struggles Continue," *Virginia Mercury,* January 6, 2020.

34.  Each state is granted two statues at the US Capitol designed to celebrate key persons or events in that state's history. Virginia's other statue is of Washington. See Robert Zullo, "Governor's Office Seeks Legislation to Replace Lee Statue at U.S. Capitol," *Virginia Mercury,* December 23, 2019.

35.  Editorial Board, "How Ralph Northam Came Back from the Political Dead," *Washington Post,* December 27, 2019.

36.  Lisa Marie Segarra, "Watch John McCain Strongly Defend Barack Obama during the 2008 Campaign," *Time,* August 25, 2018.

37.  National Conference on State Legislatures, Center for Legislative Strengthening, "State Legislative Policymaking in an Age of Political Polarization," February 2018, https://www.ncsl.org/Portals/1/Documents/About_State_Legislatures /Partisanship_030818.pdf.

38.  In 2013, I could have created chaos by objecting to the Republicans' request to introduce an entirely new budget after the deadline. Instead, I urged my colleagues not to object because we extend these courtesies to other members.

39.  This did not apply to the Rules Committee. In the Senate, there was no rule compelling proportional representation, and when Democrats retained control, they did not create one.

40.  The National Conference on State Legislatures study details how Connecticut, which currently has Democrats in control of the legislature, embodies a culture described as a "New England sense of civility." Under its informal norms, the practice of "calling the previous question" to shut off debate is simply not done (see National Conference on State Legislatures, Center for Legislative Strengthening, "State Legislative Policymaking in an Age of Political Polarization," 9). Some states, such as Wisconsin, have a stormier history with the informal norms, with the result that there is more polarization in the body.

41.  Laura Vozzela, "Va. House Speaker Kills GOP Senate Redistricting Plan," *Washington Post,* February 6, 2013.

42. William J. Howell, "Howell: For the Honor of the Institution, Amendments Ruled 'Out of Order'," *Richmond Times Dispatch*, February 7, 2013.

43. Dawn Baumgartner Vaughan, Lauren Horsch, and Paul A. Specht, "NC House Overrides Budget Veto in Surprise Vote with Almost Half of Lawmakers Absent," *Raleigh News & Observer*, September 11, 2019. In Virginia, a two-thirds vote is necessary to override a governor's veto; in North Carolina, it takes only 60 percent of those present.

44. Daniel Yudkin, Stephen Hawkins, and Tim Dixon, "The Perception Gap: How False Impressions are Pulling Americans Apart" (New York: More in Common, 2019), www.moreincommon.com.

45. This dynamic is further examined in C. R. Sunstein, *Conformity: The Power of Social Influence* (New York: NYU Press, 2019).

46. Laura Barron-Lopez and Heather Caygle, "Black Lawmakers Get Biden's Back amid 'Segregationist' Uproar," *Politico*, June 19, 2019.

47. Bryan Stevenson, *Just Mercy: A Story of Justice and Redemption* (New York: Spiegel & Grau, 2014), 17.

48. Clarence Page, "Barack Obama Is Right about Giving 'Woke' Culture a Rest. Will Progressive Democrats Listen?," *Richmond Times-Dispatch*, November 5, 2019.

49. Alan I. Abramowitz, *The Great Alignment: Race, Party Transformation, and the Rise of Donald Trump* (New Haven, CT: Yale University Press, 2018), and Ezra Klein, *Why We're Polarized* (New York: Avid Reader Press, 2020), Kindle edition, 9–10.

50. Thomas E. Mann and Norman J. Ornstein, *It's Even Worse Than It Looks: How the American Constitutional System Collided with the New Politics of Extremism* (New York: Basic Books, 2012). Pew recently reported that Republicans are more likely than Democrats to ascribe negative characteristics to people in the opposing party, with one exception: 75 percent of Democrats say Republicans are "more closed-minded" than other Americans, while 64 percent of Republicans say the same about Democrats ("Partisan Antipathy: More Intense, More Personal," Pew Research Center, October 10, 2019, https://www.people-press .org/2019/10/10/partisan-antipathy-more-intense-more-personal/).

51. "Joint Statement from Elections Infrastructure Government Coordinating Council & the Election Infrastructure Sector Coordinating Executive Committees," Cybersecurity and Infrastructure Security Agency, November 12, 2020, https://www.cisa.gov/news/2020/11/12/joint-statement-elections-infrastructure -government-coordinating-council-election.

52. Matt Zapotosky, Devlin Barrett, and Josh Dawsey, "Barr Says He Hasn't Seen Fraud That Could Affect the Election Outcome," *Washington Post*, December 1, 2020.

53. Jennifer L. Hochschild and Katherine Levine Einstein, "Do Facts Matter? Information and Misinformation in American Politics," *Political Science Quarterly* 130, no. 4 (2015): 585ff.

54.  "Polarization and the Pandemic: How COVID-19 Is Changing Us," More
     in Common (poll), April 3,2020, https://www.moreincommon.com/media
     /3iwfb5aq/hidden-tribes_covid-19-polarization-and-the-pandemic-as-released
     -4-3-20.pdf. The poll further reported that the total share of Americans who
     describe the country as unified has grown from 4 percent in 2018 to 32 percent
     in April,2020, while the percentage of Americans who regard the country as
     "very divided" had dropped from 62 percent to just 22 percent.
55.  "Full Transcript: Jeff Flake's Speech on the Senate Floor," *New York Times,* Octo-
     ber 24, 2017.
56.  Baltimore Sun Staff, "Full Transcript: Rep. Elijah Cummings' Closing State-
     ments at Michael Cohen Hearing," *Baltimore Sun,* February 28, 2019.

# Index

Abbott, Gregg, 20, 170, 174
abortion: copycat bills on, 77; in
    COVID-19 pandemic, 24, 152; culture
    wars and, 151–53, 160; *Roe v. Wade*
    on, 43, 52, 54–55, 151–53; state anti-
    abortion measures, 52, 54–55, 151–53,
    250n12; US rates of, 151, 249n6
Abramowitz, Alan I., 31–32
Abrams, Stacey, 61, 86–87
ACA. *See* Affordable Care Act of 2010
ACLU (American Civil Liberties
    Union), 118, 152, 162
Affordable Care Act of 2010 (ACA):
    backlash against, 8, 39, 75, 139–40;
    individual mandate in, 141, 142, 145–
    46; interest group targeting of, 78;
    legal challenges to, 76, 142; Medicaid
    expansion under, 35, 142–44; model
    for, 10, 69, 141; politicization of, 141–
    42; reinsurance programs under,
    147; Trump administration's under-
    mining of, 144–46, 148
AFP (Americans for Prosperity), 78, 79
air pollution, 76
Alabama: abortion restrictions in, 52,
    55, 151–53; constitution of, 43, 46, 51,
    55, 216n38; COVID-19 vaccines in,
    28; infant mortality rates in, 38; pre-
    emption of local initiatives in, 171–72;
    right-to-work laws in, 244n35; tax
    burden in, 135
Alaska: attorney general appointments
    in, 74; criminal justice policy in,

119; demographic characteristics, 61,
    62; education in, 99; home rule in,
    258–59n74; legislative representation
    in, 73; marijuana laws in, 54; natural
    resources of, 56–57; right-to-work
    laws in, 133; violent crime rates
    in, 33
ALEC (American Legislative Exchange
    Council), 77–79, 118, 199
Allen, George, 70, 222n14
Amazon, 125–27, 137
amendment processes, 51–55, 213n53,
    218n61
American Civil Liberties Union
    (ACLU), 118, 152, 162
American dream, 64–65, 105
American Legislative Exchange Council
    (ALEC), 77–79, 118, 199
Americans for Prosperity (AFP), 78, 79
American Society of Civil Engineers
    (ASCE), 262n34
apologies, power of, 193, 194
Arizona: COVID-19 response in, 20,
    26, 174; energy policy in, 180; mar-
    ijuana laws in, 54; preemption of
    local initiatives in, 169, 170, 174;
    redistricting in, 95; right-to-work
    laws in, 244n35; in 2020 presidential
    election, 2, 3, 82; water constraints
    in, 56
Arkansas: COVID-19 response in, 205–
    6n30; right-to-work laws in, 244n35;
    tax burden in, 135

and, 2, 20, 27–28, 81, 90; demographic factors in, 61; mail-in voting
for, 2–3, 11, 76, 81–82, 90–91; polling
results prior to, 1; public perceptions of, 2–4; secretaries of state and,
225n34; voter turnout in, 63, 84, 87.
*See also* Biden, Joe; Trump, Donald

undocumented immigrants, 60, 75,
157–60
unemployment, 21, 66, 139
unions. *See* labor unions
United States Capitol Building insurrection (2021), 5
United States Constitution: checks
and balances in, 187; development
and ratification of, 42; Equal Rights
Amendment and, 77; express vs.
implied powers in, 43, 45; on powers
granted to states, 161, 254n3; on
redistricting process, 91; state constitutions compared to, 42, 45, 46, 49.
*See also specific amendments*
Unite the Right riot (2017), 6, 9
universities. *See* higher education
urban-rural divide, 60, 61, 156, 167
Utah: criminal justice policy in, 119;
demographic characteristics, 58, 62;
education in, 99; election laws and
voter participation in, 83, 89, 90;
Medicaid expansion in, 52; redistricting in, 40, 95

Vadum, Matthew, 85
Vermont: constitution of, 45, 214n9;
COVID-19 response in, 28; education in, 98, 99, 108; election laws in,
89; immigration laws in, 159; marijuana laws in, 54; redistricting in,
95; reproductive rights in, 153; violent
crime rates in, 33
veto power, 71, 223n9
Virginia: Amazon headquarters in,
125–27, 137; attorneys general in, 74–
77; constitution of, 43, 45, 47–51, 53,
213n53, 215n23; COVID-19 response
in, 17–18, 22, 24–25, 27, 28, 36;
criminal justice policy in, 33, 115, 118,
193, 236n17; demographic character-

istics, 59–61; education in, 47–48,
97–103, 109, 110; election laws and
voter participation in, 32, 81–84, 88,
226n16; energy policy in, 178, 180,
182, 261n28; environmental protections in, 49–50; during federal
sequestration, 57–58; governors in,
42, 43, 69, 71; gun laws in, 33, 72, 155;
incarcerated populations in, 113–14,
116; incentive programs in, 129–32;
infant mortality rates in, 140; judicial
selection in, 121, 123, 240n66; labor
unions in, 244n46; legislative representation in, 73, 195–97; life expectancy in, 38, 140; local governments
in, 164–65; Medicaid expansion in,
72, 140, 142, 143; natural resources
of, 57, 218n1; political culture of,
63–65; ranking data for, 36–38, 127;
redistricting in, 39–41, 92, 94–96;
right-to-work laws in, 133; tax burden
in, 135; in 2020 presidential election,
1; unemployment in, 21, 139; violent
crime rates in, 33
voter participation, 81–91; automatic
registration, 89–90, 226n16; dis-
enfranchisement and, 51, 86, 87; in
early voting, 2, 3, 62, 89, 90; efforts
to increase, 89–91; by mail-in voting,
2–3, 11, 76, 81–83, 89–91; same-day
registration, 83, 90, 228n52; state
policy and, 7, 11, 35, 78, 82–84; suppression of, 84–89; turnout rates, 32,
58, 62–63, 82–87, 199; "use it or lose
it" laws, 227n33. *See also* elections
Voting Rights Act of 1965, 87, 88

wage rates. *See* minimum wage
Walker, Scott, 34–35, 40, 69, 128, 133
Walsh, Marty, 173
Warner, Mark, 70, 74, 92, 144, 193,
222n6
Warren, Earl, 73
Washington (state): COVID-19
response in, 16–17, 22, 25, 28, 173,
207n56; education in, 110; election laws and voter participation
in, 83, 89, 90; energy policy in,
178; gun laws in, 52; home rule in,